Eur - The Wall

A Guide to Unusual Sights

Anneli S. Rufus
and
Kristan Lawson

John Wiley & Sons, Inc.
New York • Chichester • Brisbane
Toronto • Singa

Publisher: Stephen Kippur
Editor: Katherine Schowalter
Managing Editor: Ruth Greif
Editing, Design, and Production: Richard Christopher & Associates, Inc.

Illustrations by Anneli S. Rufus
Maps by Kristan Lawson

This publication is designed to provide accurate and authoritative information in regard to the subject matter covered. It is sold with the understanding that the publisher is not engaged in rendering professional services in the subject matter discussed. Due to the ever-changing marketplace, we suggest that you contact the addresses given to verify information.

Copyright © 1988 by Anneli S. Rufus and Kristan Lawson

All rights reserved. Published simultaneously in Canada.

Reproduction or translation of any part of this work beyond that permitted by section 107 or 108 of the 1976 United States Copyright Act without the permission of the copyright owner is unlawful. Requests for permission or further information should be addressed to the Permission Department, John Wiley & Sons, Inc.

Library of Congress Cataloging-in-Publication Data

Rufus, Anneli S.
   Europe off the wall / Anneli S. Rufus and Kristan Lawson.
     p.   cm.
   ISBN 0-471-63737-8
   1. Europe--Description and travel--1971- --Guide-books.
I. Lawson, Kristan   II. Title
D909.L33 1988
914'.04558--dc19   87-34563
                                                                        CIP

Printed in the United States of America
88 89 10 9 8 7 6 5 4 3 2 1

Contents

Introduction   iv
How to Use This Guide   v
The Countries
    Austria   1
    Belgium   17
    Denmark   37
    Finland   49
    France   57
    West Germany   105
    Great Britain   122
    Greece   172
    Ireland   180
    Italy   189
    The Netherlands   211
    Norway   225
    Portugal   233
    Spain   245
    Sweden   267
    Switzerland   278
    Yugoslavia   298
    The Small Countries   302
        Andorra   303
        Luxembourg   304
        Monaco   306
        Vatican City   306
General Index   307
Specialized Indexes   311
Calendar of Festival Dates   314

INTRODUCTION

Welcome to *Europe Off The Wall* !

Many of us long to explore Europe's mysterious side—the weird little places that only locals know about, the frantic festivals, the intriguing eccentricities. Yet unusual things, by their very nature, are not easy to discover, and tourists find themselves reluctantly beating the well-worn paths that all the guidebooks have been signposting for generations.

Adventurous travelers have long needed a book that forgoes the standard attractions in favor of Europe's bizarre underside: the Other Europe. Forget about Big Ben, the Oktoberfest, and the Louvre. Say hello to underground cities, firewalking rituals, and the museum of tropical diseases.

We ferreted out over 750 curiosities—always searching for the strangest, the most memorable; for each entry we've given a concise description and the pertinent details of when and how to visit. All the specifics have been confirmed and reconfirmed, but prices invariably succumb to inflation, so by the time you read this some of the entrance fees may be outdated; we can only guarantee that they were correct as of the end of 1987.

One final note: all place names are given in the language native to the region wherein the item is located. Sometimes this is not the same as the national language; for example, names in northeastern Spain are in Catalan, names in Wales are in Welsh, and so forth.

Acknowledgments
We'd like to thank, in addition to our parents, the following people: Andreas Blaha, Jan de Boever, Peter Hiess, Christophe Mielle, Nadja and Ralph Palim, Valerie Robert, Rita and Steve Sneyd, and Bernadette Vandercammen.

HOW TO USE THIS GUIDE

The Guide is organized alphabetically by country, and then alphabetically within each country by city. The only exceptions are France, Great Britain, Italy, and Spain, which are divided first into regions, and then alphabetically by cities within each region.

The bottoms of the pages also serve as a quick alphabetical index to *Europe Off the Wall*: the left-hand pages list the countries; the right-hand pages list the regions or cities.

In addition to a complete index of countries and cities, the back of this Guide also contains the following specialized indexes:

>Anatomy Museums
>"American" Wild West Towns
>Eccentric Architecture
>Factory Tours
>Funny Fountains
>Holy Relics
>Postcard Towns
>Strange Art
>Unusual Churches

At the very end of the Guide is a Calendar of Festival Dates, which you can use to find the exact dates of the many strange festivals, celebrations, and customs listed in this Guide.

AUSTRIA

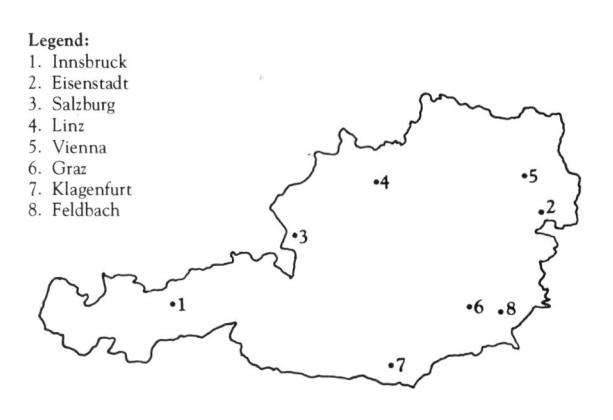

Legend:
1. Innsbruck
2. Eisenstadt
3. Salzburg
4. Linz
5. Vienna
6. Graz
7. Klagenfurt
8. Feldbach

Austria has yodelers, but so does Switzerland. Austria has the Danube. So does Romania. Austria has *lederhosen* but Germany's got the suspendered leather shorts too. Austria has very nice Alps, but absolutely *every*body's got Alps— even Yugoslavia. Austria has W. A. Mozart and the Trapp Family Singers, but so does Hollywood.

But Austria feels uniquely Austrian. There's a certain sense of security that comes from being in a country where women wear dirndls on the streets of the cities and a dumpling nestles in every pot.

In Austria you're liable to find a deposed Hapsburg or a princess behind every Alp, sipping coffee with whipped cream and muttering some sophisticated joke.

Identity problems, wholesomeness alongside old-world decadence, a bloody, complicated history that has kept the country's borders bouncing athletically around the map ... another people

Austria / 1

would be bitter about all this, or at least darkly confused. But what do the Austrians do? They throw back their heads and roar with sardonic laughter.

One thing Austrians like to laugh at is death. There's no mistaking an old-world morbidity in the way crypts and graveyards, death masks, and blood-soaked royal uniforms become objects of delighted fascination.

Visit a cemetery in an Austrian country village and you'll see constant activity as people move energetically among the carved wood and wrought-iron crosses, polishing ceramic photographs of the dead, placing newly lit candles in red glasses, trimming the weeds, and watering the flowers—all the while chatting together like neighbors over a backyard fence. This perhaps is the singularly typical Austrian experience. In death and burial are combined the elegant theatrics and the weighty sense of history that Austrians cherish. Death is one of the country's great motifs, but the people make it as beautiful and as light as a theme in a Mozart sonata.

GRAZ

Schloss Eggenburg Hunting Museum: Eggenburger Alle 90. Open daily, 9 A.M.–noon and 1 to 5 P.M. Admission: AS 20; groups, AS 15 per person. Phone: 0316-532 6416.

A hunting museum wouldn't be a hunting museum without stuffed animals, but the hunting museum in Schloss Eggenburg shines above the rest because some of the animals are freaks. Two heads, extra limbs—you get the idea. Man just loves to remind Mother Nature that she makes mistakes too.

HALLEIN
(50 miles south of Salzburg)

Salt Mines (Salzbergwerk): Take bus or train south from

Salzburg to Hallein; from there take the cable car from the Salzbergbahn next to the Salzberghalle up to Bad Dürnnberg and the salt mines. Open April 25–September 30, daily, 9 A.M.–5 P.M.; October 1–18, 10 A.M.–2 P.M. Admission: cable car and salt mine tour combined, AS 130; Students, AS 120; children under 15, AS 75; children under 4 not admitted. Phone: 06245/3511 or 06245/5285/15.

Down, down, down, 3,000 feet underground, where you put on a salt miner's outfit and behave like a hyperactive child for an hour and a half. Slide down long wooden slides, explore ancient mine tunnels, take underground boat rides, ride around on little electric trains, and pay no attention to the tour guide and his boring historical facts.

HALLSTATT
(40 miles southeast of Salzburg)

Chapel Bonehouse (Pfarrkirche Beinhaus): in the village cemetery, next to the church. Open daytime only. Admission: free.

There are no vacancies in Hallstatt's little graveyard, so to keep things going smoothly, bones are removed several years after burial and stored in the chapel. Well over a thousand skulls are stacked neatly there now. As if this weren't enough, many of the skulls are painted with such information as the date and cause of death. Somehow it's all rather cozy—like Hallstatt itself.

HINTERBRÜHL
(Six miles south of Vienna)

Underground Lake (Seegrotte Hinterbrühl): Take a train from Vienna Südbahnhof to Mödling. From Mödling take a bus (they depart approximately once an hour) to Hinterbrühl. Open daily year-round, daytime only. Phone: 022 36/263 64.

When caves and lakes team up they make for a spooky combination. Here, hidden just a few minutes from Vienna, is one of Europe's largest underground lakes. You can tour the extensive grottoes and caverns—all lit by candles, to heighten the effect—in long white boats. Don't bother to memorize all the geological and statistical trivia; just sit back and get the willies.

INNSBRUCK

Giant Chess Games: Where else but Innsbruck, a city of slow promenades in the park and pensive relaxation, would there be *four* outdoor chess games?

1., 2. In the Hofgarten (the city's central park), on either side of the main gazebo.

Classically carved, ornate $2\frac{1}{2}$-foot-tall wood pieces and plenty of interested spectators ensure a pleasant experience, whether you're watching or playing.

3. At the end of Sparkassenplatz, two blocks from the Tourist Office.

A less-used set in an obscure cul-de-sac.

4. In the suburb of Hungerburg (just across the river).

Amongst this city's frivolous amusements (miniature golf, go-carts, etc.) you'll find yet another giant chessboard.

KAAG
(Near Edelsbach and Feldbach in East Styria)

Franz Gsellmann's World Machine (Weltmaschine): house 14, Kaag. No established visiting hours; make an appointment by calling Maria Gsellmann at 03115/2983. She doesn't speak English; if you want an interpreter to arrange the visit for you, call Dr. Oskar Deissher at the Ministry of Culture: 0316/7031 2601. Admission: free, but donation suggested.

Working in secret for 23 years, Franz Gsellmann, a village farmer, built Austria's most amazing machine. The thing grew and grew, larger and stranger, and Gsellmann vowed that no one would see the Weltmaschine while its creator lived. When his widow unveiled it in 1982, two years after the farmer's death, the Weltmaschine was as big as an elephant; a giddy, whirring, flashing fantasy sculpture among whose hundreds of elements one can find a roulette wheel, a windmill from Holland, five crucifixes, a barometer, a hula hoop, toy spaceships, an oxygen tank, a model of the Brussels Atomium, a plastic Virgin Mary, a suit of armor, and enough ringing bells, winking colored lights, and bright blue iron grillwork to stop a train. Ninety percent of the moving parts still worked at the time of the 1982 unveiling; but as they break down, no one will be able to repair them, since Gsellmann deliberately left no instructions. While he was still alive, the Guggenheim Museum in New York City heard of his project and offered to buy the Weltmaschine for a staggering sum. The farmer wouldn't hear of it. "The machine only works when it is at home," he told Guggenheim.

KLAGENFURT

Minimundus: Villacherstrasse 241, on the western side of Klagenfurt, at the corner of Villacherstrasse and Süduferstrasse. Open May, June, and September, 8:30 A.M.–6 P.M.; July and August, 8 A.M.–8 P.M. Closed October–April. Admission: AS 47; children, AS 15. Phone: (0 42 22) 21 1 94.

If this place doesn't set you to singing "It's a Small World, After All," then nothing will. Minimundus is packed with perfect copies of the world's most famous buildings and structures—all $\frac{1}{25}$ their normal size. But that's not as small as you might think; the replicas range from two to 20 feet tall. Some of the models are so much like their originals that it would be impossible to tell them apart if you saw photographs of them with nothing to indicate the scale. Consequently, Minimundus is full of lazy but clever tourists taking phony souvenir snapshots: "Here I am in Venice. That's the Kremlin there. Oh, that's me with the Eiffel Tower in the background."

POTTENBRUNN
(35 miles west of Vienna)

Tin Figure Museum (Zinnfigurenmuseum): in Pottenbrunn Castle (Wasserschloss Pottenbrunn). Take train to St. Pölten, then take local commuter train one stop west to Pottenbrunn. From the Pottenbrunn train station, follow the signs to the castle, about a 20-minute walk. Open Tuesday–Sunday, 9 A.M.–5 P.M. Closed Monday. Admission: AS 30.

In this romantic, hard-to-reach, moat-encircled castle is a museum devoted entirely to little tin soldiers. Though they lack the Action Grip and bendable limbs of G.I. Joe, their modern counterpart, they have the grace and charm that he lacks as they troop silently in their glass cases.

RUST
(Ten miles east of Eisenstadt, in Burgenland)

Bird Museum: Am Hafen 2. Open in summer, 9 A.M.–noon and 1–6 P.M. (though the owner, Herbert Vargyas, says you can visit "any time"). Admission: AS 15. Phone: 02685/468.

One of Rust's proudest moments is when the storks return every year to nest on the rooftops of the old part of the city. This is a bird-loving town, and the Bird Museum has displays on more than 300 native species, including many waterfowl. If you want to combine your visit with some real-live stork viewing, come between the end of March and the end of August. That's stork-nesting season in Rust.

SALZBURG

Dwarves' Garden (Zwerglgarten): in the garden fronting Schloss Mirabell, near Schwarzstrasse. Admission: free.

Salzburg's Bishop Wolf Dietrich, who built Mirabell for the mother of his children, installed the Zwergl-garten in the spirit of what may have been humor, may have been perversity, and may have been true admiration of the dwarves. Carved out of stone, a ring of bigger-than-life dwarves, male and female, stand in various attitudes. One has an enormous goiter, another a hunchback, another a wooden leg, and still another an egg-like bump on the head. Several of them are smiling, but several more are scowling and howling, baring their teeth—their grotesque expressions fixed vividly forever in stone. This is not a place to go when very drunk, especially at dusk when the shadows play nasty tricks.

Hellbrunn Pleasure Castle (Lustschloss Hellbrunn): three miles from downtown Salzburg: take bus 55 from in front of the Rathaus, on the river, next to the Staatsbrück Bridge. Open April, 9 A.M.–4:30 P.M.; May, 9 A.M.–5:30 P.M.; June, July, and August, 9 A.M.–6:30 P.M. Admission: AS 39; students and children aged 4–15, AS 19; children under 4, free. Guided tours only (included in admission price), every half hour on the half hour. Phone: 84 16 96.

Even if the fountains here did not have minds of their own, Hellbrunn would still be a wacky wonder. Along this watery promenade, birds twitter and organs play (all operated by water power), and water jets lift balls and even a jeweled crown high into the air. The place is the brainchild of a certain bishop with an irrepressible wit, as evidenced by the squirting picnic table you'll see at the beginning of your tour. What do we mean by the fountains having minds of their own? At the risk of ruining some of Austria's wettest surprises, let's just say that water can spurt quite unexpectedly from the most innocent-looking places; one is never quite sure when, how far, or on whose head. (Hint: don't stand on any wet spots.)

House of Nature (Haus der Natur): Museumsplatz 5. Open daily, even on most holidays, 9 A.M.–5 P.M. (aquarium closes at 4:30). Admission: AS 30; students and people aged 18 and under, AS 15.

Forget about Mozart: Salzburg's premier attraction is, without a doubt, the must-see Haus der Natur. Four lower floors of great exhibits culminate in the incredible top floor. Ground floor: 30-foot-long giant squid hanging from the ceiling, aquarium with unusual fish, dioramas of Tibetan nomads and Buddhist cremation rituals (what's that doing here?); first floor (that's the way they do things in Europe—the first floor is actually the second floor): immense quartz crystals as big as barrels, naturally mummified animals; photographs of natural disasters and squished roadkill. Second floor: a reptile zoo and, believe it or not, a collection of animal feces. The third floor is the lull before the storm of weirdness above. Fourth floor: stuffed freak animals (calves with 11 legs and one eye, Siamese twin animals, and so on), a display on the mating habits of all species, including man, a horrifying collection of huge pinned insects, and a truly unforgettable exhibit of malformed human fetuses in jars of formaldehyde. Austria may not have sleazy circus sideshows, but it does have the Salzburg Haus der Natur.

Mozartkugeln Store: Spezialitäten Reber: Griesgasse 3, near Mozart's birthplace. Open Monday–Friday, 9 A.M.–6 P.M.; Saturday, 9 A.M.–noon.

Located in a tall, cool, fourteenth-century building, this shop sells only one thing: Mozartkugeln, Austria's edible homage to the musical little fellow who lies buried in a pauper's grave. The candies are chocolate outside, marzipan inside, with a hazelnut-cream heart. The composer's face is printed on the foil wrapper. Though you can buy these elsewhere in Salzburg, this store is Mozartkugeln world headquarters. Reber sells the candies—and nothing else—singly or in gift boxes of every size and shape.

Toy Museum (Spielzeugmuseum): Bürgerspitalplatz 2. Open Tuesday–Sunday, 9 A.M.–5 P.M. Closed Monday. Admission: AS 20; students, AS 10; children aged 6–15, AS 5; children under 6, free. Phone: 84 11 37.

This thoughtful museum provides more than just a look-see: not only is there a fully equipped playroom for kids and a puppet theater with performances throughout the day, but there is also a room full of vintage science exhibits that the visitor can operate, and several HO scale model electric trains set against Austrian scenery, put in motion at the push of a button. Add to this the actual toy collection, which emphasizes folk toys. You'll see examples from Russia, Portugal, Romania, and elsewhere, made of wood, bread dough, and even pine cones and moss.

STADL PAURA
(One mile south of Lambach)

Church of the Holy Trinity (Dreifaltigkeitskirche): take a bus to Stadl Paura from in front of the Lambach train station. Tell the driver you want to see the Dreifaltigkeitskirche. A road leads from the bus stop up to the church.

When Abbot Maximilian, who designed this church to fulfill a vow made during a plague year, decided to dedicate his creation to the Holy Trinity, he didn't kid around. Not only does the church interior have three walls, but it also has three altars, three organs, and a triangular skylight—everything is in threes. Even the floor tiles are based on triangles. Each of the three altars is equally elaborate: Abbot Maximilian wanted to create "three absolutely equal churches within one building." You can see the abbot in the fresco over the altar opposite the front door. Clutched in his hands are the blueprints for the church.

VIENNA (WIEN)

Bell Museum (Glockenmuseum): Troststrasse 38. Open Wednesday, 2–5 P.M. Admission: AS 20. Phone: 604 34 60.

No "tingalings" here—the bells in this private museum are huge, resounding church bells. Dating as far back as 1242, these antiques bear inscriptions, carvings, and decorations, even though they were built to be heard and not seen. The most unusual specimen is a three-foot-high Japanese bell used in Buddhist ceremonies.

Bob Hope's Portrait in Museum of Fine Arts (Kunsthistorisches Museum): Maria-Theresien-Platz. Open Tuesday–Friday, 10 A.M.–6 P.M.; Saturday and Sunday, 9 A.M.–6 P.M. No entry allowed after 5:30. Closed Monday. Admission: AS 45; students, AS 20; children under 10, free. Phone: 93 45 41.

The one thing that makes this portrait of Bob Hope different from all the others is that it was painted by Albrecht Dürer in 1511. Go to the room with the

Albrecht Dürer collection, look for a large painting of the Crucifixion entitled Das Allerheiligenbild, scan the crowd scene in the lower right-hand corner, and *voilà!* there he is, ski-jump nose and all. The man in the painting is actually a little more angular and youthful than Bob looks today, but the resemblance is still so strong as to be uncanny.

Catacombs in St. Michael's Church: Michaelerplatz, opposite the Alte Hofburg. Entrance to the crypt is to the left of the High Altar. Guided tours held weekdays 11 A.M.–3 P.M.; Sundays and holidays, one tour only at 11 A.M. Admission: AS 15.

The star attraction here is mummies—not wrapped in strips of cloth like their Egyptian counterparts, but lying like oversized dolls in their open coffins. They've lost considerable weight since they were laid to rest in centuries past, but other than that, the mummies look like rather starved, stretched-out versions of you and me, with even their eyelids and clothing intact.

Catacombs in St. Stephan's Cathedral: Stephansplatz 1. Open Monday–Saturday, 10–11:30 A.M. and 1:30–4:30 P.M.; Sunday and holidays, 11–11:30 A.M. and 1:30–4:30 P.M. Guided tours every half hour on the half hour. (Five-person minimum for required guided tour.) Admission: AS 25; children, AS 10. Pay at end of tour. Phone: 515 52/563.

These are somewhat less than lurid, as catacombs go. A cool, confusing maze of tunnels (which are actually more frightening than the bones) leads past the Mass Grave Room, where bones are heaped willy-nilly; the Black Plague Room, with thousands more bones; and the unimaginatively titled Bone House, an alcove in which former monks' bones are piled neatly, like cans in a supermarket display. These are conservative catacombs, good for the kind of person who likes a bit of thrill-'n'-chill but who worries about nightmares— the kind of person who loved *Topper* but couldn't sleep for weeks after seeing *Psycho*.

Circus and Clown Museum: Karmelitergasse 9. Open Wednesday, 5:30–7 P.M.; Saturday, 2:30–5 P.M.; Sunday, 9 A.M.–noon. Phone: 34 68 615.

Circuses and museums occupy opposite ends of the entertainment spectrum, yet the Viennese have managed to successfully combine the two. Clown suits through the ages (can't you just see someone doing their Ph.D. thesis on the history of clown suits?), circus posters, clown makeup displays, photos of famous circuses, clowns in art, circus paraphernalia, clown dolls—it's all here under the Big Top.

Clock Museum (Uhrenmuseum): Schulhof 2. Open Tuesday–Sunday, 9 A.M.–12:15 P.M. and 1–4:30 P.M. Closed Monday and holidays. Admission: AS 15; students, AS 5; children under 6, free. Phone: 533 22 65.

"Dear me, I'm late!" cried the White Rabbit as he hopped off to visit his favorite museum before it closed at 4:30. He just loves the pocketwatch section, with its amazing display of little timepieces, all hundreds of years old, in the shapes of violins, fruits, bells, and many with exquisite miniature paintings on them. Elsewhere in the museum are towering grandfather clocks, indoor astronomical clocks, indecipherable clocks from ancient China and Japan, super-accurate digital clocks, clocks whose pendulums are in the shape of a swinging child or a pair of see-sawing men, and clocks with kitschy Egyptian and Roman themes. If you're in the museum when the big hands reach 12, you'll be treated to rooms full of clonking, clanging, whistling, and tinkling as the clocks all strike the hour: one clock even features a procession of hammer-wielding monks who emerge to strike the monastery bell. Note that this museum has three floors and the top two are easy to miss inadvertently.

Esperanto Museum: 1 Hofburg, just inside St. Michael's Gate of the Imperial Palace, on the top floor. Open Monday, Wednesday, and Friday, 9 A.M.–3:30 P.M. Admission: free. Phone: 52 10 415.

The proponents of Esperanto, an artifical language invented by an ambitious Polish eye doctor named Zamenhof, once had visions of grandeur. It was inevitable, they thought, that Esperanto would become the world's language. Well, not yet. But in this museum you can get a glimpse of the brave new world they had in mind. On display are products whose labels are in Esperanto, including hair gel and pantyhose; products that are actually *named* "Esperanto"; books, from *Struwwelpeter* to the Bible, printed in Esperanto; stamps in Esperanto; pamphlets in Esperanto; and a fascinating old strategy map showing Esperanto's victories and captured territory worldwide.

Holy Lance with Holy Nail, and Holy Grail, in the Secular and Ecclesiastical Treasuries (Schatzkammer): Holy Lance is in Room 11 and Holy Grail is in Room 8, in Hofburg, Schweizerhof. Open Monday, Wednesday, Thursday, and Friday, 10 A.M.–6 P.M.; Saturday, Sunday, and holidays, 9 A.M.–6 P.M. Closed Tuesday. No entry allowed after 5:30. Admission: AS 45; students and seniors, AS 20; children under 10, free. First Sunday of every month, free admission for everyone. Phone: 533 60 46.

Somewhere in Vienna's large complex of palaces, hidden away in a corner of room 11 of the Imperial Treasury, is the Holy Lance *(Heilige Lanze)*, supposedly the very lance with which a Roman soldier pierced Jesus' side. Actually, the Imperial curators think it was probably made in the eighth century A.D., which explains its unhonored position. Believers not only think that the eighth-century metalwork was just a later addition to the original Lance, but also that a nail pulled from the True Cross is part of the added metalwork. Close inspection of the lance sheds little light on the problem, as by now only the tip is left: it's about two feet long, made mainly of iron with gold, silver, brass, and lead embellishments. In Room 8 of the same museum is an agate bowl that legend has claimed to be the Holy Grail from which Jesus drank at the Last Supper. Believers say they can see Jesus' name in the veins of the agate (we sure couldn't). The nonbelievers seem to have the upper hand in this instance, however, since they claim to have proven the bowl was not carved until the fourth century A.D..

Museum of Horseshoeing, Harnessing and Saddling, and Hoof and Claw Orthopedics (Museum für Beschlag, Beschirrung, Sattelung, und Orthopädie bei Huf- und Klauentieren): Linke Bahngasse 11, near the corner of Beatrixgasse. Enter through the driveway of the Veterinary Medicine University. Open Monday–Thursday, 1:30–3:30 P.M. Admission: free. Phone: 73 55 81/372.

Although it has several worthy competitors, this museum might just be the strangest place in Austria. At least it's the funkiest. Before you even make it to the museum, you must walk through veterinary treatment rooms and up a staircase lined with photographs of hoof surgery techniques. The first room is a warm-up, with a section on ostrich-racing (including ostrich saddles, ostrich harnesses and a real ostrich leg lying unexplained on the floor); reindeer harnessing; and spurs, riding crops and saddles. The second room is the real knockout: garishly diseased hooves, sliced in half; ill-sealed jars of malformed horse, cow, pig, and even duck feet in formaldehyde; orthopedic horsehoes; horseshoes for freak double and triple hooves; and vaguely horrifying uncovered boxes of hooves, assorted feet, and fresh, meaty parts.

Military History Museum (Heeresgeschichtliches Museum): Arsenal, Objekt 18. From Südbahnhof, walk two blocks down Arsenalstrasse, turn left into the Arsenal Complex and look for Objekt (Building) 18. Open Saturday–Thursday, 10 A.M.–4 P.M. Closed Friday. Admission: AS 30; students, AS 15; children under 10 and soldiers in uniform, free. First Sunday of every month, free admission for everyone. Phone: 78 23 03.

If it's gore you're after, take a sharp right turn as soon as you enter the museum. About halfway down the hall you'll find a room dedicated to the assassination of Franz Ferdinand (Sarajevo, June 8, 1914). Here you'll find Franz Ferdinand's death mask, of course, and that of his wife, in addition to the uniform he was wearing when shot: it's riddled with bullet holes in the chest region and positively lumpy with dried blood. Also on display is a favorite with Vienna schoolchildren: the car in which it happened. Darn those convertibles.

Private Penguin Museum: Open by appointment only. Admission: AS 20; free if you bring a penguin of some sort to donate to the collection. For directions call 96 18 093 and ask for Čik (pronounced "chick").

Stuffed penguins, glass penguins, vintage penguins, inflatable penguins. Penguins that squeak, penguins that waddle, penguins whose bellies hide tubes of roll-on antiperspirant. Let Čik show you what must be the biggest penguin collection in all of Vienna—probably in all of Austria. Each of his birds has a unique function, and the collection is growing all the time.

Royal Family Crypt (Kaisergruft): Tegetthoffstrasse 2; two blocks north of Albertinastrasse. Open daily, 9:30 A.M.–4 P.M. Admission: AS 20; students, AS 10.

Another Viennese school-field-trip standby that few foreigners know about is the underground Kaisergruft: bone-rattlingly cold rooms packed with all of Austria's deceased royalty—all the Franzes, all the Marias, all the Johanns—from the sixteenth century onward. They're sealed snugly into coffins, many of which are decked with statuary that confirms the local saying about the Viennese loving a beautiful funeral. Baroque bronze skulls leer sarcastically from coffin lids whereon bronze angels cavort and bronze banners bear sonorous warnings and mottoes. Look for the pathetic child-coffins tucked ignobly into the corners.

Sewer Tours (On the Trail of The Third Man*)*: Tours are given the first Saturday of May, June, July, August, September, and October. Reservation office opens 14 days before each tour, and tickets must be purchased at least three days in advance. Children under 14 years old not allowed. Tours leave from in front of the information booth in the Karlsplatz Passage. Admission: AS 20. Phone: 42 800/29 50 Monday–Friday, 8 A.M.–3 P.M., or go to the Excursion Bureau in the City Hall (Rathaus) (entrance at Friedrich-Schmidt-Platz 1).

Aficionados of the film *The Third Man* can reenact the famous chase through the sewers of Vienna, where Harry Lime finally met his demise. The tour concentrates on the tunnels and sewers in the area under Karlsplatz, which is where scenes from the movie were filmed. Even if you've never seen *The Third Man*, the tour is a unique way to see Vienna and learn its history from the bottom up.

Tobacco Museum (Tabak Museum): Messepalast 7. Enter from Mariahilfer Strasse 2, walk 30 feet into the courtyard and take a sharp left turn in the cafe garden. Open Tuesday, 10 A.M.–7 P.M.; Wednesday–Friday, 10 A.M.–3 P.M.; Saturday and Sunday, 9 A.M.–1 P.M. Closed

Monday. Admission: AS 20; students, AS 10; groups of five or more, AS 5 per person. Phone: 96 17 16.

This collection conjures up images of distinguished gentlemen in smoking jackets, seen through a blue haze. Of the thousands of pipes here, from all over the world, many, most notably the huge ivory pipe carved to represent a cathedral, deserve to be in a sculpture museum. Others represent famous persons, gods and goddesses, and bawdy encounters. Here too are snuffboxes made of enamel, ivory, and gemstone; real wooden Indians; old opium paraphernalia; and cigar-band mosaics. Upstairs is a unique art exhibit: all of the paintings (done in many styles over several centuries) have one thing in common: a cigarette, cigar, or pipe is depicted somewhere on the canvas.

Undertakers' Museum (Bestattungsmuseum): Goldeggasse 19, Room 17. Open Monday–Friday, noon–3 P.M. Admission: free. Phone: (0222) 65 16 31/227.

You may never meet a more enthusiastic tour guide than the English-speaking gentleman at the Bestattungsmuseum. He's one of Vienna's leading undertakers, and with a breathlessness bordering on glee he'll show you the collection of historic coffins (including one limited-edition reusable model with a trap door at the bottom); models of tram cars used for hauling plague victims; filled cremation urns; contraptions by which a person presumed dead could signal the undertaker from inside the coffin that it was merely a case of suspended animation. You'll see much evidence of Vienna's sentimental obsession with funerals. And while nearly every other museum in this city lays claim to some part of the great composers, on display here are the official death notices of Beethoven and Strauss, Haydn's death mask, and Schubert's death certificate.

WERFEN
(30 miles south of Salzburg)

Ice Giants' World (Eisriesenwelt): To get there take a train south from Salzburg to Werfen. Follow the signs from the central market plaza along the path for approximately 10 minutes to the cable railway station. Take the cable railway up to the "Dr. Oedl House," where you buy admission tickets to the caves. Food and a rest area are available at the Dr. Oedl House. From there it is a 15-minute walk to the caves. Wear sturdy shoes and warm clothes. Cameras are not allowed. Miners' lamps are provided. The whole visit takes about 5 hours. Guided tours (required) are given 30 minutes after the arrival of each cable car. Cable railway runs May 1–October 5, 9 and 11 A.M. and 2 P.M., and will also run at 10 A.M., noon, and 1, 3, 4, and 6 P.M. if at least five people are waiting (which there usually are). Round-trip price: AS 70; children under 14, AS 35. Admission to caves: AS 60; children under 14, AS 30. Phone: 06468/248.

You may never get to be an interplanetary explorer, but a visit to the Eisriesenwelt will at least make you feel like one. The scenes confronting you in some of these ice caves can only be described as unearthly. The icy configurations are actually only the very front part of one of the world's largest cave systems. Your guide leads you from one immense, phantasmagorical room to the next (don't worry about slipping—wooden steps have been installed where needed); unless you're crazy, don't go wandering off by yourself. The twisted, eerie, natural ice "sculptures" are formed when water trickles into the caves from above and freezes. Some of them have been given descriptive names, but your own imagination will run rampant. Alexander von Mörk, who discovered most of the caves, is actually entombed in white marble next to the largest cave. This isn't the cheapest sight in Austria, but it might be the most unforgettable.

BELGIUM

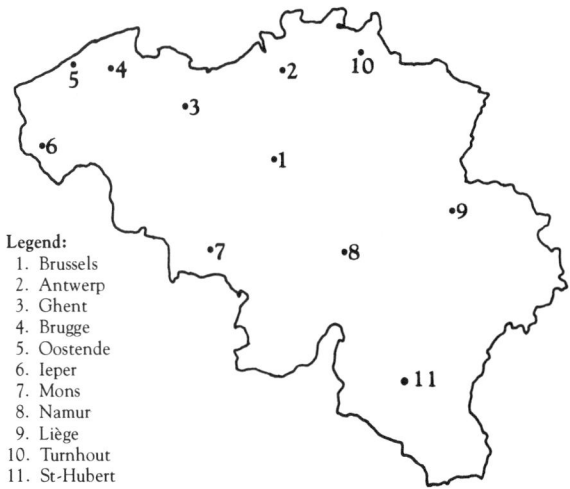

Legend:
1. Brussels
2. Antwerp
3. Ghent
4. Brugge
5. Oostende
6. Ieper
7. Mons
8. Namur
9. Liège
10. Turnhout
11. St-Hubert

"What do you think of my country?" asked our new Belgian friend. Before we could answer, she said, "*I think it's ugly.*"

And yet a week later we met Parisians who swore by Brussels, who would gladly trade a hundred croissants for a single Belgian waffle, who would jettison their champagne for a mug of Belgian cherry beer.

Belgium is too self-conscious. The Belgians shift uncomfortably from one foot to the other, scanning the horizon in search of invaders, enemy bombs and anti-Belgian jokes. Belgians purse their lips and think, sarcastically, "But of course!" when foreigners mistake famous Belgians for Frenchmen or Dutchmen: Pieter Breughel, Peter Paul Rubens, Anthony van Dyck, René Magritte, Georges Simenon—even Hercule Poirot.

Foreigners just don't know what Belgians are capable of. But this is the nation that brought you fruit-flavored beer and the patron saint of insanity: surely there's something going on here.

Belgium / 17

ANSEREMME
(One half mile south of Dinant; 50 miles southeast of Brussels)

Lesse River Kayak Trips (Descente de la Lesse): several companies provide kayaks in Anseremme, including Lesse Kayaks (Place de l'Eglise d'Anseremme 2, phone [082] 22 43 97 or [082] 22 31 20) and Kayaks Ansiaux (rue du Velodrome 15, phone [082] 22 23 25). Call at least one day in advance to reserve a kayak, especially on weekends.

Cruising down a river is an enjoyable and exciting way to spend a day—remember all the fun those guys had in the movie *Deliverance?* Luckily, you won't see any blind banjo players along the Lesse; instead, there are castles, cliffs, pasturelands, picnic areas, and a lot of other happy-go-lucky kayakers. The ride is fairly safe, and no special boat knowledge or swimming skill is required. Here's how to arrange the trip: after making a reservation by phone, show up at Anseremme sometime between 8 A.M. and 10:30 A.M., where you pay your money and lock up your belongings. Then you take one of several trains or buses to Houyet, 12 miles upstream, where your kayak is waiting for you. Paddle down to Anseremme (where you'll arrive sometime between 3 and 6 P.M.), drop off the kayak, and pick up your stuff. For the less athletic, Lesse Kayaks also has daily boats trips down the river in large, sedate barges guided by polemen. (Prices for kayaking vary from company to company and change every year, but expect to pay somewhere around BF 800.)

ANTWERP

Antwerp Zoo Bird House: in the zoo, entrance at Koningin Astridplein 26, adjacent to the central train station. Open daily 8:30 A.M.–6 P.M.; in winter, 8:30 A.M.–5 P.M. All buildings close 15 minutes before the zoo closes. Admission: BF 260; children 3–12, BF 160; children under 3, free. Phone: (03) 231 16 40.

The Antwerp Zoo, in addition to having one of the best collections of animals in Europe, has an extremely unusual Exotic Bird House. It's not the birds themselves that are the attraction here, but the way in which they are contained. In the area called the Dark Gallery, there's no wall to prevent the birds from flying away, yet they are tricked by ingenious lighting into thinking they're in an enclosed space. You can stand quite close to the birds with no barrier between you and them, but they never even try to leave their "cage of light." Also worth visiting at the zoo are the African animals housed in a mock Egyptian temple and the reptile house with simulated rainstorms.

Museum of the Wheel (Museum Het Wiel): Hopland 17. Open April 15–November 30, Wednesday and Saturday, 10 A.M.–5 P.M.; December 1–April 14, Saturday, 10 A.M.–5 P.M. and Sunday 9:30 A.M.–2:30 P.M. Admission: BF 100; seniors, BF 80; children under 12, BF 50. Phone: (03) 232 62 74.

For the moment, at least, these wheeled wonders are holding still so that you can get a good look: the world's first bicycles are here, as are motorbikes, go-carts, carriages, and steam engines; if it rolls, it's here.

BAARLE-HERTOG and BAARLE-NASSAU (Ten miles north of Turnhout, two miles inside the Dutch border).

Tourist Office phone: 00-31-42579921

Europe has its share of geopolitical anomalies, but none can compare with this bizarre situation. Inside the Netherlands is a city called Baarle-Nassau. It's a Dutch city. That makes sense. But also inside the Netherlands is a city called Baarle-Hertog. It's a Belgian city, even though it's not physically connected with Belgium. To make matters worse, the two cities have nightmarishly complicated municipal borders and are intermingled like a pair of wrestling octopi. Baarle's schizoid personality is the result of political shenanigans between some twelfth-century dukes and counts who had no inkling of the consequences of their actions. Now the city has two governments, two legal systems, two fire departments, two currencies, two sets of business hours, two of everything—one Belgian, one Dutch. You can stroll through the city and pass back and forth from Belgium to Holland dozens of times (the way to tell is by the address plates on the houses, which sport national flags). A fitting way to cap off your visit is with a drink at Cafe Het Hoekske, which straddles the border and is the site of all the city's international transactions.

BINCHE
(30 miles south of Brussels)

Binche Carnival: every year on Carnival (also known as Shrove Tuesday). Action takes place throughout the town all day.

At daybreak on Carnival, Binche's notorious *Gilles* begin to fill the streets. Wearing yellow, red, black, gold, and white costumes decorated with lions, crowns, stars, and real clanging bells, they don their immense (nearly three feet tall) ostrich-plume headpieces and dance through the streets to a slow drumbeat. At 10 A.M. everybody, including the *Gilles*, gathers in the Grand' Place in the center of town. From there a disorderly procession of countless thousands tromps through the town all day. The *Gilles* now each carry a basket of oranges, which they toss one by one to the crowd. Be warned, though, that the tossing can become pretty furious as oranges begin to fly everywhere, whomping people on the head and splattering juice all over. This tradition dates from the 1500s, when the Hapsburgs ruled Belgium and the King of Spain paid Binche a visit. A huge fiesta was staged for him, with locals dressing up like Peruvian Incas and handing out gold-colored fruit to symbolize Spain's recent "discovery" of gold in South America. Other dances, parades, and festivities take place later that evening and on the preceding Sunday.

International Carnival and Mask Museum (Musée International du Carnaval et du Masque): rue de l'Eglise 71, two blocks from the Grand' Place. Open February 1–March 31, Sunday, 2–6 P.M.; April 1–December 13, Monday–Thursday and Saturday, 10 A.M.–noon and 2–6 P.M. Admission: BF 90; students and seniors, BF 75; children 6–14, BF 55. Phone: (064) 33 57 41.

Visiting this museum is like stepping into someone else's midsummer night's dream. All the world's latent wildness and usually repressed fantasies are revealed in the form of scary masks, suits covered entirely in snails, moss, bells, or coins; shaggy false beards; and soaring headgear; Africa, Asia, the Americas, Europe, Oceania, and India are all represented here. And you thought

Europe was thoroughly civilized? The bizarre costumes from France, Italy, Greece, Spain, Portugal, Austria, and, of course, Belgium are enough to keep a horde of anthropologists scratching their heads for a long time.

BRUGGE (BRUGES)

Organ Museum (Orgelmuseum): 't Zand-Vrijdagmarkt 11, just west of downtown. Open Easter–November 15, daily, 10 A.M.–7 P.M. Admission: BF 120. Phone: (050) 33 18 55 or (050) 33 88 32.

And you thought organs were dignified creatures, made to moan sonorously in church lofts. Some do; but their less pious cousins are having a far jollier time: fairground organs, hurdy-gurdies, dance organs—even delicate music boxes round out the museum's collection. Many of the mechanical instruments are in working order, and the tour guide operates them for you.

Procession of the Holy Blood (Heilig-Bloed Processie): every year on Ascension Day, starting at 3 P.M. from the Basilica of the Holy Blood, going through the streets of the old town. Call the Brugge Tourist Office for more information: (050) 33 07 11.

In 1150 a local knight came back from the Second Crusade with a small package under his arm. Big deal, right? Well, it's the biggest deal in the world to the people of Brugge: in that package were drops of blood supposedly shed by Jesus as he was dying, and the whole city stages a huge celebration every year to commemorate the arrival of The Holy Blood. The fantastic procession, which winds through the streets, involves thousands of people, some dressed in ancient costumes acting out Bible scenes, others dressed in medieval costumes reenacting the return of the knight, others singing, dancing, marching ... everything but throwing batons in the air. The reliquary containing The Holy Blood comes at the climactic end of the procession. The rest of the year The Holy Blood is in the Basilica, in the upper chapel, where it is displayed every Friday from 8:30–11:45 A.M. and from 3–4 P.M. The blood is in a glass vial in an ornate gold and silver reliquary and is on display every day for approximately two weeks before the procession.

BRUSSELS (BRUXELLES)

Atomium: in Laeken Park, northern edge of the city. Take the metro to Heysel stop, or tram 81. Open Easter–September 15, daily, 9:30 A.M.–10 P.M.; September 16–Easter, daily, 9:30 A.M.–6 P.M. Admission: BF 90. Phone: (02) 478 48 66.

Brussels is home to many, many molecules, but only one is 165 billion times normal size. The 310-foot-tall Atomium, built in 1958 for an exhibition, looks just the way early-20th-century physicists imagined a molecule should look: geometrically arranged gleaming spheres (representing the atoms) connected by thin tubes (representing the electrical connections between the atoms). But the Atomium isn't just weird to look at: you can actually go inside and ride escalators up the tubes to the various "atoms," where there are observation platforms, a restaurant, and exhibits about famous physicists and atomic energy. Some say the Atomium is a travesty, others say it's the most futuristic structure ever built. They may both be right.

Brewers' Museum (Musée de la Brasserie): Maison des Brasseurs, on the Grand' Place. Open Monday–Friday, 10 A.M.–noon and 2–5 P.M.; Saturday 10 A.M.–noon. Closed Sunday. Admission: BF 50 (collected at end of visit). Phone: (02) 512 11 81.

Sit at a sturdy wooden table in this quaint seventeenth-century house (the world's only guild house still used for its original purpose—guild meetings) and watch a slide show about the Brewers' Guild (English soundtrack available). It is a prosperous and determined history, though at times tragic. Even if you don't like beer, the museum makes you at least respect it: "Beer is a wholesome beverage," booms the voice on the soundtrack, "born of the sap of the harvest." Afterward there's a free mug of you-know-what waiting for you in the taproom.

Brussels Gueuze Museum: rue Gheude 56, in the Anderlecht suburb, west of downtown. Take bus 20 or 47. Open October 15–April 30, Saturday only, with tours at 11 A.M., and 2 and 3:30 P.M. Admission: BF 60. Phone: (02) 520 28 91 or (02) 521 49 28.

Belgium is home to a number of eccentric beers, and this brewery/museum is the last place on earth making some of them. Consider Kriek, a beer flavored with cherries;

Gueuze, in which wheat ferments spontaneously in the bottle; and Faro, a heady 1,000-year-old recipe. The brewery also makes beer flavored with raspberries and brown sugar.

Horta Museum: rue Americaine 25, in the St-Gilles suburb. Take bus 54 or tram 37, 81, 93, or 94. Open Tuesday–Sunday, 2–5:30 P.M. Closed Monday. Admission: BF 50. Phone: (02) 537 16 92. Guided tours on request.

Art nouveau—that voluptuous blend of wrought-iron tendrils, stained and frosted glass, fluted tulip lamps, and lush curves—owes its soul to turn-of-the-century Belgian architect Victor Horta. This museum is installed in Horta's own house. Objects on display include the architect's blueprints, sinuous furniture that he designed himself, and photographs. The house itself is rich in Horta's art nouveau trademarks.

Jeanneke-Pis: at the end of Impasse de la Fidelité, which branches off Beenhouwers Strasse, two blocks from the Grand' Place.

This urinating statue, the female counterpart of the more famous Mannekin-Pis, was installed June 24, 1987. All the money she earns from donations goes toward fighting cancer and AIDS. Squatting and smiling, radiating nonchalance, pigtailed Jeanneke urinates every bit as well as her brother.

Lock and Key Museum (Musée de la Serrure): rue des Bouchers 70, two blocks from the central train station. Front of the museum is unmarked. Admission: free. Phone: (02) 511 35 91.

Along one wall of an old-time Brussels lock craftsman's shop is a diverse collection of locks, keys, doorknockers, buckles, silver spurs, and a lot of objects that must be locks and keys but sure don't look like them: studded balls, textured cylinders, etc. An interesting display details "The Language of Keys." At the rear of the shop, amid debris, a life-size waxen metalsmith labors with hammer and anvil.

Mannekin-Pis Costume Collection: in The Museum of the City of Brussels, Maison du Roi, in the Grand' Place. Open Monday–Wednesday and Friday, 10 A.M.–12:30 P.M. and 1:30–5 P.M.; Thursday, 10 A.M.–5 P.M. (10 A.M.–4 P.M. in winter); Saturday and Sunday, 10 A.M.–1 P.M. Admission: BF 50; children 6–15, BF 35. Phone: (02) 511 27 42.

If you were the Mannekin-Pis, the famous urinating statue of Brussels, wouldn't *you* want a disguise? Now you can see the little pisser dressed as an Arab sheik, a train conductor, Mickey Mouse. Over the years, dozens of kind persons and heads of state have presented Mr. Inexhaustible Bladder with costumes, and while the actual statue at the corner of rue de l'Etuve and rue du Chêne is occasionally dressed up, the bulk of his wardrobe is stored at the Maison du Roi. Among other costumes you'll see are those of a soccer player, Vincent Van Gogh, bullfighter, Portuguese fisherman, WWI soldier, Tahitian king, African chief, Chinese folk dancer, Welsh coal miner, John Bull, chef, policeman, and ancient Roman. And boy, does the Mannekin-Pis look silly as a witch.

Museum of Bookbinding: rue Bemel 21-23, in the Woluwé-St-Pierre suburb, southeast of downtown. Take bus 36. Open Tuesday–Saturday, 10 A.M.–5 P.M. Closed Sunday and Monday. Admission: free. Phone: (02) 770 53 33.

Love to read but don't have time for the whole book? The museum's collection of book coverings spans five centuries, tracing this often-overlooked art from its glorious Renaissance salad days all the way to the twentieth century.

Musical Instrument Museum (Musée Instrumental): 17 Place Petit Sablon, in the Royal Music Conservatory, south of downtown. Open Tuesday, Thursday, and Saturday, 2:30–4:30 P.M.; Wednesday, 4–6 P.M.; and Sunday, 10:30 A.M.–12:30 P.M. Closed Monday and Friday. Admission: free. Phone: (02) 512 08 48.

Some museums are just too big for their own britches. This is one of the largest collections of musical instruments in the world, but there's only space to display 1,200 of its 5,000 instruments at any one time, so you'll never know what might be on display. Many of the instruments are exceedingly rare and exotic, so you're guaranteed to see something unusual.

National Museum of Historical Figurines (Musée International de la Figurine Historique): in the Abbot's House at Dieleghem (Demeure Abbatiale), rue J. Tiebackx 14, in the Jette suburb, north of downtown. Take bus 13 or 53.

> ## BRUSSELS' ART NOUVEAU HOUSES
>
> Brussels, home of the architects who dreamed up this most sinuously feminine of modern architectural styles, sports many stunning examples of art nouveau. The following buildings were designed by Victor Horta between 1893 and 1905.
>
> Maison Tassel: rue Paul Emile Janson 12 (1893)
> Maison Wissinger: rue Hôtel des Monnaies 66 (1894)
> Maison Frison: rue Lebeau 37 (1895)
> Jardin d'Enfants: rue St. Ghislain 40 (1895)
> Hôtel Solvay: avenue Louise 224 (1895)
> Hôtel van Eetvelde: avenue Palmerston 2-4 (1897)
> Hôtel Max Hallet: avenue Louise 346 (1905)
> Les Magasins Waucquez: rue des Sables 20 (1905)

Open Tuesday–Friday and the first weekend of every month, 10 A.M.–noon and 2–4 P.M. Admission: free. Phone: (02) 479 00 52.

If only history had *really* looked like this, how cute it would have been—especially the wars. Thousands of tiny little people in metal and plastic, elaborately costumed (considering their size), are arranged in dioramas that illustrate the entire history of the civilized world. (Special emphasis is placed on Belgian history.) It's not all tin soldiers, either: kings, queens, politicians, laborers, and children take part in the Lilliputian scenarios.

Ommegang Pageant: every year on the first Thursday in July. Mostly contained in the Grand' Place. For more information, call the Brussels Tourist Office at (02) 513 89 40.

Charles V, the luxury-loving king, saw a pageant once in 1549 that impressed itself so vividly on his mind that to this day the people of Brussels reenact it every July. Local aristocrats dress up in rich, historic costumes to lead the day's parades. Also on hand are acrobats, dancers, and other performers, both serious and light-hearted—just as Charles would have ordered it. The festival climaxes in true Renaissance fashion with a human chess game played out in the Grand' Place: brightly clad horsemen in conquistador costumes are the chess pieces.

CHAUDFONTAINE
(Two miles southeast of Liège)

Western City Recreation Center (Centre Recreatif de Western City): rue Bois de la Grue 2. Open daily in summer. Cowboy stunt show on Sundays at 3 P.M. Phone: (041) 65 54 61.

All the Belgian cowpokes spend their Sunday afternoons here, practicing at the firing range for the big bank raid, getting their saddles repaired, chowing down on the "authentic Texas gastronomic specialties," and exercising their elbows at the saloon. Visitors can also rent horses at the stables, buy Wild West curios at the General Store, and wonder why a tar pit is among the town's featured attractions. Watching the Sunday afternoon shows is just like being on the set of a *Gunsmoke* episode.

COUVIN
(60 miles south of Brussels)

Grottoes of Neptune: two miles north of Couvin-Petigny on Route 180. Open Easter–September 30, daily, 9:30 A.M.–noon and 1:30–6 P.M.; in October, Saturday and Sunday, 9:30 A.M.–noon and 1:30–6 P.M. Phone: (060) 31 19 54 or (02) 731 59 67. Tours last 45 minutes.

The first half of the tour is on foot, the second half by boat. The underground explorations are brought to a big finale with a *"son et lumière"* (sound and light) show. With inspiring music filling the caves, lights and images are projected onto a gushing underground waterfall—a rather hallucinatory experience.

DRONGEN
(Four miles west of Ghent)

Glue Museum (Kolla Lijmmuseum): Antoon Catriestraat 39. Open Monday–Friday, office hours only. Admission: free. Phone: (091) 26 89 41.

Among life's unsung heroes, glue has a longstanding position. Have you ever stopped to wonder, "How did people stick things together before glue was invented?"

Well, luckily for people, glue has, in some form or another, been in use since prehistoric times. This company museum traces glue's use through the eighteenth century.

GEER
(20 miles west of Liège)

Museum of Penguin Effigies: rue de Boëlhe 17. Open by appointment only. Admission: free. Phone: (019) 58 83 78.

Geer is a long way from the South Pole, but you wouldn't know it from the number of penguins to be found waddling around this museum. The curator has collected about a thousand effigies, made of paper, fabric, metal, and plastic; depicted on plates, jewelry, posters ... you name it. The exhibits are changed periodically, but the theme is always penguins.

GHEEL (GEEL)
(25 miles east of Antwerp)

Festival of St. Dympna: every year on May 15; all over the city, especially at the tomb of St. Dympna.

To Belgians, the name Gheel means one thing and one thing only: insanity. Mentally ill people from all over the world come to Gheel in the hope of a miraculous cure. St. Dympna, the patron saint of insane people, has her shrine here, and for centuries families cursed with madness have flocked here to pray to the saint. Now Gheel is essentially an insane asylum without walls: the population is almost entirely composed of nurses, priests, health-care workers, worried families—and madmen. May 15, which is St. Dympna's feast day, is the most frenzied day of the year. Mentally ill people from all over are brought to her tomb; hysteria erupts, and anything can happen.

Museum of St. Dympna: Gasthuisstraat 1. Open May 15– August 31, Sunday, 2–6 P.M.; other times by appointment only. Admission: BF 35; students, BF 20; children, free. Phone: (014) 58 92 76.

This museum is not only about St. Dympna and her tragic life story, but also about the history of mental illness in Gheel. Photos, drawings, and dioramas describe and explain the whys and hows of Gheel's unique situation.

GHENT (GENT)

Gravensteen Castle Torture Museum: on the Sint-Veerleplein, in the center of town. Open April–September, 9 A.M.–6 P.M.; October–March, 9 A.M.–4 P.M. Admission: BF 60; children under 12, free. Phone: (02) 25 93 06.

The Belgians may have invented waffles, but you'll find yourself speculating about the original function of waffle irons when you see the human branding irons on display here. In addition to *oubliettes* (dungeons), you'll see stocks, thumbscrews, humiliating shame masks, and collars with the spikes pointing *in*. Where a bed once stood is now a similar-looking but less than comfortable bit of furniture: the rack. The museum's pitchforks were once used to keep condemned people from escaping being burned at the stake.

HAN-SUR-LESSE
(45 miles south of Liège)

Grottoes of Han-Sur-Lesse: to get to the grottoes, buy tickets and take the special tram next to the church in the center of town. The tram will take you up to the grottoes' entrance. Open Easter–September 30, daily 9–11:30 A.M. and 1–6 P.M. (trams leave every half hour during these times); October 1–Easter, trams leave once every two hours. Tours take 1 hour 45 minutes. Phone: (084) 37 72 13.

The river Lesse goes underground at Han, and has carved out an incredible series of caves and grottoes, now all fitted with eerie lighting. Part of the tour is by boat on the underground section of the river; the reechoing sounds of the water lapping against the boat and the walls only add to the creepy atmosphere. Some of the grottoes are almost 400 feet tall; in other areas you practically have to bend over. A museum at the end displays various objects found over the years in the grottoes.

HOESELT
(60 miles east of Brussels)

Witches' Festival (Heksenfeest): August 15 and the following weekend. For more information phone the Provincial Tourist Association at (011) 22 29 58.

Belgium burned all of its real witches in the Middle Ages, so the ones you see in this festival are all make-believe. The festivities climax in a parade through the streets of town. Broomstick-wielding, shaggy-haired "witches" are the star attraction, but an assortment of other weirdly dressed creatures and characters join the procession too.

HOTTON
(30 miles south of Liège)

Grottoes of 1001 Nights: One-half mile southwest of Hotton (the entry building is in the middle of a field). Open April–October, daily 9 A.M.–6 P.M. Admission: BF 150; children, BF 80. Phone: (084) 46 60 46 or (084) 46 61 71.

The name of this place should tip you off: it's one of those caves where every formation, room, or strange stalagmite has been given some colorful name. Passing the "Room of Perseverence" and "The Altar" on your way down, you come to the "Midnight Room," where several stalactites go off at inexplicable angles. Cross "The Pit" and "The Big Basins" to "The Chess Game" (we still haven't figured out this name), a shadowy maze of oozings and stalactites. Finally, you arrive at "The Balcony," a shelf with a view into the huge cavern, at the bottom of which is a river.

HULSTE
(West Flanders)

Museum of Finch-Catching (Nationaal Volkssportmuseum voor de Vinkensport): Hazenstraat 4. Open the first and third Saturday of every month, 2–5 P.M. Admission: free. Phone: (056) 66 81 98.

You're probably thinking, "Finch catching? This one *must* be a joke." But no—it *is* real. We went there. A whole museum devoted to the hobby of catching finches to use as pets—you may never find a museum on a more obscure topic.

IEPER (YPRES)
(30 miles southwest of Brugge)

Cat Festival: second Sunday in May, 3 P.M. Parade takes place on even-numbered years only; cat toss happens every year.

In 1817, Ieper's textile industry was threatened by a sudden overpopulation of ravenous rats. Cats were brought in to control the rodents, but then the cats over-reproduced and Ieper had yet another animal problem. This, they say, is the source of the annual festival in which the town jester hurls stuffed velvet cats from the belfry into the jostling crowds below. In 1817 (so the story goes), the jester's ammunition was real, live cats. The biannual cat parade hints at ancient cat worship: an enormous, towering King and Queen of Cats (and the Crown Prince Kitten, Piepertje) roll through the streets surrounded by 2,000 locals in cat suits and medieval costumes.

KALMTHOUT
(15 miles north of Antwerp)

Beekeeping Museum: Heikanstraat 51a. Open April, May, June, September, and October, Sunday, 2–5 P.M.; July and August, daily, 2–5 P.M. Admission: BF 25; children, BF 10. Phone: (03) 666 96 98.

Bees make honey, but don't fool yourself—they aren't making it for *us*. Learn how humans hoodwink bees into yielding their personal baby food for our enjoyment.

KANNE
(13 miles north of Liège, on the Dutch border)

Subterranean Museum: Schoolstraat 278. Open by appointment only. Admission: BF 45. Phone: (012) 45 11 00.

This underground labyrinth wears signs of its former occupants the way a very old phone booth wears graffiti. Prehistoric cave paintings depict animals and plants; elsewhere in the cave are Roman artifacts, nineteenth-century spelunking equipment, and fossils—displayed in the exact locations where they were found. The most modern exhibit deals with mushroom growing.

KNOKKE-HEIST
(Ten miles north of Brugge, on the coast)

Butterfly Town (De Vlindertuin): Bronlaan 14. Take bus 767 from the Knokke train station. Open Easter–mid-October, daily, 10 A.M.–5:30 P.M. Admission: BF 100; seniors, BF 80; children under 12, BF 50. Phone: (050) 61 04 72. Guided tours on request.

The butterflies' 1,300-foot-long enclosure has waterfalls, pools, and exotic flora, to convince these dumb beauties that they're not really a stone's throw from the chilly North Sea, but back in steamy Africa, Asia, or South America, where they belong. Special glass cases contain cocoons and caterpillars at various stages of development, while others illuminate various aspects of insect life. Meanwhile, the butterflies hover and glide overhead.

LEUVEN (LOUVAIN)
(15 miles east of Brussels)

Artois Brewery Tours: by appointment only. Admission: free. Phone: (016) 24 72 99.

To you, a glass of beer might be an oasis of relaxation after a hard day's work, but for some people—many of them Belgians—that glass of beer *is* a hard day's work. See beer from the brewers' viewpoint, watch its various stages of production, sample the wares—and next time you reach for a cool brewski, at least you'll feel educated.

LIÈGE

Piece of the True Cross: in Church of the Holy Cross (Eglise Sainte Croix) on rue Ste-Croix, near Place St-Lambert. Open normal church hours.

In a golden triptych, fashioned reverently in the twelfth century with bas-relief apostles and saints, angels and jewels, a piece of the True Cross rests serenely under a small glass dome. The triptych is in the church's treasury alongside other religious prizes.

LIER (LIERRE)
(20 miles north of Brussels)

Astronomical Clock and Astronomy Studio (Zimmertoren): Zimmerplein 18. Open June–August, daily, 9 A.M.–noon and 1–7 P.M.; May, September, and October, daily, 9 A.M.–noon, and 1–6 P.M.; March and April, daily, 9 A.M.–noon and 2–5 P.M.; November–January, daily, 9 A.M.–noon and 2–4 P.M. Admission: BF 30; children, BF 20. Phone: (03) 489 11 11.

Stuck in central Belgium but need to know about the next high tide? Take a gander at Lier's astronomical clock, whose 13 separate faces tell you the phase of the moon, the date, the location of the planets, the sign of the zodiac, the date of the next eclipse, the state of the tides, and more (including the time). At the stroke of noon a procession of mechanical figures files out of the little window on the tower. You can go inside the tower and inspect the studio of astronomer and watchmaker Louis Zimmer (complete with planetarium), who built the clock in 1930.

MECHELEN
(15 miles south of Antwerp)

International Apimondia Beekeeping Museum (Bijenteeltmuseum): Antwerpsesteenweg 92. Open March–October, Tuesday–Friday, 2–5 P.M.; Saturday and Sunday, 2–6 P.M.; November–February, Tuesday–Sunday, 2–5 P.M. Closed Monday. Admission: BF 33; seniors and children, BF 25. Phone: (015) 20 38 21.

Our prehistoric ancestors were a brave and sturdy lot. Not only did they have to contend with bears and wolves and the invention of fire; they also managed to get honey away from the prehistoric bees. This museum traces beekeeping from those scary days to these. Displays feature ancient and modern beekeeping equipment, hives, types of honey, and actual bees.

MONS

Battle of the Lumeçon and Procession of the Golden Carriage: on Trinity Sunday, the first Sunday after Whitsun (late May or early June). The procession starts at 10 A.M. from the Belfry on the hill, and goes down to the central square (Grand' Place), where the fight takes place at 12:30 P.M.

A crazed combination of folklore, Christian celebration, and pagan festival, the Mons Battle of the Lumeçon is hard to classify. The day starts at 10 A.M. with a parade of local groups in costume and, most importantly, the "Golden Carriage" (Car d'Or), which resembles a petite gilded Spanish galleon and which carries the reliquary housing the skull of St. Waudru, the city's patron saint. At 12:30, after the procession has arrived at the Grand' Place, a man dressed as St. George gallops out on a white horse and engages in a ferocious mock battle with the "Lumeçon," a strange, green, missile-shaped dragon. The dragon is controlled by six or eight white-garbed men, but, as expected, St. George always wins. Later that night is the "Pageant of Mons," which employs up to 2,000 actors. A three-day municipal festival follows the battle.

MORKHOVEN
(20 miles east of Antwerp)

Museum of Skulls (Schedelhof): Bertheide 12. Open Thursday–Tuesday, 10 A.M.–6 P.M. Closed Wednesday. Admission: free. Phone: (014) 22 08 12.

Six hundred skulls stare out at you with eyeless sockets. Ever wonder what a rhino's head looks like without the flesh? This is the place to find out. You can also see bird skulls, an elephant's skull, primate skulls—you've probably gotten the idea by now.

OOSTENDE

The Mercator: in the Jachthaven Mercator (Mercator Yacht Harbor), east of downtown. Open January and February, Sunday, 10 A.M.–noon and 1–4 P.M.; March, Saturday and Sunday, 10 A.M.–noon and 1–5 P.M.; April and May, Saturday and Sunday, 9 A.M.–noon and 1–6 P.M.; June and September, daily, 9 A.M.–noon and 1–6 P.M.; July and August, daily, 9 A.M.–7 P.M.; October, Saturday and Sunday, 10 A.M.–noon and 1–5 P.M.; November and December, Sunday, 10 A.M.–noon and 1–4 P.M. Admission: BF 60; students, BF 20; children 4–14 and seniors, BF 30; children under 4, free. Phone: (059) 70 56 54.

This three-masted sailing ship used to ply the seven seas. Now it houses a maritime museum, chock-full of curious exotic objects that sailors brought back from their voyages—the strange souvenirs of Belgium's lifelong affair with the sea. An off-the-wall note: before she retired, the Mercator brought home to Belgium the bodily remains of Father Damien, priest to the lepers of Molokai.

PEER
(50 miles northeast of Brussels)

The Pears of Peer: throughout the town.

This village's name, in reality, comes from a dull German word: *"Perre,"* meaning "enclosure." But locals far prefer to associate with the juicy, comfortably shaped fruit, whose Flemish name is *Peer*. The whole town glitters with images of golden pears: a huge one surmounts the cast-iron water pump; the Gothic church spire has a pear as does the town hall's tower. One of the town's prized artistic possessions is the "Madonna with Pear." Now, let's not hear any more lip about "enclosures," y'hear?

ST-HUBERT
(85 miles southeast of Brussels)

Feast of St. Hubert: every year on November 3. For more information, call the St-Hubert Tourist Office at (061) 61 20 70.

Bloodhounds in the basilica? No, the priest doesn't mind. It's all part of the celebration to honor the eighth-century saint who, while hunting in the Ardennes, met an enormous stag with a golden cross glowing between its antlers. Hubert was instantly converted and became the patron saint of hunters. Here in his town, Hubert's feast day is marked by a Hunters' Mass: red-jacketed, velvet-capped huntsmen wail away on spiraled hunting horns, while ranks of dogs stand by, waiting tensely for their masters to present them to the priest, who blesses each one.

ST-TRUIDEN
(45 miles east of Brussels)

Astronomical Clock: in the Begijnhof. Performances on the hour.

Twenty thousand mechanical parts make this one of the world's most complicated clocks. At the stroke of every hour, who should lead the parade of automata but Death himself (to make you think twice about the passage of time). Following him is a pair of medieval artisans. The clock also keeps track of the constellations, eclipses, and the earth's path around the sun.

SILLY
(25 miles southwest of Brussels)

This town, located midway between Ath and Enghien, seems unaware that its name means anything in English. Friends at home will appreciate some Silly postcards, though.

SOUGNÉ-REMOUCHAMPS
(Ten miles south of Liège)

Grottoes of Remouchamps: on the Route de Louveignée, just outside of town. Open May–August, daily, 9 A.M.–6 P.M.; March, April, September, and October, daily, 9:30 A.M.–5 P.M.; November–February, Sunday, 9:30 A.M.–5 P.M.; and by appointment. Admission: BF 245; children, BF 145. Phone: (041) 84 46 82.

After a stroll through dripping, concretion-filled caves with "fairytale lighting," climb into a little red, blue, or yellow boat for what is claimed to be the longest underground boat ride in the world. Professional cave boatmen pole you along the subterranean Rubicon river; be careful of the stalactites and low ceiling. The river runs along underneath, not next to, the caves you explore in the first half of the visit.

TILFF
(Five miles south of Liège)

Bee Museum (Musée de l'Abeille): rue du Bichet 9. Open June–August, daily, 10 A.M.–noon and 2–6 P.M.; April, May, and September, Saturday and Sunday, 10 A.M.–noon and 2–6 P.M.; other months by appointment. Admission: BF 40; children under 13, BF 15. Phone: (041) 88 22 63.

For the horrific thrill of a lifetime, press your face up against one of the museum's glass-enclosed hives of living bees. The more mature among you can look at all the exhibits about bees and beekeeping. Especially interesting is the electronic display board, which tries to unravel the meaning of bee dances.

TURNHOUT
(25 miles east of Antwerp)

National Playing Card Museum (Nationaal Museum van de Speelkaart): Begijnenstraat 28. Open June, Tuesday–Friday, 2–5 P.M.; and Sunday, 10 A.M.–noon and 2–5 P.M.; July and August, Tuesday–Saturday, 2–5 P.M. and Sunday 10 A.M.–noon and 2–5 P.M.; September–May, Wednesday and Friday, 2–5 P.M. and Sunday 10 A.M.–noon and 2–5 P.M. Admission: BF 20; children, BF 15. Phone: (014) 41 56 21.

Shuffle straight over to this full house of cards where

they have a great deal of decks. Now that I've gotten that out of my system, let's talk about the museum. The accent here is not only on playing cards, but on the machines that make them, since Turnhout has been the European card-manufacturing headquarters for over 150 years. The number and variety of decks in their archives is stupendous, with designs ranging from ancient to modern, hilarious to regal, quaint to shocking; unfortunately, only part of the collection can be shown at one time, so the exhibit is constantly rotated. Also on display are mechanical devices used in the manufacture and design of cards, and other objects relating to the business and games of cards.

VIELSALM
(30 miles south of Liège)

Witches' Festival (Heksenfeest): July 20, beginning at 9 P.M. Phone: (080) 21 50 52 or (080) 21 54 32.

If only the medieval Belgians had known how fond their twentieth-century descendants would be of witch festivals, maybe they would have let a few witches live. The Salm Valley, where Vielsalm is located, observes the Witches' Festival: about 30 locals don flowing black dresses, black kerchiefs, and hideous wild-eyed, beak-nosed masks. They leap and dance around, cutting capers that pass for the events of a witches' Sabbat. As night turns into day there is much waving of broomsticks, reading of mock proclamations, and costumed hilarity.

WEZEMAAL
(15 miles northeast of Brussels)

Lamp Museum (Lampenmuseum): Aarschotsesteenweg 196. Open by appointment only. Admission: BF 20. Phone: (016) 44 53 65.

The 500 lamps in this collection represent over 500 years. Oil lamps, gas lamps, and others—including some rare fifteenth-century lighting fixtures—trace humans' struggle against one of the scariest foes in the world: darkness.

DENMARK

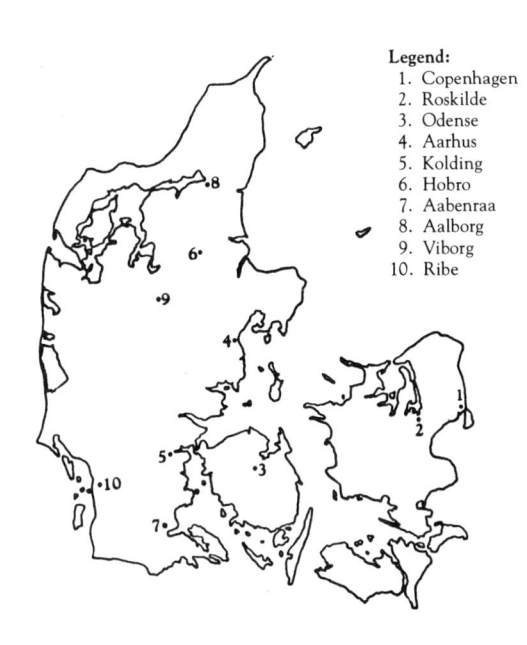

Legend:
1. Copenhagen
2. Roskilde
3. Odense
4. Aarhus
5. Kolding
6. Hobro
7. Aabenraa
8. Aalborg
9. Viborg
10. Ribe

One day in Copenhagen, the first sunny day of the summer, we saw a woman rollerskating without a shirt on. Grinning, she sped down the street—not trying to be sexy; not at all crazy. She was simply glad the sun was finally shining.

You won't see that every day in Denmark. On another day it might be a giant of a man, covered head to foot in balloons, or a huge garden in the shape of a world map. A swashbuckling Viking heritage has left the Danes self-confident. They've got imagination.

The Danes are also great storytellers. And Hans Christian Andersen was hardly the first of

Denmark / 37

his kind—a thousand years ago, his ancestors were spinning great sagas, full of violent deaths and bickering gods.

Which came first—the Danes' storytelling prowess or their love of children? Here, kids are seen as whole, worthy beings. All over the country are little paradises built for them.

Where else but Denmark would you find an entire city built of Lego blocks?

AABENRAA
(Southern Jutland, 17 miles north of the German border)

Aabenraa Museum: H.P. Hanssensgade 33B. Open May 15–September 14, Tuesday–Sunday, 10 A.M.–4 P.M.; September 15–May 14, Tuesday–Sunday, 1–6 P.M. Closed Monday. Admission: 5 kr; children, 1 kr. Phone: (04) 62 26 45.

This, the local maritime museum, has two unusual sections. One contains rows and rows of tiny ship models built inside bottles. Another section is filled with bizarre and exotic curios collected over the centuries by Danish sailors plying the seven seas.

Ride-at-the-Ring Festival (Amtsringriderfesten): usually the first weekend in July. Exact site sometimes changes, though it shouldn't be hard to find.

"Riding-at-the-ring" is an ancient tradition in southern Jutland, and it is kept up in several towns and villages in yearly festivals. But the biggest festival with the best riders is in Aabenraa. In this nonviolent form of medieval jousting, riders spear small hanging metal rings instead of their opponent's hearts. The horses go at full gallop and the lances are much heavier than they look, so it takes a great deal of skill to spear a ring. A winner is crowned every year. No betting is allowed (though everybody bets anyway). The festivites also include a big parade, marching bands, and the usual drunken revelry.

AALESTRUP
(North central Jutland, 30 miles southwest of Aalborg)

Danish Cycle Museum (Danmarks Cykelmuseum): Borgergade 10. Open May 1–November 1, Tuesday–Thursday, Saturday, and Sunday, 10 A.M.–6 P.M., and Friday noon–6 P.M. Closed Monday. Admission: 7 kr; children, 2 kr. Phone: (08) 64 19 60.

This museum has not just bicycles, but also scooters and other pedal-powered vehicles from the past that defy modern attempts at classification. The hundred-odd (take it both ways) cycles stretch back through the decades and are an unusual side of cultural history. Note the comfy "sofa bikes," a great idea that should have caught on but never did.

AERØSKØBING
(On the island of Aerø)

Bottle Ship Collection (Flaskeskibssamlingen): Smedegade 22 (in the center of the old town, near the water). Open May–September, daily, 9 A.M.–5 P.M.; October–April, daily, 10 A.M.–4 P.M. Admission: 10 kr; children, 5 kr. Phone: (09) 52 13 00.

This museum is devoted to the remarkable results of one of the world's most peculiar hobbies: the construction of miniature ships inside bottles. Some of the five-masted schooners are so detailed they must have taken years to create. The technique for making these is shrouded in mystery, and for many people (ourselves included) the mere existence of bottle ships is an unsolved enigma. The curator, a seasoned old seaman, has spent every spare minute of the last 50 years making these things, and will give you some pointers if, for some ungodly reason, you decide to take up the hobby yourself.

BILLUND
(22 miles northwest of Kolding on Jutland)

Legoland: Open May 1–third Sunday in September, 10

A.M.–8 P.M. (10 A.M.–9 P.M. from mid-July to mid-August). All rides close at 5:30 P.M. (7:30 P.M. from mid-July to mid-August.). Admission: 36 kr; children 18 kr; rides cost 6 kr each, or 40 kr for eight rides. Phone: (05) 33 13 33. (Legoland has no street address, but is so big it's unmissable.)

This is as much a pilgrimage site as an amusement park. Practically everything here is made out of Lego blocks (which, for the untutored, are small, plastic interlocking building blocks, and are one of the most popular children's toys in the world). But in Legoland, Lego transcends toyhood; it becomes an artistic medium, a building material, a form of decoration, a way of life. With over 30 million Lego blocks, specially trained Lego artists were given free reign to realize their fantasies. The results? A 20-by-40-foot replica of Mount Rushmore, a jungle of life-sized African animals, a towering Egyptian temple, an immense sculpture of Indians chasing a stampeding herd of buffalo, a miniature city, statues of famous men, a model of the space shuttle launch pad, an airport, and so on. Legoland also has rides, a western city, and other amusement park standbys, but it's the stunning, huge Lego creations that draw fascinated artists and reverential Lego fans from all over the globe.

COPENHAGEN (København)

Christiania: entrance at the corner of Prinsessegade and Badsmandsstraede, on Christianshavn, an area east of central Copenhagen. Always open. Admission: free.

Christiania, which was started in 1971 as an anarchist commune, for years struggled to survive against the wishes of the hostile Danish government. Eventually, though, the government got bored with the eviction attempts, the commune's squatters lost interest in politics, and Christiania degenerated into an alternative tourist attraction and a place to buy drugs. Now, instead of being a living monument to the revolution of the sixties and early seventies, Christiania is a depressing yet fascinating testament to the power of apathy. Mangy dogs and half-hearted drug dealers prowl the overgrown lanes between dilapidated former army barracks; bars' jukeboxes play mid-seventies hits; restaurants serve vegetarian food at not-so-radical prices, and the 1,000-or-so inhabitants scrounge for enough kroners to stay comfortable. The score: Capitalism 1, Revolution 0.

Pipe Museum: Amagertorv 9 (inside the W. O. Larsen Pipe Store). Open Monday–Thursday, 9 A.M.–5:30 P.M.; Friday 9 A.M.–7 P.M.; Saturday 9 A.M.–1 P.M. Closed Sunday. Admission: free.

Attached to Copenhagen's largest pipe store, this museum is devoted to unusual pipes and pipe paraphernalia. Among others are pipes made from seashells, pipes made from animal hooves, a meerschaum pipe in the shape of a skull, a primitive tribal pipe with three bowls, a pipe whose stem is literally tied in a knot, and a tiny pipe not much bigger than a toothpick. Note also the practical joke lighter made from a real (defused) hand grenade, and the collection of antique cigarette packages and labels.

Workers' Museum (Arbejdermuseet): Rømersgade 22. Open daily, 11 A.M.– 4 P.M. Admission: free. Phone: (01) 13 01 52.

Denmark has its kings, mermaids, and thunder gods, but *somebody* has to work for a living. This museum traces working-class history from 1850 to the present, using films, photos, and reconstructed environments (which are true to life and thus less than pretty). A 1950s room and a 1930s room are among the displays dedicated to the worker's life: its struggles, its ornaments, its mood, its grit.

FREDERIKSHAVN
(Northern edge of Jutland)

Bookplate collection (Exlibrissamling): in the Frederikshavn Art Museum, located in the downtown pedestrian street. Open Tuesday–Sunday, 10 A.M.–5 P.M. Closed Monday. Phone: (08) 42 32 66.

"This Book Belongs To...." No matter what language they speak, bookworms all over the world respect that message. This unique collection treats the *ex libris* as art, exhibiting specimens from Denmark and the rest of the world, spanning several hundred years. Also featured here are diverse bookmarks.

HILLERØD
(20 miles northwest of Copenhagen)

Aebelholt Abbey: Four miles from town on the road to Frederiksvaerk. Take bus 324 from Hillerød train station. Open May–August, Tuesday–Sunday, 10 A.M.– 4 P.M.; September, Tuesday–Sunday, 1–4 P.M.; and April and October, Saturday and Sunday, 1–4 P.M. Admission: 10 kr; children free. Phone: (02) 11 03 51.

The skeletons on display here, disinterred from the convent cemetery, bear silent and gruesome witness to medieval illnesses and their treatments. The building that houses the skeletons also houses a collection of medical implements found during excavations at the site of this now-ruined twelfth-century hospital-monastery: implements so crude they inspire much sympathy for the previous owners of the skeletons. Just be glad you can't hear them scream.

HOBRO
(Northern Jutland)

World Map Garden: on the southern tip of Klejtrup Lake, next to the town of Klejtrup, six miles southwest of Hobro. Take bus 55 from Hobro and tell the driver you want to get off at the World Map stop. Open May–August, daily, 9 A.M.–8 P.M.; September, daily, 9 A.M.– 6 P.M. Admission 10 kr; children, 5 kr. Phone: (08) 54 61 32.

Yes, it's a small world after all, but you probably never expected it to be *this* small. For 25 years a local eccentric named Soren Poulsen made artificial islands off the southern shore of Klejtrup Lake in the exact shape of the continents, and eventually a complete and very accurate model of the world. A bridge connects the mainland with the southern tip of Africa, and from there you can migrate your way to Tierra del Fuego or Burma. Crossing the Bering Strait takes just one step, but getting to Madagascar requires a substantial leap. If you want, you can now putt your way around the world on the newly installed miniature golf course.

HØJER SLUSE
(Southwest corner of Jutland)

Flood Museum: Open Saturday–Thursday, 10 A.M.–4 P.M. Closed Friday. Admission: 10 kr; children 5 kr. Phone: (04) 74 29 11.

The surrounding delicate marshland is flood country; if you want a safe but scary glimpse of what happens when Mother Nature decides to take a bath, look at the photos showing the effects of the devastating floods that struck the area in 1976 and 1981. Also on display is wreckage collected in the wake of the floods.

MØNSTED
(Seven miles west of Viborg on Jutland)

Limestone Caves with Bat Museum (Mønsted Kalkgruber): on Kalkvaerksvej. Buses running between Holstebro and Viborg stop at Mønsted; caves are one mile from the bus stop. It is also possible to call the caves from the Viborg, Holstebro, or Skive train stations (ask for Mrs. Balslev) and someone will come and pick you up. Open April–October, daily, 10 A.M.–4 P.M.; June and July, daily, 10 A.M.–6 P.M.; other times by appointment only. Admission: 16 kr; children, 8 kr. Phone: (06) 64 50 02.

The Vikings, armed with pickaxes and muscles, hewed this maze of caves so that they might obtain chalk for their buildings. Now the caverns are home to 200 tons of Danish cheese, which flourishes in the subterranean climate. An English-speaking tour guide leads you around and tells the story of the caves and their denizens: Vikings, cheese, and all the rest, including bats—of which more stuffed specimens are on display here than in the Copenhagen Zoology Museum. Don't miss the startling Sumatran "Flying Dog" bat.

ODENSE
(On the island of Funen)

Rescue Museum (Falckmuseet): Klostervej 28 (a 10-minute walk from the train station). Open Tuesday–Saturday, 10 A.M.–4 P.M.; Sunday and holidays, 1–5 P.M. Closed Monday. Admission: 12 kr; children under 14, 8 kr. Phone: (09) 12 75 20.

Life in the land of fairy tales has its emergencies, too. The Falckmuseet houses ambulances, fire trucks, and other rescue equipment from various periods of Danish history. Life-saving scenarios give this museum a bit of the old blood-'n'-guts, while illustrating the importance of speedy rescue in a country that has, among other things, one of Europe's highest suicide rates.

RIBE
(Southern Jutland)

Debtors' Prison Museum: V. Støckens Plads. Open May–September, Monday–Friday, 1–3 P.M. Admission: 5 kr. Phone (05) 42 00 55.

Ribe is proud of its medieval quaintness, but an unsavory part of its medieval history is the town's Debtors' Prison, wherein are preserved the once well-used executioner's axe, spiked maces, antique guns, and various items from the days of primitive law enforcement when missing a loan payment was a punishable felony.

Night Watchman: rounds start at Torvet Square in front of the Weis' Stue Inn, in the town center. May 1–September 15, daily, 10 P.M.; rounds take one hour. Admission: free. Phone: (05) 42 15 00.

Although he may be a tourist attraction now, the Ribe night watchman is an authentic remnant of an earlier era when most towns had night watchmen. You can tag along as he strolls through the streets carrying his lantern, making sure everything is in its proper place, singing the watchman's song, and telling interesting and occasionally bawdy tales about various sites passed along the way. Luckily he knows English, so if you tell him ahead of time he'll translate much of the patter as he goes along.

ROSKILDE
(20 miles west of Copenhagen)

Lejre Research Center (Oldtidsbyen): near the town of Lejre, just west of Roskilde. A bus runs directly from the Roskilde train station to the Lejre Research Center every hour at 43 minutes after the hour, and returns to the station from Lejre at 15 minutes after the hour (last bus leaves at 5:15). Open April–September, daily, 9 A.M.–5 P.M. Admission: 31 kr; students, children, and seniors, 14 kr. Phone: (02) 38 02 45.

Watch Stone Age and Iron Age families doing what comes naturally—cooking over fires, making tools and cloth—and feel free to ask them questions as you explore their historically-accurate dwellings. Lejre casts an effective spell, largely because you can participate in the ancient shenanigans yourself. Grind wheat berries with a mortar and pestle and bake your simple cakes over a fire; row a dugout canoe in the lagoon; dance in the spiral labyrinth. In the park's Iron Age sacrificial bog, the flayed skins of two horses hang from poles. Ancient animal breeds raised at Lejre include four-horned sheep. A section of the center is dedicated to agricultural life in the 1800s. Lejre workshops, held throughout the summer, feature ploughing, dyeing, archery, dancing, pottery making, rope making, and other activities of the Stone Age, Iron Age, and nineteenth century.

Mechanical Clock: on the Roskilde Cathedral (Domkirke) in the exact center of town. Mechanical figures are just above the main entrance. Performances every hour on the hour.

On the hour, St. George gallops out of this 500-year-old clock on his horse and attacks the Dragon. The Dragon then roars in rage, which causes the figure named Per Døver ("The Deafener") to swing wildly at the bell to strike the hour. This scares the fourth figure, called Kirsten Kimer ("Ringer") to shake her head in surprise or fear. Every 15 minutes, Kirsten comes out and delicately tinkles her bell.

Museum of Old Tools (*Håndvaerksmuseet*): Ringstedgade 68. Open Monday–Friday, 7 A.M.–4:30 P.M.; Saturday, 8 A.M.–noon. Closed Sunday. Admission: free. Phone: (02) 35 00 57.

Streamlined testaments to man's need to shape, build, and create, the diverse woodworking tools on display here come from ancient Egypt, Greece, and Rome, as well as medieval and Renaissance Europe. Axes, bores, lathes, saws, and other implements show both their users' ingenuity and the development of woodcraft.

Playing Card Museum (*Spilkammeret*): Sct. Hansgade 20 (one third of a mile northwest of the cathedral). Open Monday–Wednesday, 3–5 P.M.; Sunday 1–6 P.M. Admission: 10 kr; children under 15, 2 kr. Phone: (02) 35 18 08.

Scandinavia's largest card collection includes more than 2,500 decks. The owner, Danish tarot authority K. Frank Jensen, arranges changing thematic exhibits in the museum (such as children's playing cards, eroticism on playing cards, and of course tarot cards). Cards from all corners of the earth and dating back several centuries offer a colorful look at games and—even more interestingly—at the many strange symbols that move us and continually fascinate us. Note the round and oval decks from India and Japan, the 1984 Teddy Bear Tarot, and the body-organ deck.

Roskilde Sommerland: $2\frac{1}{2}$ miles south of Roskilde in the town of Vindinge, the northeast corner of town. Signs point the way. From Roskilde train station take bus 603. Open May–June 19, 10 A.M.–6 P.M.; June 20–August 9, 10 A.M.–7 P.M.; August 10–30, 10 A.M.–6 P.M. Admission: 40 kr; children under 3 free. Phone: (02) 35 70 75.

Also known as Vindinge Naturpark, the Roskilde Sommerland is a combination amusement park and animal reserve—a weird idea to Americans, but the Danes take it in stride. Don your cowboy hat, hop on a complimentary horse at the western town, and ride out to check on the herd of rare Danish deer and rabbits. Paddle out onto the lake among the swans in your swan-shaped paddle boat (camouflage, you see). Ride in the bizarrely decorated Filipino taxi-bus to the gigantic chess game or the not-always-functional Gold Mine. Sure it doesn't make sense—that's what makes it enjoyable.

RUDKØPING
(On Langeland Island, south of Fyn)

Prairie Wagon Holidays: Bystraedet 3. Rental fee for one week: 2,959 kr. Phone: (09) 51 14 44.

On this isolated island it is possible to rent a covered wagon and horses for a week of traveling the old-fashioned way. The price of 2,959 kr gets you everything you need for the care of the horses and the wagon. You travel on special roads generally not used by cars, and you sleep in the wagon. Up to four people can go with each wagon, so it actually can be a much cheaper way to spend your holiday than staying in a hotel room in a city. You need no special knowledge or experience with horses: a quick training session before you leave is sufficient. Once you're out in the countryside you're totally alone. It's quiet, peaceful, slow, sedate, and so different from the typical American whiz-bang tourism pace that it definitely ranks as off the wall from our point of view.

RY
(Central Jutland)

Himmelbjerget ("Sky Mountain"): two miles west of Ry, which is 18 miles west of Aarhus on Jutland. To get there, either walk (the "mountain" is an unmistakable destination), or take bus 311 from downtown Ry. Phone: (06) 89 34 22.

Himmelbjerget is the second highest point in Denmark—450 feet tall. Okay, so this isn't Switzerland. However, though Himmelbjerget may be pathetic as far as mountains go, the rest of Denmark is so absolutely flat that the view from the tower on top is startling: there's nothing to obstruct the panorama, and it's possible on clear days to see all the way to the sea and a huge section of central Jutland.

VINDERUP
(Ten miles southwest of Skive, on Jutland)

Stone-Age Open Air Museum: on the Moors of Hjerl (Hjerl Hede) on Hjerl Hedevej 14. From Vinderup train station, buses leave for Hjerl Hede at 11 A.M. and

3 P.M. (the distance is 3 1/2 miles). Open April–October, daily, 9 A.M.–5 P.M.; December, Saturday and Sunday. Admission: 30 kr; children, 12 kr (prices higher in December). Phone: (07) 44 80 60.

Summer is the best time to visit Hjerl Hede, for that is when families occupy most of the museum's 40 lakeside Stone Age and Iron Age dwellings. Clad in skins and homespun garb, the families go about their primitive chores for your (and their) enjoyment. They'll willingly answer your questions about the things they are doing—making flint and stone tools, weaving cloth, raising (and eating) animals. Some of the houses are also occupied on the December weekends.

FINLAND

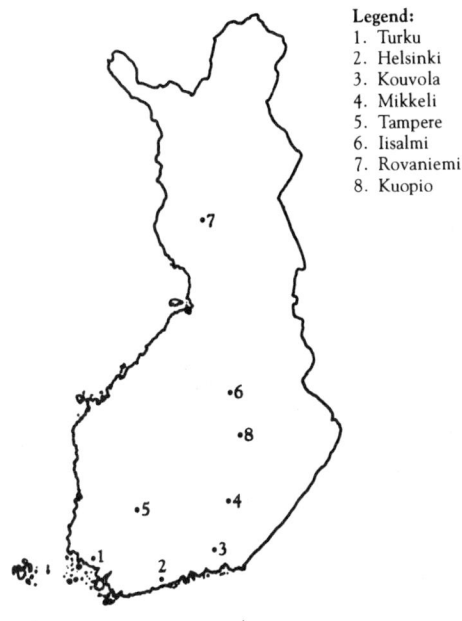

Legend:
1. Turku
2. Helsinki
3. Kouvola
4. Mikkeli
5. Tampere
6. Iisalmi
7. Rovaniemi
8. Kuopio

Finland is Europe's great mystery. Its borders play footsie with Russia and the Arctic Circle; its eastern half has more lakes than solid ground. Finland has gold, reindeer, blood pancakes, and bread baked with fish inside. What can you say to riches like that?

And take the Finnish language. This dense forest of double k's, double a's, i's, and l's is completely unrelated to every other language on earth, save one, and that one is Hungarian. Biologically, also, the Finns are unrelated to their Scandinavian neighbors, and are well aware of their uniqueness.

Every Finn lives a little like a frontiersman (the climate demands it)—in touch with the land and the elements, and with a sense of humor that

Finland / 49

is unusual in Scandinavia. Wry wit is everywhere in Finland, glowing like a campfire on an arctic winter night. You'll see it in the country's earthy poetry, its art, and in the way a Finn looks at you when he serves you your first plate of blood pancakes.

ALAHÄRMÄ
(140 miles north of Tampere)

Härmäland Trollpark: just south of Alahärmä toward the town of Härmä, off Highway 67. Alahärmä has a train station. Open in May, 11 A.M.–7 P.M.; June, July, and August, 10 A.M.–9 P.M. Theater performances begin daily at 2 P.M. Phone: 964-845 045.

In the olden days, as legend has it, real trolls used to roam these woods; now they're extinct, and the only reminders left are the goofy waist-high troll statues here in Härmäland. As you wander through the section of forest enclosed within Härmäland, you come across dozens of odd little troll scenes: Viking trolls in their ship; tree trolls; camping trolls; and right near the entrance, Himmi and Hiski, a guitar-playing troll and his troll groupie. At 2 P.M. in the Troll Theater, some of the trolls come to life and perform a play in Finnish.

HELSINKI

Alko Shop Museum: Tallberginkatu 2B. Take bus 65 A or 66 A from the bus or train station. Open by appointment only. Admission: free. To arrange for an English-speaking tour guide, call (90) 60 911.

In Finland, when you go down to the store for a bottle of "wodka," you needn't worry about which shop has the best prices. Ever since 1934, the government-owned Alko Company has controlled all Finnish alcohol sales. The company's museum focuses on the business end of alcohol, with advertising props and gimmicks and artifacts related to the sale of alcohol in Europe since the Middle Ages. A reconstructed 1934 liquor store conveys a sense of irrepressible joy.

Dairy Museum (Meijerimuseo): Meijeritie 6, northwest

of downtown. Take bus 45 or 39 from Simonkenttä. Open by appointment only. Admission: free. Call Mr. Hakkarainen at (90) 568 2482 to arrange for an English-speaking guide.

If you've come to love Finnish dairy products, investigate their source. This museum is part of the headquarters of Valio, Finland's cooperative dairy association. While you can't meet any Finnish cows here, you can inspect many years' worth of equipment. The English-speaking tour guide can explain how the various implements work together with the cows to produce milk, cheese, the yogurt-like *viili*, and other northern dairy standbys.

Kreisi Restaurant: Bulevardi 7. Open daily, 11 A.M.–11 P.M. Phone: (90) 611 081.

The name of this restaurant is not just another inscrutable Finnish word. Pronounce it phonetically and what have you got? "Crazy"—and that's the spirit of the place. Guests can choose from among several dining rooms, each of which is furnished and decorated according to a different theme. The Airplane Room has seats from old planes at the tables. The Beach Room has lively tropical murals on its walls. The Jungle Bar and Sauna Room are also available, but the local favorite is Kreisi's Prison Room, with bars on the windows, stone walls, spiders and spiderwebs, and a pervasively punitive ambience.

Veterinary Medicine Museum (Eläinlääketieteen Museo): At the College of Veterinary Medicine, Hämeentie 57, northeast of downtown. Take tram 6 from the center of the city. Open by appointment only. Admission: free. Phone: (90) 711 411. You can also appear in person and ask the receptionist to let you see the museum. (All the buildings on the campus have the same address, so the best way to find the museum is by asking directions once you get there.)

Let's face it, some people will be satisfied by nothing less than two-headed animal fetuses. Freaks and deformities of the animal kingdom are to be found aplenty in this museum's Pathology section. The museum's pride and joy is its collection of historical Finnish veterinary implements, but that doesn't stop college students and curious Helsinkiites from heading straight to the pathology section every time.

IISALMI
(In the center of Finland)

Bottle Museum (Kansainvälinen Pullomuseo): Museum is in nearby Sonkajärvi (ten miles northeast of Iisalmi), and is located on the church garden. Open June 1–August 30, Tuesday–Sunday, 10 A.M.–8 P.M. Closed Monday. Admission: Mk 10; students, Mk 5; children under 7, free. Phone: (977) 614 70 or (977) 615 51.

From amphorae to ampules, beer bottles to medicine bottles, wide mouths, narrow mouths, new bottles, old. The hundreds of bottles and other containers in this collection illustrate the ways in which bottle shape and size lend themselves to the vessels' function.

JYVÄSKYLÄ
(125 miles north of Helsinki)

Sauna Village: located $6\frac{1}{2}$ miles south of Jyväskylä in the village of Muurame. Saunas are available for private use by prior arrangement. Appointment not necessary to visit museum. Phone: 731 087.

A proper sauna is a steamy nude bask punctuated by quick dips in an icy lake or rolls in the snow. Muurame's Sauna Village includes a Sauna Museum with 20 different saunas, some of them over 150 years old. All are available for detached, fully dressed observation as well as the all-out, invigorating experience for which they were designed.

MIKKELI

Dinosauria: three miles east of Mikkeli in the resort village of Visulahti. Open May, daily, 11 A.M.–3 P.M.; June 1–August 16, daily, 9 A.M.–9 P.M.; August 17–31, daily, 11 A.M.–3 P.M. September, Saturday and Sunday, 11 A.M.–3 P.M. Admission: Mk 30; children 6–14, Mk 20; children under 6, free. Phone: (955) 362 881.

Finland is about the last place you'd expect to find a forest full of life-size dinosaurs. Dinosaur-park addicts will find their Scandinavian fix here. A stunning 90-foot-long brontosaurus strides through trees that hadn't even evolved when he was around. You'll also find very realistic stegosauri, a hungry Tyrannosaurus Rex, and many others—some over 30 feet tall—whose scientific names elude us at the moment. We just call them "Sir."

MiniLand (Minimaa): three miles east of Mikkeli in the resort village of Visulahti. Minimaa is on the eastern edge of Visulahti. Open May, daily, 10 A.M.–6 P.M.; June 1–August 16, daily, 9 A.M.–9 P.M.; August 17–31, daily, 10 A.M.–6 P.M., September, Saturday and Sunday, 10 A.M.–6 P.M.,. Admission: Mk 20; children 6–14, Mk 10; children under 6, free. Phone: (955) 362 281.

Finland likes to celebrate itself, so in Minimaa you won't find the Eiffel Tower or the Statue of Liberty. A typical Finnish wooden house and sauna, Sibelius' house, rural churches—that's the kind of stuff you'll see reproduced here on a one-to-twenty scale. Children tower over some of the buildings, and others are as big as Volkwagens.

Wax Museum (Vahakabinetti): three miles east of Mikkeli in the resort village of Visulahti. Open daily, 9 A.M.–9 P.M. Admission: Mk 25; children 6–14, Mk 15; children under 6, free. Phone: (955) 362 881.

What better way to give famous Finns their proper place in history than to meet them—practically in person. In the Finnish history section, somberly clad figures illustrate what's been happening in Finland during the last 100 years; other sections of the museum are far less dignified: Swedish import Pippi Longstocking is a little too angelic. An array of the world's performers brings us Charlie Chaplin, the Beatles, and a Humphrey Bogart who could easily lend his head to Peter Lorre without raising suspicion. Strangely, all the entertainers look as though they are about to be hanged.

NAANTALI
(10 miles west of Turku)

Sleepyhead Day Festival: July 27. Harbor dunk at 7 A.M. in the city's yacht harbor at the western edge of town, next to the tourist office. Phone: (921) 755 388.

Naantali's yearly party starts early in the morning—really early—as revelers go through the city making as much noise as possible. Sometime around 6:30 A.M. they arrive at the home of that year's "Sleepyhead" (some local celebrity who has been secretly awarded the "honor"), who is roused rudely out of bed, taken down to the yacht harbor, and, at the stroke of seven, tossed into the chilly waves. The rest of the day is taken up with performances, the wearing of outlandish costumes, and the revival of an ancient Naantali custom: a town drummer declaring "the proclamation of public peace."

ROVANIEMI
(On the Arctic Circle)

Santa Claus Land (Joulumaa): located just north of Rovaniemi (which has both a train and a bus station). Open daylight hours year-round. Phone: (960) 17 203 or (960) 17 201.

The reason you see Santa only once a year is that he's so busy in his permanent home, here in Finnish Lappland. Santa Claus maintains his office here, directly on the Arctic Circle, surrounded by workshops, playgrounds, ski slopes, a North Pole conquest museum, and an arctic botanical park. Not only can you talk with Santa, but you can also write postcards or letters here and give them to Santa's helpers, who will mail them for you at Christmastime (no matter when you write them). The letters arrive in time for Christmas, with a North Pole postmark.

SALO
(28 miles east of Turku)

Helisnummi Chapel (Helisnummen Kappeli): at the city cemetery, near Uskela Church on the southern edge of town. Open May–August, daily, 10 A.M.–6 P.M., and by appointment other months. Phone: (924) 137 60.

This triangular church is only 24 years old. The shape, as in other triangular churches, represents the Holy Trinity. The most notable aspect of the Helisnummi Chapel is its pyramidal roof, which touches the rest of the building at only three points, and which required some very ingenious engineering techniques.

TAMPERE

Haihara Doll Museum: Just east of town in the suburb of Kaukajärvi. Take bus 24 from downtown Tampere. Open May–September, daily, noon–6 P.M.; February–April and October–November, Saturday–Thursday, noon–4 P.M. Closed Friday. Admission: Mk 10; children, Mk 2. Phone: 630 350.

In this, Finland's largest doll museum, the charming folk toys reveal many aspects of life in this country—which has little in common with its Scandinavian neighbors. Note the unusual native dolls from the mysterious Finnish Lappland.

Women's Gymnastics Museum (Varala Museo): Varalankatu 36, on the west side of town, past Pyynikki Park. Take bus 15 from downtown Tampere. Open in summer, Tuesday, 6–8 P.M., and Sunday, 1–4 P.M. Also open by appointment. Admission: Mk 5; children, Mk 1. Phone: 35 200.

The photos show generations of women leaping, rolling, bending over backwards, and contorting their bodies into a hundred improbable positions. Antique gymnastic equipment lets you ponder just how it was done; rows and rows of photos of earnest-faced human pretzels in floppy bloomers make this an art museum of a different kind.

TANKAVAARA
(140 miles north of Rovaniemi and the Arctic Circle)

Gold Museum, Gold Village, and Gold Panning World Championships: Gold Museum is at the end of the road that passes through Tankavaara Gold Village. Open June 1–August 15, daily, 9 A.M.–6 P.M.; August 16–September 30, daily, 9 A.M.–5 P.M.; October 1–May 31, by appointment only. Phone: 9693 46 171.

The museum has two sections. The main part is about prospecting and gold—with a definite Finnish slant. Some of the prospecting mock-ups and other displays are outdoors. The other part is an impressive gold, precious stone, and mineral collection. Elsewhere in Gold Village, you can take gold-panning lessons and make arrangements to do some real panning out in the wilderness. Some years, the Gold Panning World Championships are held here in August. To find out if the Championships will be held during your visit, you can call 9693 46 158 or ask in Helsinki.

TURKU

Medieval Banquet: in Turku Castle, on Linnankatu at

the passenger-ship docks, on the western edge of town. Held during August every year. Call (921) 511 211 for exact dates and to make reservations. Price: Mk 270; children 4–14, Mk 135; children under 4, free.

The one-year reign of Duke John (Juhana) of Finland is well remembered for its lavish parties. Every year in August the clock is turned back and it's party time once again. John and his wife Katarina are there, as are authentically clad entertainers and servants—all quaffing, singing, and telling jokes in many languages (including English). The meal, consisting of historically accurate sixteenth-century Finnish fare (eaten without the benefit of silverware), is followed by songs and old-style dancing. Guests are encouraged to join in.

Pharmacy Museum: Läntinen Rantakatu 13, right across from the river, next to the municipal Tourist Office. Open May 1–September 9, daily, 10 A.M.–6 P.M.; October–April 30, daily, 10 A.M.–3 P.M. Admission: Mk 5; children and students, Mk 2. Phone: (921) 303 300.

A lone leech glides about in an aquarium, and women in period costume flit about like so many ghosts of the pharmacist's wife. In this former pharmacist's home, laboratory, and shop are hundreds of antique apothecary jars, many of them filled with the original medicines—asafoetida, quinine bark, saxifrage.... Strangely pleasant smells waft from the old jars and the bunches of herbs hanging from the ceiling. Some of the old ingredients are unnerving: what kind of disease called for arsenic or crushed red coral?

TUUSNIEMI
(30 miles east of Kuopio)

Mechanical Music Museum (Mekaanisen Musiikin Museo): call (971) 751 219 for exact directions. Open March–August, Tuesday–Sunday, 11 A.M.–6 P.M. Closed Monday. Admission: Mk 15; children 4–6, and groups, Mk 8.

Back before compact discs, before stereo, before LPs, even before electricity, there were record players and recorded music. This museum has a collection of more than 100 record players, dating as far back as the 1880s. Most of them still work, and the guide will play for you cylinders and odd-sized disc records from the late 1800s.

FRANCE

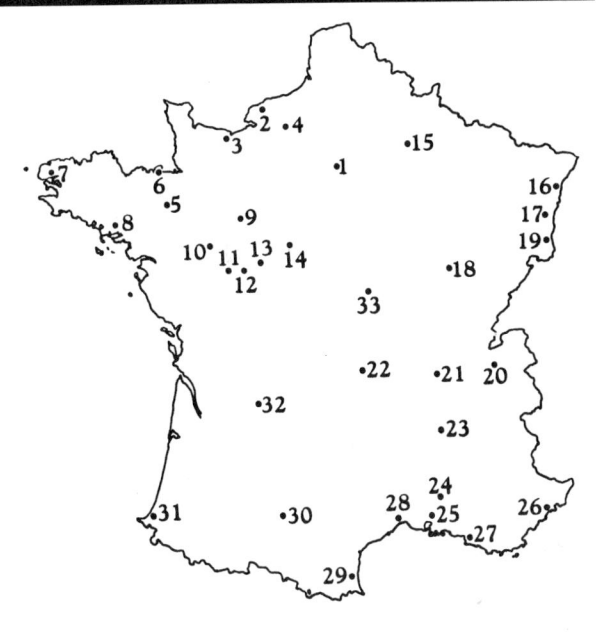

Legend:
1. Paris
2. Fécamp
3. Caen
4. Rouen
5. Rennes
6. St-Malo
7. Brest
8. Vannes
9. Le Mans
10. Angers
11. Saumur
12. Chinon
13. Tours
14. Blois
15. Reims
16. Strasbourg
17. Colmar
18. Dijon
19. Mulhouse
20. Annecy
21. Lyon
22. Clermont-Ferrand
23. Valence
24. Avignon
25. Arles
26. Nice
27. Marseille
28. Montpellier
29. Perpignan
30. Toulouse
31. Biarritz
32. Périgueux
33. Nevers

When you go to Europe, you're bound to overhear a conversation like this one between two young Americans at least four or five times during your trip:

"Have you ever been to France?"
"Oh yes, I lived there for a while."
"Really? Where?"
"In Paris."
"For how long?"
"Three days."
"Oh. What was it like?"

France / 57

At this point the dialogue can go in one of two directions. One possibility is "...hated it...so rude...expensive..."; another is "...my favorite place in the world...so beautiful...delicious...." The range of opinions is vast. Yet how can similar experiences evoke disgust in some people and adoration in others?

France is the place where fantasies come true. If you arrive in Paris *expecting* waiters to be rude, *expecting* nobody to speak English, *expecting* chauvinism and snobbishness...then that's exactly what you'll get. The French are sensitive, and can pick up subtle clues. If you expect generosity, helpfulness, patience, good food, and make heartfelt blundering attempts to speak the language, then the French will sense your positive attitude and treat you accordingly: you may never want to leave.

Similarly, if you arrive in France expecting to see art, castles, and beaches, you can be assured of seeing plenty of each—and plenty of other tourists looking for the same thing. But if you arrive, *Europe Off The Wall* in hand, looking for catacombs, hairdo museums, and nude cities, you're guaranteed to find France the strangest, most fascinating country in Europe.

PARIS

Bread Museum (Musée du Pain): 25 bis rue Victor-Hugo in the Charenton suburb, southeast of the center, just south of the Bois de Vincennes. Metro: Charenton-Ecoles. Open Tuesday and Thursday, 2–4 P.M. Closed mid-July to September 1. Admission: free. Phone: 43 68 43 60.

In France, bread inspires a certain kind of passion. This museum focuses on bread's history, displaying ancient loaves and wafers from Asia and the Middle East; 2,600-year-old paintings depicting bread; dioramas of ancient bakeries; baking equipment from the Byzantine Empire and ancient Rome; and a whimsical array of European baking molds (including one shaped like Napoleon Bonaparte). Other exhibits explore bread in the works of famous artists, songs about the joys of bread, and many oddly shaped loaves.

Catacomb Tours: entrance is at 1 Place Denfert-Rochereau, 14th arrondissement. Metro: Denfert-Rochereau. Tours given Tuesday–Friday, 2–6 P.M.; Saturday–Sunday, 9–11 P.M. and 2–4 P.M. Phone: 43 22 47 63.

These underground streets and passages, permanent home to more than five million deceased Parisians, are a great favorite with live Parisians: an eighteenth-century nobleman staged a banquet down among the bones; the French Resistance held their secret meetings here; nowadays punks and art students love the place. The tour winds its chilly way past walls of bones and piles of bones and artfully arranged skulls.

The Crown of Thorns: in Notre Dame Cathedral, in the Treasury (toward the back; entrance is in the right-hand wall), 4th arrondissement. Metro: Cité. Open daily 8 A.M.–7 P.M. Admission to Treasury: 15F; students, 10F; children, 3F. Phone: 43 26 07 39.

The Crown of Thorns? You bet—none other than the one Jesus wore on his last day. The crown is displayed almost casually in the back room of the Treasury, on the left wall in the center of a case containing other relics. The crown is in a doughnut-shaped glass-and-metal reliquary, but is placed so high up that it's hard to see the crown clearly. To compensate for this, church officials have courteously placed a photograph of the crown where it's easy to see. Every year during Lent the crown is presented to the public in an official ceremony, and every year on Good Friday the crown is presented with two other relics—a piece of the True Cross and a nail from it—which are never displayed except at this time.

Edith Piaf Museum (Musée Edith-Piaf): 5 rue Crespin-du-Gast, 11th arrondissement. Metro: Ménilmontant. Open Monday–Thursday afternoons by appointment only. Closed July. Admission: free. Phone: 43 55 52 72.

This shrine to the delicate *chanteuse,* installed in the rooms of a private apartment, covers every aspect of Piaf's life in loving detail. You'll see the Little Sparrow's shoes, clothes, portraits, furniture, sheet music, knickknacks, show posters, records, fan mail, photos, and the costumes she wore on stage.

Eyeglasses Museum (Musée des Lunettes et Lorgnettes de Jadis): 2 Avenue Mozart, 16th arrondissement. Metro:

La Muette. Open Tuesday–Saturday, 9 A.M.–1 P.M. and 2–7 P.M. Closed Sunday, Monday and August. Admission: free.

Among the famous four-eyes whose glasses you can see here are Sofia Loren, Audrey Hepburn, and the Dalai Lama. Clumsy medieval lenses are ugly ducklings compared to super-hip modern specimens and aids for the nearsighted-but-vain—such as lenses cleverly hidden in fans and walking sticks, or encrusted with enough jewels to make everybody *else* go blind.

Eyeglasses Museum of Pierre Marly: 85 rue du Faubourg St-Honoré, 8th arrondissement. Metro: St Philippe-du-Roule or Champs-Elysées. Open Tuesday–Saturday, 9 A.M.–noon and 2–7 P.M. Closed Sunday and Monday. Admission: free. Phone: 42 66 65 54.

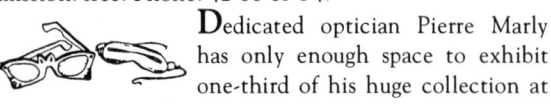

Dedicated optician Pierre Marly has only enough space to exhibit one-third of his huge collection at any one time, so he rotates the displays periodically. You might see (among other things) ancient Chinese eyeglasses, Renaissance specs, Eskimo slit-in-the-wood sunglasses, or Sarah Bernhardt's ruby-studded monocle.

Freemasons' Museum: 16 rue Cadet, 9th arrondissement. Metro: Cadet. Open Monday–Saturday, 2–6 P.M. Closed Sunday and September 1–15. Admission: free. Phone: 45 23 20 92.

If you're wondering just who the Freemasons *are*, this is the place to find out. Founded hundreds of years ago, the Freemasons are a secret mystical brotherhood that may or may not have changed the course of history. Masonic symbolism is explored in depth at this museum, with all kinds of artifacts—swords, medals, aprons—relating to their rituals, displayed alongside paintings of initiations, portraits of famous Masons, scores of famous musical works with secret Masonic themes, and a section dedicated to female masonry. Rumors and legends about the Masons are explained, but no real secrets are revealed. For that kind of information, you have to join.

Giant Golden Baby: in front of the Jouets & Cie toy store, 11 boulevard de Sebastopol, 1st arrondissement, half a block up from rue de Rivoli. Metro: Rambuteau or Etiènne Marcel. Baby is visible anytime.

"Look at the size of that baby," we gulped, coming upon this towering fiberglass infant, 18 feet high, detailed and lifelike except for its great size and overall gold patina. The huge sculpture was installed as a permanent advertisement for a toy store. It could just as easily be an ad for hallucinogens.

Hairstyle Museum "Intercoiffure": in the Maison des Nations, 11 *bis* rue Jean Goujon, 8th arrondissement. Metro: Champs-Elysées. Open Tuesday and Friday afternoons by appointment. Admission: free. Phone: 43 59 15 40 or 43 59 05 15. Ask for Madame Mommega.

The combined collections of two longtime French hairstylists include dozens of historic hair-design sketches, labyrinthine wigs, diverse and elaborate hair ornaments, and snippets from famous (and even crowned) heads. The snippets are encased in heart-shaped plastic reliquaries, and thus we learn the secrets that, previously, only their hairdressers knew for sure: Princess Anne's hair, for example, is hopelessly thin and wispy, while Sophia Loren's is healthy. (Also on display are sample tresses from Elizabeth Taylor, Princess Grace, Jackie Kennedy, and Jean Cocteau.) The most riveting part of the museum is a collection of jewelry made of intricately woven human hair: rings, pendants, spherical earrings, inch-wide bracelets—even belts. This was actually a fashion among Victorian widows.

Jardin d'Acclimatation: in the Bois de Boulogne, just north of Avenue du Mahatma-Gandhi, 16th arrondissement. Metro: Les Sablons. Open daily, 10 A.M.–6:30 P.M. (no entry after 5:45). Admission: 6.50F; children under 3, free. Phone: 46 24 10 80.

Okay, we admit it, the Jardin d'Acclimatation is for kids. Even so, it has many unusual features, and if you go at off-peak times you will find it a refuge from other tourists. The Jardin's Hall of Mirrors has a few outstandingly disorienting funhouse mirrors, including one that reflects three heads to your one, two of which are *not* reversed the way they're supposed to be. A giant chess game is near the park's southern edge; pick up the foot-tall chess pieces from the entrance next to the bowling alley. There's also a doll museum, a clock made of living flowers growing out of the ground, carnival midway games, miniature golf, and a miniature train, among dozens of other kid-oriented attractions. This is the ideal place for disillusioned poets and for spy rendezvous.

Jim Morrison's Grave: in Père-Lachaise cemetery, east of the center. Main entrance is on boulevard de Ménilmontant, near Avenue Gambetta, 20th arrondissement. Metro: Gambetta, Philippe-Auguste, or Père-Lachaise. Open in summer, 9 A.M.–6 P.M.; spring and fall, 7:30 A.M.–6 P.M.; winter, 8:30 A.M.–5:30 P.M. Follow the scrawled "Jim" signs.

"Jeem" Morrison may or may not really be dead, but his grave is by far the most popular in a cemetery whose dozens of famous tombs include those of Molière, Chopin, and Edith Piaf. Morrison's grave, topped by a luridly painted plaster bust, almost always has young (and not-so-young) pilgrims hanging around it, mooning about the long-lost sixties. Doors fans from all over the world have, over the years, covered Jim's tomb and those around it with a blanket of impassioned graffiti; tidbits of sixties philosophy; "Break on through to the other side"—that kind of thing.

Lock Museum (Musée de la Serrure): in the Hôtel Libéral Bruant, 1 rue de la Perle, 3rd arrondissement. Metro: Chemin-Vert or Rambuteau. Open Tuesday–Saturday, 10 A.M.–noon and 2–5 P.M. Closed Sunday and Monday and August. Admission: 10F; students and children, 5F. Phone: 42 77 79 62.

Ever since drawbridges went out of fashion, castles have had to use locks and keys to keep undesirables out. This museum has gold-plated locks from Versailles, the Tuileries, and many French *chateaux*. Also on display are Renaissance door knockers, ancient Roman keys, giant keys, and finely crafted specimens from all over the world. Note the trick locks—designed to give lock pickers a nasty surprise.

Medical History Museum (Musée de l'Histoire de la Médecine): 12 rue de l'Ecole de Médecine, in the Ancienne Faculté de Médecine, near boulevard St-Michel, 6th arrondissement. Metro: Odeon. Open during the school year (late September–June), Wednesday and Friday, 2–6 P.M. and Saturday, 2–5 P.M. Closed July–September. Admission: free. Phone: 43 29 21 77, ext. 448.

When they say history, they aren't joking: surgical and medical implements here come from ancient Egypt, Rome, and medieval Europe. One room is dedicated to the practice of trepanning—drilling holes in people's heads to relieve the pressure inside (or to let the demons escape). Keep an eye out for the fascinating "animal table."

Museum of Advertising (Musée de la Publicité): 18 rue de Paradis, 10th arrondissement. Metro: Chateau d'Eau or Gare de l'Est. Open Wednesday–Monday, noon–6 P.M. Closed Tuesday. Phone: 42 46 13 09.

If you watch TV just to see the commercials or read *Vogue* just for the ads, this museum will satisfy. Monthly changing exhibits are drawn from a collection of over 50,000 international advertising posters and 25,000 TV and radio commercials. The collection spans 300 years, and among the poster artists whose work is included here, you'll find Toulouse-Lautrec, Mucha, and Erté. Their lesser-known colleagues prove themselves just as clever.

Museum of Blindness (Musée Valentin-Haüy): 5 rue Duroc, 7th arrondissement. Metro: Duroc. Open Tuesday and Wednesday, 2:30–5:30 P.M. and by appointment. Closed July–August. Admission: free. Phone: 47 34 07 90. Ask for Mr. Balphin.

The alphabet known as Braille was actually invented by Louis Braille's compatriot, Valentin-Haüy. Braille perfected the idea and made it famous. This museum explores the uses for such an alphabet, displaying interesting Braille typewriters, Braille playing cards, and games specially designed for the blind. Another section features crafts made by blind artists, and still another displays the personal possessions of famous blind people.

Museum of Counterfeits (Musée de la Contrefaçon): 16 rue de la Faisanderie, 16th arrondissement. Metro: Port-Dauphine. Open Monday and Wednesday, 2–4:30 P.M.; Friday 9:30 A.M.–noon. Admission: free. Phone: 45 01 51 11.

You'll find yourself scrutinizing the labels on your jeans long after visiting this museum. All the audacious fakes on display here were (at various times and places) passed off on the public as real. You'll see counterfeit designer clothes, purses, cigarettes, coffee, candy, cookies (all displayed alongside the real thing), and a hilarious array of counterfeit perfumes. For example: Chenel #19, Chinarl #5 and Christal Door. Among the bogus Cointreau offerings you'll see Coindreau (a Canadian effort) and Coinfreau (Yugoslavian).

Museum of Popular Arts and Traditions (Musée National des Arts et Traditions Populaires): 6 Avenue du Mahatma-Gandhi, in the Bois de Boulogne, just past the entrance to the Jardin d'Acclimatation. Metro: Les Sablons. Open Wednesday–Monday, 10 A.M.–5:15 P.M. Closed Tuesday. Admission: 15F; 8F on Sundays and holidays. Phone: 47 47 69 80.

The magic and witchcraft section (way in the rear) contains a tantalizing sampling of French charms against rabies and lightning, and divining rods, witches' spellbooks, and the like. The studio of a modern Parisian clairvoyant (a real person) is reconstructed here, with all his original furnishings and paraphernalia: a stuffed owl, tarot cards, strange paintings, etc. The push of a button activates a taped narrative (in French), in which the clairvoyant himself explains the significance of various items in the room.

Museum of Public Health (Musée de l'Assistance Publique): 47 Quai de la Tournelle, 5th arrondissement. Metro: Gobelins or Maubert. Open Wednesday–Sunday, 10 A.M.–5 P.M. Closed Monday, Tuesday, and August. Admission: 2F; students, free. Phone: 46 33 01 43.

Tracing 1,000 years of hospital history, the museum has exhibits on childhood diseases, prostitute health, abandoned babies, and new health laws. The museum's prized possessions are the forceps and uterine specula of famous Parisian doctors.

Museum of Women and Automatons: 12 rue de Centre, in the Neuilly suburb northwest of the center. Metro: Pont de Neuilly. Open Wednesday–Monday afternoons: one guided tour per day at 3 P.M. Closed Tuesday. Admission: 10F; students and children, 5F. Phone: 47 45 29 40.

What a combination: women and robots! The proprietor runs this place with a straight face, displaying nineteenth-century robots alongside an array of the personal effects of female human beings: clothes, letters, intimate things. The museum is especially proud of Marie-Antoinette's corset, a seashell-shaped bed that used to belong to a famous Paris prostitute, and (to show that they like all kinds of women) religious offerings made by the martyred St. Julie.

Perfume Museum (Musée de la Parfumerie): 9 rue Scribe, 9th arrondissement. Metro: Opera. Open Monday–Friday, 9:30 A.M.–5:30 P.M.; Saturday, 9:30 A.M.–2:30 P.M. Closed Sunday. Admission: free. Phone: 47 42 93 40. Guided tours on the half hour.

Paris knows perfume. You'll see flacons of all shapes and

sizes and amazing atomizers—made of gold, silver, crystal, and even more original media. The heady stuff itself is looked at in terms of both its religious and amatory uses.

Plans-Reliefs Museum: on the fourth floor of the Musée de l'Armée, which is in the Hôtel des Invalides, in the southern part of the building close to avenue de Tourville, 7th arrondissement. Metro: Varenne or Latour-Maubourg. Open April–September, daily, 10 A.M.–6 P.M.; October–March, daily 10 A.M.–5 P.M. Admission: free, once you're inside the Musée de l'Armée. Phone: 47 05 11 07.

These 1/600-size scale models of cities, buildings, and countryside were once all highly sensitive classified military secrets. Consequently, the precision of these models, some of which are over 300 years old, is astounding. If you like miniaturized things or want to see what all those old buildings looked like before age took its toll, then this is the place for you.

Police Museum (Le Musée des Collections Historiques de la Préfecture de Police): in the Police Department building, 1 *bis,* rue des Carmes, 5th arrondissement. (Entrance is on rue de la Montagne-Ste-Geneviève.) Metro: Maubert. Open Monday–Thursday, 9 A.M.–5 P.M. and Friday 9 A.M.–4:30 P.M. Admission: free. Phone: 43 29 21 57.

A squad of mannequins in police uniforms creates an unsettling mood as you enter. Head straight for the section dedicated to crime, where you'll see, among other things, a revolution-era guillotine blade (and toy guillotines with tiny severed heads in baskets), a perfume-bottle bomb, a flowerpot bomb, an explosive book, metal straps for robbing collection boxes, and other curios confiscated by the Paris police. One interesting exhibit is a human skull with a hole in it, displayed alongside the very hammer that made the hole and murdered the skull's former occupant.

Rat Trap Shop's Display Window: shop is E. Aurouze, 8 rue des Halles, 1st arrondissement. Metro: Pont-Neuf. Window is visible anytime.

Animal lovers, stay away. In fact—animals, stay away. This display window, designed to boast Monsieur Aurouze's trapping prowess, contains a bear trap, stuffed mole, and several dozen dead rats (big ones), hanging in rows with traps on their necks. A placard reads, "Sewer rats—captured in Les Halles in 1925." This is a consummately gross window, and the only people who should go to see it are vicious ghouls with bad taste. We know you're out there.

Sewer Tours (Les Égouts): across the street from 93 Quai d'Orsay, next to Pont de l'Alma, on the left bank of the Seine, 7th arrondissement. Metro: Alma-Marceau. Open Monday and Wednesday and the last Saturday of every month, 2–5 P.M.; tours (50 persons) leave every 20 minutes and last one hour. Admission: 8F. Phone: 47 05 10 29. (Note: sewers are usually closed when it is raining and when the Seine is very high.)

"Today's itinerary: the Louvre, the Eiffel Tower, and then the sewers." Does that sound like a day of Parisian fun? No? Then skip the Louvre and the Eiffel Tower and head straight for the sewers. The tour begins with a small museum and film (English headphone translation available), explaining the history and function of the sewers. From there, the guide leads you through the illuminated, slippery tunnels of Paris's waste disposal system. As you might expect, it smells pretty bad. Make sure to wear rubber-soled walking shoes, as water and sludge are everywhere—as are tubes, wires and the occasional mutant.

Tobacco Museum (Musée de la SEITA): 12 rue Surcouf, 7th arrondissement. Metro: Invalides. Open Monday–Saturday, 11 A.M.–6 P.M. Closed Sunday. Admission: free. Phone: 45 55 91 50.

Rare smoking paraphernalia here include an ancient Aztec pipe, Native American peace pipes, and old Parisian "Tabac" signs. This is Paris, after all, so of course art gets into the act: a slide show explores tobacco and smoking in artwork of the last 200 years.

Waiters' and Waitresses' Race (Course des Garçons et des Serveuses de Café): future dates not set, but race is generally held around June 21 every year, usually at 3 P.M.; starting and finishing at the Hôtel de Ville. Metro: Hôtel de Ville. For exact time and place, call the tourist office in May or June: 47 23 61 72.

They're off! This isn't just any old race: it's the national championship for French waiters and waitresses. Dressed up in aprons, starched shirts, and bow ties, with white towels over their arms, they dash through the streets balancing a bottle of beer and a full glass on a small tray.

They're not allowed to spill a drop, and must keep a proper waiterly posture the whole way. The winner gets a big tip from the mayor.

PARIS ENVIRONS

CHARTRES

Mosaic House (Maison Picassiette): Impasse du Repos, 22 rue de Repos. Open in summer, Wednesday–Monday, 10 A.M.–noon and 2–6 P.M. Admission: 6F. Phone: 37 36 41 39.

Raymond Isidore, a cemetery worker, mosaicked his house inside and out with countless bits of broken plates. Covering one outside wall is a view of the city of Chartres in mosaic, and the cathedral as seen from various angles. Elsewhere—even on the floor—you'll see flowers, birds, people, stars, religious things, and motifs based on the Chartres cathedral's stained-glass windows. The skilled artistry and sheer amount of mosaic work show the late Monsieur Isidore as dedicated, passionate, and obsessed.

CONFLANS-SAINTE-HONORINE
(15 miles northwest of Paris)

Barge Museum (Musée de la Batellerie): in the Chateau du Prieuré, on Place Jules-Gévélot. Open in summer, Wednesday, Saturday, and Sunday, 3–6 P.M.; in winter, 2–5 P.M. Admission: free. Phone: 39 72 58 02.

Conflans-Sainte-Honorine is barge headquarters for the river Seine, and this museum deals not only with barges but with the people who live and work on them. Models and photos show the difference between barges from various regions, including some very exotic examples. The subculture of bargemen and their families is explored, and the walls are adorned with barge-oriented artwork.

COUPVRAY
(25 miles east of Paris)

Louis Braille Museum: on rue Louis-Braille, in nearby Esbly. Open April–September, Wednesday–Monday, 10 A.M.–noon, and 2–6 P.M.; October–March, Wednesday–

Monday, 10 A.M.–noon and 2–5 P.M. Closed Tuesday. Phone: 60 04 22 85.

This is Louis Braille's actual birthplace, the house where an accident blinded him at the age of three. On display are personal possessions as well as examples of works in the Braille alphabet.

THOIRY
(20 miles west of Paris)

Museum of Gastronomy: in the castle, off the A30 road. Open April–September, daily, 10 A.M.–5:15 P.M.; October–November, Monday, Wednesday, and Thursday, 10 A.M.–5:15 P.M. Admission: 18F. Phone: 34 87 40 67.

The masterpieces of France's best pastry chefs are mounted and displayed here. Among other creations, you'll see some delicate, long-stemmed roses made of sugar. The museum houses many other gastronomic wonders, in the form of both real food and replicas.

BRITTANY AND NORMANDY

BALLEROY
(20 miles west of Caen)

Balloon Museum (Musée des Ballons): on the castle grounds. Open April–September, Thursday–Tuesday, 9 A.M.–noon and 2–6 P.M.; closed Wednesday and October–March. Admission: 8F; children 7F. Phone: 31 21 60 61.

Dioramas, real balloon gondolas, pictures, and books illustrate the history of hot-air ballooning from the days of the Montgolfier brothers to now. The museum is the brainchild of American magazine magnate Malcolm Forbes.

CARNAC
(15 miles west of Vannes)

Two Thousand Nine Hundred Thirty-five Standing Stones (Alignments): just north of town. For more information call the Carnac Tourist Office at 97 52 13 52.

This is the world's greatest megalithic site. Standing stones (menhirs) form a two-mile avenue across the heath; the whole area is studded with stone tables (dolmens), tombs, mounds, and huge lone megaliths. No one has been able to fix an accurate date to the erection of these monuments, but most agree it was over 4,000 years ago.

COSSÉ-LE-VIVIEN
(Nine miles southwest of Laval, which is midway between Angers and Fougères)

The Strange Museum of Robert Tatin (Etrange Musée Robert Tatin): in the center of town in the farm called La Frénouse. Open in summer, daily, 10 A.M.–noon and 2–6 P.M.; in winter, 10 A.M.–noon and 2–5:30 P.M. Admission: 8F; students and children, 4F. Phone: 43 98 80 89.

Self-taught ceramicist Robert Tatin filled his farm with large, funny figures in ceramic and cement. The work is an intoxicating blend of pagan and Christian, east and west. Gazing at you with goggle eyes are innumerable dragons, Madonnas, water goddesses, tiki heads, fish, birds, and disembodied faces. Surprises lurk everywhere.

FÉCAMP

Benedictine Museum and Distillery: 110 rue Alexandre-le-Grand. Open daily, Easter–November 11, 9:30–11:30 A.M. and 2–5:30 P.M. Admission: 15F (includes samples). Phone: 35 28 00 06.

This ancient liqueur has a recipe even more complicated than Dr. Pepper's. The guided tour provides a glimpse and a whiff of the many tantalizing ingredients (which include saffron, cinnamon, hyssop, myrrh, coriander, thyme, nutmeg, and 20 other spices). The museum has exhibits about the monastery that made the drink famous, medieval distillation equipment, and more than 700 counterfeit bottles of Benedictine. The modern distillery shows how Benedictine is made today, and the tour concludes with a sample—in a glass, on a crepe, or on ice cream.

Holy Blood: in Trinity Church (l'Eglise de la Trinité), next to rue des Forts. Open normal church hours. Phone: 35 28 17 73.

On display here in the church is a reliquary containing a small amount of Jesus' blood. Pilgrims used to come from all over Christendom to see it, but now only devout

Catholics and *Europe Off The Wall* devotees visit this unusual relic.

GRANVILLE

Seashell Fairyland, Mineral Palace, and Butterfly Garden: all in the Marine Aquarium complex, on the Pointe du Roc at the far western tip of the city. Open daily, Easter–November, 9 A.M.–noon and 2–7 P.M. Admission to each section: 12F; children under 14, 9F. Phone: 33 50 03 13 or 33 50 19 10.

Some French people find *coquillage* tacky, but we love it: it's the art of making sculptures and mosaics out of shells. The Seashell Fairyland offers prime examples: life-size Roman columns, masks, replicas of Angkor Wat and the Cairo mosque are just a few of the wonders here, built entirely of shells. The Mineral Palace is a variation on that theme, with many large creations made out of semi-precious stones: a unicorn, a Japanese tea garden, an exploding volcano, a blue dragon, flowers, mosaics, etc. And the Butterfly Garden's huge, dead, colorful specimens are arranged in curious geometric dioramas, enhanced by butterfly-wing mosaics, carved tiki heads, and taped jungle animal noises.

ÎLE D'OUESSANT
(12 miles off the western tip of Brittany)

The Île d'Ouessant Local Museum (Ecomusée de l'Île d'Ouessant): in the hamlet of Niou Huella, half a mile west of Lampaul, where the ferries arrive from Brest. Open April–June, Wednesday–Monday, 2–6 P.M.; July and August, daily, 11 A.M.–6:30 P.M.; September, Wednesday–Monday, 11 A.M.–6:30 P.M. Admission: 10F; children, 5F. Phone: 98 68 87 76 or 98 48 86 37.

Every region of France has its own "ecomusée," a museum illustrating the rural lifestyle of the area. The Île d'Ouessant's ecomusée is unusual because life there is unusual: the island has no trees or wood, the men spend most of their lives at sea, and the women do the farming. The museum, made up to resemble the archetypical Ouessantine house, contains furniture made out of wood washed up from shipwrecks, and interesting shrine-like decorations. The people are so maritime-minded that the insides of their homes are arranged and organized like ships' cabins.

LISIEUX

St. Thérèse's Relics: in the Salle des Reliques, to the left of the main door of the Carmel Chapel, on rue du Carmel. Open daily, 7 A.M.–7 P.M. Admission: free. For more information call the Lisieux Tourist Office at 31 62 08 41.

They don't keep her body in a glass case, but the relics on display here include many things St. Thérèse used during her short life: a penitential thorned cross and thorned bracelet, rough ceramic eating utensils, and two pairs of shoes: her little white satin wedding-to-Jesus shoes and her clumsy wooden clogs, worn in the convent. Best of all is a vast sheaf of golden hair—about three feet long—cut off on the day Thérèse took her vows. It still curls.

LOUVIERS
(55 miles northwest of Paris, just south of Rouen)

Robert Vasseur's Mosaic House: 80 rue du Balchampêtre. Open Monday–Saturday, 5–9 P.M. and Sunday in the afternoons (but this is a private residence, so on occasion no one will be home and you'll only be able to see the outside). Phone: 32 40 22 61.

Robert Vasseur started his career as a milkman, but then he caught Mosaic Fever. For 35 years now he has covered every available surface of his house and property with mosaics made of shells, pieces of pottery and broken plates. Floors, walls, ceilings, furniture, doorways, patios, fountains, sculptures, windowsills—all completely covered with intricate, exacting, colorful geometric mosaics. It takes a driven man to make something as overwhelming as this.

MORLAIX

Waiters' Race (Course des Garçons de Café): every year on a Sunday in early September, at 2 P.M. in the place du Marc'hallac'h. For current date and more information, call 98 88 02 40.

Everybody knows French waiters take themselves seriously. This annual footrace lets them put their skills to the test: balancing a tray with a full glass and bottle of beer, contestants run around a specified course, careful not to spill a drop. The winner gets to compete in the big Paris Waiters' and Waitresses' Race.

PAIMPONT FOREST
(23 miles west of Rennes)

Forest of Legend (Brocéliande): the area north and west of Plélan-le-Grand, east of Tréhorenteuc and around the town of Paimpont. For more information, call the Brocéliande Tourist Office at 99 06 86 07.

Few people know that many of the legends and stories surrounding King Arthur, Merlin the Magician, and the Knights of the Round Table take place not in England, but here in Brittany. The Paimpont Forest is the modern-day remnant of the Forest of Brocéliande, home of Merlin and stomping grounds of Lancelot, Vivian, and other Arthurian characters. Legendary and mystical sites dot the landscape: signs at road intersections and villages indicate a self-guided walking tour of interesting places, and the Brocéliande Tourist Office (in the Plélan-le-Grand Town Hall) sells maps and gives tours of the area several days a week (call tourist office for exact times). Here's a list of some of the more remarkable sites. *The Fountain of Youth:* just southwest of the village of St-Malon sur Mel, southwest from the Etang (lagoon) de la Marette, in a small grove of trees, next to a large fence. (It's somewhat hard to notice, as it's just a small water hole, so be careful: Ponce de León took a wrong turn here and ended up in Florida.) *Merlin's Tomb:* just southeast of the Fountain of Youth; across the road in a field under a tree is a standing stone that supposedly marks where Merlin's body is buried (despite conflicting legends that he never physically died). *Tréhorenteuc Church:* an Arthurian-related church listed separately in this chapter. *The Valley of No Return:* just southwest of Tréhorenteuc on the eastern edge of the forest. Go south on road D141 and take a path branching off to the west. At the end of this dead-end valley is the Fairy's Mirror, where legend has it that Merlin's spirit (and/or body) remains trapped in a prison of air made by Vivian. *Barenton Fountain:* a path leads north to it from the village of Folle Pensée. Also known as Merlin's Spring, this was a Druidic ritual spot; the water supposedly has magical powers. Vivian met Merlin here, too. (It's a good idea to get a map before venturing into the forest.)

PLOUHARNEL
(18 miles southwest of Vannes)

Le Galion Shellcraft Museum: just south of Plouharnel on the road leading out to the Quiberon Peninsula; the galleon is next to the water in its own little square pool. Open April–September, daily, 10 A.M.–noon and 2–6 P.M.

Two of the great mysteries of Brittany are, one, why is a huge, unseaworthy galleon stranded in a 50-foot-long manmade pool; and two, why does this galleon contain a museum of crazy comical sculptures and designs made of shells? More proof for the existence of paranormal phenomena.

RY
(Ten miles east of Rouen)

Galerie Bovary: in the Old Cider Mill. Open Easter–October 31, Saturday–Monday, 11 A.M.–noon and 2–7 P.M. Admission: 15F; students, 10F; children, 8F. Phone: 35 23 61 44.

Ry is the city Flaubert chose as the setting for his novel *Madame Bovary*. In the old mill, numerous mechanized figures act out scenes from the book in appropriately tear-jerking fashion.

ST-MALO

Exotarium: on place Vauban, opposite the aquarium in the city walls. Open in summer daily, 9 A.M.–11 P.M.; in winter, daily, 9 A.M.–noon and 2–6 P.M. Admission: 16FF; students and children 7–16, 11F; children under 7, free. Phone: 99 40 91 86.

Across the street from the dank, fish-filled catacombs that serve as St-Malo's municipal aquarium is its neglected sister exhibit, the Exotarium. Advertised by a funky homemade sign featuring a smiling chameleon, this is an exotic zoo in miniature. You'll find reptiles, insects, and other crawlies as you wander through steamy-hot shadowy halls, and you'll come face-to-face with big spiders and little alligators, venomous frogs, and clicking cockroaches. The last time we visited, the highlight was a tankful of nightmarish insects known as Australian Scorpion Ants—but since we arrived just in time to see the mother scorpion ant being devoured by her swarming

Brittany and Normandy / 73

offspring, the entire species might by now be a victim of rampant cannibalism.

Sculptured Rocks (Rochers Sculptés): three miles northeast of town in Rotheneuf. From St-Malo take bus 1 or 4 from next to the tourist office to Rotheneuf, and follow the signs from the corner of rue Abbé-Fouéré and Chemin des Rochers Sculptés (bear right). Open daily, 9 A.M.–9 P.M. Admission: 7F. For more information call 99 56 64 48.

Carved by hand, these wind-lashed cliffs take the shape of sea monsters, rearing heads, and strange human figures. Abbé Fouéré, a nineteenth-century religious hermit, spent years sculpting the seaside rocks to illustrate local tales, blending fact with fiction. You can walk along paths cut into the rock to get an up-close look at the figures and niches.

ST-MICHEL-DE-MONTJOIE
(35 miles southwest of Caen)

Museum of Granite: in a park in the middle of town (no street address). Open June 15–September 15, 10 A.M.–noon and 2–6:30 P.M.; rest of the year, Saturday and Sunday only, 2–6 P.M. (other times by appointment). Admission: 9F; children, 5F. Phone: 33 59 84 94 or 33 59 84 80.

Respect for rocks—that's what we like to see. This museum (the first of its kind) shows how granite has been extracted and worked for the past several hundred years. On display is a surprising variety of useful and artistic objects made of granite.

ST-PIERRE-SUR-DIVES
(18 miles southeast of Caen)

International Museum of Miniature Furniture: in the Orangerie of the Chateau de Vendeuvre, which is just southwest of St-Pierre-sur-Dives. Open June 1–September 15, daily, 2–7 P.M. Phone: 31 40 93 83.

Satin, brocade, tiny silk pillows, and intricately carved chair legs the size of pencils ... we're not talking Barbie's Dream House here. French craftsmen have been known to spend hundreds of hours making a single small object, lavishing on it the most expensive materials, the most painstaking detail—just to prove they are masters of their craft. This collection is full of examples of such

TLC: tiny four-poster beds and tiny divans are enhanced by minuscule framed paintings and infinitesimal bouquets.

LE TERTRE ROUGE
(23 miles southwest of Le Mans; two miles southeast of La Fleche)

Unusual Zoo (Parc Zoologique et Musée des Sciences Naturelles de Jacques Bouillault): just southeast of Le Tertre Rouge, next to the Route de Savigné. Open in summer, daily, 9:30 A.M.–7 P.M.; other months open 9:30 A.M.–dusk. Admission: 31F; children, 18F. Phone: 43 94 04 55.

France's answer to Dr. Doolittle, Jacques Bouillault, owns and operates this private zoo. Bouillault cares for and feeds all the animals himself, has given nicknames to every one, and seems to have a special way of communicating with them. He enters the enclosures of even the most dangerous animals with no fear, and they all treat him like a friend. Though it is small, the zoo has a full range of residents: elephants, lions, tigers, giraffes, camels, black panthers, many kinds of monkeys and apes, birds, reptiles, tapirs, water buffaloes, bears, etc. Watching Bouillault at work is fascinating, and he's almost always there, except when he's off to parts unknown to bring home some new friends. Also inside the zoo is a small natural history museum about local animals.

TRÉGASTEL
(Eight miles north of Lannion, on the north Britanny coast)

Aquarium in a Grotto: corner of route de l'Ile Renot and boulevard du Coz-Pors. Open in summer daily 9–8. Phone: 96 23 88 67.

Fish, lobsters, and coral aren't the first inhabitants of this pink-and-grey hulk of stone. In years past, the grotto served as a church and even as a family home.

TRÉHORENTEUC
(28 miles west of Rennes)

Church with Bizarre Decorations: in the center of the village of Tréhorenteuc, ten miles west of Plélan-le-Grand, on the edge of Paimpont Forest, on road D141. Open all year, regular church hours. If the door is closed, ask at the house next door and they will give you the key. Admission: free. Call 99 07 81 37 or 99 06 86 07 for more information.

Pagan legend and Christian piety get inextricably mixed here in the region where the Knights of the Round Table and the Twelve Apostles garner equal respect. The local priest has covered the church with mosaics of local Round Table stories, paintings with Celtic pagan themes, and strange inscribed symbols and runic-seeming markings. Lest the congregation forget entirely that this is a Christian church, he included scenes of Jesus at the Stations of the Cross, but even these have hints of Arthurian influence. The church stands right next to the Valley of No Return and other mystical sites: see the Paimpont Forest entry for a description of the area.

VILLEDIEU-LES-PÔELES
(16 miles east of Granville)

Bell Foundry (Fonderie des Cloches): rue du Pont-Chignon, two blocks up from the church. Open daily 8 A.M.–noon and 2–6 P.M. Admission: 8F; children under 12, 5F. Phone: 33 61 00 56.

The chime of bells can sound more heavenly than earthly. To see how mere mortals create those divine peals, visit the foundry, which still employs old-fashioned methods and tools, such as a windlass. Homemade chimes have been ringing in this valley for over 200 years.

Copper Museum (Musée du Cuivre): rue Général Huard. Open June 1–September 15, daily, 9 A.M.–noon and 2–7 P.M. Admission: 8F. Phone: 33 61 00 16.

Local legend recalls the clang of smiths' hammers in these streets 900 years ago, when the Knights of Jerusalem came to town and shared their metalworking secrets. The very name of the village—Les Pôeles—means "panmakers." The museum displays a huge array of sturdy yet radiant pans, tubs, jugs, and weathercocks. Also on exhibit is an old-fashioned copper workshop.

LOIRE VALLEY

AMBOISE

Mechanical Puppet Exhibit: in the Amboise Castle. Open daily, 9 A.M.–noon and 2–6 P.M. (in winter, 9 A.M.–noon and 2 A.M.–dusk). Admission: 20F; students, 10F; children 7–16, 8F. Phone: 47 57 09 28 or 47 57 00 98.

The Amboise puppets are never advertised or mentioned, even during the tour, and so they take most people by surprise. After the tour you'll leave the castle via an old spiraling passageway. It's lined with niches and eerie cave-like little rooms, each one housing an assemblage of automated marionettes. Activated electronically every few minutes, the creatures spastically mimic the whole range of human activity. Spooky lighting and whimsical, rich costumes on the puppets will haunt your memory.

BLOIS

Poulain Chocolate Factory Tours: the factory is right near the train station. Four guided tours per day, Monday–Friday, in the summer, at 8:45 and 10 A.M.; 1:30 and 2:45 P.M. Two per day in winter, at 10 A.M. and 2:45 P.M. Admission: free. Reservations required. Phone: 54 78 39 21.

For an hour and a half, you're immersed in chocolate. Well, not physically, but the very thorough tour includes a film and an explanation of Poulain's complicated chocolate-making machinery. And, in the true French spirit of generosity, there are plenty of free samples.

Robert Houdin Magic Museum: in the Blois chateau, on Place du Chateau, inside the chateau's archaeology museum. Open July–August, daily, 9 A.M.–6 P.M.; other months, daily, 9 A.M.–noon and 2–6 P.M. Combined admission to castle and museum: 20F; admission to museum only: 5F. Phone: 54 78 06 62.

No, not Harry Houdini, but Robert Houdin, the great nineteenth-century French stage magician and godfather of modern performance prestidigitation. Erich Weiss renamed himself Harry Houdini in honor of his idol, Houdin. This museum traces Houdin's career, and has many of his stage tricks on display. Houdin also made innovative mechanical devices and toys; several of these can be seen here too.

CHEILLÉ
(Three miles west of Azay-le-Rideau)

Beardless Jesus: in the village church. Open regular church hours.

If there's one thing Christians and non-Christians agree on, it's that Jesus had a beard. This salient fact, however, eluded the anonymous sculptor who crafted Cheillé's life-size crucifix, and the result is just about the world's only representation of a beardless adult Jesus.

CHEVERNY
(Seven miles southeast of Blois)

Feeding the Dogs (Soupe des Chiens): at the castle. Feeding times: October–March, Monday and Wednesday–Friday, 3 P.M.; April–September, Monday–Friday, 5 P.M. Phone: 54 79 96 29.

With its 2,500 sets of antlers and mounted animal heads, Cheverny castle is sort of a Louvre for hunters. The castle's owner feeds his contingent of 70 purebred hunting dogs a sumptuous meal every day, amid elaborate ritual. The dogs' chowtime has become something of a local spectator sport, as crowds flock to Cheverny just to see the valuable hounds gobbling meals fit for a king, as hunting horns blare.

CHINON

Animated Wine and Barrelmaking Museum (Le Musée Animé du Vin et de la Tonnellerie): 12 rue Voltaire, in the center of town. Open May–September, Friday–Wednesday, 10 A.M.–noon and 2–6 P.M. Closed Thursday. Admission: 12F (minimum of two people); children under 7, free. Phone: 47 93 25 63 or 47 93 32 87.

Before you enter make sure to request the tape-recorded narrative in English; as you pass from room to room, strategically placed speakers tell the story. Carefully constructed scenarios illustrate the old-fashioned style of winemaking, from harvesting to tasting. The twist here is that homemade automata stiffly work with the old tools, making both wine and barrels. Of course it wouldn't be a proper wine museum without the requisite free taste. In the final scenario, an old robot couple quotes Rabelais about the necessity of drinking wine every day and "pissing away gravel."

Echo: go up the hill to the castle, and continue on to the route de Tours behind the castle. You'll come to a large sign reading "Clos de l'Echo Vent" and pointing to the right. Don't follow the sign. A smaller sign points up a small road branching to the left. Go up this road—rue de l'Echo—200 yards to a small raised cement platform.

The Chinon echo is so well known hereabouts that the local newspaper is actually named "l'Echo." Follow the above directions and shout toward the castle; you'll be rewarded with the sound of your own voice, bouncing off the castle walls and coming back to you, clear as day. The echo is only as amusing as you are.

DÉNEZÉ-SOUS-DOUÉ
(11 miles west of Saumur)

The Sculpted Cavern (La Caverne Sculptée): signs point the way from the center of the village. Open Easter–June, daily, 2–7 P.M.; July–August, daily, 10 A.M.–7 P.M.; September–October, daily, 2–7 P.M. Phone: 41 59 08 80 or 41 59 15 40. Guided tours available in English.

Four hundred years ago, a mysterious brotherhood of masons went to work on the walls of this cavern. The result is a compelling array of over 300 figures, among whom is the first American Indian ever carved in Europe. The masons may have been trying to leave a coded message for future generations, or they may simply have wanted to create a folk-art masterpiece in a place where rain and wind could never wear it away.

LA FOSSE
(Ten miles west of Saumur)

Troglodyte Hamlet (Hameau Troglodyte): La Fosse is one mile southeast of Dénezé. Open daylight hours, March–June and September–October, Tuesday–Sunday; July–August, daily; February, Saturday and Sunday afternoons only. Closed December and January. Phone: 41 59 00 32.

The houses and even some of the furniture are carved right out of the stone. Three families lived in this semi-subterranean place up until the turn of the century; now one family lives here. You can explore this bizarre kind of architecture. Note the fairytale quality of grass growing out of the roofs and chimneys poking out of the ground.

MONTPOUPON
(Six miles south of Chenonceau and 20 miles east of Tours)

The Home of the Gentlemen Hunters (Demeure de "Gentilshommes Chasseurs"): inside the castle. Open April 1–June 15 and October, Saturday–Sunday, 2–6 P.M.; June 15–October 1, daily, 10 A.M.–noon and 2–7 P.M. Admission: 12F. Phone: 47 94 23 62.

Just see if your heart doesn't get all fluttery when you hear the tape-recorded hunting horns here at the museum. The horn calls—complicated and forceful—are called *les fanfares* here. The question is, do they make you want to grab a rifle–or scamper up a tree?

NANTES

Jules Verne Museum: 3 rue de l'Hermitage, in the southwestern part of the city next to the river. Open Wednesday–Monday, 10 A.M.–12:30 P.M. and 2–5 P.M. Closed Tuesday. Admission: 5F; children free; free for everyone on Saturday and Sunday. Phone: 40 89 11 88.

Jules Verne, the influential originator of modern science fiction and adventure novels, was a native of Nantes. This museum is the city's tribute to him. Besides the typical writer-worship displays (furniture from Verne's study, manuscripts, personal knickknacks), the museum has interesting models of futuristic machines and vehicles described in Verne's novels (Captain Nemo's submarine, Phileas Fogg's balloon) and illuminated scenes from the stories. Plenty of first editions and Jules Verne curios round out the collection.

NEVERS

Bernadette's Body: in the Convent of St. Gildard, on rue de Lourdes, north of the train station. Open Monday–Saturday, 9 A.M.–5 P.M. For more information call 86 59 07 03.

Bernadette Soubiros' life changed in 1858 when she told the world that the Virgin Mary had appeared to her in a grotto at Lourdes. At that time Bernadette was a 14-year-old peasant. Later on she became a nun in Nevers, where she died in 1879. Now Bernadette is a saint and you can see her embalmed body in a glass case in a special chapel at the convent. Well-preserved as the body is, it doesn't look a bit like Jennifer Jones (who played Bernadette in the movie version of her story). It doesn't even look like a *dead* Jennifer Jones.

PLESSIS-BOURRÉ
(Ten miles north of Angers)

Strange Ceiling: in the castle's Salle des Gardes. Open Friday–Tuesday, 10 A.M.–noon and 2–5 P.M., and Thursday 2–5 P.M. Guided tours at 10:45 and 2:30. Price of tour: 21F; children 7–15, 11F. Phone: 41 32 06 01.

Louis XI's minister of finance, Jean Bourré, commissioned a painter to decorate his ceiling in such a way that, even 500 years later, it radiates Bourré's eccentricity. The two dozen panels show scenes from French fables—a few of which are funny, a few bawdy, a few both—as well as cryptic occult illustrations that have kept French art students wondering for half a millennium.

ROCHEMENIER
(12 miles southwest of Saumur)

Troglodyte Village: in Rochemenier, half a mile northeast of Louresse, which is four miles northwest of Doué-la-Fontaine. Open April–June, Tuesday–Sunday, 9:30 A.M.–noon and 2–7 P.M.; October, Tuesday–Sunday, 2–6 P.M.; November–March, Saturday–Sunday only, 2–6 P.M. (Opening hours are variable in December.) Phone: 41 59 18 15 or 41 59 35 91.

Dug out of the soft stone are several farms, dozens of subterranean houses, and a chapel. Until the last century most of these were occupied, and now one of the underground houses is furnished in a modern style to prove that subterranean living is still as practical as ever. Bushes sprout from the houses' roofs. In most of the buildings you can see locally made furniture and implements.

SAUMUR

Mushroom Museum (Musée du Champignon): two miles northwest of town, just past St Hilaire-St Florent on the left bank of the Loire. Take local bus from Saumur's Place Roosevelt to St Hilaire-St Florent and walk half a mile from the last stop. Open March 15–November 15, daily, 10 A.M.–noon and 2–6 P.M. Guided tours only. Admission: 12F; children, 7.50F. Phone: 41 50 31 55.

Mushrooms are best cultivated underground, so this is an underground museum, allowing you to see a bit of the 300 subterranean miles dug into the soft stone of the Saumur region. As well as fossils and old wine presses, you can see thousands of living mushrooms—which are cultivated in plastic bags nowadays. That may seem funny to you, but who are we to argue with the people who invented mushroom quiche?

SAVONNIÈRES
(Eight miles southwest of Tours; two miles east of Villandry)

Petrifying Grottoes (Grottes Petrifiantes): just northeast of town. Open February 8–March 31, Friday–Wednesday, 9 A.M.–noon and 2–6 P.M.; April–October, daily, 9 A.M.–7 P.M.; November–December, Friday–Wednesday, 9 A.M.–noon and 2–6 P.M. Admission: 16F; children, 9.50F. Phone: 47 50 00 09.

Anything left in the waters of these caves eventually becomes covered with a coating of mineralized stone. The caves have bizarre, wiggly stalactites, waterfalls turned to stone, and plenty of interesting mineral formations. The museum of petrifaction next to the cave contains petrified objects, cameos and artwork carved from layers of calcite, and other inscrutable cave curios. Part of these caves extend underground all the way to the nearby Villandry castle. The touch of modern comical chintziness is added by the stone sculptures of animals and prehistoric creatures that supposedly inhabited the area.

TOURS

Museum of Master-Craftsmanship (Musée du Compagnonnage): entrance at 8 rue Nationale. Open January–March and October–December, Wednesday–Monday, 9 A.M.–noon and 2–5 P.M.; April–September, Wednesday–Monday, 9 A.M.–noon and 2–7 P.M. Admission: 5F; students, 2.50F. Phone: 47 61 07 93.

Talk about going to great lengths to prove a point. Objects on display here were created for one reason only: to prove their makers' consummate skill. You'll see a six-story pagoda made of cake icing, a basketwork bust of

Napoleon, a quilted satin *coquille St-Jacques* (scallop), a sugar castle (complete with swan ponds and lighted windows), the world's most perfect clown shoes, and an unforgettable chocolate violin (life-size and a dead-ringer for the real thing). Other incredible items on display are testament to the talents of blacksmiths, bakers, confectioners, coconut carvers, staircase-makers, rope-knotters, rubberstamp-makers, upholsterers....

TRÉLAZÉ
(Five miles east of Angers)

Cointreau Tours: in the factory, on Carrefour Molière, just outside of Trélazé in the village of Saint-Barthélemy d'Anjou. Tours operate Monday–Friday at 10 A.M. and 2:30 P.M. Admission: free. Reservations required. Individuals must be matched up with a group tour; the Cointreau people will work this out for you. Phone: 41 43 25 21.

Can't afford to buy it by the bottle? You're in good company, pal. But at least you can emerge from the factory tour knowing a lot more about the stuff than most of the people who *can* afford it. The tour reveals an ingenious mixture of old equipment and new methods. Your studiousness will be rewarded with a free sample.

USSÉ
(18 miles west of Tours)

Sleeping Beauty's Castle: Open March 15–September 30, daily, 9 A.M.–noon and 2–7 P.M.; October–November, 10 A.M.–noon and 2–6 P.M. Admission: 30F; students, 18F; children 8–18, 14F. Phone: 47 95 54 05.

Taller and whiter than most of its neighboring castles and boasting more towers and a prime location at the edge of the dark Chinon forest, Ussé castle inspired French author Charles Perrault to write his fairytale *La Belle au Bois Dormant*. We know the tale as *Sleeping Beauty*. A visit to the castle includes a scene from the fairytale, with incorrectly dressed mannequins posing in a tower.

SOUTHWEST

AGDE
(25 miles southwest of Montpellier)

Aquatic Jousting: on the canal just opposite the cathedral, in the center of town. Jousts take place in early July on Saturday and Sunday evenings, and late July and August on Saturday and Sunday afternoons. For more information, call the Agde Tourist Office at 67 94 29 68.

Summer afternoons find the local menfolk out on the canal, proving their virility by knocking each other out of boats with ten-foot poles. See the Sète entry for more description.

AMPLEPUIS
(28 miles northwest of Lyon)

Sewing Machine Museum (Musée Machine à Coudre): on place de l'Hôtel de Ville, in the old chapel. Open July–August, daily, 2:30–6:30 P.M.; September–June, Saturday, Sunday, and holidays, 2:30–6:30 P.M. Admission: 5F; children 4F. Phone: 74 89 08 90.

Amplepuis is the hometown of Barthélemy Thimonnier, inventor of the sewing machine in 1830. Seventy sewing machines, including the oldest one in existence, are shown here in a display tracing their history. The first ones were quite primitive, but the basic underlying design has remained unchanged. We'll admit that even after seeing this museum, we *still* can't figure out how sewing machines work.

ANDOUZE
(25 miles northwest of Nimes)

Bambouseraie: 1½ miles east of Andouze, near the D907 road (follow the signs). Open April–June, daily, 9:30 A.M.–noon and 2–7 P.M.; July and August, 9:30 A.M.–7 P.M.; September and October, 9:30 A.M.–noon and 2–7 P.M. Admission: 20F; children under 13, 10F. Phone: 66 61 70 47.

The Far East comes alive in southern France, where this park is home to 100 kinds of bamboo, including some giant species. The trees are artfully arranged around life-size Asian stilt homes, which visitors may explore inside and out. Also here are tiny bonsai trees, a Japanese tea garden, and a water garden complete with huge voluptuous pink hyacinths.

BORDEAUX

Customs Museum (Musée des Douanes): 1 place de la Bourse, near the Quai de la Douane, on the river. Open May–September, Tuesday–Sunday, 10 A.M.–noon and 1–6 P.M.; October–April, Tuesday–Sunday, 10 A.M.–noon and 1–5 P.M. Closed Monday. Admission: 6F; students and children, 3F. Phone: 56 44 47 10 or 56 52 45 47.

Through pictures and actual specimens of contraband, the museum traces the history of smuggling (and attempted smuggling) from ancient Roman times to the present. Clever smuggling devices are on display, and famous cases are illustrated.

CAP D'AGDE
(28 miles southwest of Montpellier)

Nude City (Quartier Naturiste): on the eastern edge of Cap d'Agde, which is three miles south of Agde. Bus 273 runs from both Agde and Cap d'Agde to the Quartier Naturiste. Always open (except when it gets cold). Admission: 10F; children under 15, free; to bring your car in costs 40F, but it is pointless to do so since you have to park it right near the entrance anyway. Phone: 67 26 45 61.

A nude beach and then some: this resort cape boasts an entire nudist city, with a population of 25,000 in the high season. And there's no need to ever leave or get dressed: shops, hotels, banks, apartments, restaurants, theaters, nightclubs, doctors, even a post office—all nude—cater to your every whim. Though you may be informed otherwise, a large sign at the entrance reads "Nudity Obligatory," so remember to bring extra sunscreen.

LA CHAISE-DIEU
(38 miles southeast of Clermont-Ferrand)

Echo Room (Salle de l'Echo): in the St. Robert Abbey. Open in summer, daily, 9 A.M.–noon and 2–7 P.M.; open the rest of the year Wednesday–Monday, 10 A.M.–5 P.M. Phone: 71 00 01 16 or 71 00 06 06.

In this room, two people can stand in opposite corners, each facing the wall, and without raising their voices can have a clear conversation. The amazing acoustics made the room very useful in medieval times for terminally ill contagious people who wanted to make their confession without infecting the priest. Nowadays you can still test the echo.

CLERMONT-FERRAND

Petrifying Fountain (La Fontaine Petrifiante): at the corner of rue Gaultier-de-Biauzat and rue du Perou, just north of central Clermont. Open July and August, daily, 8 A.M.–7:30 P.M.; September–June, daily, 9 A.M.–noon and 2–6 P.M. Phone: 73 37 15 58.

The waters of this naturally occurring fountain cover everything they touch with a smooth, ivory-like coating. The process takes about three months, and for hundreds of years people have "petrified" objects by putting them in the path of the fountain's water. During the visit, you can see the petrifying process in action, as well as the results of past petrification. What's peculiar is the things people have chosen to petrify: real stuffed animals, life-size statues of people, bas-relief carvings of local folkloric scenes, portraits to be made into cameos ... if it was up to us, we'd be petrifying wigs, guitars, and hamburgers.

CONDOM
(60 miles northwest of Toulouse)

"Condom" doesn't mean the same thing in French as it does in English, so this town thrives, unaware of its prophylactic namesake. A quick postcard from here to your grandmother will set family matters askew in no time.

FOIX
(45 miles south of Toulouse)

Labouiche Underground River Boat Trips: near the village of Vernajoul, three miles northwest of Foix (follow the signs). Open: April and May, Monday–Saturday, 2–6 P.M.; Sunday and holidays, 9 A.M.–noon and 2–6 P.M.;

June, July, and September, daily, 10 A.M.–noon and 2–6 P.M.; August, daily, 9:30 A.M.–6 P.M.; October, Sunday only, 10 A.M.–noon and 2–6 P.M. Last tour leaves at 5 P.M. Phone: 61 65 04 11.

Subterranean mariners will be in their element here: this is one of the longest underground river trips we have encountered, a 1½ hour ride that takes you up and back a mile's worth of the subterranean Labouiche (which itself continues for at least two miles more). Spookily lit stalactites set the scene.

GANGES
(24 miles north of Montpellier)

Les Demoiselles Grotto: three miles south of Ganges on the D986 road, next to the village of St-Bauzille-de-Putois. Open April–September, daily, 8:30 A.M.–noon and 2–7 P.M.; October–March, daily, 9:30 A.M.–noon and 2–5 P.M. (last funicular leaves one hour before closing time). Admission: 25F. Phone: 67 73 70 02 or 67 58 44 12.

An underground funicular ride takes you to a series of caverns, the largest of which is called the Cathedral. The Cathedral is filled with phantasmagorical stalagmites and concretions; all have been given religious names, and the concept of an underground cathedral is taken to its fullest extent. One immense stalagmite, said to resemble a statue of Mary and Jesus, is called "Virgin and Child." A series of elongated petrified drippings are the cathedral's "organ." Other stalagmites are the "columns" that hold up the ceiling. Strange protruding formations are the cathedral's "gargoyles." Whether or not you can envision this comparison, the shapes and colors certainly are impressive.

LA GRANDE MOTTE
(12 miles east of Montpellier)

Unusual Architecture: throughout the city.

La Grande Motte is a new, artificially created resort built by the French government to promote tourism in the area and to cope with all the people heading south for their summer vacations. The government hired some "visionary" architects to design the apartment complexes and hotels, and nobody bothered to rein in their fantasies. The result is a string of vast, bizarrely shaped buildings lining the coast. Zigzaggy pyramids, roller-coaster frames, cylinders and cones, towering circles and curves—it's fascinating and weird, even if you're just driving through.

MONTPELLIER

Anatomy Museum: on rue Ecole de Médecine, in the Faculté de Médecine, next to the cathedral. Open Monday–Friday, 2:15–5 P.M. Phone: 67 60 73 71.

This, the oldest functioning medical school in the world, has one of the oldest and most extensive anatomy collections anywhere. Freaks, mummies, jaw-dropping monstrosities, wax models of anatomical specimens made for teaching purposes, genetic defects ... little more need be said. If you like this sort of thing, this is the sort of thing you'll like.

ORADOUR-SUR-GLANE
(15 miles northwest of Limoges)

Oradour-Sur-Glane is a unique monument to the tragedy and cruelty of WWII, and is guaranteed to bring tears to your eyes. On June 10, 1944, SS stormtroopers marched into Oradour-Sur-Glane and, with no provocation and apparently no reason, massacred the entire village of unarmed civilians (including 300 children), either by shooting them or burning them alive. To ensure that this inhuman slaughter not be forgotten, the French have never repaired or rebuilt the city. It still stands exactly as it did that day, burnt-out and empty buildings lining the streets, cars rusting away, the church (where many of the people were killed) standing in ruins.

ORGNAC
(22 miles northwest of Orange)

Forestière Grotto: four miles northwest of Orgnac on the D217 road. Open April–September, daily, 10 A.M.–7 P.M. Phone: 75 04 08 79 or 75 38 63 08.

The stalagmites at Forestière are unlike any we've ever seen. They look like the arms of some subterranean Lovecraftian octopus emerging from his lair. Weird bumps and lumps seem almost alive, like taste buds or suction cups. Strange, globular concretions lurk just on the surface of still pools. Meanwhile, hairy crystals sprout from the ceiling. Perhaps the entrance to the cave is the vast maw of some very clever creature.

PALAVAS
(Five miles south of Montpellier)

Aquatic Jousting: on the town canal. Jousts take place in June and July on Saturday and Sunday afternoons. For more information, call 67 68 02 34.

Palavas, like Agde and Sète, also has summertime boat jousts. See the Sète entry for more description.

POITIERS

Futuroscope Park: five miles north of Poitiers on the N10 road, near the town of Jaunay-Clan. Open daily, 10:30 A.M.–6:30 P.M. Admission to park and Kinemax theater: 50FF; children 5–18 30FF; admission to park only: 20FF: children 5–18, 10FF. Phone: 49 41 21 24.

This ambitious project was still being built when we visited, but it should be mostly completed by 1988. Futuroscope is a huge complex devoted to—what else?—the future. Dozens of high-tech displays explain futuristic ideas and machines. The "Village du Futur" is a simulated space-age village where George Jetson would feel at home. The "Lac du Futur" has a floating theater on it. A different theater, the Kinemax, has a separate admission fee, and if you see it you'll realize why: the screen, which they claim is the largest in Europe, is absurdly gigantic. Futuroscope will be spawning more and more new sections in the months to come: keep an eye on your radar screen for future developments.

ST-AMBROIX
(32 miles north of Nimes)

Cocalière Grotto: one mile northeast of St-Ambroix, near the D904 road. Open: April–October, daily, 9:30 A.M.–noon and 1:30–6 P.M. Phone: 66 24 01 57.

This is the cave that has everything: crazy-looking stalagmites, prehistoric remains, underground lakes and crystal-clear pools, a mock-up of some cave explorers, mineralized blobs dripping from the ceiling, an underground bicycle-riding path (really!), its own train that picks you up at the exit and brings you back through a countryside dotted with dolmens and tumuli, mysterious tunnels that go off for dozens of miles underground, and plenty of souvenir shops at the entrance. What more do you need?

ST-EMILION
(22 miles east of Bordeaux)

Church Carved from Solid Rock (Eglise Monolithe): underneath part of the town. Guided tours only. Tours leave from the Tourist Office on place des Créneaux daily at 10 A.M. (tours last 45 minutes). Admission: 18F; children, 12F. Phone: 57 24 72 03.

The caves in the hill on which the town now stands were used as a sanctuary by Saint Emilion in the eighth century. Later, monks dug out an underground ossuary, tunnels, and eventually a large church. The tour takes in most of St-Emilion's subterranean sites, but the church is the undisputed climax. The inside is built to look like a regular church (columns, arches, etc.), even though none of the architectural features are structurally necessary since the church is made of a single piece of rock.

ST-GUILHEM LE DÉSERT
(20 miles northwest of Montpellier)

Clamouse Grotto: one mile south of St-Guilhem le Désert on the D4 road. Open April 1–November 15, daily, 9 A.M.–noon and 2–6 P.M.; November 16–March 31, Sunday and holidays only, 2–5 P.M. Admission: 25F. Phone: 67 57 71 05.

This grotto, formed by an underground river, has as its speciality countless intricate, twisted, mineralized squiggles, delicate crystals, multicolored concretions, and elongated tapering orange stalactites that look like mutated carrots growing down from the ground above. The half-mile underground walk would take all day if you stopped to look at every interesting shape.

SÈTE
(15 miles southwest of Montpellier)

Aquatic Jousting: on the Sète canals which pass through the center of town. Jousts take place throughout the summer, especially on Sundays in late June and near Bastille Day (July 14); the most action takes place in the second half of August. Admission: free. For exact times and more information, call the Sète Tourist Office at 67 74 73 00.

Americans are fond of saying, "I wouldn't touch that with a ten-foot pole," but the men of Sète love touching things with ten-foot poles so much they spend their summers knocking each other out of boats with them. They've been doing it for 300 years now, though nobody knows why. Two teams, one in a red-and-white boat, another in a blue-and-white boat, row out onto the canal as hundreds of spectators cheer; musicians at the back of each boat play the old jousting song, while the two contestants, each on a special prow platform, joust wildly at each other. The last dry man is the winner.

SORGES
(Ten miles northeast of Périgueux)

Truffle Museum (Ecomusée de la Truffe): on le Sentier des Truffières. Open Wednesday–Monday in the afternoon (no set hours). Closed Tuesday. Phone: 53 05 90 11.

The truffle, that rare and delicate fungus, is one of the few remaining foodstuffs that man has been unable to grow in a controlled environment. All truffles have to be gathered in the wild; and the only way to find them is with specially trained dogs or pigs. This musem, in the heart of truffle country, is all about how and where to find truffles, the history of truffle-hunting, and of course the importance of truffles in French *haute cuisine*. Photos, films, and dioramas illustrate the different truffle species, what they taste like, and how the world would be a sadder place without them.

LA VILLEDIEU
(18 miles west of Montélimar)

The Little Museum of the Bizarre (Le Petit Musée du Bizarre): in the village of La Villedieu, which is $3\frac{1}{2}$ miles west of Villeneuve de Berg on the N102 road. Open by appointment. Phone: 75 94 83 28.

The proprietor has collected every piece of bizarre artwork that he could get his hands on, so the museum offers a varied and weird array of sculpture, painting, folk art, furniture, and knickknacks. Most of these are the work of self-taught artists.

PROVENCE AND THE RIVIERA

ANSOUIS
(15 miles north of Aix-en-Provence)

Extraordinary Museum of Undersea Discoveries (Musée Extraordinaire de Georges Mazayer): rue du Vieux Moulin. Open in summer, Wednesday–Monday, 2–7 P.M. Closed Tuesday. Other months open Wednesday–Monday, 2–6 P.M. Phone: 90 79 20 88.

Georges Mazayer spent most of his life as a professional diver and undersea explorer. In 35 years he discovered many strange things on the ocean floor, and he has now put them all in his museum: odd pieces of coral, strange rocks and shells, mysterious objects that have yet to be identified, and pictures made by Mazayer of the unexplainable scenes he has encountered under the waves.

CHATEAUNEUF-LES-MARTIGUES
(12 miles north of Marseille)

El Dorado City: one mile southeast of Chateauneuf-les-Martigues, just south of the A55 road, to the east of the road to Carry-le-Rouet. Open March 16–May 31 and September 16–November 15, Thursday–Saturday, noon–7 P.M. (with no stunt show) and Sunday 10 A.M.–7 P.M. (with stunt show at 2:30); June 1–September 15, daily, 10 A.M.–dusk (with stunt show at 3); November 16–March 15, Sunday only, noon–dusk. Admission: 37F; children under 14, 27F. Phone: 42 79 86 90.

This here ain't no sham Western town, nosireebob. Everything in El Dorado City is meant to be as authentic as possible. The buildings are duplicates of actual old Western buildings; the actors playing the cowboys, Indians, Mexicans, showgirls, and townfolk are all convincingly costumed. There's a dance hall, saloon, steam train, haunted gold mine, rifle range, and elaborate and exciting stunt shows in the center of town.

CUGES-LES-PINS
(14 miles east of Marseille)

OK Corral: two miles east of Cuges-les-Pins on the N8 road. Open in March, Sunday only, 10:30 A.M.–6:30 P.M.;

April–May, Thursday, Saturday, and Sunday, 10:30 A.M.–6:30 P.M.; June, daily, 10:30 A.M.–6:30 P.M.; July and August daily, 10:30 A.M.–7:30 P.M.; September, Thursday, Saturday, and Sunday, 10:30 A.M.–6:30 P.M.; October, Sunday only, 10:30 A.M.–6:30 P.M. Most rides close between noon and 1:30 P.M. Admission: 50F; children under 10, 40F. All rides are free once you're inside the park. Phone: 42 73 80 05 or 42 73 82 75.

At this all-American Wild-West theme park, you can get your face painted like an Indian brave's, watch French cowboys gun each other down at the "Western Spectacles" (usually starting around 1 P.M.), and ride any of the dozens of amusement-park rides—some with strangely non-Western names. A goofy Boot Hill cemetery has comical tombstone epitaphs that may require a French dictionary to be appreciated in full.

GRASSE
(Eight miles north of Cannes)

Fragonard Perfume Factory Tours: 20 Boulevard Fragonard. Tours given daily, 10 A.M.–noon and 2–5 P.M. (6 P.M. in summer). Tours available in English. Phone: 93 36 44 65.

Grasse's factories produce most of the world's perfume essences. Guided tours show you perfume-making processes, and a museum on the premises (Maison Fragonard) traces the use of scent from ancient times.

Galimard Perfume Factory Tours: 73 route de Cannes. Open business hours only. Admission: free. Tours available in English. Phone: 93 36 08 10.

The tour shows how lavender and other choice local flowers are pressed, crushed, dissolved, and made into perfume. A visit to the in-house perfume history museum is included in the tour.

Molinard Perfume Factory Tours: 60 boulevard Victor-Hugo. Tours given July–September, Monday–Saturday, 8:30 A.M.–6:30 P.M.; October–June, Monday–Saturday, 8:30 A.M.–1 P.M. and 2–6 P.M. Phone: 93 36 03 56.

Besides good smells, this tour offers views of the factory's fine old distilling machinery and provides step-by-step explanations of what the employees are doing. On exhibit here is an extensive collection of Lalique perfume bottles.

TARASCON
(Seven miles north of Arles)

Tarasque Parade: every year on the last Sunday in June, at about 3 P.M. Parade route includes the Avenue de la Republique, Course Aristide Briand, Boulevard Victor-Hugo, Boulevard Gambetta, and Boulevard Itam. For more information call 90 91 03 52.

The Tarasque was a bloodthirsty monster, half-lion and half-dragon, that terrorized the region until St. Martha (Mary Magdalene's sister) came to town in 48 A.D. and vanquished the beast. Good King René established this festival in the fifteenth century: through the streets marches a 15-foot tarasque, green all over, with evil red spikes, an almost-human nose, and eyes "redder than cinnabar," as local poet Frederic Mistral once wrote. Costumed characters aid the monster's dipping, swooping progress, while throngs of spectators shriek with joy.

VENCE
(12 miles north of Cannes)

Matisse Chapel (Chapelle du Rosaire): 46 Avenue Henri-Matisse, one mile from the center of town. Open Tuesday and Thursday, 10–11:30 A.M. and 2:30–5:30 P.M. (Open slightly later in summer.) Closed November–mid-December. Phone: 93 58 03 26.

The whole chapel is the work of local boy Matisse, inside and out—from the tall spire of a cross on the roof to the black-and-white pictures on the interior walls.

VILLEFRANCHE-SUR-MER
(Six miles east of Nice)

Jean Cocteau Chapel (Chapelle St-Pierre): overlooking the harbor. Open in summer, Saturday–Thursday, 9:30 A.M.–noon and 2:30–7 P.M.; in winter, Saturday–Thursday, 9:30 A.M.–noon and 2–4:30 P.M.; spring and fall, Saturday–Thursday, 9 A.M.–noon and 2–6 P.M. Closed November 15–December 15. Admission: 5F. For more information call 93 80 73 68.

Huge disembodied staring eyes are an unsettling part of this chapel's interior decoration. Surrealist film director, poet, and artist Jean Cocteau restored and redecorated the entire chapel in honor of St. Peter, patron saint of fishermen. The lighthearted wall paintings depict scenes from the saint's life—with a profusion of fish and eyes.

VILLENEUVE-LOUBET
(Six miles west of Nice)

Culinary Arts Museum: the Auguste Escoffier Foundation, 3 rue Escoffier. Open in summer, Tuesday–Sunday, 2–6 P.M.; winter, Tuesday–Saturday, 2–6 P.M. Admission: 10F; students and children, 5F. Phone: 93 20 80 51.

Installed in the former home of master French chef Escoffier, the museum has on display some amazing and unlikely things crafted in sugar and chocolate—the work of prize-winning confectioners. The museum's collection also includes 1,000 different menus.

——— THE RHONE AND THE ALPS

ANNECY

Bell Museum (Musée de la Cloche): 3 chemin de l'Abbaye in Annecy-le-Vieux, one mile north of Annecy. Open June 1–September 15, Monday–Saturday, 10 A.M.–noon and 2:30–6:30 P.M.; Sunday, 2:30–6:30 P.M.; September 16–November 30 and January–May, Tuesday–Saturday, 10 A.M.–noon and 2:30–5:30 P.M. Closed December. Admission: 15F; students and children, 12F. Phone: 50 23 60 86.

The biggest bells in France were made here at the Paccard foundry—and so was our own Liberty Bell. On display at the museum are ancient bells, carillons, chiming clocks, bell molds, and an audio-visual program.

BOIS D'AMONT
(40 miles north of Annecy)

Wooden Box Museum (Musée de la Boisselerie): in the Town Hall. Open in summer, Saturday and Sunday, 3–6 P.M. Phone: 84 60 04 92.

Remember that wooden box you made in shop class in seventh grade? Well, these are better. Bois d'Amont has been a box-making town for 200 years now, and the museum displays the work of local artisans: clock cabinets, food boxes, chests, postal boxes, and more. A reconstructed box-making studio is also on display.

CHAMONIX

Ice Sculpture Cave (La Grotte de Glace): at the Mer de Glace. Take the Montenvers Rack Railway from Chamonix to the Mer de Glace (round trip price: 41F). Once there, follow the signs to La Grotte de Glace. Open July–September, daily, whenever trains arrive (approximately 9 A.M.–6 P.M.). Exact hours depend on weather conditions. Admission: 7.50F. Call 50 53 12 54 for more information.

Most people come up here for the stunning view over the Mer de Glace glacier. But not us. We head straight for the viewless ice caves and their crazy, kitschy, permanent ice sculptures. Rooms carved into the glacier are fully furnished: ice piano, ice bed, ice couch, ice chairs—enough to fill a living room and a bedroom. The rent is low but there's no central heating.

HAUTERIVES
(17 miles north of Romans-sur-Isere, which is 12 miles northwest of Valence)

The Ideal Palace (Palais Idéal): in the middle of the village. Open in summer, daily, 8 A.M.–8 P.M.; in winter, daily, 8 A.M.–6 P.M. Closed January. Admission: 11F; children, 5F. Phone: 75 68 81 19.

It's part Hindu temple, part French chateau; a Mecca for surrealists, a palace gone wild. Palais Idéal, a massive monument swarming with hundreds of stone animals, people, plants, and other fantastic shapes, represents the lifework of a French mailman who taught himself masonry and created this wonder from the ground up, using stones and bits of things he found while on his rounds. The mailman, Joseph Ferdinand Cheval, intended the Palais as a monument to himself, and the result is very, very personal indeed.

LYON

Museum of Textile History (Musée Historique des Tissus): in the Villeroy Mansion, 34 rue de la Charité, 2nd arrondissement, six blocks from the Lyon-Perrache train station. Open Tuesday–Sunday, 10 A.M.–noon, and 2–5:30 P.M. Admission: 12F. Phone: 78 37 03 92.

Lyon, long a fabric center, celebrates the art of cloth with incredibly beautiful samples from all ages and all corners of the world: Coptic tapestries, Japanese screens, Persian carpets, Renaissance Spanish and Italian textiles, fourth-century Egyptian weavings. Compare these with the layest Lyon silks and abstract patterns. After this you'll really think twice about wearing polyester leisure suits.

Public Hospital Museum (Musée des Hospices): Hotel-Dieu, place de l'Hôpital, 2nd arrondissement. Take bus 8 or 28 from downtown. Open Monday–Friday, 1:30–5:30 P.M. Admission: 5F. Phone: 78 37 36 46.

Science, history, charity, and the macabre come together in the form of antique bedpans and a padded cell, terrifying old surgical instruments, and a centuries-old doctor's uniform which, although it could pass for a carnival costume, was designed to protect its wearer against the plague.

NYONS
(35 miles northeast of Avignon)

Olive Museum (Musée de l'Olivier): place des Tilleuls (in the Olive Co-op). Open July and August, Thursday–Saturday, 3:30–6:30 P.M.; September and winter, Saturday, 3:30–6:30 P.M. Admission: 5F; students, free. Phone: 75 26 12 12.

Nyons is France's olive capital, so its museum is naturally all about olives and the subculture of olive growers. Displays show what it's like to spend your life planting, growing, harvesting, and selling olives. And I bet you never thought there were so many different kinds, colors, and uses for this odd little fruit.

OYONNAX
(Ten miles north of Nantua)

Museum of Combs and Plastic: La Grenette, 3 rue de la Victoire. Open July and August, daily, 2:30–7:30 P.M.; September–June, Tuesday and Saturday only, 2–5 P.M. Phone: 74 77 44 55.

That modern miracle—plastic—gets the attention it deserves here in Oyonnax, long a plastic manufacturing town. On display at the museum are lovely examples of the plastic maker's craft: eyeglass frames, clasps, hair combs, multitudinous hairpins, and some rare celluloid dishes and cowhorn utensils. Early plastic-and comb-making machinery traces the industry from 1939 onward.

ROMANS-SUR-ISÈRE
(12 miles northwest of Valence)

Shoe Museum (Musée de la Chaussure): 2 rue Sainte-Marie. Open Wednesday–Saturday and Monday, 9 A.M.–noon and 2–6 P.M.; Sunday, 2:30–6 P.M. Closed Tuesday. Admission: 10F; students, 5F; children under 7, free. Phone: 75 02 44 85.

No one dares go barefoot in Romans, chief shoemaking town in a nation that loves good shoes. Shoes on display in the museum include many stunning French creations (including Art Deco shoes) as well as the footwear of five continents and 4,000 years: Roman sandals, musketeers' boots, Venetian slippers, baby shoes, soldier's shoes, shoes for Chinese bound feet (*pieds mutilés*, they say here), Indian moccasins, and don't miss the Australian aboriginal shaman's sandal.

LES ROUSSES
(20 miles north of Geneva)

Canadian House (La Maison Canadiènne): located three miles southwest of Les Rousses, in the town of Prémanon. Open December–October, daily, 10 A.M.–noon and 2–6 P.M. Closed November. Phone: 84 60 76 20.

A maple-leaf flag flies over La Maison Canadiènne, and the surrounding terrain looks a lot like parts of Canada. Inside you'll find exhibits on Canadian life, Canadian animals (including Canada geese and sled dogs) and Canadian Indians. The collection includes some elaborate Canadian Indian clothing.

ST-CLAUDE
(35 miles south of Besançon)

Pipe Museum: just to the left of the cathedral. Open June–September, daily, 9:30–11:30 A.M. and 2–6:30 P.M. Phone: 84 45 04 02 or 84 45 17 00.

Workers in St-Claude crank out three million pipes every year, and they've been doing so for well over a hundred years. The local specialty is briarwood pipes, but the museum displays specimens from all corners of the world.

ST-PAUL-TROIS-CHATEAUX
(18 miles north of Avignon)

Truffle and Wine Museum (Maison de la Truffe et du Tricastin): in place de la République. Open April 15–October 15, Monday, 3–6:30 P.M.; Tuesday–Saturday, 9:30 A.M.–noon and 3–6:30 P.M.; Sunday 10 A.M.–noon and 3–6:30 P.M. The rest of the year the afternoon times are 2:30–6 P.M. Phone: 75 96 61 29.

Everything you always wanted to know about nature's most elusive fungus: the museum has exhibits on the growth and life cycle of truffles, as well as methods for hunting them and serving them once you've caught them.

SEYSSEL
(50 miles northeast of Lyon)

Museum of Wood (Musée du Bois): on place de la République. Open July and August, daily, 10 A.M.–noon and 3–6 P.M. Admission: free. Phone: 50 59 26 27.

This is not so much a museum of wood but rather of things made from wood: a collection that shows just how versatile the medium can be. Included here are an amazing model of an engine, a miniature suspension bridge and intricate stairway, cars, instruments, buildings, and statues—all made of wood.

NORTH AND EAST

ARNAY-LE-DUC
(18 miles northwest of Beaune)

Museum of the Arts of the Table: 15 rue St-Jacques (in the ancient Hospices St-Pierre). Open April–June, Tuesday–Sunday, 10 A.M.–noon and 2:30–6:30 P.M.; July–August, daily, 10 A.M.–noon and 2:30–6:30 P.M.; September–October, Tuesday–Sunday, 10 A.M.–noon and 2:30–6:30 P.M.

Admission: 10F; students and children, 5F. Phone: 80 90 11 59 or 80 90 03 44.

Changing exhibitions all revolve around food and the distinctly French rituals of preparing it, serving it, and eating it.

BÈZE
(Ten miles northeast of Dijon)

Underground Boat Rides: at the source of the Bèze River. Open April and October, Saturday–Sunday, 10 A.M.–noon and 2–7 P.M.; May–September, daily, 10 A.M.–noon and 2–8 P.M. Closed November–March. Admission: 13F; students and children, 8F. Phone: 80 95 20 87.

Ancient peoples regarded river sources as magical places. The boat ride lets you decide for yourself as you experience the eerie sensation of traveling along subterranean waters, with no sky above.

CHALON-SUR-SAÔNE

Nicephore Nièpce Museum: 28 Quai des Messageries, on the river. Open Wednesday–Monday, 9:30–11:30 A.M. and 2:30–5:30 P.M. Closed Tuesday. Admission: 1F; students, 0.50F. Phone: 85 48 41 98.

It's a tragedy that Nicephore Nièpce, one of the most important inventors who ever lived, remains in almost total obscurity to this day. It was Nièpce who invented photography—not Daguerre (who capitalized on Nièpce's work), and not Henry Fox Talbot (who made an art out of it). Nièpce took the world's first permanent photograph (which you can see at the museum) at the incredibly early date of 1826, which was 13 years before anybody else. The museum also has the world's first camera and photographic equipment (from Nièpce's lab), the first color photos ever made, the first microfilm (used in the 1870 war), futuristic cameras used in space flights, and rotating exhibitions of important modern photographers.

DIJON

Grey Poupon Mustard Shop: 32 rue de la Liberté. Open Monday–Saturday, 9–11:45 A.M. and 12:45–7 P.M.

This company has been making mustard for over 200 years, so they know their stuff. This store displays antique mustard jars and containers, and of course rows and rows of countless varieties of mustard. The sheer number of different flavors (beer, thyme, vinegar, etc.) is amazing. But be careful what you buy: some of the flavors will have you breathing fire after the first taste.

MULHOUSE

Museum of Textile Printing (Musée de l'Impression sur Etoffes): 3 rue des Bonnes Gens, two blocks from the train station. Open Wednesday–Monday, 10 A.M.–noon and 2–6 P.M. Closed Tuesday. Admission: 22F; students, 15F; children under 10, free. Phone: 89 45 51 20.

The scarf-and-handkerchief collection of brilliantly printed specimens from Europe and the United States alone could fill a whole museum. (No runny noses allowed.) The rest of the museum displays sumptuous fabrics from all over the world, decorated with the most creative motifs. Among the ten million samples (spanning 200 years), you'll see Japanese silks, African and Indian cottons, French cashmere, and more.

Wallpaper Museum (Musée du Papier Peint): 28 rue Zuber, in the Rixheim suburb just northeast of downtown. Take bus 10. Open Wednesday–Monday, 10 A.M.–noon and 2–6 P.M. Closed Tuesday. Admission: 22F; students, 15F; children under 10, free. Phone: 89 64 24 56.

Two hundred years of wall coverings makes for an unusual view of history. The museum's 130,000 samples come from everywhere, and constitute the world's largest wallpaper collection. Indonesian batiks, panoramas painted on panels, and many Alsatian wallpapers are among the exhibits here.

ORNANS
(12 miles southeast of Besançon)

Vouivre Country: in the upper Loue River valley, which runs southeast from Ornans through Mouthier.

In a half-forgotten corner of Europe's mythological bestiary dwells the Vouivre, a ferocious winged reptilian monster who once supposedly preyed on travelers and locals throughout the Jura mountains. Today, as legend has it, the Vouivre's last stronghold is in the cliffs, still pools, and secluded chasms of the upper Loue valley. Cryptozoologists will find the town of Ornans the perfect base for exploratory expeditions into the rugged surrounding countryside. In Ornans you can even find locally made books about the Vouivre and its mythical companion, the Fouletot—a French-style goblin that lurks in the region's fir-tree forests.

PREZ-SOUS-LAFAUCHE
(35 miles north of Dijon)

Zoo of Wood (Zoo de Bois): in a farmhouse with no street address in Prez-sous-Lafauche, which is a village between Chaumont and Neufchateau on the N74 road, about 18 miles northeast of Chaumont. Once you reach the town, ask directions to the Zoo de Bois. Open June 1–September 15, daily, 3–6 P.M. (usually). Admission: 30F; students and children, 25F. Phone: 25 31 57 66.

Many museums claim to be unique, but rarely are their claims substantiated. The Zoo of Wood (also known as the Musée aux Branches) does nothing to promote itself, yet it is undoubtedly the only museum of its kind in the world. The museum's owner and curator, Monsieur Chaudron, has spent his life collecting tree branches that are naturally formed in the shapes of animals. You'd think it would be once in a lifetime that you'd find a branch in the shape of an elephant or a dog, yet Chaudron has a large number of them on display here. Where he gets them is a mystery.

RONCHAMP
(43 miles northwest of Besancon)

Le Corbusier Chapel (Chapelle Notre-Dame du Haut): on a hill overlooking the countryside. Open March 15–November 15, daily, 9 A.M.–7 P.M. Closed November 16–March 14. Phone: 84 20 65 13.

The chapel's unusual shape and billowy concrete roof is the work of adventurous modern architect Le Corbusier, who finished the chapel in 1955. Blindingly white, rounded, and deliciously asymmetrical, the chapel looks a little like a Greek cottage gone to heaven.

ST-DIZIER
(35 miles southeast of Chalons-sur-Marne)

Marcel Dhièvre's Petit Paris: on avenue de la Republique (no number). Visible anytime.

Marcel Dhièvre's bright painted birds and plants would

ALSATIAN ST. JOHN FIRES

To celebrate St. John's feast day (and a much more ancient holiday, the summer solstice), many Alsatian towns and villages build 30-foot pyramids of logs, which they set ablaze on the hillsides after dark. This makes for an entrancing spectacle. The towns tend to stagger their burnings over a week or so, so that people can attend more than one. The dates vary slightly from year to year, but they always fall on or near June 21. For the current schedule of St. John fires (Feux de St-Jean), call the tourist offices in Strasbourg (88 32 57 07) or Colmar (89 41 02 29). The following is a list of towns that regularly put on St. John fires.

ALBE ($\frac{1}{2}$ mile north of Villé, which is 20 miles northwest of Colmar)
ANDLAU (15 miles north of Colmar)
BELMONT (20 miles north of Cernay, which is seven miles northwest of Mulhouse)
DAMBACH-LA-VILLE (16 miles north of Colmar)
KIENTZHEIM (Five miles north of Colmar)
RIQUEWIHR (Six miles north of Colmar)
SÉLESTAT (12 miles north of Colmar)
WISSEMBOURG (30 miles north of Strasbourg)

---

look almost Pennsylvania Dutch if they weren't quite so intense—and so dense. Dhièvre filled the days of his retirement decorating his house's facade with paintings, mosaics, and bas-reliefs. The name "Petit Paris" alludes to mosaicked miniature versions of the Arc de Triomphe, the Eiffel Tower and other Parisian monuments over Dhièvre's front door. If only the *real* monuments had Dhièvre's cheery, candy-colored look.

STRASBOURG

Astronomical Clock: inside the cathedral, in the center of town. Performances daily at 12:30 P.M. Admission: 4F. (Buy tickets at the tourist office or the cathedral's cashier after 11:30 A.M.)

The 15-minute performance stars delicate, mechanical versions of Jesus, the apostles, angels, and Death. The clock, made in Strasbourg 150 years ago, has several faces, which give details about the state of the heavens.

Water Jousting: Monday and Friday evenings throughout July and August, at 8:30 P.M., at the Corbeau Bridge (Pont de Corbeau), just south of the cathedral. For more information call 88 35 03 00.

In a test of both manliness and balance, brave men try to knock each other out of boats with long wooden poles, while the River Ill, and many eager spectators, wait breathlessly to see who will take an unwanted bath.

TURCKHEIM
(Three miles west of Colmar)

Town Crier (Veilleur de Nuit): between May and the fall grape harvest, every night at 10 P.M. For more information call 89 27 38 44.

With a tall spear in one hand and a glowing lantern in the other, Turckheim's solemn town crier makes his rounds. He's one of the last of his kind in Europe, and his three-cornered hat and black cloak enhance the crier's quaintness.

WEST GERMANY

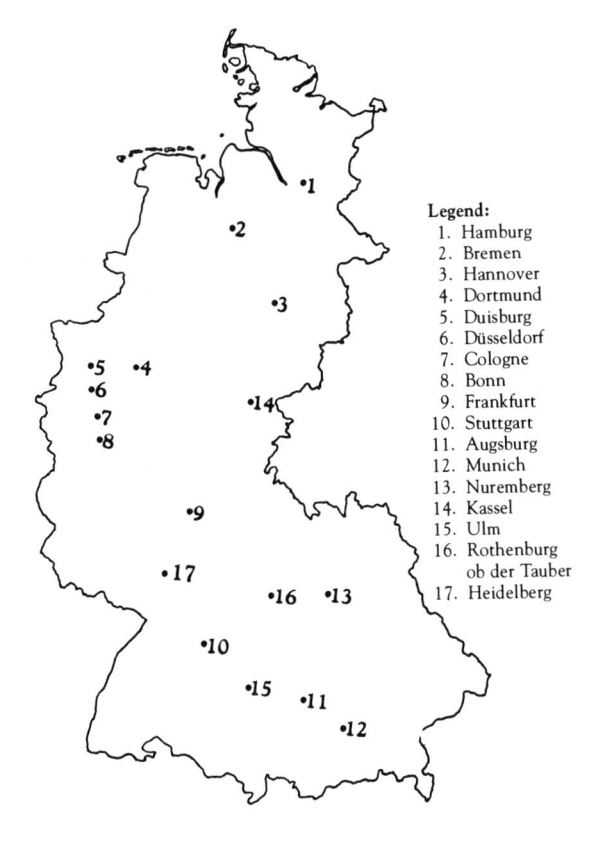

Legend:
1. Hamburg
2. Bremen
3. Hannover
4. Dortmund
5. Duisburg
6. Düsseldorf
7. Cologne
8. Bonn
9. Frankfurt
10. Stuttgart
11. Augsburg
12. Munich
13. Nuremberg
14. Kassel
15. Ulm
16. Rothenburg ob der Tauber
17. Heidelberg

Germans might resent what everyone's always saying about them—namely, that they work too hard, are too inhibited to have any fun, and care far too much about taking baths. Even so, your average Hans or Hilda is not about to wallow in filth, take a week off work without pay, strip and do the hula just to prove everybody wrong. *Nein.*

There's something comforting about all that

West Germany / 105

straight-faced German doggedness, that driving need to organize and label, the bristling energy that results from a good, solid, liverwurst-rich breakfast.

For one thing, it leads to great museums. Germany probably has more museums per capita than any other nation in the world; it's part of the national character. Museums of fine art and big-time history are here, yes; but we are more concerned with the innumerable museums dedicated to every imaginable aspect of life, death, food, wallpaper, bugs, footwear, cigars...well, the list goes on and on (as you'll see). Museums on subjects you've always taken for granted (but how much do you *really* know about shoes, anyway?) stand side-by-side with museums on startling, disturbing themes. And Germans take their museums about as seriously as they take their sausages, which is *very*. While a wackier, more slipshod people might milk such subjects as Faust and torture for a laugh now and then, the Germans seldom take these opportunities, and the poker face reigns supreme, which is actually the beauty of German museums.

Of course, they're also very, very clean.

AUGSBURG

Fred Rai Western City: 15 miles east of Augsburg, off Bundesstrasse 300; technically within the jurisdiction of Dasing, but actually eight miles northeast of Dasing. Open Palm Sunday (late March) until the end of October, Tuesday–Sunday, 9 A.M.–6 P.M. Closed Monday. Admission (which includes all performances): DM 5; children, DM 3. Phone: (08205) 225.

Fred Rai, a German country-and-western crooner, built this wild-west theme park as the realization of a lifelong dream. As with other German wild-west cities, Rai crammed everything west of the Mississippi into one place: cowboys, farmers, Mexicans, saloons, cavalry forts, gun-happy sheriffs, every Indian tribe he could think of, modern country music, conestoga wagon rides, and a nice big American flag with too many stars. You can pan for gold, ride horses, practice your lasso technique, and, after some chow in the "Mexican Cafe," take in the Wild West Show, featuring "Lex Randy, King of the Cowboys." On Sundays, Fred Rai himself gallops into town on his trusty horse, Spitzbub, and belts out some songs about his lonesome days on the prairie.

Medieval Banquet (Mittelalterliches Schlemmermahl): at Stiermann House (Stiermann-Haus), Maximilianstrasse 83. Open evenings (except holidays) at 7:30 P.M. Price ranges from DM 35.50–DM 58.50. Advance reservations required. Phone: 08231/2020 during weekday working hours.

Rough handmade platters arrive at your table filled with delicacies made from real fifteenth- and sixteenth-century German recipes. But the authenticity doesn't end there, as you are given only a stiletto with which to eat and old-style mead and natural dark beer to drink. Medieval dining customs are strictly upheld by the staff, who have a great time chastising diners who break the rules. But it's all in fun, they say.

Statues in the Augustus Fountain: in the Rathausplatz, opposite City Hall.

Here's the wet nurse's fantasy: breasts that never run dry.

BAD HOMBURG
(Five miles north of Frankfurt)

Saalburg Restaurant: in the Römerkastell, outside the city near the Roman excavations. Open every night at 7:30 P.M. Phone: (06175) 1007.

If you fantasize about an evening of ancient Roman revelry but are leery of fraternity toga parties, then take a chariot ride out to the Saalburg Restaurant. Each evening at 7:30 they stage a four-hour-long Roman banquet, with real Roman food, Roman costumes, and Roman eating utensils; and the waiters even attempt some Germanicized Latin. You must call in advance to make a reservation. (Don't worry—they speak English too.)

BUENDE
(60 miles west of Hannover)

Tobacco Museum: Funfhausenstrasse 15. Open Tuesday–Saturday, 10 A.M.–noon and 3–5 P.M.; Sunday, 11 A.M.–12:30 P.M. Closed Monday. Admission: free.

In this self-proclaimed "Tobacco Town," formerly but no longer a center for that industry in Germany, you can learn legends, lore, and history of the Devil's weed, and inspect a cigar as big as a baseball bat.

COLOGNE (KÖLN)

Eau de Cologne Museum (Kölnischwasser 4711 Museum): located in the company's administration building; call 4711 for address and to make an appointment.

Currently you must make a prior appointment to view the lovely old bottles and cologne-making equipment—and even then, you must demonstrate a "valid reason" for wanting to see it. But in 1989, the 4711 Company will open a museum for the public at its central store on Glockengasse, just west of Tunisstrasse.

Silverware Museum (Kabinettmuseum Glaub): Burgmauer 68. Open Tuesday–Friday, 3–6 P.M.; Saturday, 11 A.M.–2 P.M. Closed Sunday and Monday. Admission: free. Phone: 13 41 36.

Those who love to eat and/or fight in style will appreciate this collection of historical and artistic knives and serving ware. Included are art nouveau goblets, jeweled napkin rings, and other gleaming trinkets that would look as good in the jewelry box as in the kitchen.

Shrine of the Three Wise Men: in the Dom (cathedral); at the eastern end of the building, in the high altar. Open daily, 7 A.M.–7 P.M. Admission: free.

"We three kings of Orient are...." Ever wonder what became of those guys after their brush with fame way back when? Well, they ended up in Cologne, brought there from Italy in 1164. By now, though, they're just bones, housed in a condominium-style triple coffin in Cologne's dominating cathedral. Sorry, the Little Drummer Boy has not been afforded the same honor.

DUISBURG

Urinating Statue: directly behind the train station, to the left of the rear door as you exit.

Brussels' famed Mannekin-Pis has an earthy cousin here in Duisburg; immortalized in bronze, he is forever pulling up his shirt and looking down to observe the tinkle. Local pranksters make sure he usually has a real cigarette dangling from his parted lips to give him that air of sophistication.

DÜSSELDORF

Conch and Snail Museum (Löbbecke-Museum): between Speldorfer and Brehmstrasse, next to the river in the Nordpark. Open Tuesday–Saturday, 10 A.M.–5 P.M. Closed Sunday and Monday.

The Düsseldorf pharmacist Theodor Löbbecke loved snails and conches. Here in newly remodeled surroundings is his collection of more than 150,000 shells—more than enough whorls and swirls to hypnotize or dizzify. (Speaking of exoskeletons, Löbbecke's insect collection is an added attraction here.)

Neander Valley and Neanderthal Museum: Ten miles from town. Take bus 743 (bus sign will read "Mettmann") from the stop around the corner to the right of the train station. Usually open Tuesday–Sunday, 10 A.M.–5 P.M. Closed Monday.

A reconstructed skeleton marks the spot where Neanderthal Man was discovered in 1856, and a small museum nearby tells the story. The adjacent park—about 2,500 acres—is stocked with animals Mr. and Mrs. Neanderthal knew in their time: old breeds of bison, wild cattle, wild ponies, and deer.

ESSEN

Poster Museum (Deutsches Plakatmuseum): Rathenhauserstrasse. Open Tuesday–Sunday, noon–8 P.M. Closed Monday. Phone: 0201/884 114.

Americans love posters so much they buy and sell millions of them every year; Germans show their affection for posters by making a museum of them. The displays here come from many countries, and some of the posters are well over 100 years old.

FRANKFURT

Struwwelpeter-Museum: Hochstrasse 45-47 (a 15-minute walk from the central train station). Open Tuesday–Sunday, 11 A.M.–5 P.M.; Wednesday 11 A.M.–8 P.M. Closed Monday. Admission: free. Phone: 069/28 13 33.

Meet Struwwelpeter (Slovenly Peter), Germany's best-known children's-book hero. This stubborn little boy, created in the nineteenth century by author Heinrich Hoffman, refuses to cut his hair or his nails, and the result is a startling, tangled, twisted mess. This museum, founded in 1982, adores Struwwelpeter and his author, displaying dozens of editions in many languages, including Japanese and Yiddish. The English edition was translated by Mark Twain. Note also the *Struwwelpeter* parodies, *Struwwelhitler* (1941) and *Tricky Dick* (1974), and a set of supermodern paintings of an updated Struwwelpeter: "Struwwelpunk '84."

GARMISCH-PARTENKIRCHEN

Linderhof Castle: Take bus from in front of Garmish-Partenkirchen train station (departure times, Monday–Friday, 8:50 and 10:15 A.M., 12:10 and 1:10 P.M.; Saturday and Sunday, 10:15 A.M. and 1:10 P.M. Bus costs DM 9.60 round trip (free with Eurailpass). Castle is open 9 A.M.–5 P.M. in summer, 9 A.M.–4 P.M. in winter. Admission: DM 6; students, DM 3. Phone: (08822) 5 12.

King Ludwig II of Bavaria was nicknamed "Mad King Ludwig"; if a passion for wedding-cake rococo and things heavily Wagnerian are cause for madness, then Ludwig was definitely off his rocker. But oh, what fun to have the money for indulging one's tastes: among other crazy delights, Linderhof features the Grotto of Venus, an artificial cavern whose walls bear an enormous painting of a scene from a Wagner opera. Ludwig used to float about the underground lake in a golden boat, which you can still see.

Neuschwanstein Castle: Take bus from in front of Garmish-Partenkirchen train station (departure times: 8:00 A.M., 12:10 and 4:30 P.M.). Bus costs DM 21 round trip; DM 12.80 one way (free with Eurailpass). One way takes approximately two hours. Easy connections from Füssen, running all day. Castle is open 8:30 A.M.–5:30 P.M. in summer, 10 A.M.–4 P.M. in winter. Admission: DM 6; students, DM 3. Phone: (083 62) 8 10 35.

It is said that Neuschwanstein Castle was the inspiration for Sleeping Beauty's Castle at Disneyland. At any rate, Neuschwanstein and its neighbor, Hohenschwangau, are the stuff of fantasy piled high atop imagination: Mad King Ludwig's imagination, that is, with dizzying evidence of his obsession with medieval legends. You may have seen postcards and jigsaw puzzles of this lofty castle, but nothing beats seeing it in person.

GERSTHOFEN
(North of Augsburg)

Balloon Museum: in the center of town, in a five-story

tower—you can't miss it. Open Wednesday, 2–6 P.M. and Saturday, Sunday, and holidays, 10 A.M.–6 P.M. Closed Monday, Tuesday, Thursday, and Friday. Phone: (0821) 49888-21.

A hundred years before the Wright Brothers were born, people were flying—in balloons. Gersthofen's museum does its best to remind us of balloons' now-forgotten role in history: first controlled flight, first object into space, first aerial warfare and bombing—all in balloons. You can also see displays on balloon fashion fads and balloon art. And if this whets your appetite for a little floating around, you can rent a balloon of your own at one of the many ballooning fields around Gersthofen.

HASSLOCH

"Holiday Park": Two miles south of Hassloch, which is 30 miles west of Heidelberg. Open from early April–early October, 9 A.M.–6 P.M. Phone: 0 63 24/5 84 74.

It can be a shock to see a crazy amusement park like this in a place like Germany. Lion tamers, spiral roller-coasters, magic shows, trained dolphins, and a dizzying whirl of other attractions make up one of the largest amusement parks in Europe. Don't miss the embarrassing-but-still-cute "Carmens Hunde-Revue," which has dogs dressed in frilly clothing pushing each other around in baby carriages and performing other humiliating tricks.

HEIDELBERG

Apothecary Museum (Deutsches Apothekenmuseum): located inside the castle (above the Old Town), in the Otto Heinrich building (entrance to the museum is under the stairs of the Otto Heinrich wing). Open Saturday, Sunday, and holidays, 10 A.M.–5 P.M.; November–March, 11 A.M.–5 P.M. Admission: DM 1.50.

It's nice to know that for several centuries, people have had pharmacists to care for them; this museum's array of utensils and vessels from the sixteenth to nineteenth centuries and its reconstructed pharmacist's lab are a testament to that helpful profession. But among the rows of prescriptions and ingredients on display here are some that seem to tread a thin line between curing and killing.

Student Jail (Studentenkarzer): Augustinerstrasse 2. Open Monday–Saturday 9 A.M.–5 P.M.; closed Sunday and holidays. Admission: DM 0.60.

From 1712 to 1914 these cells were the fate of Heidelberg university students who misbehaved. Usually the crime was nothing more sinister than drunk-and-disorderly conduct or too-outrageous pranksterring; and in typical college-student fashion, the jailbirds emblazoned their personalities all over these walls with much graffiti and even self-portraits, which you can still see, laboriously executed in soot and other makeshift substances.

HEROLDSBACH

Erlebnispark Schloss Thurn: 12 miles north of Nuremberg. By car: take Road A73 north to the Baiersdorf Nord-Heroldsbach exit, then west three miles. By train: take train from Nuremberg to Forchheim, then take bus 8922 to Heroldsbach and walk three blocks (across the train tracks) to Schloss Thurn. The whole park is open daily from Easter–September 15, 9 A.M.–6 P.M.; ticket booth closes at 4:30; all rides open 10–5. Admission: DM 10; DM 6 on Fridays. Phone: 09190/555.

Whoopee! A pint-sized Disneyland without the Disney. Schloss Thurn is a picturesque seventeenth-century castle around which has been built Erlebnispark ("Adventure park"), an amusement empire with several distinct regions: fairytale land, deer park, mini stock-car racetrack, medieval jousting arena, petting zoo, monorail, kids' funland, adults' dance hall, miscellaneous rides and entertainments, and the park's premier attraction: Western City. Westernstadt, as they call it in these parts, will either make you laugh or cry, depending upon how homesick you are for the ol' prairie. The Germans have a strange obsession with the "Wild West," and all the local Urban Deutschescowboys come here for their fix: a fake bank raid and shoot-out every day at 11:30 and 4. Be sure to take a gander at the tragic Western Museum, with its "authentic" dioramas of Sioux Indians camped out in the shade of saguaros and totem poles.

HOCKENHEIM
(Ten miles southwest of Heidelberg)

Tobacco Museum (Tabakmuseum Hockenheim): Open Monday–Friday, 2–4 P.M.; Sunday, 10 A.M.–noon. Closed

Saturday. Phone: 06205/21 291.

You won't see any "No Smoking" signs here. This museum explores tobacco and all its uses.

KASSEL

Brothers Grimm Museum: in the Kulturamt, in Schloss Bellevue, at Shöne Aussicht 2. Open Tuesday–Sunday, 10 A.M.–5 P.M. Closed Monday. Admission: free.

Up here in Northern Germany, they take Grimm's Fairy tales very seriously—as evidenced by this museum, which houses original manuscripts and drawings, important letters, and more miscellany about Mr. and Mr. Grimm than you'll see anywhere else.

Wallpaper Museum (Tapetenmuseum): inside Hessisches Zentralmuseum, near Wilhelmshoherstrasse. Open Tuesday–Friday, 10 A.M.–5 P.M.; Saturday and Sunday, 10 A.M.–1 P.M. Closed Monday. Admission: free. Phone: 0561/775712.

You may never have thought it possible that someone could put together an interesting museum about wallpaper, but here it is. See what the inside walls of sixteenth-century houses *really* looked like.

KNITTLINGEN
(20 miles northwest of Stuttgart)

Faust Museum: on Marktstrasse. Open Tuesday and Wednesday, 9 A.M.–noon and 1:30–5 P.M.; Saturday and Sunday, 10 A.M.–6 P.M. Phone: 07043/3027.

Faust may or may not have been a real person, and he may or may not have sold his soul to the Devil, but the controversy doesn't stop Knittlingen from proclaiming itself as Faust's hometown. They even have a statue of him, as well as the museum full of Faust paraphernalia.

MITTENWALD
(South of Munich on the Austrian border)

Violinmakers and Folklore Museum (Geigenbau- und Heimatmuseum): Ballenhausgasse 3. Hours change seasonally and from year to year. Phone: 0 88 23/84 18.

Way up here in the Alps, the Mittenwalders have spent many a long winter making—of all things—violins. The local museum about regional lifestyles is therefore understandably mainly about how violins are made and the people who make them. No Stradivariuses here, but the local product plays a waltz just as prettily.

MUNICH (MÜNCHEN)

Bavaria Filmstadt: Bavaria Filmplatz 7 (take tram 25 from main train station or downtown Munich south to the Bavaria Filmplatz stop, or take subway line U8 to Silberhornstrasse station and transfer to tram 25 there). Open March–October, 9 A.M.–4 P.M. Admission: DM 10; students and groups, DM 9; children aged 4–14, DM 6. Phone: (089) 64 90 67.

This self-proclaimed "Bavarian Hollywood" has a Germanic version of the famed Universal Studios tour in Los Angeles, except that here you get to see the sets of *Das Boot, Berlin Alexanderplatz,* and *The Never-Ending Story* instead of *Jaws, Psycho,* and *The Munsters.* You can ride around from set to set in cute little train cars, and maybe if you're lucky see some actual filming going on.

Fotomuseum: in the Munich Stadtmuseum: St-Jakobsplatz 1. Open Tuesday–Saturday, 9 A.M.–4:30 P.M.; Sunday and holidays, 10 A.M.–6 P.M. Admission: DM 4; students, DM 2; families, DM 6; children under 6, free. Free entry for everyone on Sunday and holidays. Phone: 233/23 70. (Admission price also includes entry into the Puppet-Theater Museum and Musical Instrument Museum.)

The fun here is of the hands-on and eyes-on variety: after "Susi," a winking, kiss-throwing hologram greets you at the door, a camera obscura, zoetrope, the optically illusionary fotoskulpture, and many other early-photography landmarks stand waiting to be experienced. Of special interest is a huge nineteenth-century round-robin 3-D photo viewing arcade featuring travelogue scenes. Many of the hands-on items are placed at kid-level for easy operation.

Hunting and Fishing Museum (Deutsches Jagd- und Fischereimuseum): Neuhauserstrasse 53. Open April–October, Tuesday–Sunday, 9:30 A.M.–5 P.M.; November–March, 9:30 A.M.–4 P.M. Closed Monday. Admission: DM

3; students, DM 1.50. Phone: 22 05 22.

While the museum overall will not appeal to vegetarians, the cult of the hunt gets its tribute here: a palatial hall is lined with trophy heads, antlers, and hunt-related paintings; taxidermed game animals pose against impressionistic backgrounds; stuffed fish and big guns are here, as well as the world's largest collection of fish hooks. Note also the jewel-and-hoof royal hunting jewelry (a Bavarian specialty), a feel-the-animal exhibit with explanations in Braille, and a flock of stuffed Wolpertingers, Bavaria's answer to the American jackalope: who *says* a rabbit can't have wings and deadly fangs?

Karl Valentin Museum (Valentin-Musäum): in the Isartor Gate tower (Isartorturm), on Isartorplatz (get off at Isartorplatz subway station). Open Monday, Tuesday, and Saturday, 11:01 A.M.–5:29 P.M.; Sunday, 10:01 A.M.–5:29 P.M. Admission: DM 1.99; Students and children, DM 0.99. Phone: 22 32 66.

Karl Valentin was an absurdist German comedian popular in the '20s and '30s, and this museum is devoted to him and his career. So far, so good. Unless you know German, this place will make you dizzy. Apparently, Valentin thought the whole world was one big joke, so his museum is one big joke: a cramped, illogical layout, indecipherable displays, and a kooky, nearly inaccessible cafe on the top floor. Germans think this place is absolutely hilarious, but the few Americans who find themselves here search in vain for something they can understand. Though some of the humor is lost because it is based on puns in German, a good deal of it falls flat simply because of an unbridgeable cultural gap between the German and American psyches. To the Germans, an admission price of 1 mark and 99 pfennigs is a total crack-up, but in America, everything is $1.99, and it's never funny. You may end up laughing, but you won't be sure why.

Musical Instrument Museum: in the Munich Stadtmuseum, St-Jakobs-platz 1. Open Tuesday–Saturday, 9 A.M.–4:30 P.M.; Sunday and holidays, 10 A.M.–6 P.M. Admission: DM 4; students, DM 2; families, DM 6; children under 6, free. Free entry for everyone on Sunday and holidays. Phone: 233/23 70. (Admission price also includes entry into the Puppet-Theater Museum and Fotomuseum.) Videos daily, 10:30–11:30 A.M. and 2–3 P.M.

From a Bolivian ten-string guitar made from an armadillo's shell to a seven-foot trombone—this collection sets the lips and fingers a-twitching. While the collection is markedly low on modern items—a 1982 Japanese computerized guitar is about it—the many hundreds of historic instruments here are delightful proof of the human need to entertain and be entertained.

Puppet Theater Museum (Puppentheatermuseum): in the Munich Stadtmuseum, St-Jakobs-platz 1. Open Tueday–Saturday, 9 A.M.–4:30 P.M.; Sunday and holidays, 10 A.M.–6 P.M. Admission: DM 4; students, DM 2; families, DM 6; children under 6, free. Free entry for everyone on Sunday and holidays. Phone: 233/2370. (Admission price also includes entry into the Fotomuseum and Musical Instrument Museum.)

The grotesque world of marionette theater has flourished for centuries in Germanic Europe, where the local imagination has proved itself hungry for the funny-sad antics of ludicrous puppets. In this museum you'll see Beowulf and Grendel as puppets; Jesus and the Devil as puppets; abstract impressionist puppets; the Beatles as enormous puppets (all four of them, for some reason, are playing guitars); five full-sized real vintage puppet theaters; and row upon row of disembodied puppet heads. It all makes you wonder what happens late at night when the visitors are gone and the lights are off.

Toy Museum (Spielzeugmuseum): in the old Rathaus tower, Marienplatz 2. Open Monday–Saturday, 10 A.M.–5:30 P.M.; Sunday and holidays, 10 A.M.–6 P.M. Admission: DM 3; children, DM 1; families, DM 5. Phone: 29 40 01.

All along the steep spiral staircase in the tower are rooms filled with kaleidoscopes, dolls, a doll zoo with impressive elephant gates, and Christmas tree ornaments. Best of all is the miniature church altar complete with tiny, detailed tin crucifix, chalice, censers, pictures of the Passion and somber doll-nuns.

NUREMBERG (NÜRNBERG)

Fountain of Virtues: in Lorenzerplatz, next to St. Lorenz church.

The "virtues" here are four bronze female figures, fully dressed except for their breasts, the nipples of which are squirting out milky water at a furious rate.

Industrial Arts Museum (Gewerbemuseum): Gewerbemuseumsplatz 2. Open Tuesday–Friday, 10 A.M.–5 P.M.; Saturday and Sunday, 10 A.M.–1 P.M. Closed Monday. Admission: DM 2; students, DM 1. Phone: 09 11/20171.

The industrial arts in this quiet museum are confined mostly to beer steins—but after all, this is Germany. Note also the nineteenth-century cabinet decorated with anatomically accurate, lovingly executed bugs.

Medieval Torture Chamber (Lochgefängnisse): under the old Town Hall on Rathausplatz, directly behind St. Sebaldus Church. Enter through the middle door of the Old Town Hall building. Open May 2–September 30, Monday–Friday, 10 A.M.–4 P.M.; Saturday, Sunday and holidays, 10 A.M.–1 P.M. Admission: DM 3; students and children, DM 1.

The stretching racks, spiked wrist clamps, and tongue pliers send chills down the most stoic of spines, and the dark, clammy cells make Alcatraz look like the Holiday Inn. Unfortunately, the guided tours, which provide the really gory details, are conducted in German only. An information sheet in English gives you the basics, but your imagination is the best guide here.

PIRMASENS
(50 miles west of Heidelberg)

Shoe Museum (Schuhmuseum): in the Altes Rathaus (old Town Hall), Hauptstrasse 24. Group guided tours only. Open Thursday, 3–6 P.M.; Sunday, 10 A.M.–1 P.M. Phone: 06331/841 842.

Pirmasens is a shoemaking center, so it's no wonder that most of the local museum is dedicated to footwear of all kinds—from shoes made of human hair to shoes made specifically for the bound feet of Chinese women. Try walking a mile in *those* shoes.

ROTHENBURG OB DER TAUBER

Doll and Toy Museum (Puppen- und Spielzeugmuseum):

Hofbronnengasse 13. Open March–December, daily, 9:30 A.M.–6 P.M.; January–February, 11 A.M.–5 P.M. Admission: DM 3.50; students, DM 2; children under 10, DM 1.50. Phone: 09861/7330.

The 300 dolls in this collection were all made between 1780 and 1940. Most are displayed inside exquisite doll houses furnished in such lavish detail as to make you wish *you* were four inches tall and could drink from the pea-sized teacups. Note the fully equipped doll shops, doll schoolroom, doll circus and doll carousel.

Holy Blood: in St. Jacob's church (St-Jakobs-Kirche), on Kirchplatz. Open Easter–October, 9 A.M.–5 P.M.; November–Easter, 10 A.M.–noon and 2–4 P.M. Phone: 09861/3057.

On the second floor of this old Protestant church, upstairs from an oddly out-of-place African sculpture exhibit, is the intricately carved Altar of the Holy Blood. On the altar is a thirteenth-century cross, and set in the cross is an oval rock crystal reliquary that supposedly contains drops of blood bled by Jesus on the cross. The reliquary, being at least ten feet above the floor, is a little hard to see, but it's faith that counts here, not visibility.

"The Mayor's Drink" (Der Meistertrunk): held every Pentecost weekend twice each on Saturday, Sunday, and Monday, usually at 10 A.M. and noon. Admission: DM 11-14. Phone: (09861) 404 92.

In 1631, the city was threatened with an attack by mean General Tilly. But a former Rothenburg Mayor, Herr Nusch, made a deal with Tilly that if Nusch could quaff a near-gallon mug of wine in one go, Tilly would retreat. Nusch drank it, Tilly beat it, and Rothenburg commemorates this event every year with a dramatic play. The dialogue is entirely in German, but if you know the plot, as you now do, thanks to us, it's still fun to watch.

Medieval Criminal Museum (Mittelalterliches Kriminalmuseum): Burggasse 3, Open April–October, daily 9:30 A.M.–7 P.M.; November–March, 2–4 P.M. Admission: DM 3.50; students, DM 2.50; children under 13, DM 2. Phone: (09861) 53 59.

A specialty here is shame masks—humiliating medieval headgear designed to punish all manner of sinners, from bad musicians to blabbermouths. These appear alongside such terrifying devices as iron maidens, chastity belts, ducking cages and dunce caps. The museum, with its emphasis on punishment, is really more about morality than criminality. While the displays are grisly fun, they will make all redheads, herbalists, blasphemers, and people with unusual birthmarks glad the Middle Ages are long gone.

RÜDESHEIM AM RHEIN
(35 miles west of Frankfurt)

Rheingau Museum of the History of Wine: Rheinstrasse 2. Open daily, 9 A.M.–12:30 P.M. and 1:30–6 P.M. Admission: DM 2.50; students, DM 2. Phone: 0 67 22/2348.

In the moist heart of Germany's Rhine wine region, in a labyrinthine eleventh-century castle, lurks Europe's largest wineglass collection: Roman, Greek, Syrian, Cretan (1500 B.C.), primitive European, and glamorous modern European glasses are represented here. It's a castleful of viniana: with labels, punchbowls, pig- and poodle-shaped decanters, a room devoted to barrelmaking, and some very witty corkscrews.

Siegfried's Mechanical Music Cabinet (Siegfried's Mechanisches Musikkabinett): Oberstrasse 29, in the Bromserhof. Open mid-March–mid-November, daily 10 A.M.–10 P.M. Admission: free. All visitors must join a complimentary group tour. Phone: 06722/4217.

If you thought recorded music began with Edison's phonograph, think again. The tinkling, tooting, wheezing machines in this privately owned collection date back to the early 1700s, and just about all of them are in perfect working order. One *"Koncertorgel"* as big as a two-car garage can play old waltz favorites loudly enough to shame any ghetto-blaster. An innocent-looking chair produces the faintest delicate lullaby when sat upon by an unsuspecting visitor. The tour (which is required since only the tour guides know how to operate the machines) includes many other crazy music- and noise-producing contraptions, and is climaxed by an amazing Bechstein player-piano that uses a unique piano-roll system never since duplicated. The piano plays songs the way a real-live concert pianist would play them, with soft tones, largatos, and beautiful phrasing.

SCHWETZINGEN
(Seven miles west of Heidelberg)

Schwetzingen Castle Gardens: take bus 7007 from Heidelberg train station (free with Eurailpass or InterRail). Open daily, 7 A.M.–8 P.M. Admission: DM 2; students, DM 1. Phone: 0 62 02/49 33.

Like Mohammed and his mountain, Schwetzingen's prince elector decided to bring the world's tourist sights to his backyard rather than go visit them in person. As a result, the Schwetzingen Castle Gardens are overflowing with spectacular replicas of buildings from the four corners of the world: a mosque, a Greek temple, a Chinese bridge, Versaille's gardens, fake ruins, Roman aqueducts, and so on. Every one is a rococo sham, but there's nothing like that "around the world in 80 minutes" feeling.

SOLINGEN

Blade Museum (Deutsches Klingenmuseum): Wuppertaler Strasse 160 (take bus 682 or 683 from the Solingen-Ohligs train station, or bus 683 from the Wuppertal train station). Open Tuesday–Sunday, 10 A.M.–1 P.M. and 3–5 P.M. Closed Monday. Phone: (0212) 591 313.

If it's sharp, this museum has it, from stone-age meat hackers to modern designer butter knives. Sword lovers will drool over the collection of medieval and Renaissance swords. Amazing scissors, too.

SPEYER
(15 miles southwest of Heidelberg)

Wine Museum: in the Domplatz (take bus 7007 from Heidelberg train station). Open daily, 9 A.M.–noon and 2–5 P.M. Admission: DM 1.50; students, DM 0.50.

The star attraction here is the world's oldest known vintage: a container of Roman wine from the year 300 A.D. It's just for looking at and not for sipping, however: there's not a loaf of bread in the world, and certainly not a thou, old enough to go with this wine.

STUTTGART

Bible Museum: Balingerstrasse 31, in the Stuttgart suburb of Möhringen. Open Monday–Friday, 8 A.M.–4 P.M.; Saturday, 10 A.M.–1 P.M. Closed Sunday. Admission: free. Phone: 0711/7200 30.

The Bible Museum houses thousands of editions of one of the most important books ever written. And since this is Martin Luther territory, it is fitting that they have an exceedingly rare "Luther Bible," dating from 1545.

Playing Card Museum (Deutsches Spielkarten-museum): Schönbuchstrasse 32, in the Stuttgart suburb of Leinfelden-Echterdingen. Take tram 6 from the Stuttgart central station in the direction Echterdingen to the stop called Spielkartenmuseum. Open Tuesday–Friday, 2–5 P.M.; Sunday and holidays, 10 A.M.–1 P.M. Closed Monday and Saturday and holidays. Phone: 0711/7986-335.

Here you will see not just poker-faced jacks, kings, and queens, but a diverse collection of illustrated cards. Among these are decks made in Europe, Asia, and India over the past three centuries. And not just playing cards, but tarot cards too; so that card sharks as well as fortune tellers will appreciate this one.

ULM

Bread Museum (Deutsches Brotmuseum): Fürsteneckerstrasse 17. Open Sunday–Friday, 10 A.M.–1 P.M. and 2–5 P.M. Closed Saturday. Admission: DM 2.50; students, DM 2. Phone: 0731/30561.

That bread is the staff of life is what the folks at this museum would very much like you to believe. And the displays do a good, wholesome job of convincing you, as they show the importance of bread in Egyptian, Mayan, Roman, and early Christian cultures: actual primitive bread ovens; dioramas illustrating breadmaking techniques across the centuries; devotional art honoring grain deities. For all the abundance depicted in this museum, the undercurrent is hunger, and bread's effectiveness in fighting it. Note the bread-rationing coupons from Nazi Germany, and the world hunger map.

Giant Chess Game: In Ehinger Anlagen Park, south of the train station, near the Bread Museum.

The large, attractive, well-made pieces are so heavy that they have internal handles for lifting. The board is big, to match the set, and the park is green and sedate.

WANK

Postcard Town: take train or car to Garmisch-Partenkirchen, then take the "Wank-Bahn" cable car from the north end of the city on Wankbahnstrasse.

Send a postcard from here to your British pen-pals; they may never write back.

GREAT BRITAIN

Legend:
1. London
2. Plymouth
3. Newquay
4. Exeter
5. Brighton
6. Bristol
7. Oxford
8. Norwich
9. Birmingham
10. Cardiff
11. Swansea
12. Stoke-on-Trent
13. Nottingham
14. Sheffield
15. Leeds
16. York
17. Liverpool
18. Newcastle-upon-Tyne
19. Edinburgh
20. Glasgow
21. Gloucester
22. Bournemouth
23. Portsmouth
24. Manchester

To date, there have been 79 million novels, 218 trillion poems, and 695 thousand travel guides written about Britain—and we're supposed to say something new about it here. Fat chance. We could say Britain is beautiful, ugly, old, new, exciting,

122 / *Great Britain*

depressing, fat, skinny, smooth, lumpy ... but it wouldn't matter, because someone, somewhere, would have already written it.

Britain is densely packed with fascinating places to visit. ("Wait—didn't I just read that somewhere else?") Whether you stay in thronging central London or the most out-of-the-way hamlet ("I've heard *that* before."), you're sure to find something strange or eccentric—if you look hard enough. ("That's what they all say.") But we know that most travelers don't have the time to be rooting around for unusual sights. ("Amen.") So we've dug up a couple hundred of the oddest places to see in Britain—and we're handing them to you on a silver platter. ... Ah, I see we've left you speechless.

LONDON

Anniversary Press: 46 The Market, South Row, Covent Garden WC2. (Tube: Covent Garden.) Open Monday–Friday, 9:30 A.M.–5 P.M. Phone: 01-379 7779.

Hidden in a warehouse in Kent are more than one million old newspapers. At the Covent Garden office of Anniversary Press you can order a genuine, complete, yellowed newspaper from any date in the last 173 years: your grandfather's birthday, the day you were conceived, *any* date; and they'll have it ready for you the next morning. They've got the *London Times*, the *Telegraph*, and the *Guardian*.

Anything Left-Handed: 65 Beak Street W1. (Tube: Oxford Circus.) Open Monday–Friday, 10:30 A.M.–5 P.M.; Saturday, 10 A.M.–2 P.M. Phone: 01-437 3910.

Left-handed boomerangs? Indubitably. Lefties will appreciate this shop's thoroughness; righties will flush crimson with guilt when they realize how much they take for granted everyday implements that, for southpaws, are just plain backwards. On sale here are left-handed corkscrews, playing cards, knives, nail-file kits, teapots, even clocks.

Brompton Cemetery: Lillie Road SW6. (Tube: West Brompton or Earls Court.) Opening times: Monday–Friday, 9 A.M.; Saturday–Sunday, 1:30 P.M. Closing times:

November–January, 4 P.M.; February and October, 5 P.M.; March and September, 6 P.M.; April–August, 7 P.M.

This vast, aged boneyard, with its thousands of overgrown graves and mournful weeping willows, fulfills every fantasy ever inspired by horror films and Victorian ghost stories. Its long, quiet avenues are dreamily eerie; a posted list of rules at the gate—warning against secret and illegal burials—completes the picture.

Clockmakers' Company Collection: located inside the Guildhall Library, Aldermanbury EC2, northeast of St. Paul's Cathedral. (Tube: Bank.) Open Monday–Saturday, 9:30 A.M.–5 P.M. Admission: free. Phone: 01-606 3030.

Arrive on the hour to hear the clocks clanging and chiming—and although this is a library, nobody hisses "Shhh!" On exhibit are London's lordliest grandfather clocks, ships' chronometers, and diverse watches. Don't miss the clockmaking milestones: one of the world's first electric clocks (circa 1846), and a "gas clock" that operates via hydrogen gas pressure.

Coram Foundation for Children: 40 Brunswick Square WC1. (Tube: Russell Square.) Open Monday–Friday, 10 A.M.–4 P.M. Admission: 50p. Phone: 01-278 2424. Occasionally the building is rented out for conferences and thus is closed to the public, so it's a good idea to call before visiting.

Thomas Coram, a good-hearted eighteenth-century sea captain, cared so much about the growing numbers of children turning up abandoned on London doorsteps that he created this foundling hospital in 1739. Today the foundlings are gone, but on display at the foundation are trays laden with tokens left with abandoned babies by their mothers: lockets, signet rings, jewelry, and notes, meant as goodbye gifts and the vaguest of identity badges.

Cuming Museum: 155-157 Walworth Road SE17, in the Southwark borough. (Tube: Elephant and Castle.) Open Monday–Wednesday and Friday, 10 A.M.–5:30 P.M.; Thursday, 10 A.M.–7 P.M.; Saturday, 10 A.M.–5 P.M. Closed Sunday. Admission: free. Phone: 01-703 6514. Due to insufficient staff, the museum is subject to periodic unscheduled closures; it is a good idea to call ahead.

Lightning will never strike the Cuming Museum, nor will the museum ever drown, for within its walls lurks the Lovett Collection of London Superstitions. Amulets and charms abound here, and each one was actually used by some superstitious Londoner in the days preceding WWI. You'll see charms to ward off a sore throat, rheumatism, hexes, and other mishaps. Prized exhibits are a baby's caul sewn up in a bag (protection against drowning) and a bull's heart pierced with a pin. The latter curio was involved in a local case: the owner of a murdered bull pierced the animal's heart with the pin in the hope of magically forcing the anonymous killer to confess. Supposedly, it worked.

Druid Spring Equinox Ceremony: March 21, noon, on Tower Hill, next to the Tower of London, EC3. (Tube: Tower Hill.)

London's ancient order of Druids celebrate the coming of spring every year with long white robes, mystical banners, incantations, swords, staffs, and the planting of seeds.

Embassy of Texas on an Uncharted Street: on Pickering Place, off St. James's Street between King Street and Pall Mall, SW1. Look for a thin covered passageway next to Berry Bros. and Rudd Ltd. at 3 St. James's Street (Nearest tube: Green Park.) Always open. Admission: free.

On Pickering Place, Londoners always remember the Alamo. Unfortunately, they have all but forgotten Pickering Place. Even on the most detailed maps of London, Pickering Place is omitted, and it would rank as the most inconsequential street in the city were it not for one unusual past tenant. During Texas's brief sojourn as an independent nation (1842–45), it established an embassy in London—on, of all places, Pickering Place. A plaque halfway up the covered passage marks the spot.

Geological Museum: Exhibition Road SW7. (Tube: South Kensington.) Open Monday–Saturday, 10 A.M.–6 P.M.; Sunday, 1–6 P.M. Admission: £1; children, 50p. Phone: 01-589 3444.

The "Story of Earth" exhibition, on the ground floor, puts you right in the middle of what the insurance companies call Acts of God: an animated model volcano spurts lava convincingly while a filmstrip shows real eruptions. Most unsettling of all is the earthquake section, in which the floor shakes and jolts underfoot in scientifically programmed simulation of a 4.0 earthquake.

London / 125

Highgate Cemetery: entrance on Swain's Lane N6, northern London. (Tube: Archway.) Guided tours of old cemetery, daily, April–September, 10 A.M.–4 P.M., October–March, 10 A.M.–3 P.M., every hour on the hour. Admission: voluntary donation. The old cemetery can be visited without a guide from 1–5 P.M. on the first Sunday of May, June, August, September, and October. New part of cemetery is open to the public 9 A.M.–5 P.M. daily (last admission, 4:45).

Swain's Lane divides Highgate Cemetery into two halves: the larger part, to the east, is still actively in use as a cemetery and can be visited without a guide. Among the dozens of famous and unusual tombs here are those of Karl Marx and the pianist Thornton, whose gravestone is in the shape of a baby grand piano. It was also in this half where, according to rock-'n'-roll legend, Rod Stewart worked as a gravedigger. The older half, west of Swain's Lane, filled up years ago and is now visitable by guided tour only. The extremely knowledgeable and personable guides lead the way through the jungle-like cemetery, which for years lay abandoned. The guides point out some of the innumerable strange tombs and tell amusing and chilling tales of the notorious cemetery's history. No two tours are the same; repeated visits reveal new treasures every time.

Hunterian Museum: in Royal College of Surgeons of England, Lincolns Inn Fields WC2. (Nearest tube: Holborn.) Open during school term only, Monday–Friday, 10 A.M.–5 P.M. Admission: free. Phone: 01-405 3474. Admission is strictly limited to serious types. Your best bet is to apply in writing to the curator or call ahead. Either way, you must prove that you're a member of the medical profession, or be very, very persuasive. But boy, is it worth it.

Your chances of getting to see this incredible collection are rather slim, so we feel guilty about tormenting you with a description. Still, it's one of the most fascinating places in the city, so we'd feel even guiltier leaving it out. Suffice to say that, among other things, the Hunterian has the skeletons of executed criminals as well as medical anomalies, human and animal freaks, and many other exhibits dealing with the weird and gruesome side of the healing profession. This alone might be good enough reason to sign up for medical school.

Jeremy Bentham's Body: in University College; entrance

on Gower Street, one block south of Euston Road WC1. (Tube: Euston Square.) To find Jeremy, enter through the main Gower Street gate, and go through the right-hand door of the large building facing you (door is just to the right of central stairs). Once inside, go right through another set of doors, and his large wooden case will be on your left. Open daily during the school term. Case is generally locked in summer, but you can go downstairs one floor and ask the Beadle to open it for you. Admission: free.

Jeremy Bentham, one of the founders of London's University College, requested in his will that his colleagues dress his preserved skeleton in his Sunday clothes, then place the dressed skeleton in Bentham's favorite chair near the entrance to the college. When Bentham died in 1832, his instructions were carried out unflinchingly. To this day you can see his fully clothed skeleton sitting serenely in a box, in a building near the main gate. His head (now a wax duplicate) sports a snappy straw hat. Any student will gladly point the way to "our Jeremy."

London Dungeon: 28/34 Tooley Street SE1. (Tube: London Bridge.) Daily 10 A.M.–5:30 P.M. Admission: £3.50; children under 14, £2. Phone: 01-403 0606.

England's goriest (and thus most cherished) memories come together here. Who ever said the British were genteel? We see plagues, tortures, executions, superstitions, and medieval amputations sharing the stage with royal murder. Famous Britons like Thomas à Becket and Mary, Queen of Scots suffer alongside anonymous peasants and criminals—all brought to you via the magic of glorious technicolor waxwork, with no holds barred: not a drop of blood or pus spared. The newest exhibit, dedicated to Henry VIII, gives us a look at that old British sport, beheading.

Museum of Garden History: St. Mary-at-Lambeth, Lambeth Palace Road SE1. Museum is located next to Lambeth Palace. (Tube: Lambeth North.) Open Monday–Friday, 11 A.M.–3 P.M.; Sunday, 10:30 A.M.–5 P.M. Admission: free. Phone: 01-261 1891.

The garden museum, created inside a formerly condemned derelict church, is the first of its kind, based on the collections of John Tradescant Sr. and John Tradescant Jr., seventeenth-century royal gardeners who traveled all over Europe and the colonies collecting what were then strange and unknown plants. Some of their discoveries—notably the plane tree—took to the English climate so well that they are often thought to be native species. On the museum grounds are a faithful replica of a seventeenth-century garden and the actual grave of the *Bounty*'s Captain Bligh.

Museum of Mankind: 6 Burlington Gardens W1. (Tube: Green Park.) Open Monday–Saturday, 10 A.M.–5 P.M.; Sunday, 2:30–6 P.M. Admission: free. Phone: 01-437 2224.

Life-size replicas of corners of the Third World employ convincing sound effects and authentic furnishings—assembled by the British Museum's ethnographical department. Explore a realistic African marketplace, a bit of Amazonian rain forest, an Indonesian rice barn and—the newest section—a Madagascar House. The emphasis here is on lifestyle—the moving, fluid pulse of people's lives.

Museum of the United Grand Lodge of England: Freemasons' Hall, Great Queen Street WC2. (Tube: Holborn.) Open Monday–Friday, 11 A.M.–4 P.M. Guided tours (required) depart every hour on the hour. On Saturday, one tour only at 10:30 A.M. Admission: free. Phone: 01-831 9811.

Glimpse the strange, secret world of the Freemasons—a centuries-old brotherhood that is heavy on symbolism and mystical rites. This collection is the world's most comprehensive on the subject of Freemasonry, and includes many ritual implements and domestic objects: swords, jewelry, sundials, wristwatches, banners and more, all bearing the mysterious Mason symbolism. The collection spans three centuries. A tour of the museum also takes in the Masonic temple, notable for its elaborate mosaics.

Musical Museum: 368 High Street, Brentford, Middlesex. Take British Rail to Kew Bridge. Open Saturday–Sunday, 2–5 P.M. Admission: £1.50; children, £1. Phone: 01-560 8108.

If you've always thought real musicians were too temperamental, you'll love the violins, pianos, and Wurlitzer organ at the Music Museum: they play all by themselves. The guide sets many of the instruments in motion during the tour—including a Steinway piano that faithfully reproduces the subtlety of a human hand—but there are no temper tantrums here.

Natural History Museum: Cromwell Road SW7. (Tube:

South Kensington.) Open Monday–Saturday, 10 A.M.–6 P.M.; Sunday, 1–6 P.M. Admission: £2; children, £1. Phone: 01-589 6323.

A dignified place like this is hardly where you'd expect to fulfill those guilty fantasies about returning to the womb. But when opportunity knocks.... The museum's Hall of Human Biology features (among other more cerebral pursuits) an alcove decked out to resemble an enormous human womb. Walk right in. Thrill to the recorded sound effects: the squishy sound of a beating heart, the familiar rhythms. Brings back memories.

Odontological Museum: 35 Lincolns Inn Fields WC2. (Tube: Holborn.) Open business hours, Monday–Friday, and by appointment. Admission: free. Phone: 01-405 3474, ext. 75.

Historic custom-made dentures, diseased jawbones, skulls, and antique tooth-pulling instruments that will make your blood run cold. As is usually the case with these serious, scholarly museums, it's all very real and very scary.

Old St. Thomas' Operating Theatre: Chapter House, St. Thomas Street SE1 (near Southwark Street), in a church. (Nearest tube: London Bridge.) Open Monday, Wednesday, and Friday, 12:30–4 P.M. Phone: 01-407 7600, ext. 2739.

If anybody needed to have an operation 150 years ago, not only would they have to endure the procedure without the benefit of anesthesia, but they'd also have scores of medical students watching the action at close range and breathing their germs all over the incision. You can relive those grand old days of medicine by visiting this, the last old-style operating theatre left anywhere. See the short, unpadded operating table, the spectators' gallery and the authentically abrupt rules of behavior in the operating room. Nearby are displays about nineteenth-century herbal medicine and nursing to soothe your jangled nerves.

Sir John Soane's Museum: 13 Lincolns Inn Fields WC2. (Tube: Holborn.) Open Tuesday–Saturday, 10 A.M.–5 P.M. Admission: free. Phone: 01-405 2107.

The idiosyncratic house and collections of Sir John Soane, architect, have remained untouched since the day Soane died in 1837. It's fascinating to walk through the house and see the kinds of things a man of Soane's day would collect and how he would display them. The house is a visual cacophony of ancient statuary, columns, vases, architectural models, drawings, and busts. There's even an Egyptian sarcophagus from Thebes (Soane bought it at an auction for £2,000), housed in Soane's own creation, the "Sepulchral Chamber." Also built into the house is the "Monastic Cell," painted ceilings, and a dome.

Tragical History Tours: Meet the bus outside the Temple tube station at 7 P.M. In summer, tours depart every weekday; in winter, three days a week; in December, Wednesday only. Price: £8.50; students, £7; children under 16, £5.50. Phone: 01-857 1545 or 01-467 3318.

The tour guides are London actors and actresses, well-versed in giving you the creeps. In three hours, the tour touches on London's most enthusiastically bloody, violent, and scary stories, going on beyond Jack the Ripper and Sweeney Todd to a cavalcade of lesser known killers, ghosts, gangsters, and mutilated corpses. The entire tour is conducted with a lip-smacking relish, and climaxes with a visit to a seventeenth-century haunted house, whose resident ghost is still looking for a woman to bear his heir.

The Wellcome Tropical Institute Museum: 183 Euston Road NW1. (Nearest Tube: Euston Square.) Open Monday–Friday, 9 A.M.–5 P.M. Admission: free. Phone: 01-387 4477, ext 3240. (This is not to be confused with the Wellcome Institute for the History of Medicine, which is a library located in the same building, or with the Wellcome Tropical Institute Head Office across the street at 200 Euston Road, or with the Wellcome Museum of the History of Medicine, which is housed inside the London Science Museum on Exhibition Road.)

Because this is a research museum, and thus in theory only open to researchers, the displays are satisfyingly uncensored and shockingly graphic. The topic here is desease, especially tropical disease. Hundreds of horrible diseases are described in full, with details on their history, symptoms, method of transmission, cures (if any) captioned photographs of the afflicted, and plenty of genuine human extremities and organs floating in jars of formaldehyde or encased in clear plastic. You can pick them up for a closer look. The intestinal parasite displays are particularly effective, and don't miss the cancerous foot. Remember: ghouls will be turned away at the door.

Wimbledon Lawn Tennis Museum: The All England

Club, Church Road SW19. (Tube: Southfields is closest, but still makes for rather a long walk.) Open Tuesday–Saturday, 11 A.M.–5 P.M.; Sunday 2–5 P.M. Closed Monday. Admission: £1.50; children under 17 and seniors, 75p. Phone: 01-946 6131.

From now on you'll be grateful for your cool, roomy tennis shorts and cushy sneakers. This museum's life-size dioramas trace tennis history from Victorian times to the present. In the "Victorian Garden Party" exhibit, mannequins stand covered neck-to-ankles in yards of fabric, clutching antique racquets and looking faint. A theatre in the museum shows films of actual tennis matches. Also, from inside the museum, visitors have an unobstructed view of the coveted Center Court.

WALKING TOURS

London teems with pilgrims, who come from all over to retrace the steps of heroes, or to finally *see* the London they've learned to love through literature. They come to search for traces of mythic, classic, essential England. With these pilgrims in mind, a number of companies conduct walking tours with special themes: Sherlock Holmes, Jack the Ripper, sixties rock, ghosts, and the like. Here's a list of some of the more unusual tours.

SHERLOCK HOLMES

<u>The London of Sherlock Holmes</u>: June–January, Saturdays, 2 P.M. Meet the guide at the Monument tube station (Fish Street Hill exit). Price: £2.50; children under 14, free if accompanied by an adult. Walk lasts $1\frac{1}{2}$–2 hours. Phone: 01-882 3414.

You can see the place (in London's oldest hospital) where Holmes met Dr. Watson for the first time. A plaque marks the spot. The tour also visits places that formed the scenes of "The Man With the Twisted Lip" and other great London cases.

<u>In The Footsteps of Sherlock Holmes</u>: June–January, Sundays, 11:30 A.M. Meet the guide at the Covent Garden tube station (main entrance). Price: £2.50; children under 14, free if accompanied by an adult. Walk lasts $1\frac{1}{2}$–2 hours. Phone: 01-882 3414.

This is Holmes' West End. Covered on the tour are Old Scotland Yard (Holmes' jeering ground) and the great detective's favorite restaurant. The tour ends up at the Sherlock Holmes Pub and Museum, a veritable Mecca for Doyle fans.

<u>On the Trail of Sherlock Holmes</u>: June–January, Mondays, 11 A.M. Meet the guide at the Baker Street tube station. (That's the station with Holmes' silhouette on all the wall tiles.) Price: £2.50; children under 14, free if accompanied by an adult. Walk lasts $1\frac{1}{2}$–2 hours. Phone: 01-882 3414.

There really *is* a 221B Baker Street. The tour explores this as well as other Holmes-and-Watson hangouts, and is narrated by a longtime Arthur Conan Doyle scholar.

JACK THE RIPPER

<u>Jack the Ripper's Trail of Terror—an 1880s Mystery Pub Walk</u>: Fridays at 7 P.M. Meet the guide at the Tower Hill tube station. Price: £3; students and seniors, £2.25; children under 14, free if accompanied by an adult. Phone: 01-937 4281 or 01-278 3720.

Darkened mean streets, a great unsolved murder mystery, and pubs: this is one of London's favorite combinations. The tour includes stops in some watering holes associated with Jack The Ripper's legend.

<u>Jack the Ripper—East End Murders</u>: Thursdays at 2 P.M. Meet the guide at the Tower Hill tube station. Price: £2.25; students £2; children under 16, free if accompanied by an adult. Walk lasts $1\frac{1}{2}$–2 hours. Phone: 01-882 2763 or 01-644 5401.

A creepy trip back in time to the Ripper's reign of terror. The message here seems to be: autumn, 1888. That's just about one hundred years ago. Does history repeat itself?

<u>The London of Jack the Ripper</u>: March–October, Monday, 7:30 P.M. Meet the guide at the Whitechapel tube station. Price: £2.50; children under 14, free if accompanied by an adult. Walk lasts $1\frac{1}{2}$–2 hours. Phone: 01-882 3414.

Stroll through Jack-The-Ripper landscapes both physical and psychological. The guide presents many of the current, hot theories regarding the Ripper's true identity.

Jack the Ripper and the Elephant Man: Sundays at 11 A.M. Meet the guide outside the Aldgate tube station. Price: £3; children under 12, free if accompanied by an adult. Phone: 01-504 9159.

From the Londoners' imagination springs a series of bizarre connections between the mysterious murderer and the deformed man. As you stroll along, theories and anecdotes abound.

GHOSTS

A Ghost Walk—The Haunted City: Thursdays at 7:30 P.M. Meet the guide at the St. Paul's tube station. Price: £2.25; students and seniors, £2; children under 16, free if accompanied by an adult. Phone: 01-882 2763 or 01-644 5401.

As shadows creep about St. Peter's Cathedral, you prowl in search of the neighborhood's celebrated specters, while the guide regales you with tales of mayhem and romance.

Haunted London—A Ghost Walk: Fridays at 7:30 P.M. Meet the guide at the Covent Garden tube station. Price: £2.50; children under 14, free if accompanied by an adult. Phone: 01-882 3414.

London's ghosts love the theater as much as London's tourists do. This tour investigates some Theatre District hauntings, and ends up in a pub that has its very own ghost story.

Ghosts, Ghouls, and Haunted Taverns: Sundays at 7 P.M. Meet the guide at the St. Paul's tube station. Price: £3; students and seniors £2.25; children under 14, free if accompanied by an adult. Phone: 01-937 4281 or 01-278 3720.

Savor the chills along haunted byways, past ghost-infested buildings, and into several old pubs where ghosts have been counted among the customers.

MISCELLANEOUS

London's Rock Routes and the Swinging Sixties: Tour times vary. Price: £3; students and seniors, £2; children under 14, free if accompanied by an adult. For current times and location, phone 01-937 4281.

From the skiffle and trad-jazz scenes through the mods 'n' rockers up through the late-seventies punk scene, this Soho-based tour touches on the careers of London's most important bands. Among others, you'll learn about the Who, the Yardbirds, the Beatles, the Stones, the Kinks, Small Faces, Pink Floyd, and the Sex Pistols.

<u>Murders, Radicals, and Haunted Taverns</u>: Halloween or thereabouts, 7 P.M. Meet the guide at the Whitechapel tube station. Price: £3. For current exact date, call 01-550-5587 or 01-253 5066.

If trade unionists haunt your nightmares alongside ghosts and the Elephant Man, then this catch-all Halloween tour is for you. Haunted taverns, highwaymen, killers, and socialists all come together in this East End romp.

<u>Underworld London—Fagin's Friends</u>: Tour times vary. Price: £3; students and seniors, £2. Phone: 01-937 4281.

Wending through the oldest part of London, the tour follows the footsteps of criminals great and small, with visits to prisons, execution sites, and low-life rendezvous.

SOUTH OF LONDON

BRAMBER
(Eight miles northwest of Brighton, near Steyning, West Sussex)

House of Pipes: on the High Street. Open daily, 9 A.M.–6:30 P.M. Admission: 45p; children 4–14, 15p. Phone: (0903) 8 12 122.

You might end up wanting to take up smoking—if only just to carry around bizarre pipes like the ones shown here. The owners rave on and on about the uniqueness of a pipe museum; we know better, but still, the 40,000-item collection is impressive, containing many pipes made out of truly unlikely materials.

GODSHILL
(South-central Isle of Wight)

Model Village: in the Old Vicarage Gardens. Open April–September, Monday–Saturday, 10 A.M.–5:30 P.M.; Sunday, 2–5:30 P.M. Phone: (0983) 270.

This is a model village with a twist: inside the model village is a model of the model village. Inside *that* is a model of the model of the model village. Pretty complicated stuff. If you can't handle it, or if you forgot to pack your microscope, be content with the large one-tenth-scale stone churches and thatched cottages.

MAIDSTONE
(30 miles southeast of London)

Dog Collar Museum: in Leeds Castle, just southeast of town. Museum is located in the castle's gatehouse. Take British Rail to Beersted; buses travel from there to Leeds Castle. Open April–October, daily, 11 A.M.–5 P.M.; November–March, Saturday and Sunday, noon–4 P.M. Admission (includes visit to castle and grounds): £3.85; students and seniors, £3.35; children 5–15, £2.85; children under 5, free. Phone: (0622) 65400.

Gold and silver collars, brass and tooled leather—this is exactly the kind of eccentric museum you'd expect to find in the land that brought you Yorkshire Terriers, Scotties, Welsh Corgies, and the Hound of the Baskervilles. Some of the collars here are nearly 500 years old, and one of them contains an inscription written by Alexander Pope.

TONBRIDGE
(27 miles southeast of central London)

Milne Museum of Electrical Appliances: located in the Slade. Open Tuesdays only. Admission: free. Phone: (0732) 36 47 26.

Homesick for your toaster? Nostalgic for those great kitchens of the fifties? Many of the appliances on display in this museum really work. They range in age from 25 to 180 years. Dad and junior will get a big kick out of the lawnmower section.

WILMINGTON
(Five miles northwest of Eastbourne, East Sussex)

The Long Man: on the north face of Windover Hill, one-half mile south of town. Always open. Admission: free.

He might be the world's largest human likeness at 231 feet tall, carved into the white chalk hillside and clearly visible against the grass. In each hand he holds a staff even taller than he is; some speculate that these were originally spears. The Long Man's age is an absolute and total mystery, as is his identity. The Norse god Woden has been suggested; but then, so have Apollo and St. Paul.

SOUTHWEST ENGLAND

BOLVENTOR
(Ten miles northeast of Bodmin)

Potter's Museum of Curiosity: located in Jamaica Inn, which is just northwest of the village of Bolventor, on the north side of the A30 road in Bodmin Moor. Open daily, 10 A.M.–6 P.M. Admission: £1. Phone: (0566) 86250.

Nineteenth-century taxidermist Walter Potter poured his heart and soul into stuffing hundreds of cute, fuzzy (dead) animals, standing them on their hind legs and dressing them in human costumes. They're arranged in human tableaux, to wit: the Kittens' Wedding; the Rabbits' School; the Kittens' Tea and Croquet Party; and many more. The animals, dressed in jewelry, tiny neckties, and tiny maids' uniforms, even have human facial expressions. Potter's incredible attention to detail and snide sense of humor has made this a cult museum for nearly a century. (Note: the museum, originally located in Arundel, Sussex, moved here to Cornwall in 1987.)

BUCKLAND-IN-THE-MOOR
(20 miles southwest of Exeter, in Dartmoor)

"My Dear Mother" Clock: on St. Peter's Church in the center of town.

This old church has a new clock donated by a loyal local churchgoer as a memorial to his mother. The letters "M Y D E A R M O T H E R" are substituted for numbers on the clock face. Oops, it's T past D—gotta go!

CERNE ABBAS
(Seven miles north of Dorchester, Dorset)

Cerne Giant: on a hill half a mile northeast of town.

Carved into the hillside, outlined in vivid white against the green, is a heck of a man, 180 feet tall and 45 feet wide. How he got there is a mystery. For over 1,000 years, local women have been camping on his huge body in hopes of curing their infertility. It's easy to see why the Cerne Giant is a fertility symbol: the 120-foot club he grips in his left hand isn't the only big, stiff pole the giant's got. (You know what I mean.)

CHRISTCHURCH
(One mile east of Bournemouth)

Tricycle Museum: on the Quay Road. Open Easter–May and October, Saturday and Sunday; June–September, daily. Admission: 65p; children, 35p. Phone: (04252) 3240.

One of the great things about the old days was that adults could ride tricycles without being accused of childishness. This museum houses several dozen adults' and children's three-wheelers, ranging over the past hundred years. Many seem so sturdy and sensible that you'll wonder whatever possessed you to "graduate" to ten-speeds.

COMBE MARTIN
(Five miles east of Ilfracombe, on the north Devon coast)

The Pack of Cards Inn: on the town's one main street (you can't miss it). For more information, call (027188) 3319.

Eighteenth-century gambler George Ley won a fortune at cards, and so built this inn and settled down. As a memorial to his luck, he not only named the inn "The Pack of Cards," but he actually designed it to resemble (physically and symbolically) a house of cards. It has four floors (four suits), 13 doors on each floor (13 cards in each suit), and 52 windows (the number of cards in a deck). Each floor is slightly smaller that the one below it, which is how a house of cards would look. To give the occupants a scare, stand a few yards back and blow real hard.

DARTMOOR

Letterboxing: throughout the 365-square-mile wildlife reserve.

A strange and typically British sport erupted in this wild, vast moorland over a century ago. Here's how it works: at odd, unmarked locations throughout the reserve are about 1,000 metal boxes. Inside each box is an official rubber stamp, stamp pad, and visitors' book. Since the locations of the boxes are all secret, the sport is like a big, windswept, grown-up Easter egg hunt. The usual practice is this: carry around a pocketful of stamped, dated, self-addressed postcards, and when you find a hidden box, leave your card inside so that the next person who finds the box will stamp it with the rubber stamp and mail it. The fun, apparently, lies in seeing how long it takes for someone else to find the box (sometimes years go by), and in collecting as many different stamps as possible. Make sure to sign the visitors' book, too. Here's a clue for the impatient among you: one of the boxes stands at Cranmere Pool, a few miles from Okehampton.

DORCHESTER
(22 miles west of Bournemouth)

The Dinosaur Museum: Icen Way. Open daily, 10 A.M.–5:30 P.M. Phone: (0305) 69880.

You won't find many tyrannosauri elsewhere in Britain. No wonder Dorchester prizes its herd of life-size model dinos, which are augmented in this museum by electronic educational displays. Visitors are even encouraged to touch the big guys—but did dinosaurs *really* have such sallow complexions? No wonder they became extinct.

EXMOUTH
(11 miles southeast of Exeter, Devon)

A la Ronde: two miles north of town, on Summer Lane. Buses travel to A la Ronde from both Exmouth and Exeter.

Open Easter–October, Monday–Saturday, 10 A.M.–6 P.M.; Sunday, 2–7 P.M. Admission: £1.50; children, 50p; seniors, £1. Phone: (0395) 265514.

The Misses Jane and Mary Parminter spent many a late-eighteenth-century evening sticking seashells in beautiful patterns all over the Shell Gallery in their 16-sided house. The Parminters' eccentric sense of decoration went even further: friezes (of the ladies' own design) are crafted with feathers and seaweed, and the central hall is octagonal. There are grottoes and views here, too.

GOONHAVERN
(Five miles south of Newquay)

World in Miniature: south of Goonhavern on the B3285 road. Take bus 57, 87, or 87A. Open mid-March–late October, daily, 9 A.M.–dusk. Phone: (0872) 572828.

Six- to 20-foot versions of the world's great structures include the Leaning Tower of Pisa, Egyptian pyramids, the Great Sphinx, an impressive Taj Mahal, the Eiffel Tower, Swiss chalets, Dutch windmills, Chinese pagodas, and so on and on on—11 acres of them. America is faithfully represented here by Tombstone, where animated cowboys hunker down in the saloon, stagecoach depot, stables, and barber shop.

LOOE
(15 miles west of Plymouth)

Monkey Sanctuary: four miles northeast of town. Follow the signs on the B3253 Plymouth–Looe road. Open July–August and Easter week, Sunday–Thursday, 10:30 A.M.–5 P.M.; April 12–June 30 and September, Sunday, Wednesday and Thursday, 10:30 A.M.–5 P.M. Phone: (05036) 2532. Visits not advisable for children under 4.

Rare South American woolly monkeys are successfully bred here, but that doesn't mean the monkeys are in a good mood. You can watch the little fellers in their natural habitat, walk among them in the gardens, observe their treetop shenanigans, and learn about their habits from the expert staff. This is not a zoo, however, and while monkeys will often come right up to visitors, the animals are still quite wild.

MINEHEAD
(22 miles northwest of Taunton)

Hobby Horse: Parade begins at 6 A.M. on May 1 every

year. Parade route starts at Dunster Castle, then winds through the streets of Minehead and Dunster. Hobby Horse can also be seen on the evening of April 30.

Less famous than the Padstow 'Obby 'Oss (see Padstow in this chapter), Minehead's long-tailed May beast is six feet tall, made of brightly dotted canvas and streaming ribbons, balanced on a man's shoulders. His annual parade might be the remnant of an ancient fertility rite, but local legend offers a more bizarre explanation: after an eighteenth-century shipwreck, a cow washed ashore. Some people cut off its tail, attached it to a stick, and used this to cajole money out of their neighbors.

NEWQUAY

Tunnels Through Time: St. Michael's Road (near the pedestrian walkway). Open Easter–October, daily, 10 A.M. till evening (closing times not fixed). Phone (0637) 873379.

"See PIRATES and WRECKERS who brought terror to the sea..." "PUNISHMENTS for nagging wives and drunken men..." "MERLIN making magic in his secret hideaway..." "The extraordinary undersea city of LYONESSE...." Only Americans can appreciate great kitsch like this. Of course these aren't actual tunnels through time, but a series of wax figure scenarios about Cornwall's historical and legendary (mostly legendary) past. Ghouls and children are encouraged to pay special attention to the Dungeon of Despair, with its outstanding torture scenarios.

PADSTOW
(Eight miles west of Wadebridge, north Cornwall coast)

'Obby 'Oss": every year on May 1, unless May 1 falls on a Sunday, in which case the festival takes place April 30. Parade begins around 10:30 A.M. For more information, call (0637) 87 13 45.

"'Obby 'Oss" is local dialect for "Hobby Horse," and the morning of the festival finds a strong local man covered head-to-foot in a horse costume, six feet in diameter. He bobs and swirls down the streets of town, occasionally "catching" women under his costume, occasionally sinking "dead" to the ground, only to be revived by his attendants' loving pats. Accordions wheeze and people sing songs as the 'Obby 'Oss keeps up his dance all day, casting a seductive spell over the crowds who come to watch him.

SARK
(Channel Island eight miles east of Guernsey)

Sark is accessible by boat from Guernsey and Weymouth, and by hydrofoil from Jersey and St. Malo in France.

Back in the Middle Ages, England had a feudal system of government in which land was controlled by lords and worked by vassals and serfs. But that's all gone now, everywhere but one place: Sark. This tiny channel island, just a few miles off the coast of France, is the last feudal fiefdom in England—and probably the world. Seigneur Michael Beaumont is Sark's benevolent hereditary ruler, and everyone on the island is his subject. Sark has different laws from England (for example, there is no income tax, and no divorce), and used to have its own language, Sercqais, which is closer to French than English, but which has practically died out in the last 50 years. In theory, at least, Sark is an independent state attached to the Bailiwick of Guernsey, though it never has done much to assert its independence, except maybe rigorously enforce its island-wide ban on cars. Farming vehicles are allowed, though, so some locals use their tractors as taxis to bring people up from the port.

SHEBBEAR
(20 miles northeast of Launceston, in Devon)

Turning the Devil's Stone: every year on November 5 in the evening. The ritual takes place at the town square.

The Devil lies buried under an old oak in Shebbear's town square. That's what the locals say, and to keep him from wreaking havoc on the town, once a year they turn the boulder that marks his grave. In fact, they didn't turn the boulder in 1917, and that year many of the soldiers from Shebbear died in battle. So the enormous struggle to turn the heavy stone with ropes and crowbars is worth the effort. Meanwhile, churchbells clang noisily to make extra-sure the Evil One gets no peace.

SIDMOUTH
(12 miles east of Exeter)

Donkey Sanctuary: just east of town on the A3052 (Sidmouth–Lyme Regis) road. Open daily, 9 A.M.–dusk. Admission: free, but donations are welcome. Phone: (03955) 6391.

These softhearted Britons have rescued nearly 3,000 donkeys from cruel owners. (It isn't very comforting to think that in the country that produced James Herriot, people mistreat their beasts.) At the sanctuary you can roam among the sweet-faced creatures, who are guaranteed TLC and veterinary care for the rest of their lives. They've had a rough time of it; maybe your visit will cheer them up.

SOUTH MOLTON
(12 miles southeast of Barnstaple, in Devon)

Quince Honey Farm: on the A361 road. Take red bus 7 from Barnstaple. Open Easter–October, daily, 8 A.M.–6 P.M.; November–Easter, daily, 9 A.M.–5 P.M. Admission: £2; children, 75p. Phone: (07695) 2401.

If you've always admired bees but never knew how to get close to them, Quince Honey Farm has the answer: clever glass booths positioned inside a 25,000-square-foot indoor apiary, so that you can safely watch wild honeybees soaring and zooming all around. Whew—who needs roller coasters? Also here are open hives and some that are covered with glass on one side, revealing all aspects of that unfathomable bee society. Even the queen bee is visible.

STREET
(Six miles south of Wells)

Shoe Museum: on High Street in the Clark Shoe Factory. Open Easter Monday–October, Monday–Friday, 10 A.M.–4:45 P.M. and Saturday, 10 A.M.–4:30 P.M. Admission: free. Phone: (0458) 43131.

For some people, shoes are just a way to cover the feet; others see shoes as works of art and as important cultural artifacts. The Clark Shoe Company sees shoes as a business, which means they understand shoes from all points of view. So, in their museum there are displays about the manufacturing of shoes (modern machines, old-fashioned tools), advertisements and placards illustrating the history of shoe fashion, and of course shoes, shoes, and more shoes, some 2,000 years old and some from this season, and countless others from all the years in between.

WELLS

Astronomical Clock: on the cathedral's north transept, in the center of town. Performances every hour on the hour. Admission: free.

The Wells astronomical clock dates from the fourteenth century, but was restored recently to look as spiffy as new. Every hour four knights gallop out and engage in a miniature jousting tournament, while a fifth figure, nicknamed "Jack Blandivar," marks every quarter hour and registers his applause by kicking bells with his heels; he clangs out the hour with a big hammer.

Wookey Hole Caves: two miles northwest of Wells. Open in summer, daily, 9:30 A.M.–5:30 P.M.; in winter, daily, 10:30 A.M.–4:30 P.M. Admission: £2.95; seniors, £2.45; children 4–16, £1.95; children under 4, free. Phone: (0749) 7 22 43.

The proprietors got themselves a hole and couldn't decide what to do with it, so the Wookey Hole complex became home to a collection of strange bedfellows: a functioning paper mill, a giant waterwheel, an old-fashioned penny arcade, fairground rides, and a detailed exhibit about Madame Tussaud (done, appropriately enough, in wax). And we mustn't forget the caves, which include underwater lakes, evidence of early human habitation, grottoes, and even a big stalagmite they claim is the petrified Witch of Wookey. (No; no one *really* expects you to keep a straight face.)

WEST PUTFORD
(18 miles southwest of Barnstaple)

The Gnome Reserve: on the Bidford Road, toward the town of Bradworthy. Follow the signs. Open April–May and September–October, Sunday–Friday, 10 A.M.– 1 P.M. and 2–6 P.M.; June–August, Sunday–Friday, 10 A.M.–1 P.M. and 2–9 P.M. Admission: 60p; children 4–15 and seniors, 40p; children 2–3, 20p. Phone: (040 924) 435.

Are you the type who gets a kick out of little kids' birthday parties? That's the spirit at the Gnome Reserve, where more than 1,000 pottery gnomes pose unsteadily about several acres of wooded countryside, accompanied by the necessities of gnome life: waterwells, wheelbarrows, butterflies, and large polka-dotted mushrooms. Also on the premises are two acres' worth of pixies, which the proprietors insist are not the same species as gnomes. Admission price includes the free loan of a peaked cap (small heads only).

YELVERTON
(Five miles north of Plymouth)

Paperweight Centre: at Leg O' Mutton Corner, across from the Leg O' Mutton Inn, on Buckland Terrace. Open Easter–October 31, Monday–Saturday, 10 A.M.–5 P.M.; November–Easter, Wednesday, 1–5 P.M.; some Saturdays in December, 10 A.M.–5 P.M. Admission: free. Phone: (0822) 85 42 50.

This place is home to more than 800 glass paperweights from many ages and places. No two are alike. Their dazzling color and mandala-like designs show why the paperweight has been called "the executive's crystal ball."

WALES

ABERCRAF
(16 miles northeast of Swansea, on the A4067 road)

Dan-yr-Ogof Showcaves: two miles northeast of Abercraf, just north of the village of Craig-y-nos. Open April–October, daily, 10 A.M.–5 P.M. Admission: £2.65; children, £1.65. Phone: (0639) 730284 or (0639) 730693.

In Britain, if something's called a "showcave" you can rest assured that the cave is the least interesting thing there. Dan-yr-Ogof has an excellent dinosaur park with "life-size" dinosaurs (funny how every "life-size" triceratops in Europe is a different size), featuring a great nine-foot-tall prehistoric flightless bird. Next to the dinosaurs is a snowless ski slope on which you can practice your slaloms on a sweltering summer afternoon. There's also a museum of excavated items, and, oh yes, the caves, rendered safe with floodlighting and waterfalls, and a Bone Cave wherein dwelt prehistoric Welshmen.

BEAUMARIS
(Five miles north of Bangor)

Beaumaris Jail (Jêl Beaumaris): on Steeple Lane. Open May–September, daily, 11 A.M.–6 P.M. Phone: (0248) 723262 ext. 138.

Yes, people suffered here, and you can stroll through the scenes of their misery: prison cells, scaffold, gallows, treadwheel (Britain's only one left in its original position), and punishment room. The jail was built in 1829 by the inventor of the Hansom cab.

CALDICOT
(Ten miles east of Newport)

Medieval Banquets: at Caldicot Castle (follow the signs on the Newport-Chepstow road). Banquets held Monday–Saturday at 8 P.M. To make reservations (which are necessary), call (0291) 421425.

They don't check family trees at the door, so even if you haven't a single earl, duke, or lady-in-waiting in your bloodline, you can still eat at the castle. Bright-faced men and women in yards and yards of green-and-gold velvet serve the meal, which includes cups and cups of mead. Afterwards, in the candlelight, they play the Welsh harp and other nostalgic instruments.

CARDIFF
(Surrounding villages)

Mari Lwyd: from Christmas to January 6. For more information, call the Cardiff Tourist Office at (0222) 27281.

Villages adorn a horse skull with ribbons, bells, gold braid, and glass eyes, and they put it on a pole, which is carried by a man wrapped in a white sheet. From door to door in the villages near Cardiff the Mari Lwyd ("Gray Mare") and his company go, snapping the skull's jaws and begging to be let in. Homeowners sing songs about why they can't let him in, but eventually everybody relents, and the strange parade lasts well into the evening.

HAY-ON-WYE
(20 miles west of Hereford)

If you're the kind of person who can't walk past a shelf

KING ARTHUR

King Arthur's adventures are thrilling enough in print. But to actually visit the haunts of Arthur, Guinevere, Merlin, and the Knights...! Forsooth, it is possible.

<u>Cadbury Castle:</u> near South Cadbury, ten miles northeast of Yeovil, in Somerset. This has long been thought by many to be the location of Camelot, and recent excavations have proven that it was indeed occupied during the Arthurian period.

<u>Dozmary Pool:</u> in Bodmin Moor, south of Bolventor and the Jamaica Inn, in Cornwall. This is one of three English pools claiming to be the bottomless one into which Sir Bedivere, Arthur's steward, threw the sword Excalibur. The misty silent atmosphere seems just right.

<u>Glastonbury Abbey:</u> six miles southwest of Wells, Somerset. Glastonbury is said to be Arthur and Guinevere's burial place—the Isle of Avalon. Many centuries ago, local monks uncovered a pair of skeletons (the female had golden hair, it is said), together with a cross inscribed with the royal couple's names. The bones were buried near the abbey's high altar (which is marked with a plaque), but the abbey is in ruins now, and the condition of the bones is uncertain.

<u>Slaughter Bridge:</u> one mile north of Camelford, in Cornwall. Slaughter Bridge is said to be the site of Arthur's last tragic battle against his nephew Mordred. A plaque nearby (on private property) indicates the place where Arthur fell.

<u>Tintagel Castle:</u> six miles northwest of Camelford, in Cornwall. This dramatic cliffside ruin (accessible via rugged foot trail) is Arthur's supposed birthplace. It was here, say the legends, that Uther hoodwinked Igraine into conceiving Arthur. "Merlin's Cave" is also an attraction here.

<u>Winchester Castle:</u> on Castle Avenue, off the High Street, Winchester, in Hampshire. On the Great Hall's west wall you can see the Round Table, or at least *a* round table; a pretty convincing one. It's divided into 24 green and gold sections, inscribed with the knights' names.

For more Arthurian sites, refer to the Paimpont Forest entry in the Brittany section of France.

of used books without perusing every one, allow a year's visit in Hay-on-Wye, Wales, population (humans): 1,000; (second-hand books): more than 1 million. The main purveyor of these is Richard Booth, Ltd. (on Lion Street). Listed in the *Guinness Book of World Records* as the world's largest used bookstore, Booth's miles of shelves occupy about five buildings. A dozen other bookstores also make their homes in little Hay-on-Wye, which is known in England as "The Town of Books."

LLANFAIRPWLLGWYNGYLLGOGERYCH-WYRNDROBWLLLLANTYSILIO-GOGOGOCH
(Five miles west of Bangor on the A5 road)

The name alone says it all. This city's name, commonly abbreviated to Llanfair P.G., is actually 58 letters long (as you can see), and means, "The church of St. Mary in a hollow of the white hazel near to the rapid whirlpool and to St. Tysilio's church near to a red cave." To commemorate your visit to this utterly unpronounceable place, have your picture taken in front of one of the town signs (there's one at the old train station and another above a newsagent's), or buy a special souvenir train "platform ticket," which is good for nothing but framing.

PEMBROKE
(50 miles west of Swansea)

National Museum of Gypsy Caravans, Romany Crafts, and Lore: on Commons Road. Open Easter–September 30, Sunday–Friday, 10 A.M.–5 P.M. Closed Saturday. Admission: £1.50; seniors, £1.20; children, 60p. Phone: (0646) 68 13 08.

Gypsy culture is mysterious; gypsies are elusive. This museum unravels some of the mystery, with a large collection of carts and wagons (rebuilt and restored on the premises), photos, artifacts, and handicrafts made by the traveling people themselves.

PORTMEIRION
(25 miles south of Bangor, and two miles southeast of Porthmadog)

Town open April–November, daily, 9:30 A.M.–5:30 P.M. Admission: £1.80; children, 80p. (Leave your car outside unless you're staying at the hotel.) Phone: (0766) 770228.

"Who are you?" "The new Number Two." "Who is Number One?" "You are...Number Six." "I am not a number. I am a free man!" Fans of the classic television show *The Prisoner* often wonder what town was used as the set for the Village, the surrealistic prison camp for ex-spies, where every episode took place. Portmeirion is it, and because of all the free publicity has become the only city in Great Britain to charge admission. If you've seen *The Prisoner* you know what Portmeirion looks like: lush with subtropical plants, white and pastel buildings seemingly transported from the southern Italian coast, brimming with statues, colonnades, promenades, quaint cottages, and striking towers. Designed and built by eccentric Welsh architect Sir Clough Williams-Ellis from 1925 to 1975, Portmeirion is the perfect artificial village. If you've got money to spare or a fantasy to fulfill, you can actually stay in Portmeirion in its ritzy hotel or in one of the aforementioned cottages (just like Number Six). A Prisoner Information Centre and gift shop caters to pilgrims and fanatics.

RUTHIN
(17 miles south of Rhyl)

Medieval Banquets: in Ruthin Castle, on the western side of town. Daily starting at 7:30 P.M. Phone for reservations: (08242) 3435.

True, most people in Wales during the Middle Ages lived in hovels and ate gruel. These festive evenings ought to be called "Royal Medieval Banquets" to be more sociologically correct. Ruthin's proprietors trick visitors into thinking they're having a good time by getting them drunk on free-flowing wine, stuffing them with good food, and entertaining them with costumed harpists, singers, and jesters. Well, maybe it isn't a trick after all.

CENTRAL ENGLAND

ABBOTS BROMLEY
(20 miles southeast of Stoke-on-Trent)

Abbots Bromley Horn Dance: every year on the first

Monday after the first Sunday after September 4 (but never on Monday, September 5), 8 A.M.–8 P.M. For more information call (0283) 840 558 or the Lichfield Tourist Office at (0543) 252 109.

Reindeer in Staffordshire? A man dressed as Maid Marion? This is one of England's most ancient rituals, and they say it has something to do with hunting and fertility. Six men in quasi-Tudor costume take six reindeer heads out of the village church (where they have been stored for several hundred years, taken out only for the annual horn dance). They clutch the heads against their chests, so that the antlers reach way up above the dancers' heads. All through the parish, all day, the dancers clomp along, accompanied by a man with a horse's head, a Fool, Robin Hood, some Merry Men, and that broad-shouldered, thick-legged Maid Marion.

BATH

Museum of Bookbinding: on Manvers Street, across the street from the bus station. Open April–September, Monday–Friday, 9 A.M.–1 P.M. and 2:15–5:30 P.M. Admission: £1. Phone: (0225) 66 000.

Nowadays, machines can bind book pages together with glue and paper at the rate of 8 billion per minute. But it wasn't always that way. Bookbinding used to be an art, and the bookbinder was more important than the printer, author, and publisher combined. Okay, that's an exaggeration, but you just can't find beautiful bindings anymore. A diorama showing the tools and mood of a nineteenth-century bindery is the museum's focal point. Several elegant and intricate bindings are displayed in the manner of art treasures.

BRISTOL

Harvey's Wine Museum: 12 Denmark Street. Open Friday, 10 A.M.–noon. Admission: £1. No one under 18 admitted. Phone: (0272) 277 661.

For just two hours a week, Harvey's, the guiding light of winos the world over, opens its doors to the public. Inside are hundreds of bottles, labels, and wine glasses. A special section is devoted to the company's own technique for making wine. The museum also has many unusual samples of the most crucial wine-related tool: the corkscrew.

BROCKWORTH
(Three miles east of Gloucester)

Cheese Rolling: on Coopers Hill, every year on Spring Bank Holiday Monday, which is usually the last Monday in May. Rolling begins at 6 P.M. For more information call the Gloucester Tourist Office: (0452) 421 188.

You think it's easy to roll cheeses down a hill? Well, maybe it is; but how about rolling cheeses *up* a hill? Little kids, old ladies, even the mayor takes part in the annual Coopers Hill event, which involves rolling the cheeses up, then down the hill, and is somehow connected with preserving the people's sheep-grazing rights. The ritual is 400 years old. A total of six cheese-rolling races punctuate the day. The rolling can get pretty rough and wild.

CHIPPING CAMPDEN
(11 miles south of Stratford-upon-Avon)

Cotswold Olimpick Games: on a Friday in very late May or very early June; date varies from year to year. Call the Chipping Campden Tourist Office for current date: (0386) 840 289. Games take place on Dover's Hill, about one mile northwest of town.

No 400-meter relay or javelin throw here, no siree. These aren't the Olympic Games—they're the *Olimpick* Games, the world championships of such obscure English rural sports as shin-kicking, greased-pole climbing, rabbit chasing, leapfrogging, and cudgel fighting. The games originated in the early 1600s, died out for a while, and have now been revived. A character dressed as Robert Dover, the games' original organizer, presides over the chaos. Despite their seemingly frivolous nature, the competitions are serious, with winners, losers, and plenty of injured contestants. The Cotswold Olimpick Torch is a big bonfire built to mark the end of the games and the beginning of the night's drunken revelry.

GLOUCESTER

The Pack Age Revisited (Robert Opie Collection): Albert Warehouse, Gloucester Docks (a large brick building with a big sign reading "Pack Age"). Open Tuesday–Sunday, 10 A.M.–6 P.M. Closed Monday. Admission: £1.50; children, 75p. Phone: (0452) 32 309.

This museum displays advertising as folk art: its stupendous collection of products, packages, and ads from the last two centuries will show you how sophisticated modern packaging techniques really are. Consider the names of some of the foods marketed in decades past: Bile Beans, Motoring Chocolate, Belgravian Boiled Ox Tongues, Duraglit. For British senior citizens this is nostalgia; for Americans it is ethnology about a thoroughly foreign culture. To make the experience even more effective, a number of TVs are constantly running, showing an endless stream of vintage commercials.

Severn Bore: visible from various points along the river Severn, but is most striking from the village of Stonebench, near Elmore, which is five miles southwest of central Gloucester. The Bore is strongest at high tide during a full moon, especially during the spring and autumn equinoxes.

The Severn Bore is an authentic tidal wave that courses up the river Severn when conditions are right. (Local Gloucester newspapers publish the times when the Bore is likely to be highest.) The mouth of the Severn is shaped like a big, long funnel, and as the river gets thinner and thinner, the tidal waters rushing in from the sea have less and less room. Finally, near Stonebench, where the river reaches its narrowest point, the mass of water propelled forward by the tide becomes a five- or six-foot-high wall of liquid, gushing upstream. Remember, though, that sometimes the Bore can be a bore, and make sure to read the papers or call the Stroud Tourist Office at (04536) 4252 before going out to see it.

HALLATON
(13 miles east of Leicester)

Bottle Kicking and Hare Pie Scramble: every year on Easter Monday. Action takes place on Hare Pie Bank on the outskirts of town, at the village church, and all over the place.

If you arrived at Hallaton on the Monday after Easter completely unaware of what was about to happen, you'd think the town was an asylum for madmen. It all started in 1770, when Hallaton's rector was given a piece of land; the only rent he had to pay for it was two hare pies, some bread, and some ale, which was to be distributed among the poor. Back in those days the rector just tossed the pie, bread, and ale out in front of the church and let the villagers scramble for their share. Now, over 200 years later, the same thing happens—in essence at least. One of the pies is blessed and handed out at the church gate by the current rector. The other pie is carried to Hare Pie Bank, where it is flung wildly all over. Then three ale kegs (two full and one empty) are brought out, and chaos breaks loose. The men from the nearby village of Medbourne arrive in their rugby gear; the Hallaton men put on kneepads and cleats; one of the barrels is tossed between them, and oomph! The struggle is on to get the barrel across each team's "goal line," which are a couple of streams one mile apart. This rugby-keg match has no rules, no referee, and no time limit, and can get hysterical and violent. After a score, the next barrel is used. If each team gets one full barrel across its stream, then the empty keg is used as a tiebreaker. Afterward, of course, the kegs are opened and heartily chugged.

ILKESTON
(Five miles west of Nottingham)

The American Adventure: just north of Ilkeston, next to the A6007 road (signs point the way). Open May 25–September 31, daily, 10 A.M.–6 P.M. Admission: £4.95 (includes most rides). Phone: (0773) 769 931.

What is America? This theme park will help you understand America as you've never understood it before. The attractions here run the gamut from the authentic to the ludicrous, with plenty of incongruities tossed in for good measure. Consider this abbreviated list: The New England Village's "Sioux-venir" shop; "Tennessee Tentacles" octopus ride; "Kool Hand Luke's Ice Cream Parlour"; the Hill Billy Shootout in Fort Laramie; the San Francisco Wharf containing the El Paso Cantina and the New England Tavern (with Mississippi steamboats paddling past); toilets whose doors read "Señoras" and "Caballeros"; "Dutch Cassidy's" windmill; the Forty-Niners' *Silver* Mine; Medicine Man Island with teepees, totem poles and grizzly bears. It's just like home, isn't it?

KILPECK
(Seven miles southwest of Hereford)

Sheila-na-gigh: among the stone carvings on the village church.

What's this gal doing in a church? A Sheila-na-gigh is a squatting, goggle-eyed female figure who holds her cavernous private parts wide-open for all the world to see. Possibly ancient goddesses, fertility symbols, or both, these show-offs are occasionally found on old churches in the British Isles.

MOW COP
(Seven miles north of Stoke-on-Trent and 1½ miles west of Biddulph)

Mow Cop Folly: on a crag outside of town. Best seen from a distance.

A folly is a fake ruin. Mow Cop's weathered tower, broken-down walls, and hollow gothic arch have looked this way—torn and destroyed—ever since they were built in 1750. Follies were a fad among eighteenth-century British landowners, who were full of romantic longings and built fake ruins like this to improve the views on their property, or simply to further their own fantasies.

NORTHAMPTON

Museum of Leathercraft: in the Old Blue Coat School, on Bridge Street in the center of town. Open Monday–Saturday, 10 A.M.–1 P.M. and 2–5:30 P.M. Admission: free. Phone: (0604) 34881.

Are you into leather? This museum demonstrates the supple stuff's great versatility, with leather clothing, book covers, sports equipment, saddles, and diverse luggage. Some of the specimens date back to ancient Egypt. Prized possessions here are diarist Samuel Pepys' wallet and a saddle used by Queen Victoria.

NORWICH

Colman's Mustard Museum: in the Mustard Shop, 3 Bridewell Alley. Open Monday–Wednesday and Friday–Saturday, 9 A.M.–5:30 P.M. Closed Thursday and Sunday. Phone: (0603) 627 889.

Relive the last 150 years in the life of mustard, with the help of photos and examples of nineteenth-century packaging and advertisements. Special emphasis is given to the Colman company's own history. Also on view are types of mustard with obscure and surprising ingredients.

NOTTINGHAM

Caves: a visit to the Castle Museum includes a tour of the caves. Open daily, in summer, 10 A.M.–5:45 P.M.; in winter, 10 A.M.–4:45 P.M. Admission: free, except Sunday. Phone: (0602) 411 811.

In 1330, a man named Mortimer crept into the cavern under the castle, hurrying toward a rendezvous with a royal lady. But Mortimer had been followed down there, and when he left the cavern he was headed straight for the gallows. Nottingham's extensive limestone caves and passageways have been used as religious sanctuaries, air-raid shelters, and fugitives' hiding places. Mortimer's Hole—as the trysting place is now called—is a high point of the subterranean tour.

OLNEY
(12 miles southeast of Northampton)

Pancake Race: 11:45 A.M. on Shrove Tuesday (in February). Starts in the market square and ends at the parish church. For more information call (0604) 226 77.

When the church bell started clanging on Shrove Tuesday morning, 1445, summoning villagers to church, a certain housewife was in the midst of cooking breakfast. Still clutching her frying pan (which had a pancake in it), she dashed off to church. Olney commemorates the legendary event with a race. Contestants must be adult females, must wear an apron and a kerchief, and must flip a pancake at least three times while they run. The question is, do Reeboks clash with plaid aprons? An identical race is run simultaneously in Liberal, Kansas. The international winner is determined immediately afterward via a long-distance telephone call.

RANDWICK
(Nine miles south of Gloucester)

Randwick Wap and Cheese Rolling: every year in early May. Cheese blessing is first Sunday in May; wap and cheese rolling are second Saturday in May. For more in-

154 / *Great Britain*

formation call the Stroud Tourist Office at (04536) 4252 or (04536) 3942.

A wap is a fair. That's the easy part. To kick off the annual Randwick Wap, villagers roll two big cheeses down the hill amid much hilarity. These are sanctified cheeses: on the Sunday preceding the wap, these two and a third cheese are blessed in church and festooned with ribbons. The third cheese is sliced up and distributed free to all present; the other two live on to be chased down a hill.

REDDITCH
(Ten miles south of Birmingham)

National Needle Museum: on Needle Mill Lane, just north of town off the A441 road. Open April–October, Monday–Friday, 11 A.M.–4:30 P.M.; Saturday, 1–5 P.M., and Sunday, 11:30 A.M.–5 P.M. Admission: £1; seniors and children, 50p. Phone: (0527) 62509.

On the premises of an eighteenth-century needle-making forge (complete with the world's only remaining water-driven needle mill), life-size mannequins show you the hundreds of uses for needles, as well as the old methods of manufacturing them. You are quite welcome to visit; but please, don't bring your haystack.

RUSHTON
(15 miles northeast of Northampton)

Rushton Hall: one-half mile north of town. Open April 1–October 15, Monday–Saturday, 9:30 A.M.–6:30 P.M.; Sunday 2–6:30 P.M. Admission: 75p; seniors, 55p; children, 35p.

Every aspect of this building revolves around the number three, true to its owner's fascination with the Holy Trinity. The building has three sides, three stories, shamrock-shaped windows, and triangular windowpanes. Even the chimney has three sides. The Latin inscription on the wall contains 33 letters. It's as mystical as all get-out. The place was built in 1593, but the devout Sir Thomas Tresham, for whom it was built, insisted that the date on the wall read only: "93". But of course.

STONE CIRCLES

Prehistoric Britons went to great lengths to build their stone circles—finding just the right places, dragging the too-heavy stones, setting them upright, lovingly shaping them. Whether they built the circles as star-gazing arenas or as sacred temples, their labors were more than worthwhile. Even today, after thousands of years of wind and rain have battered the circles, a certain magic still stirs within them. Stonehenge and Avebury are too famous and too crowded to include here, but the following is a list of some of the other interesting and beautiful stone circles. If you're interested in this kind of thing, there are hundreds more circles to be found in England.

<u>Callanish Standing Stones:</u> Isle of Lewis, outer Hebrides, Scotland. Stones are 15 miles west of Stornoway.

Thirteen rugged stones form a circle around a central one, 15 feet tall. A cairn resides within the circle, and a 275-foot stone avenue leads away. Local legend tells of a generous, magical white cow that once worked a miracle within the circle. The legends also say the stones are petrified pagans, turned to stone by a saint when they refused to accept his religion. Scientific types call Callanish a 4,000-year-old observatory.

<u>The Hurlers Stone Circle:</u> one-half mile north of the village of Minions, on the eastern edge of Bodmin Moor, Cornwall.

These three Bronze Age circles—ranging from 100 to 130 feet in diameter—were originally shaped and placed very carefully. Legend has it the stones are all that remains of a group of men who dared to play the Cornish ball game called "hurling" one Sunday long ago.

<u>Long Meg and Her Daughters:</u> four miles northeast of Penrith, Cumbria, on a narrow country lane just north of Little Salkeld.

More an oval than a circle, this collection of 27 stones measures 330 feet across and is one of England's largest. The stones are thus named because, according to folklore, they are a petrified coven of witches. "Long Meg," some yards away, is a 12-foot sandstone monolith—the hard, cold remains of the coven's priestess.

> **Ring of Brodgar:** Orkney Island, Scotland, between Loch Harray and Loch Stenness, five miles northeast of Stromness.
>
> You'd be hard-pressed to find a more striking circle, both in terms of location and appearance. It's 360 feet in diameter—one of England's largest. Of the original 60 stones, 36 slender ones remain. The tallest measures 15 feet. The stones were already old when the Vikings passed through here and left their runic graffiti. The Ring of Brodgar is in the middle of an area loaded with standing stones, great tombs, and megaliths.
>
> **Rollright Stones:** stones are three miles northwest of Chipping Norton, which is 20 miles northwest of Oxford, Oxfordshire. Stones are just off the A34 road.
>
> Decide for yourself: this weathered, 90-foot circle is all that remains of a king and his army, turned to stone by a riddle-loving witch; or it's a sophisticated observatory.
>
> **Stanton Drew Circles:** circles are just east of the village of Stanton Drew, which is $2\frac{1}{2}$ miles southeast of Chew Magna, Avon.
>
> The largest of this group of neolithic circles measures over 320 feet across, and is also one of England's biggest. Local legend says a wild wedding party took place on this spot long ago. The partiers danced right into Sunday morning, and thus were turned to stone.

STANSTED
(30 miles north of London)

Mountfitchet Castle Torture Chamber: Castle is just off Lower Street. Open March 15–November 15, daily, 10 A.M.–5 P.M. Admission: £2.50; children and seniors, £1.50. Phone: (0279) 81 32 37.

A Norman castle just wouldn't be a Norman castle without a torture chamber full of horrible devices. The waxwork "victims" stare at us through mild, contemplative eyes as their bloody bodies are torn, stretched, and even hung. Even the bodyless heads impaled on stakes appear to be thinking over some interesting mathematical problem.

STRATFORD-UPON-AVON

Butterfly Farm and Jungle Safari: Tramway Walk, Swan's Nest Lane, across the river from the Royal Shakespeare Theatre. Open daily, in summer, 10 A.M.–5 P.M.; in winter, 10 A.M.–3:30 P.M. Admission: £1.75; children, £1. Phone: (0789) 299 288.

Sick to death of iambic pentameter? You won't find a bit of it at the Butterfly Farm, a vast fake jungle stocked with live butterflies and birds, which fly around your head like *The Tempest* itself. Also on the premises is Insect City—not exactly the Forest of Arden—where you can meet the world's largest species of spider. When you go home and everybody asks if you saw the Globe Theatre, ask them if *they've* seen the world's largest species of spider.

STROUD
(Eight miles south of Gloucester)

Brick and Rolling Pin Throwing Contest: every year on the third Saturday in July. For more information call (04536) 4252.

There's a Stroud in Oklahoma and a Stroud in Australia, and yet another Stroud in Canada. All four Strouds hold simultaneous throwing contests, and they all run to the telephone immediately afterward to discover who are the international winners. The idea of a simultaneous brick-throwing contest bloomed 20 years ago when the mayor of Oklahoma's Stroud pointed out that both his Stroud and the English Stroud had flourishing brick-producing industries. "But *we* have a rolling-pin industry," piped up Australia's Stroud. So a rolling-pin throwing contest was established for the women.

SYMONDS YAT WEST
(18 miles west of Gloucester)

Jubilee Maze and Maze Museum: just off the A40 road. Open April–October, daily, 11 A.M.–5:30 P.M. Admission: 80p. Phone: (0600) 890 360.

In 1977, all over England, people commemorated Queen Elizabeth II's 25th anniversary jubilee in many ways, but few were as unique as this: the construction of a huge hedge maze in her honor. Once you've struggled your way in and out, you can head over to what is, as far as we can tell, the world's only maze museum, full of displays about the history of this labyrinthine horticulture.

WEST WYCOMBE
(30 miles northwest of central London)

Hell Fire Caves: from London, take British Rail to High Wycombe. From there, take bus 291 or 791 to West Wycombe village (two miles north of High Wycombe). Open Easter–October 30, daily, 11 A.M.–6 P.M. Admission: £2; seniors and children, £1. Phone: (0494) 24411. Cave entrance is halfway up West Wycombe Hill.

Eighteenth-century libertine Sir Francis Dashwood and his pseudo-satanic Hell Fire Club allegedly held their meetings in these caves, which are located on the old Dashwood property. As you wander through the Labyrinth, the Hall of Statues, the Treasure Chamber, and the Inner Temple (all constructed between 1748 and 1752), pay your respects to the debauched waxworks that illustrate scenes from the Hell Fire story. A tape-recorded narration provides more juicy details.

NORTHERN ENGLAND

BRADFORD

The Color Museum: in Perkin House, 82 Grattan Road. Take bus 665, 667 or 668 from Bradford Interchange. Open Tuesday–Friday, 2–5 P.M.; Saturday, 10 A.M.–4 P.M. Closed Sunday and Monday. Admission: free. Phone: (0274) 725 138.

Hands-on experiments and optical illusions really make you think about color: how we perceive it, use it, are seduced by it, and take it for granted. A professional designer put together the exhibits, so they are sharp and relevant, touching on such subjects as animals' color perception, the meaning of colors in cosmetics, and our psychological need for colorful food. It's every bit as interesting as its name promises.

"Curry Tours"—Asian Weekends: Call Enterprise Travel at (0274) 547 038 or the Bradford Tourist Office at (0274) 753 678 for current details. Prices start at about £50 for a two-night tour.

London is famous for its Indian and Pakistani communities. However, few non-Britishers know that Bradford, population 300,000, has a greater percentage of

Indians than any city outside of Asia. Entire neighborhoods of Bradford have nothing but Indian and Pakistani restaurants, hotels, and shops. Local tour operators have capitalized on this by organizing "Asian Weekends" in which native Brits and tourists take a little trip to India, or at least a reasonable Yorkshire facsimile. Guests stay in the Indian part of town at an Indian hotel, and are taken to authentic Indian restaurants and Indian dance performances. They are introduced to the wares in the most interesting Indian shops. And *some* people say the industrial North is boring. Humph.

Walking-Stick Collection: in the Gem Museum, Lister House, 13 Heaton Road, northwest of downtown. Take bus 627 or 629. Open Tuesday–Sunday, 10 A.M.–6 P.M. Closed Monday. Admission: 35p; seniors, 25p; children under 17, 15p. Phone: (0274) 493 761.

This museum's well-traveled curator couldn't quite confine himself to gems, so he installed the Walking Stick Hall. Among the hundreds of jeweled, carved, inlaid, and funny-handled specimens are sticks owned by Winston Churchill and Charlie Chaplin.

CASTLETON
(12 miles west of Sheffield)

Speedwell Cavern: just west of Castleton on the A625 road. Open daily, 9:30 A.M.–5:30 P.M. Boats depart every 15 minutes. Admission: £2; children, £1.50. Phone: (0433) 20512.

What do you do with an abandoned lead mine? You take tourists through it on a boat. The trip continues for about a mile—completely underground—and ends up at the cave's *pièce de resistance,* a forbidding pit that the proprietors claim is bottomless.

CRAGG VALE
(Five miles southwest of Halifax)

Forged Coin Collection: in Hinchliffe Arms pub, in the center of the hamlet Cragg Vale. Open normal pub hours. Admission: free.

In 1770 Cragg Vale suddenly became the headquarters for a gang of notorious forgers. Their specialty was forged gold Portuguese coins, since they assumed (correctly) that nobody in England would know what a Portuguese coin was supposed to look like anyway. When the local economy started going haywire, word got out and the forgers were eventually caught and hanged. The few remnants of Cragg Vale's moment of glory can be seen in the Hinchliffe Arms, which has on display some of the counterfeit coins and the counterfeiters' tools. The only other place some of the coins can be seen is in the Heptonstall Old Grammar School Museum, in Heptonstall, next to Hebden Bridge (six miles northwest of Halifax).

EGREMONT
(Five miles south of Whitehaven, Cumbria)

Crabapple Fair and World Ugly-Face-Making Championship: the Saturday nearest October 18. For more information call the Whitehaven Tourist Office: (0946) 5678.

It's not just ugly-face-making, or "gurning," as the outrageous sport is known around here. It's "gurning through a braffin": making ugly faces with a horse harness around your head. And it's not just making ugly faces with a horse harness around your head, it's making *uuugly* faces: swallowing your nose, eradicating your chin, the whole bit. Top-flight gurners who turn up for the championship give new meaning to the phrase "facial expression." Great photo possibilities here.

HOLMFIRTH
(18 miles southwest of Leeds)

Postcard Museum: Huddersfield Road (next to Victoria Park, one block southwest of the tourist office). Open Monday–Saturday, 10 A.M.–5 P.M.; Sunday, 1–5 P.M. Admission: free. Phone: (0484) 682 231.

"Dear Buffi,

I had to stay with my cousins in this out-of-the-way town in northern England, and I thought I was gonna be bored till I found a museum all about postcards. Isn't that weird? There are zillions of 'em here, most of them really old and strange. Some are supposed to be nasty or funny, but I can't figure them out! The museum even has ancient silent movies and special boxes for looking at slides that are even more ancient. Like I said, it's really weird and I went there four days in a row 'cause it was free. I wish I had brought that *Europe Off The Wall* book like you suggested so that I would know about more places like this.

                           Love, Jessica."

KENDAL
(Cumbria)

Levens Hall Topiary Garden: five miles south of town on the A6 road. Open Easter–October, Sunday–Thursday, 11 A.M.–5 P.M. Admission: £2.20; children, £1.10. Phone: (05395) 60321.

The bushes are specially clipped to look like mushrooms, doughnuts, birds, a coach, horses, and so on, and they've been this way for nearly 300 years, ever since the French topiary genius Beaumont laid out this fanciful garden. But what we want to know is, is Beaumont responsible for those two bushes that look like a coffeepot and a popsicle?

KESWICK
(25 miles south of Carlisle, Cumbria)

Cumberland Pencil Museum: next to the Cumberland Pencil Factory. Open March–October, Monday–Friday, 9:30 A.M.–4:30 P.M. Admission: 70p; children, 35p. Phone: (07687) 73626.

During an uncomfortable silence at your next cocktail party, you can exclaim, "Did you know the world's largest pencil is in Keswick?" Once the ice has thus been broken, you can continue by explaining that the pencil is seven feet long, and that the pencil museum that owns it also has a James-Bondesque spy pencil containing a minuscule compass and map. Also on display are centuries-old pencils and many other pencil curiosities.

KNARESBOROUGH
(16 miles west of York)

Old Mother Shipton's Cave and Petrifying Well: just across the river from the train station; entrance is on the A59 road. Open Easter–October, daily, 9:30 A.M.–6 P.M. East tour departs at 5:15. Admission: £1.95; seniors, £1.50; children 5–17, £1.20; children under 5, free. Phone: (0423) 864 600.

The Petrifying Well is actually a waterfall containing minerals that, when absorbed, turn porous substances to stone. The process takes a few months. Hanging from hooks all over this "well" today are half-petrified teddy bears. For nearly 300 years—ever since someone discovered a petrified cow at the foot of the falls—people have been hanging things up in the water for fun. Thus on display is an historic array of stone derby hats, stone gloves, and the like. How convenient for the entrepreneurs now running this place that Mother Shipton, a fifteenth-century prophetess, was allegedly born in a cave right nearby! Today the cave finds a replica Mother Shipton duded up in ludicrous "witch" garb (including glowing eyes), displayed along with various Shipton paraphernalia.

LIVERPOOL

Beatles Convention: the last Friday, Saturday, Sunday, and Monday in August. For exact prices, times, and place, and to arrange reservations, call (051) 630 4062 or (051) 653 7080, or the tourist office at (051) 709 3631.

Every year on what the English call August Bank Holiday, the entire city of Liverpool braces itself for the annual Beatles Convention. Beatlemania reigns supreme, with bands impersonating the Beatles, star appearances by people associated with the Beatles, countless records and memorabilia for sale, concerts by other Liverpool bands, trivia competitions, and dozens of official and unofficial parties. Anybody caught not worshipping the Fab Four will be run out of town.

Beatles Museum: scheduled to open at the Albert Dock on the waterfront. For hours and price call (051) 709 3285.

The Beatles Museum has returned to Liverpool in 1988 after a long absence. The museum has the single largest collection of original Beatle objects anywhere: personal possessions, instruments, rare photos, and tidbits to titillate rabid Beatle fans.

Beatles Tours: Bus tours depart from the tourist office (29 Lime Street) daily, at 2:30 and 5 P.M. Price: £3.50. Phone: (051) 709 3631. Tours last two hours. Other bus and walking tours are given at various times.

If your soul will not rest until you see Penny Lane, Strawberry Fields, and Paul McCartney's grammar school, this is the tour for you. The bus goes to every site in Liverpool even vaguely associated with the Beatles.

Festival Park: on Sefton Street, two miles south of downtown, opposite St. Michael's station on the Merseyrail Line. Open late May–early September, daily, 11 A.M.–6 P.M. Admission: £1.50. Phone: (051) 728 9888.

Inside this big dome-shaped futuristic greenhouse is "The Magic Garden," a typical backyard grown all out of proportion: 30-foot-tall sunflowers, eight-foot mushrooms, shovels as big as billboards, and a pitchfork that the Jolly Green Giant might use to toss his salad. There's even some appropriate backyard garbage in the form of a towering Pepsi can. Come and get a bug's-eye view of things. Nearby is a full-scale model of the Beatles' Yellow Submarine, which you can climb inside and pilot to Pepperland.

MALTON
(20 miles northeast of York)

Eden Camp: on the A64 road, just where it passes north of Malton, at the intersection of the A169 road. Open daily, 10 A.M.–5 P.M. Admission: £2.50; children, £1.50. Phone: (0653) 697777.

Eden Camp is a theme amusement park with the least likely theme imaginable: the British civilian experience of WWII. "Share the laughter and tears of the family in total war." *Oy vey.* The park is actually laid out like a grim POW camp, with rows and rows of rectangular huts and guard towers. Each hut has a different theme, such as food rationing, a simulated blitz bombing, wartime fashions, a grotesque forties vaudeville act performed by puppets, and—for a cheery switch—the experience of being in a torpedoed German submarine. In the last hut you can actually crawl out through an escape tunnel. Whoopee!

MASHAM
(17 miles north of Harrogate)

Fake Stonehenge: just outside the village of Ilton, which is southwest of Masham, on the edge of the moors. Always open. Admission: free. For more information call the Ripon Tourist Office at (0765) 4625.

"Wait a minute, I thought Stonehenge was in *southern* England." True, and that was just too far away for local nineteenth-century mystical eccentric William Danby. He wanted his own personal Stonehenge, so he built one. The copy is not exact, and it's a good deal smaller than the original, but it has the undeniable advantage of being covered with luminous lichen and moss that glow in the dark. Go at night.

MORPETH
(13 miles north of Newcastle-Upon-Tyne)

Bagpipe Museum: in the castle, in the center of town. Open Monday–Friday, 9:30 A.M.–5:30 P.M. Admission: 50p; children, 25p. Phone: (0670) 511 323.

If you can't tell one set of bagpipes from another, then this place will turn you into a connoisseur o' the pipes. Scottish bagpipes, as well as those from France, Spain, and even more exotic locations, are displayed and explained in such a way that you can trace the instrument's history and see how one type of bagpipe evolved from another.

NORTHWICH
(18 miles southwest of Manchester)

Salt Museum: just outside of town on London Road. Open July–August, Tuesday–Saturday, 10 A.M.–5 P.M.; rest of year, Tuesday–Sunday, 2–5 P.M. Phone: (0606) 41331.

For the people of Northwich, "the salt of the earth" is no mere abstract expression, nor is "back to the salt mines," for salt has been the major industry around here for hundreds of years. The museum uses slide shows, tapes, photos, old tools, and lots of real salt to tell the story of the mineral and the industry. Exhibitions change periodically, but they always relate to salt. Note the odd collection of salt sculptures.

RIPON
(11 miles north of Harrogate)

The Hornblower of Ripon: every night at 9 P.M. in the market square.

"Nine o'clock and all's well!" If only all of us had a wakeman to watch over our sleep. Ripon's solemn hornblower (called The Wakeman), dressed in three-cornered hat, gold-buttoned suit, and white gloves, every night blows a horn four times in the square. This Ripon tradition is about a thousand years old, dating all the way back to Saxon times. The town's motto is printed on the Town Hall: "Excepte ye Lord Keep ye Cittie, the Wakeman waketh in vain."

Prison and Police Museum: on St. Marygate Street. Open May–September, Tuesday–Sunday, 1:30–4:30 P.M. Phone: (0765) 3706.

Police and prisoners go hand-in-hand—hand-in-handcuff, actually. Effectively housed in the cells of an old prison, the exhibits include real murder weapons, police uniforms, and mannequins dressed as jailers and prisoners. Scary pictures give a glimpse of law-and-order English style over the last 300 years. Some of the cells are furnished exactly as they were when occupied by prisoners; visitors are heartily encouraged to step inside and feel desolate.

WEST WITTON
(15 miles southwest of Richmond, North Yorkshire)

Burning Bartle: the Saturday following August 24, in the evening. For more information call the Richmond Tourist Office at (0748) 3525 or (0748) 5994.

On the shoulders of village men, a giant straw-and-rag effigy (the "Bartle") makes its way down the street. Crowds gathered on both sides of the road chant vindictive rhymes about the Bartle; their chant ends with "At Grassgill End, we'll make his end." Sure enough, when the procession reaches the little street called Grassgill End, the giant is stabbed viciously and set afire. Everyone sings merrily, watching him burn. Exactly whom the Bartle represents is not clear. Some say he was a hated pig thief, caught and brought to justice, vigilante style, many years ago. Others point out that the festival might have something to do with St. Bartholomew, whose feast day is August 24.

SCOTLAND

AYR
(30 miles southwest of Glasgow)

The Electric Brae: 9 miles south of Ayr on the A719 road, just south of the town of Dunure. For more information call the Ayr Tourist Office at (0292) 284 196.

An optical illusion? A curse? A mystery spot with unfathomable powers? Or just a case of mass hallucination? The Electric Brae (*brae* means hillside in Scottish) is a sloping section of road between the coast and the Carrick Hills whose bizarre properties have so far defied ex-

> # POSTCARD TOWNS
>
> England is chock-full of towns with names that strike Americans as funny. The joy is not only in finding them, but in actually going to them and mailing postcards home with the towns' postmarks on the back. However, everyone seems to have their own idea as to what is a funny name. So, instead of giving you an "authoritative" list of the towns we think are funny, we'll just give a sampling of some pretty remarkable ones to start you on the search for your own postcard towns.
>
> <u>Great Snoring:</u> 27 miles northwest of Norwich, Norfolk (Little Snoring is one mile south).
>
> <u>The Mumbles:</u> four miles south of Swansea, Wales.
>
> <u>New York and Boston:</u> just eight miles apart; Boston is 32 miles southeast of Lincoln and New York is eight miles north of Boston.
>
> <u>Pity Me:</u> two miles north of Durham.
>
> <u>Ugley:</u> 34 miles north of London, and four miles north of Bishop's Stortford, Essex.
>
> <u>Westward Ho!:</u> 11 miles west of Barnstaple, Devon.

planation. Drive your car down the hill and come to a full stop. Then release the brake. What happens next is a matter of opinion. Many people claim to see their car rolling back uphill. Others claim this is simply an optical illusion, but they're just party poopers. The fun is in devising explanations for the apparent miracle: the Scots say the brae is electric, or that a local witch cursed the place long ago. Americans tend to get more mystical.

BLANTYRE
(Eight miles south of Glasgow)

David Livingstone Centre: on Station Road, north of the train station. Open Monday–Saturday, 10 A.M.–6 P.M. and Sunday, 2–6 P.M. Admission: £1; children, 50p. Phone: (0698) 823 140.

A touch of the Zambezi in Scotland, the David Livingstone Centre is dedicated to the life and works of Blantyre's most famous son. The Africa Pavilion, a series of three connected small buildings arranged to resemble African huts, offers information about Livingstone's discoveries as well as a socially conscious exhibition about modern-day Africa. Next to the pavilion is Livingstone's actual birthplace, which was once a miserable tenement. Now it's a museum of Livingstone's life and the conditions in which he grew up. A great fountain featuring a huge globe and sculptured panels illustrates Livingston's adventures. Be forewarned, though, that the trick of showing up here in a pith helmet and intoning, "Dr. Livingstone, I presume?" has already worn very thin.

COMRIE
(Six miles west of Crieff, Perthshire)

Museum of Scottish Tartans: on Drummond Street. Open Easter–September, Monday–Saturday, 10 A.M.–5 P.M.; Sunday, 2–4 P.M.; October, Monday–Friday, 10 A.M.–4 P.M.; Saturday, 10 A.M.–1 P.M. Between November and Easter, hours are variable. Admission: 90p; seniors and children, 50p. Phone: (0764) 70779.

Tartan tells many a tale, as you'll see here. The world's largest tartan collection includes over 1,300 different samples, as well as details on every known tartan. You can search for your plaid roots among the museum's archives, take one of the museum's plaid quizzes, watch the resident weaver at work, or wonder what the heck it *is* that Scottish men wear under their kilts.

DUNMORE
(Two miles north of Airth, Stirlingshire)

The Dunmore Pineapple: one mile south of Dunmore on the B9124 road (which branches to the west from the A905). For more information (such as on how to rent the pineapple), call (031) 226 5922.

A 40-foot carved stone pineapple, smug as you please, sits atop a house in a peaceful garden. The big fruit was built in 1761 for the eccentric (what else?) Earl of Dunmore, who later went on to become governor of New York, Virginia, and the Bahamas. Pineapples were rare indeed in Scotland when this one was built. It's a gloriously true-to-life and well-preserved specimen, replete with spikes and a fountainlike stem. You can almost smell the tropics.

EDINBURGH

Camera Obscura: in the Outlook Tower, Castle Hill between the castle and Lawnmarket. Open April–October, Monday–Friday, 9:30 A.M.–5:30 P.M.; Saturday–Sunday, 10 A.M.–6 P.M.; November–March, Monday–Friday, 9:30 A.M.–5 P.M.; Saturday–Sunday, 10:30 A.M.–4:30 P.M. Admission: £1.25; seniors and children, 60p. Phone: (031) 226 3709.

Since 1850, this amazing optical device has been projecting live views of Edinburgh onto a round observation table. The effect is rather like that of watching a film, as the image is moving. You see exactly what's happening outside, projected on the table. Cars move; flags flutter; people scuttle along. Also on display here are scenic photographs of Edinburgh taken with tin-can "pinhole" cameras.

LAMB HOLM ISLAND
(1½ miles south of St. Mary's on the main Orkney island, and connected by a causeway to the main island)

Italian Nissen Hut Chapel: just east of the road leading from St. Margaret's Hope to Kirkwall, on the small island of Lamb Holm. Always open. Admission: free. For more information call the Kirkwall Tourist Office at (0856) 2856.

As a strange form of punishment, the British Army in WWII built a prisoner-of-war camp for captured Italian soldiers on a cold, tiny Orkney island way, way up north. The homesick Italians spent their chilly hours converting two prefab Nissen huts into a beautiful southern-Italian-style Catholic chapel, using mostly junk and driftwood as construction materials. The project impressed the Italians' captors, who promised to preserve the chapel after the war. It's still there, and although the outside doesn't look like much, the inside is truly amazing, decorated with large geometric mosaics and delicate filigree arches.

LARGS
(On the coast, 50 miles west of Glasgow)

Viking Festival: every year in early September. For current date call the Largs Tourist Office at (0475) 67 37 65.

Winged helmets gleam and outraged bellowing fills the streets as costumed men reenact the thirteenth-century Battle of Largs. As that battle pitted the Norwegians against the Scots, this is no sissy fight.

LERWICK
(Shetland Island)

Up-Helly-Aa: every year on the last Tuesday in January. Torchlight procession begins at 7 P.M. For more information call the Lerwick Tourist Office at (0595) 3434.

One of England's rowdiest festivals climaxes with a gorgeous 30-foot Viking ship going up in flames, ritually burned by townspeople in full Viking dress. The burning is preceded by a torch-lit march through the streets in which the people sing "Up-Helly-Aa!" The words, according to some scholars, mean "up-ending the holy days." Modern Shetlanders' ancestors were Norse pagans, forced to observe Christian holidays against their will. This fiery festival commemorates the pagans' rebellion against somber Christmas celebrations.

OBAN

McCaig's Folly (a.k.a. Skyline Folly): on Battery Hill, clearly visible from the harbor.

For some reason, one hears a lot more hoopla about the Colosseum in Rome than about the one here in Oban. Oban's colosseum is round, not oval like the Italian version. And its arches are gothic and pointed, not rounded like Rome's. It came about when local banker John McCaig thought he might counteract the unemployment problem by hiring a lot of men to build him a museum in the shape of a huge colosseum. McCaig died before the construction was finished, and so now the incomplete hulk, striking in silhouette, is known as McCaig's Folly.

PAISLEY
(Three miles west of Glasgow)

Paisley Museum and Art Gallery: on the High Street. Open Monday–Saturday, 10 A.M.–5 P.M. Closed Sunday. Admission: free. Phone: (041) 889 3151.

Those elaborate, flowery, languid teardrops—that's paisley, named after Paisley, where the fabric design became an art. The museum houses over 750 paisley shawls. With these as well as designers' sketches and photographs, the history of the pattern and of the shawl-making industry are detailed.

PERTH

Caithness Paperweight Museum: just north of town at the Inveralmond Industrial Estate, on the A9 road. Open Monday–Saturday, 9 A.M.–5 P.M.; Sunday, 11 A.M.–5 P.M. Admission: free. Phone: (0738) 37373.

The specialty here is millefiori, the dazzling, no-two-alike design that features colored whorls and chunks floating in crystal-clear spheres. The hundreds of paperweights on display here were all made at the Caithness glass factory.

SOUTH QUEENSFERRY
(Eight miles west of Edinburgh)

Burry Man: every year on the second Friday in August. For more information call the Edinburgh Tourist Office at (031) 577 2727.

In the heat of August, he wears a flannel body suit that even covers his face. Every inch of the flannel is stuck with prickly burrs, and his head is crowned with many roses; the Burry Man is completely unrecognizable. For seven miles he lumbers along, traveling the Queensferry boundaries as Burry Men before him have done since 1740. His costume and flower-covered staffs are so oppressively heavy that two helpers (dressed in ordinary clothes) must walk alongside him. From house to house they go, silently begging for money. The Burry Man remains mute all day—eerily so—and he finishes his sojourn, exhausted, in the late afternoon.

GREECE

Legend:
1. Athens
2. Piraeus
3. Thessaloniki
4. Corfu
5. Corinth
6. Patras
7. Lesbos
8. Rhodes
9. Crete
10. Thera
11. Naxos
12. Mykonos

In Greece, antiquity is ubiquitous. If it's not a Temple of Diana, it's a Minoan fresco or a Byzantine Church. If you added up the ages of all the ancient things in Greece, you would end up with a very large number. Very, very large. The thought of it wearies me.

So, in our search for the unusual Greece, we have avoided the ancient. If we had found a 2,500-year-old building dedicated to the god of blacksmiths in Denmark, we would have leaped for joy; in Greece, however, one can't take 15 steps without bumping into yet another 2,500-year-old building dedicated to the god of blacksmiths; they cover the landscape here, like mosquitoes and sheep.

The Greeks, undoubtedly in an attempt to provide distractions from all the Old Things, have cultivated more than their fair share of peculiar local customs and celebrations, the strangest of which we have included here. And to counterbalance the transitory nature of the festivals, we have included some remarkable natural curiosities, which, in their own way, are so old as to predate the ancient.

ATHENS

The Athens Center of Reptiles (Reptilarium): Adrianou 99, in the Plaka. Open daily, 11 A.M.–9 P.M. Admission: 200 dr; students, 100 dr. Phone: 01-3228 965.

At the Reptilarium, Athens feels comfortingly familiar, full of American-style side-show spirit. Dozens of serpents lie quietly in their cages, while signs scream at you from every angle: "Please do not touch danger!" And sexy-girl-in-black-Corvette posters line the wall, inappropriately, if hilariously. It's true that all the heavy-duty species are here—cobras, cottonmouths, mambas, and more, with wide-eyed pseudo-scientific information about their eating and reproductive habits. But are you really going to visit a reptilarium in the glitzy Plaka, land of cheap souvlaki and souvenir plastic satyrs, to gather data? No; you'll go there to chuckle at the posters, to admire the sleek, incongruous snakes, and to wonder, as we did, why every cage has a slot on top, into which giggling Greek youths slip coin after coin, often hitting the snakes on the head, but even so, seldom bestirring them.

Shadow-Puppet Theater (Karaghiosis): in Lysikrates Square (Plateia Lysikrati), in the Plaka. Nightly, usually at 8 P.M. Admission: Dr 250. For program and current showtimes, call 4129-050.

Heroes and villains, tricksters and fools: they cavort and battle as in days of yore on the stage of what is quite possibly, by this time, the last remaining theatre of its kind in Greece. The puppets, two feet tall and fully jointed, are entirely two-dimensional. Actually, they are lavishly colored, but as the silhouette's the thing, shows are strictly in black and white. If you prefer colors, you can buy actual shadow puppets in the craft and antique shops around Lysikrates Square and put on some shows of your own.

AYIA ELINI
(Three miles north of Seres)

Fire-Walking Festival (Anastenaria): Take K.T.E.L. bus from Thessaloniki to Seres, and local bus from Seres to Ayia Elini. Event is held every May 21, 22, and 23 at dusk (usually around 7 P.M.).

In this tiny village, men and women dance across live coals to commemorate an event associated with the village's patron, St. Helen. See Langadas entry for detailed description.

KALIMNOS
(City on the Dodecanese island of Kalimnos, just north of Kos, off the coast of Turkey)

Sponge Week Festival: one week after Easter. Ferries run to Kalimnos from Piraeus and nearby islands.

The economy of Kalimnos is based on one thing: sponges. Not those rectangular foam things you wipe the counter with, either, but real, living sponges that grow on the bottom of the sea, which the menfolk sail off to harvest for five months starting a week or two after Easter. Preceding their departure, the town goes sponge-mad, singing sponge songs, making the kids do the Sponge Dance, holding sponge-related religious events, and in general whooping it up spongewise. The spongemen's last night on the island is called the Night of the Lovers, and needs no further description.

LANGADAS
($7\frac{1}{2}$ miles northwest of Thessaloniki)

Fire-Walking Festival (Anastenaria): Buses bound for the village of Langadas leave every half-hour from the K.T.E.L. bus stop at 17 Irinis Street in Thessaloniki. Event is held every May 21, 22, and 23 at dusk (usually around 7 P.M.).

To the beat of a sacred drum and the whine of a one-stringed fiddle, the strange brotherhood called Anestarides ("groaners") dance barefoot, unharmed, across a bed of live coals. As they step rhythmically along, they wave blood-red scarves and clutch icons. They say they're possessed by St. Constantine, whose feast day this is, and that the Saint protects their feet. They say the ritual commemorates a medieval miracle in which the icons of St. Constantine and St. Helen, trapped inside a church during a fire, wept aloud until the citizens rescued them. But certain persons, notably, the local priests, suspect that the firewalking is more pagan than orthodox. After all, this region *was* once the cradle of Dionysus worship, and there *is* a lot of dedicated drinking going on among the firewalkers. In other Greek villages a black, uncastrated ram is sacrificed on St. Constantine's feast day. Hmm. Gets you wondering. The ritual takes on a lively, party atmosphere, although the procession that precedes it is a creepy affair, with participants gasping and sighing, in imitation, they say, of the crying icons.

LESBOS

Petrified Trees: on the western end of the island in the area between the cities of Sigri, Andissa, and Eressos. Take ferry to Lesbos from either Piraeus or Thessaloniki.

What look at first like bizarre, crumbling columns of some lost civilization are actually trees—million-year-old trees that have simply turned to stone. Arizona's Petrified Forest is a mere pile of broken logs in comparison; here on Lesbos, the trees are up to 20 feet tall, some still with branches and roots, each one with layers of colors. Some of these trees may be up to 20 million years old. The only way to reach them is via hiking boot. Use Sigri, Andissa, or Eressos as your base.

MARKOPOULO
(On the island of Kefalonia)

Assumption Day Snakes: in the village church, all day August 15. Call Kefalonia Tourist Office for more information: 0671/22. 847.

Is there any underlying significance to this strange combination of natural phenomenon and religious ceremony, or is it just a coincidence? Only Mother Nature knows for sure. Either way, Assumption Day is the biggest holiday in Markopoulo; and it just so happens that on that day, and sometimes on the preceding day as well, countless thousands of harmless little snakes with black, cross-shaped markings on their heads come writhing in from the hills to the town and the church, where the faithful hug them and include them in the religious celebration. The snakes seem to time their arrival perfectly every year, though nobody knows how or why; it's an unparallelled biological-religious conundrum.

MONOKLISIA
(15 miles southwest of Seres)

Women's Domination Day (Gynecocratie): Take K.T.E.L. bus from Thessaloniki to Seres, and then a local bus from Seres to Monoklisia. Every year on August 1. For more information call 0321-88262.

Ladies' Day in Monoklisia is not just a sissy affair, with breakfast in bed and a bouquet from the menfolk. The women literally take over the town, serving as the police force, TV repairpersons, and everything, while the men cower at home doing housework. If a man so much as ventures out of doors, he risks being chased down the street and doused with cold water by merciless women. Harking back to a time when the Mother Goddess was revered in the land, Monoklisia's women play it to the hilt, if only for a day; performing such unheard-of (in Greece) feats as swaggering into bars and playing boisterous card games. Come sundown, all is forgiven, and the men creep away from dishtowel and diaper to join the women in a feast. Someday, however—*someday*—the women might decide not to let their husbands out of the kitchen.

NEA PETRA
(Near Seres)

Women's Domination Day (Gynecocratie): Take K.T.E.L. bus from Thessaloniki to Seres, and then a local bus from Seres to Nea Petra. Every year on August 1. For more information, call 0324-41369.

Women take over the village for a day and perform the traditional male roles of filling political offices and wallowing in smoke-filled tavernas. Men, meanwhile, are confined to the house and must beat rugs, cook meals, and be otherwise domestic—risking a chase scene and a brisk encounter with a savagely thrown bucket of cold water if they dare step outside. (See also Monoklisia.)

PANAGIA
(On the island of Thassos)

Hanging of Judas Festival: To get to Thassos, take K.T.E.L. bus from 59 Langadas Street in Thessaloniki to Kavala (buses depart every hour on the hour, from 6 A.M. to 8 P.M.; the ride takes three hours). From Kavala take ferry to Thassos. Panagia is on the northeast side of the island. Event occurs yearly on the Monday after Easter.

Here is religion at its most gruesome. The day after Easter, the residents of Panagia turn their attention to the darker side of the picture and "celebrate" the suicide of Judas by hanging him in effigy in the streets of the town. Vigilante justice, Greek style.

PARIKIA
(On the island of Paros)

Valley of Butterflies (Petaloúdes, or Psihopania): the valley is near Parikia, the island's main port. Ferries connect Paros with Piraeus regularly. Summer is the best viewing time.

Want to feel as if you're walking through a *National Geographic* photo essay? Every summer, thousands of multicolored fragile butterflies cover this area like a Persian carpet.

PERAMA
(Four miles north of Ioanina, in Epirus region)

Goritsa Cave: just north of Perama, in Mt. Goritsa. Call (0651) 234.40 or (0651) 215.21 for current hours and prices.

Goritsa Cave, discovered 50 years ago—recent by Greek standards—is one of the most beautiful caverns in Greece. What makes it unusual is neither its beauty, nor its small underground lakes, nor its outstanding limestone formations, but instead a single stalagmite which, inexplicably, is in the shape of a cross—the only such stalagmite known in the world.

PHILIPPI (Filipi)

Roman Latrine: at the archaeological site in Philippi. From Thessaloniki, take K.T.E.L. bus from 59 Langadas Street to Kavala (buses depart every hour on the hour, from 6 A.M. to 8 P.M.; the ride takes three hours). From Kavala, take local bus toward Drama and get off at the Philippi stop.

Europe is covered with Roman ruins, and guidebooks are more than willing to tell you about the theaters, arches, and aqueducts. But where can you find out about the really interesting ruins, like the latrines? Here, that's where. Among Philippi's famous ruins is a huge, extremely well-preserved second-century latrine. Be warned, however, that nowadays it's an archaeological site, so relieve yourself elsewhere, despite temptation to "do as the Romans did."

PIRAEUS
(Six miles southwest of Athens)

Blessing of the Waters: to reach Piraeus, take subway from Monastiraki station in Athens or bus 040 from Filellinon Street in Athens. Event occurs yearly on the morning of January 6, on the pier. For exact time, call Piraeus information: 413. 5716 or 413. 5730.

As Greece's busiest harbor, Piraeus holds the grandest version of the water blessing, an Epiphany tradition observed at every port, river, and spring in Greece. The Archbishop of Athens and All Greece, in full regalia, consecrates the less-than-limpid waters of the harbor. Then he ceremoniously throws in a large cross, which is retrieved by divers amid the ear-splitting wail of ship sirens.

PIRGOS DIROU
(30 miles south of Kalamata)

Glifada Cave: three miles north of Pirgos Dirou. Call 0733/522 22 for current hours and prices.

A smooth, cool, underground river runs through Glifada

Cave, and visitors are allowed to explore it on their own in rented boats. Weave your way through fantastic stalagmite and stalactite mazes. Part of the cave can also be explored on foot, but keep an eye out for Injun Joe.

RHODES (RODOS)

Valley of Butterflies (Petaloúdes): 15 miles southwest of Rhodes City. Take a bus to the valley from downtown Rhodes City. June usually is the best month to visit. For more information, call (0241) 236.55 or (0241) 232.55.

Why do butterflies love the Greek isles so much? Well, they're not such stupid creatures, after all. Rhodes's Valley of Butterflies is home to a velvety red-and-black species, which at the right time of year seem to cover every leaf of every tree in the valley. Local rumor has it that the numbers are actually diminishing year after year; make sure you visit Petaloúdes before it becomes just another colorful Greek myth.

VAÏ
(On the island of Crete)

Natural Palm Grove: on the town beach. Vaï is at the extreme eastern tip of Crete. Buses run there from Agios Nikolaos and Sitia.

One generally associates palm trees with swaying hula dancers or Saharan nomads. Palm trees are not indigenous to Europe; in fact, here on Crete are the only naturally growing palm trees in Europe, apparently brought by birds or waves from North Africa thousands of years ago. The beach at Vaï—a Tahitian oasis in Greece—is a great place for prank snapshots.

IRELAND

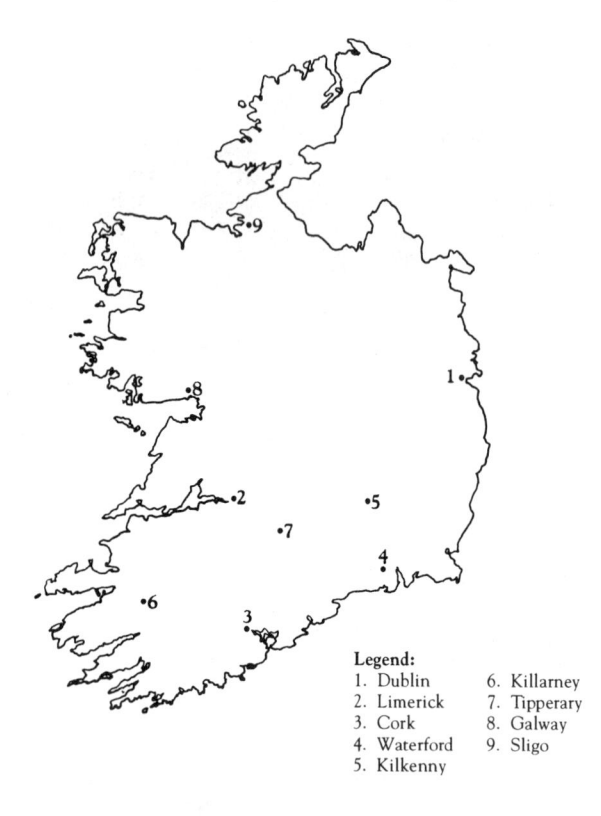

Legend:
1. Dublin
2. Limerick
3. Cork
4. Waterford
5. Kilkenny
6. Killarney
7. Tipperary
8. Galway
9. Sligo

If only poetry were a better-paying job; if only poets did not lead such impassioned, short lives—then Ireland would be as sophisticated and smooth as the rest of northern Europe.

But who's complaining?

While all of Europe wallowed stupidly through the Dark Ages, Ireland alone burned the candle of literacy in her monasteries and convents. Why is Ireland forever cursed/blessed with an artist's temperament, staying up late at night, rising late; bristling with good stories and rebellion?

Ireland, too, has the poet's surface stillness. Its ancient rocks and ruins are profoundly silent; its cities anything but modern. But through the collective imagination roams a panoply of magnificent beings, alive as you and I: the mythic Children of Lyr, turned cruelly to swans; St. Brendan, setting out to cross the Atlantic in a leather boat; fairies reveling within the hills; mermaids at sea; ghosts swirling and swooning down the ruined halls.

BUNRATTY
(County Clare; seven miles northwest of Limerick)

Medieval Banquets: at Bunratty Castle. Nightly at 5:45 P.M. and 9 P.M. Price: Ir£24.90. Phone: (061) 61788.

The velvet-gowned serving girls dole out a lot of heady mead, and before long you're convinced that it's the fifteenth century and you're the Earl of Thomond's legitimate cousin who has just dropped by for dinner. What the heck—the castle dates from 1460 and the harpists play their hearts out—even the furniture is 500 years old. Professors might find a few inaccuracies somewhere between the machine-made dishware and the semienforced audience participation; but how often does one get a chance to eat in a castle, anyway?

CORK
(County Cork)

Traditional Bowling: on the roads leading out into the countryside from the city of Cork. Most often played on Sundays. For more information, call the Cork Tourist Office at (021) 273251.

Out on the rough, hilly country roads around Cork, a prehistoric, rustic form of bowling still thrives. The games usually start outside an inn or pub. Men heave metal balls considerable distances on very rough terrain in an attempt to either outdistance each other or to come as close as possible to a certain target; the rules are rarely explained and are lost in the mists of time. Games can go on for hours and extend for over a mile down the road. This form of bowling is now extinct everywhere else in the world: folklore students take note. *Hint:* In this area, "bowling" is pronounced "boweling."

DUBLIN

Bloomsday: June 16. James Joyce Tower is located on the seashore at Sandycove, half a mile south of Dun Laoghaire. For more information, call the tower at (01) 809265.

On the anniversary of Leopold Bloom's sojourn through Dublin in James Joyce's *Ulysses,* Joyce fans from all over the world flock to the tower. Bloomsday commences at 8 A.M. with a special James Joyce breakfast at a nearby restaurant, followed by readings and festivities in the tower, where Joyce himself once lived. Walking tours, which follow Bloom's route through the city, start in front of Dublin's Central Post Office (on O'Connell Street) at 2:30 P.M. on Bloomsday and the preceding Sunday (and every Thursday the rest of the year). The price for the tour is Ir£3.

Kilmainham Jail: on Inchicore Road at the intersection of South Circular Road, just southwest of Heuston Station. Take bus 21, 23, or 78. Open Sunday 3–6 P.M. Admission: 50p; children and students, 20p. Phone: (01) 535990.

Many a tragic scene was played out for real in this gloomy, dank prison. Occupied between 1792 and 1924, it served as the last home to many political prisoners, who were executed here. A museum has been installed in the old jail to tell the story behind the cells, bars, and other forbidding remains on display here—as if just seeing them wasn't creepy enough.

Mummies under Saint Michan's Church: on Church Street next to May Lane. Tours given Monday–Friday, 10 A.M.–12:45 P.M. and 2–4:45 P.M.; and Saturday, 10 A.M.–12:45 P.M. Admission: 80p; children under 12, 40p. Phone: (01) 724154.

After a quick tour of the church (which contains an organ used by Handel), the guide leads you through creaking metal doors down into the crypt where catacombs, burial vaults, and mummies await you. Bram Stoker, whose family is buried down here, saw in this crypt the corpse of a suicide that had a wooden stake stuck in its chest (an old Irish custom to keep the soul from wandering). It is said that this was in part his inspiration for writing *Dracula*. There are no suicides here now, but there are plenty of mummified corpses on view. You can even *touch* the hand of a desiccated 900-year-old knight—for good luck. If the guide's in a cheery mood he'll even let you fondle some of the skulls and bones lying about. No one can agree why so many bodies placed down here don't decompose, but the current theory is that something in the wood of the coffins does the trick.

Mummified Cat and Mouse: in the crypt of Christ Church Cathedral, on Christchurch Road just south of the river. Entrance to the crypt is inside the cathedral at the rear of the right-hand aisle. Open May–August, Monday–Friday, 10 A.M.–5 P.M.; September–April, Tuesday–Friday, 10 A.M.–12:45 P.M. and 2:15–4:30 P.M.; Saturday, 10 A.M.–12:45 P.M. Admission: 50p; children, 25p. Phone: (01) 778099.

No one knows how the cat and mouse became trapped in the disused organ loft, but when they were finally discovered, they had been naturally mummified. The animals, probably about 150 years old, are housed in a glass case. Dry as beef jerky, they look as if death came suddenly: the cat's in mid-pounce while the mouse cowers. You'll find the glass case in a cobwebby alcove. The crypt itself reeks with that great, cool, subterranean smell.

Museum of Childhood: 20 Palmerston Park, in the Rathmines suburb. Take bus 6. Open July and August, Tuesday–Sunday, 2–5:30 P.M.; last admission at 4:45. Closed October. Rest of year open Sunday only, 2–5:30 P.M. Admission: 75p; children under 12, 50p. Phone: (01) 973223.

Two floors dedicated to children and children only, with an array of toys, dolls, and games; the museum is notable for its deliciously elaborate doll houses.

GALWAY
(County Galway)

Festival of the Tribes: every year in May or June. For current date and more information, call the Galway Tourist Office at (091) 63081.

A bit of Irish blood in the veins makes the tribal spirit run deep. Every year for three days, Galway's streets are thronged with visitors bearing the old Galway names:

Flaherty, Daly, O'Donnell, O'Shaughnessy, McHugh, McNevin (and others). People with these names are welcomed for festivities, lectures, roots research, and discovery of long-lost distant relatives. The Galway air crackles as American, British, and Australian accents blend with down-home Irish ones.

GLENEALY
(County Wicklow)

Horse-Drawn Caravans: Dieter Clissmann Horse-Drawn Caravans, Carrigmore Farm. Price: from May 2–June 19 and from August 22–September 26, Ir£250 per week; from June 20–August 21, Ir£380 per week. For more information, call (0404) 8188.

Ireland's gentler east coast is the scene for these equestrian adventures: you care for the horse, and he pulls you and your gypsy-style wagon along very obligingly, past green hills and sandy beaches. You make your own itinerary—no need to follow a set route.

GORT
(County Galway; 20 miles north of Limerick)

Coole Park with Autograph Tree: entrance is $2\frac{1}{2}$ miles north of Gort on the N18 road to Galway. Open every day, daylight hours. For more information, call the Galway Tourist Office at (091) 63081.

A huge beech tree—which has outlasted Lady Augusta Gregory's house, destroyed in 1941—bears the carved initials of many famous Irish writers. Lady Gregory, friend to W. B. Yeats, Sean O'Casey, George Bernard Shaw, Oliver Gogarty, Frank O'Connor, J. M. Synge, and others, urged her guests to leave their marks in her tree. The initials remain, surrounded by Lady Gregory's ruined walls and stables.

KILLARNEY
(County Kerry)

Transport Treasures of Ireland: located in Scotts Gardens, next to Scotts Hotel on East Avenue Road. Open March–October, daily, 10 A.M.–9 P.M. Admission: Ir£2; children, Ir£1.50. Phone: (064) 31060 or (064) 31870.

Baby carriages count as modes of transportation, too, and they stand here alongside bicycles, cars, coaches, carriages, and dozens of other notable vehicles. Some of these really are treasures in the financial sense: note the car belonging to Countess Markiewicz, and the Blue Max. Also on display is an extensive magazine collection—all the periodicals are on the subject of transportation.

KILCULLEN
(County Kildare; southwest of Dublin)

Pickled Arm at the Hideout Restaurant: in the center of Kilcullen at the intersection with the town's only traffic light. Open normal pub hours. Phone: (045) 81232.

What's that over the fireplace, amidst all the stuffed tropical animals and exotic knickknacks? Why, it looks like a human arm, but surely.... Well, yes, it actually is a human arm, the right arm of Dan Donnelly, an Irish boxing champion who defeated his English rival in a legendary 1815 match. The owners of the restaurant won't really explain why the arm is preserved and how it found its way to the restaurant; we can only recommend you read the menu very carefully, just to be sure.

KILLINABOY
(County Clare; 35 miles northwest of Limerick)

Sheila-na-gigh: over the south door of the ruined monastery. For more information, call the Ennis Tourist Office at (065) 28366.

No one knows why these exhibitionistic female figures appear, carved in stone, on old churches all over the British Isles. Naked as they are, legs and genitals spread, the Sheila-na-gighs might be vestiges of goddess-worship that managed to sneak into the decor of Catholic churches when no one was looking. Their smiles are contagious.

KILLORGLIN
(County Kerry; 15 miles west of Killarney)

Puck Fair: Every year for three days in August. For current exact dates and more information call (066) 61195 or (064) 31633.

This ancient festival finds a long-horned goat standing on a platform, wearing a gold crown, draped in purple robes, and munching greenery with a superior air as he overlooks the town. Townspeople and thousands of visitors fill the streets with music and hilarity as they pay half-serious homage to the duded-up goat known as King Puck. Modern-day revelers can only guess at the meaning of the rite.

KINVARA
(County Galway; 17 miles south of Galway city)

Medieval Banquets: at Dunguaire Castle, half a mile northeast of town. May–September, nightly at 5:45 P.M. and 9 P.M. Price: Ir£24.90. Phone: (061) 61788 or (091) 37108.

The castle itself, perched beside deep-blue Galway Bay, inspires flights of fevered poetry. The banquet here features costumed actors performing snippets of Ireland's most Irish drama and poetry, including works of local literati Yeats, Lady Gregory, Synge, and Oliver Gogarty (who used to own the place).

LISDOONVARNA
(County Clare; 40 miles northwest of Limerick)

Matchmaking Festival: Every year for three weeks in September. For more information, call (065) 74005.

In the old days, exhausted farmers used to head for this spa town after the annual harvest, in search of rest and romance. Now it's a large-scale, organized event, harvest or not. Women come from all over the world in search of a Paddy or Mike to call their own, and professional matchmakers are busy as bees for the duration of the festival. Of course it's all in fun and there are no guarantees, but many a lifelong romance has been sparked at Lisdoonvarna.

LOUGH GUR
(County Limerick; 12 miles southeast of Limerick)

Prehistoric Site and Interpretation Center: off the R512 road to Kilmallock. Open May–September, Monday–Saturday, 10 A.M.–1 P.M. and 2–6 P.M. Closed Sunday. Admission: Ir£1.20; children, 75p; students and seniors, 85p. Phone: (061) 85186 or (061) 317522. Guided walking tours available.

If you want to hear the ancient stones speak, this is the place. Stone Age men and women thrived on the shores of crescent-shaped Lough Gur, and the area is rich in prehistoric leavings: stone circles, standing stones, dolmens, stone burial chambers, artificial islands, cairns, and the like. The stone circle, 140 feet in diameter, is Ireland's largest, and dates from 2000 B.C. The Interpretation Center, modeled on a neolithic house, presents artifacts and films, cajoling those Stone Agers to live again.

MURRISK
(County Mayo; six miles southwest of Westport)

Croagh Patrick Mountain-Climbing Pilgrimage: on Croagh Patrick. To get there, take bus 264 from Westport to Murrisk. The ascent takes at least an hour. Held every year on the last Sunday in July. Pilgrimage begins at dawn and lasts all day. For more information, call the Westport Tourist Office at (098) 25711.

Ireland's beloved St. Patrick spent 40 days on this mountain in 441 A.D., fasting for Lent. That's the explanation given by most of the 60,000 pilgrims who annually climb the rocky, slippery 2,510-foot peak. Their distant ancestors celebrated an important harvest festival—Lughnasa—by climbing the mountain at this time of year. Hmmm. At any rate, the pilgrimage is a spectacle; Croagh Patrick is a mist-wreathed cone rising by the sea, swarming with determined climbers. Priests celebrate mass all day at the top of the mountain; those who make the climb barefoot pray the loudest of all.

QUIN
(County Clare; 15 miles northwest of Limerick)

Craggaunowen Project: six miles east of Quin off the Sixmilebridge/Quin road. Open April–October, daily, 10 A.M.–6 P.M. Admission: Ir£2; children, Ir£1.20. Phone: (061) 72178.

In the shadow of the castle stand homes of a far more ancient kind: cross a wooden bridge to the Bronze Age crannóg, an artificial island constructed for safety purposes, with reed houses on it. Also on the castle grounds are a reconstructed fourth-century A.D. farmhouse and an ancient "kitchen" (*fulachta fiadha*), where you can still see people grinding grain the old-fashioned way and preparing ancient recipes. Yet another prized historical tidbit on display is "Brendan," the animal-skin boat in which Irishman Tim Severin recently recreated St. Brendan the Navigator's amazing sixth-century A.D. voyage to North America (don't tell Christopher Columbus).

Medieval Banquets: at Knappogue Castle. May–September, nightly at 5:45 P.M. and 9 P.M. Price: Ir£24.90. Phone: (061) 61788.

The entire history of Ireland passes before your eyes in the course of a single meal. As diners sit at long, long tables, an array of musicians, mimes, actors, and storytellers cavort about the hall, telling Ireland's romantic, poetic, heart-rending life story.

THURLES
(County Tipperary; 36 miles east of Limerick)

Piece of the True Cross in Holy Cross Abbey: four miles directly south of Thurles on the west bank of the Suir River. Open daily, 9 A.M.–8 P.M. Admission: free. Phone: (0504) 43241 or (0504) 43118.

This isn't called the Holy Cross Abbey for nothing: here, inside a seven-inch-tall silver cross, is a piece of the True Cross. It's on display on the left side of the main altar in the Abbey Church. Eight hundred years ago this was the object of huge pilgrimages. Now, after traveling around a bit, the piece of the True Cross is back in its own abbey, but the number of pilgrims has dropped off considerably.

TRALEE
(County Kerry)

Horse-Drawn Caravans: Slattery's Horse-Drawn Caravan Centre, Lisardboula, Farmer's Bridge, Tralee. Price: May 3–June 19, Ir£200 per week; June 20–August 21, Ir£240 per week. Shorter stints also available. Phone: (066) 22364.

As if living in a gypsy wagon weren't exotic enough, this company's routes lead you along the Dingle Peninsula, one of Ireland's most actively Gaelic-speaking regions. The horse does most of the work; this is more economically sound than a Winnebago vacation.

ITALY

Legend:
1. Genoa
2. Milan
3. Verona
4. Venice
5. Bologna
6. Ascoli Piceno
7. Perugia
8. Arezzo
9. Florence
10. Siena
11. Pisa
12. Viterbo
13. Rome
14. Naples
15. Brindisi
16. Reggio di Calabria
17. Messina
18. Palermo
19. Trapani
20. Gubbio

Kidnap 100 historians. Lock them in a room. Tell them you won't let them out until they can all agree on one country as the most influential in the world's history. What will be their choice? Without a doubt: Italy. Other countries may have their moments of glory, but in the end they all fade.

Italy / 189

Italy's greatness has stamina. The Etruscan civilization was the most advanced in Europe for its time. During the Roman Republic, the Italians developed democracy, revolutionized architecture, and colonized half of Europe. During the Roman Empire, Italy was the center of the known world—politically, economically, and intellectually. The Italian monks of the Middle Ages transcribed and preserved ancient written knowledge—their enduring legacy to the post-Roman world. The geniuses of the Italian Renaissance are too numerous to mention. Italian inventors of the eighteenth and nineteenth centuries, by explaining the concepts of electricity and radio, helped usher in the age of science. And in the twentieth century: Sophia Loren. Need we say more?

So it's understandable that the modern Italians are simply Not Impressed. They glance wearily at enthusiastic tourists and think, "If we Italians hadn't civilized your ancestors, you'd all still be barbarians." And they are probably right. The Italians don't need to be reminded of their glorious history; they know it so well, they are practically bored by it.

A land with so much history is heaven for tourists. Nearly everything in the country is worth a visit. And that makes the search for unusual attractions difficult. It's like trying to find the one tortellino in a bowl of ravioli. Italy has plenty of strange things lurking in plain sight: easy to see, hard to recognize. Hopefully this chapter will show you not just where to look, but how.

Oops—those historians must be getting hungry. Where did I put that key?

NORTH

AREZZO

Joust of the Saracen (Giostra del Saracino): first Sunday in September, in the Piazza Grande, behind the Santa Maria della Pieve Church.

For some reason, the towns of central Italy have an uncontrollable urge to relive their medieval and Renaissance pasts with jousts and palios (horse races). In this ferociously nostalgic festival, horsemen chosen from the city's four neighborhoods joust with a wooden, stationary but armed Saracen figure, undoubtedly reenacting some heroic battle against invading Saracens centuries ago. The jousting is dangerous and requires a great deal of skill. All of this is done in medieval dress, with lots of flag-waving, parades, and celebration before and after the joust.

ASCOLI PICENO

Giostra della Quintana: in Piazza del Popolo. First Sunday in August, in the afternoon.

Part of Ascoli Piceno's medieval Quintana Festival is a human chess game: each piece is represented by an actor in a fifteenth-century costume. The main square is divided to create a life-size chessboard. For the best view of the game, get a seat in one of the windows in the buildings that surround the piazza.

COLLODI
(30 miles northwest of Florence)

Pinocchio Park (Parco di Pinocchio): 50 yards from the town square. To reach Collodi, take a Lazzi bus from Florence to Pescia, and from there take local bus 1 to Collodi. Open daily 8 A.M.–7:30 P.M. Admission: L 3000; children 3–10, L 2500; children under 3, free. Phone: (0572) 429 342.

Carlo Collodi used this village's name as his pseudonym, and in 1956 the village returned the favor by building a park dedicated to Collodi's most famous character, Pinocchio. Visitors to the park's Paese dei Balocchi section stroll past modernistic bronze sculptures illustrating scenes from the book. These sculptures are the stuff of troubled dreams: rabbit pallbearers haul a Pinocchio-sized coffin; a coiled serpent leers menacingly, and the Blue Fairy has a gaping hole in her chest. Also in the park are a big shark fountain, a deceptively innocent-looking maze, a moody pirate's lair, and mosaics depicting still more scenes from *Pinocchio*.

Pinocchio Park—Shark Fountain: This immense dome-shaped shark sculpture, sitting in its own little sea, is as big as a house, with double rows of teeth, bulging eyes, and skin patterned with artistically broken bottle glass. He spurts water out of his blowhole (Whale? Shark? It seems even Carlo Collodi was confused), spraying mist on anyone who happens to be crossing his sea on its cement lily pads. Climb inside the fish and see poor Gepetto waiting to be rescued.

FLORENCE (FIRENZE)

Lombardo Taxidermy and Embalming Shop (Imbalsamazione Lombardo): via della Scala 34r. Open normal business hours. Phone: 216 960. Enter through the computer store next door.

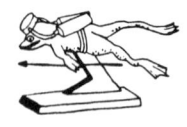

"Darling, your hall closet is *crashingly* drab. You simply *must* send away for one of those deer-foot coat racks." And the Lombardo Taxidermy Shop is the place to get it. If you tire of hanging your coat from wild-animal hooves, you can always come back for a stuffed frog decked out with a tiny snorkel, mask, and rubber swim fins; a leaping baby mule; a mounted shark face; or a simple, unadorned yak tail.

Santa Maria Novella Pharmacy (Officina Profumo Farmaceutica de Santa Maria Novella de Firenze): via della Scala 16, a three-minute walk from the train station. Open Monday–Friday, 8:30 A.M.–12:25 P.M. and 3–6:55 P.M. Closed Saturday and Sunday.

Have you ever had a strange dream about buying seasickness pills in an art museum? The world's oldest still-functioning pharmacy has frescoed walls and ceilings, stained-glass windows, statuary, and paintings by the Italian masters. Associated since the Middle Ages with the monks of nearby Santa Maria Novella Church, the pharmacy has occupied its present location since 1612. Medicines and perfumes for sale here are still made according to recipes developed by monks in the seventeenth century.

Pratolino Sculpture Garden: north of the city on via Bolognese. Take city bus 25 from in front of the train station. (The ride takes half an hour.) Open weekends only, 9 A.M.–7 P.M. Admission: L 2000. On the evenings of June 2 and July 25 (or the weekends nearest them), admission is L 3000. Concerts usually begin at 5:30 P.M. For program of events call 055/2760524-526.

There's more to Pratolino than romance and concerts under the stars. There's also the thrill that goes down your spine as you blink up at the park's star attraction, a glowering, towering sculpture of a man, carved out of a natural rock outcropping. "Appenino" is almost as big as the mountains for which he is named. His beard is a jagged cascade of stone; and one leg, uncarved below the knee, waits forever to turn from mountain into man.

GUBBIO

Palio of Archers (Palio della Balestra): last Sunday in May. In the courtyard of the Palazzo dei Consoli, between via Baldassini and via dei Consoli. Call 927 36 93 for exact time of competition, which varies from year to year.

Go watch this event, if only to see dozens of full-grown Italian men in multicolored leotards and miniskirts. These medieval costumes are part of an all-medieval day in which Gubbio invites a team of archers from the nearby city of Sansepolcro for a head-to-head, miniskirt-to-miniskirt archery competition. And it's not bows they use, but medieval *balestre*, stationary mounted crossbows which, except for this competition, now exist only in museums. Before and after the competition, there are parades and parties throughout the town.

LUCCA
(10 miles northeast of Pisa)

Santa Zita's Mummy: in the Basilica of San Frediano, at the northern edge of the city. The mummy is in an alcove to the right of the main entrance.

Zita was a poor child of Lucca, a servant in one of the city's wealthiest households, eventually canonized for her devotion to helping other poor people. Now her preserved body lies in a glass case, clothed in a blue satin gown and lace veil that are probably far nicer than what she wore in life. What grabs your attention first is not her clothes, it's her sunken cheeks and the brown hands folded across her chest. Fine clothes always look their most decadent on a mummy.

PERUGIA

Underground City: via Baglioni Sotteranea. Call 075 233 27 for current hours.

Under Perugia's streets, inside the hill, is a city that never sees the light of day. Starting 500 years ago, people began to build new houses on top of the old ones (due to quirks in the city's hilly layout), and before long the street level was 40 feet or more higher than it used to be. The old city, naturally entombed, has survived intact to this day. Its main drag is via Baglioni Sotteranea (which means "subterranean"), underneath part of the modern via Marza, where there is an entrance. But there are other areas too, reachable by stairs, tunnels, and escalators, with entrances too numerous to mention.

PESCIA
(12 miles east of Lucca)

Urinating Statue: at western end of the train station.

This little lad is about as risqué as they get here in the modest little town of Pescia. The train station mascot, only one and a half feet tall, relieves himself into his own pool, oblivious of the passing trains.

PISA

Battle of the Bridge (Gioco del Ponte): yearly on June 28. Battle takes place on the Ponte di Mezzo (between Piazza Garibaldi and Piazza XX Settembre) at 6:30 P.M., and is preceded by a costumed parade (Sfilata Storica) through the streets of town at 4:30 P.M. For more information, call 56 04 64.

Nowadays you'll see residents of all parts of Pisa acting darned civil to each other. But their forebears weren't so free with the handshakes. The rough-and-tumble Gioco del Ponte re-enacts old rivalries between the Mezzogiorno neighborhood south of the Arno River and the Tramontana district north of the Arno. The battlers show off their sixteenth-century costumes in a parade, then proceed to get leotards and tunics hopelessly dirty in the fight as onlookers cheer their own neighborhoods—for old times' sake.

PONTEDASSIO
(Four miles north of Imperia, on the Riviera)

Spaghetti Museum (Museo Storico degli Spaghetti): via Garibaldi 96. Buses run to Pontedassio from Imperia-Oneglia (bus station is next to the train station); the ride takes 15 minutes. Open Wednesday, 10 A.M.–noon and 6–8 P.M.; Saturday, 10 A.M.–noon; and by appointment. Admission: L 2000. Phone: (0183) 64.617 or (0183) 650.421.

This museum would like to shake everybody by the shoulders and yell this message at them: pasta was Italy's own invention. The guide will proudly show you a copy of an Italian manuscript that mentions pasta many years before Marco Polo left for China. Other displays show seventeenth-century noodle-making machinery; photographs of old-time pasta factories (with yards and yards of lasagna hung out to dry in the sun like wet laundry). A diorama shows Marco Polo at a Chinese banquet. "They're eating noodles, *too*," the explorer exclaims, "just as we do at home!" Best of all is the exhibit on obscure pasta shapes.

SARZANA
(35 miles northwest of Pisa)

Holy Blood: displayed the first Friday of every month at 5 P.M. in the Santa Maria Church.

Only for a short time each month is it possible to see Sarzana's pride and joy, a small reliquary containing some drops of Jesus' blood. After a half-hour showing in Santa Maria, a mass is held in honor of the relic, after which it is secreted away for another month.

SIENA

Palio of Siena: in the Piazza del Campo, July 2 and August 16.

Whole books have been written about the wild Palio of Siena. On one hand, it's just a simple horse race. On the other, it's intra-city warfare tempered by a dizzying set of rules, a series of ancient pagan rituals, and a fantastic mob scene. If you want to see this, the most famous of palios, we recommend two things: do some research beforehand so you can make sense of the madness; and commute from a nearby city (such as Florence or Arezzo), since rooms in Siena during the Palio are reserved up to a year in advance.

VIAREGGIO
(15 miles north of Pisa, on the coast)

Carnival (Carnevale): most of the action (parades, fireworks) takes place on the Promenade and other streets closest to the beach. Yearly, in the days immediately preceding Ash Wednesday. For more information, call the Carnival Commission at 42568.

Italy's own Mardi Gras has floats that are huge and hilarious, each one made up of dozens of figures. The Italian knack for color and design is at its most flamboyant as these elephantine pirates, dancing girls, and animals glide down the street. Carnival in Viareggio also features madcap masked parades and, on the final night, fireworks exploding in the sky over the beach where Percy Bysshe Shelley drowned.

ROME AND ENVIRONS

ANZIO
(36 miles south of Rome, on the coast)

Big Fish Fry: yearly, during August. To reach Anzio from Rome, take a train or Acotral bus from via Tito Labiero in Rome. For exact date and location, call 98.46.119.

Anzio gets so excited about the abundance of a local fish called *pesce azzuro* (blue fish) that sometime during August every year the town holds a festival in the fish's honor. But the guest of honor is also on the menu, as *pesci azzuri* are consumed in huge quantities. For the occasion, the people haul out a Herculean frying pan many feet in diameter (*padellone al borgo marinaro*) that is used only for this purpose. Nero, Anzio's famous native son, would have loved this.

BOLSENA
(55 miles northwest of Rome)

The Mysteries of Santa Cristina (I Misteri di Santa Cristina): yearly on July 23–24. Santa Cristina's Eve procession (July 23) begins at 10 P.M.; the procession the following day begins at 10 A.M. For more information, call 34.79.5.

The residents of Bolsena believe they would be pagans to this day were it not for Santa Cristina, whose father, the local Roman prefect, tortured and eventually killed her for her Christian beliefs. Now every year the people of Bolsena perform Cristina's story. Dressed in period costume, the actors proceed through the streets of town, stopping at intervals so that the girl portraying Cristina can act out her tortures: being boiled in oil, stretched on a Catherine wheel, bitten by snakes, etc. Half the tortures are performed the first night, the other half on the following day.

BOMARZO
(45 miles north of Rome)

Bomarzo Monster Park (Parco dei Mostri): one mile northwest of the city. A marked road leads to the park from the northern edge of town. To get to Bomarzo, take a train to Attigliano (three miles from Bomarzo), and then a local bus. Open daylight hours. Admission: L 3500; children 6–10, L 3000; children 2–5, L 2500. Phone: 0761/4202.

This, the largest conglomeration of huge grotesque sculptures this side of Easter Island, was created in the sixteenth century by Pier Francesco Orsini, a local nobleman. The park, also known as The Sacred Grove (*Sacro Bosco*), has—in addition to dozens of other horrifying monsters—giants attacking people; dragons; rampaging elephants; mysterious, sinister deities; a house of optical illusions, and "Mascherone," a vast monstrous head whose gaping mouth is framed by a dire warning carved in Latin. Around every corner is another heart-stopping scene and another wry Latin epigram.

CAPRANICA PRENESTINA
(35 miles east of Rome)

Animal and Machinery Blessing: January 17, in the center of town. Acotral buses depart for Capranica Prenestina from the end of Via Cavour in Rome, near the Termini train station.

It's a ritual as old as agriculture: the yearly blessing of domestic work animals to ensure their well-being in the upcoming year. Nowadays, though, even in the secluded hills east of Rome, modernization has set in, so the local priest blesses tractors, threshers, and other farm machines along with the animals.

FRASCATI
(13 miles east of Rome)

Three-Breasted Cakes (Pupazze): to reach Frascati, take an Acotral bus from Piazzale di Cinecittà in Rome. For futher information, call (06) 94.20.331.

Frascati has been home to sophisticated villa-dwellers since Cicero's time. Still, there's no denying the downright pagan earthiness of the city's traditional honey cakes. They're baked in the shape of people and animals, and the ones shaped like women invariably sport three breasts. The favorite local theory about the triply endowed cakes is that they used to be eaten as fertility charms. Pick up a few at a Frascati pastry shop and see what happens.

GENZANO
(18 miles south of Rome)

Festival of Flowers (Infiorata): takes place along via Berardi every year during Corpus Christi, usually in early to mid-June. Acotral buses run to Genzano from in front of Rome's Cinecittà metro stop. For exact date, call 92.21.323 or 93.20.298.

For two weeks before the festival day, women and children gather $4\frac{1}{2}$ tons of fresh flowers in the nearby fields, then separate them according to color. Other townspeople design the patterns which, on the day of the festival, will be laid out entirely in petals along the main street of Genzano. The actual spreading of the flowers on festival day takes only a few hours, as the whole town cooperates, with practiced precision. Thirty-foot-by-60-foot religious scenes, words, emblems, and even huge pictures of flowers carpet the street, looking like vast soft paintings. Late in the day, a procession travels down the flower-strewn street.

MONTECOMPATRI
(16 miles east of Rome)

Mummy: in St. Sylvester Church, at the shrine of St. Sylvester, one mile from the city, up Monte Salomone. Acotral buses run to Montecompatri from Rome's Cinecittà metro stop. For more information, call 94.20.331.

In Egypt the mummies—even the mummies of royalty—wear only plain linen. Italy, though, is a fashionable place, so the mummies get to wear fine silk. The pious Giovanni di Gesù e Maria, now dead for 370 years, lies here in his finery for all the world to see.

NETTUNO
(35 miles south of Rome)

Santa Maria Goretti's Mummy: at Santa Maria della Grazie shrine. Nettuno is accessible by train or by Acotral bus, which departs from in front of Rome's Subaugusta metro stop.

Also known as the Virgin of the Swamp (Vergine della Palude), Maria Goretti was a pre-teen from Ancona who in 1902 was attacked by a would-be rapist, a neighbor boy. When Maria tried to defend herself, the boy stabbed her to death. Now she is seen as both a heroine and a victim of the poverty in which her family lived. Her preserved body, looking childishly rounded, is on display near Nettuno. It is an object of pilgrimage every July 6.

ROME

Catacombs of Priscilla: via Salaria 430, near Villa Ada (but not *in* Villa Ada, as most city maps indicate). Ring the doorbell. Open 8:30 A.M.–noon and 2:30 P.M.–5 P.M., Tuesday–Sunday. Closed Monday. Admission: L 3000. Guided tours only (guide speaks English).

Dating back to the middle of the second century, these are the oldest catacombs in Rome. So says the tour guide, a frail nun wearing a hooded down jacket over her habit. Among the things you get to inspect are a third-century tomb with a series of paintings of a Roman lady—at her wedding, her husband's funeral, and finally her own funeral; the oldest known painting of the Virgin Mary; and walls honeycombed with empty tombs, a great many of them child-sized. Electric lights make Priscilla the luxury spot among catacombs.

Catacombs of San Lorenzo: in Basilica di San Lorenzo, a few yards west of Piazzale San Lorenzo, off via Tiburtina on the western edge of the city. Open daily, 3:30–6:30 P.M. Admission: free, but donation suggested at end of tour. Tours every 30 minutes.

The guide here knows a smattering—and only a smattering—of every language under the sun, and enthusiastically points out the sites at San Lorenzo in what might be called pidgin Esperanto. Before you know it, he'll have you reading Latin inscriptions on the tombstones taken from the catacombs and set into the cloister walls. Then the tour goes underground to the catacombs, where you can see the pick-marks of ancient tunnel-diggers, tombs broken open by medieval looters, heart-wrenching children's skeletons, and unexplained passages leading off to who knows where.

Catacombs of Sant' Agnesi Fuori le Mura: via Nomentana 349. Door is on the left inside wall of the church as you enter. Open Monday–Saturday, 9 A.M.–12:30 P.M. and 3:30–6 P.M.; Sunday, 3:30–6 P.M. Admission: L 2000.

Guided tours in Italian only.

The catacombs of Sant' Agnesi Fuori le Mura ("Saint Agnes Outside the Walls") are among the most confusing in all of Rome. Although the tour only covers a small area of the miles and miles of catacombs here, the parts covered are impressive enough: dark passageways barely wide enough for one person, hidden cul-de-sacs containing second-century tombs and bones, and a variety of spooky nooks and crannies. Would you let a weird old man with a flashlight lead you down pitch-dark underground tunnels? Sure you would.

Cemetery of the Capuchin Monks (Cimitero dei Cappuccini): side entrance of the Chiesa Immacolata Concezione, via Veneto 27. Open daily, 9 A.M.–noon and 3–6:30 P.M. Admission: voluntary donation.

Hooded mummies and the bones of 2,000 Capuchin brothers are arranged in the shapes of arches, wheels, and flowers. Each of the rooms has a fantastic array, with cowled mummies posed here and there for added drama. Lamps made of shoulder bones hang overhead, lighting your way. One room is done mostly in scapulas and vertebrae. In the last room, a princess' skeleton stares down from the ceiling, brandishing a sickle and a pair of scales.

Criminal Museum: via Giulia 52, one block from the river, just northwest of Isola Tibertina. Used to be open Sunday only, 9 A.M.–noon, but has been undergoing remodeling. For current hours, prices, and other information, call the Rome Information Office, at 463.748.

We were lured to the Criminal Museum by promises of bloodstained guillotines, the relics of Mussolini's murdered mistress, a whole room dedicated to suicide. In all of passionate Rome, this seemed the goriest corner of all. But we arrived to find the museum closed for remodeling, due to reopen by the beginning of 1988. See you there.

Exotarium: downstairs below the main train station, in the Termini metro stop. Open daily, 8 A.M.–9 P.M. Admission: L 4000; students, L 2000.

The large single room is filled mainly with reptiles—poisonous frogs, exotic turtles, mini-crocodiles, dozens of

Rome and Environs / 201

> ## Ice Cream
>
> The Italians make the best ice cream in the world. Italian strawberry gelato tastes more like strawberries than a strawberry. Luckily, strawberry isn't their only flavor. That's just the tip of the ice-cream-berg. They have imparted into ice cream such flavors as have never even flitted across the American culinary imagination. While we Americans vary our ice cream flavor range by concocting unwieldy combinations of the basics ("Chocolate-Mocha-Nut-Fudge-Caramel-Swirl"), the Italians broaden their flavor horizons with unlimited numbers of pure tastes. The following sampling of Italian ice cream flavors should pique your interest: papaya, marzipan, chestnut, fig, popcorn, kiwi, whisky, rhubarb, pear, watermelon, sherry, mare azzuro (bubblegum), cassis, malaga wine, peanut, smurf (creme soda), rice, chocolate rice, mulberry, crenshaw melon, cream, nougat, hazelnut.

snakes—with the added bonus of funny dinosaur mockups (one has a stegosaurus battling a mammoth), snake skeletons, and stuffed piranhas. If you're stuck at the train station with a couple of hours to kill, a visit to the Exotarium beats bench-warming.

Holy Relics: in Church of the Holy Cross in Jerusalem (Chiese San Croce in Gerusalemme), in Piazza San Croce in Gerusalemme, southeast of the train station. Open normal church hours. Admission: free. The holy relics are all housed in the Capella della Croce; entrance is on the left wall at the far end of the church.

This chapel holds more physical remnants of Jesus' last day on earth than does any other single place. Six reliquaries are displayed at eye-level in the chapel, all clearly visible. They are:

1. In the center, in a cruciform reliquary, three large hunks of the True Cross (one about seven inches long and two about four inches long, each) that, combined, are the largest portion of the True Cross in any one spot;

2. On the right, two vicious-looking thorns from the Crown of Thorns;

3. On the left, in a finger-shaped reliquary, the index finger with which St. Thomas the Apostle touched Jesus' side in his final moments;

4. On the lower left, a five-inch nail from the True Cross;

5. In the lower middle, a piece of the sign on the cross that read: "Iesus Nazarenus Rex Iudaeorum" (all that is visible here is part of "Nazarenus");

6. In the lower right corner, a Holy Miscellany–a piece of the Pillar of Scourging, a rock from the Stable of Bethlehem, and fragments of the Holy Sepulchre.

Holy Stairs (Scala Santa): housed in a wide sixteenth-century building in Piazza di Porta San Giovanni, diagonally across from the Basilica of San Giovanni Laterano. Open daily, 6:30 A.M.–12:30 P.M. and 3:30–7 P.M.. Admission: viewing is free, but a small donation is suggested if you want to climb the stairs. Stairs are most popular (i.e., most crowded) on Fridays during Lent.

These steps are allegedly from Pontius Pilate's own house, and Jesus ascended and descended them several times. Brought to Rome in 326 and installed in this location in 1589, the marble stairs have brown stains, allegedly Jesus' bloodstains, visible through glass windows set in the wooden covering. For Romans, climbing the Scala Santa is a pilgrimage, but strict rules apply: all climbing must be done on the knees; and once you start an ascent, you cannot turn back. A duplicate staircase was recently built next to the original Scala Santa to avoid knee-traffic jams.

Museum of the Souls of the Dead (Museo delle Anime dei Difunti): Lungotevere Prati 12. Museum is located inside the Sacred Heart of Suffrage Church (Chiesa del Sacro Cuore del Suffragio), directly across the street from the Tiber on the west side of the river. Open 6:30 A.M.–12:30 P.M. and 5–6:30 P.M. Ask the sacristan to let you in and to give you the typed information sheet in English. Admission: free. Phone: 654.05.17.

After seeing this museum—actually a single glass case in an alcove—you'll never be quite sure of anything again. The relics here are alleged proof that souls waiting impatiently in Purgatory will occasionally reach from their world into ours with burning hands to hasten their loved ones' prayers. Burned hand- and fingerprints on bedclothes, books, and shirtsleeves, left by the ghostly, urgent hands of dead souls and dating as far back as 1696, rank as Rome's most unsettling enigmas.

Six-Hour Clock: in the courtyard of Palazzo Conservatore at Borgo S. Spirito 3, just in front of the Vatican.

Few people know that when French revolutionaries adopted the metric system, they also declared that all clocks have 12 hours on them and that the big hand should go around twice each day. Before 1789, clock designs were left to the whim of clockmakers. Here, in front of the Palazzo Conservatore, you can see an extremely rare pre-Revolution six-hour clock, whose hand must go around *four* times a day. They just don't make 'em like they used to.

Taberna Ulpia: Piazza Foro Traiano 2 (between Trajan's Baths and the Forum). Open nightly except Sundays. Phone: 67.96.271 or 67.89.980.

After viewing the staid columns and stolid, no-nonsense architecture left behind by the ancient Romans, you might think there was no word in Latin for "whoopee." But there is: it's *"evohe,"* and that's what is painted on the wall at Taberna Ulpia. Ancient-Roman-style whoopee has been the basic idea here since 1880. The waiters wear togas; the decor would have been in style 2,000 years ago; the menu includes such Bacchanalian indulgences as fusilli alla vodka; and the writing on the wall also urges *"Bibe!"* ("Drink!").

Traffic Blessing: traffic circle around the Coliseum. March 1, 11 A.M.

This city of daredevil drivers is lucky to have the annual auto blessing. Every year on Santa Francesca Romana's feast day, a priest stands in a prominent (and safe) place on the sidewalk and blesses each passing car and its driver.

Wax Museum: Piazza Venezia 67 (near Piazza S.S. Apostoli). Open daily, 9 A.M.–8 P.M. Admission: L 2000; children, L 1200. Phone: 67.96.482.

The Louvre has the Venus de Milo, the Florence Accademia has Michelangelo's David, and the Rome Wax Museum has ... I Pooh. Just who are I Pooh? An extremely popular Italian rock band who remain completely obscure outside of Italy. Yet you'd think they were the new Beatles if you saw all the pomp and fanfare surrounding the unveiling of their duplicates at the Wax Museum. "The Pooh" are now the museum's pride and joy, overshadowing every other important personage in the place.

Wax Museum Annex: Piazza della Repubblica 12, near the train station. Open daily, 9 A.M.–9 P.M. Admission: L 2000. Phone: 06/47.51.509.

Famous Italian inventors, popes, and noble people, fashioned a little less hyper-realistically than the Pietà, wait patiently for you under spooky red lights. Incredibly bad portraits line the walls, forming the backdrop to such scenes as a political summit in which Kruschev grins like a maniac, sporting Dumbo ears. On a chair nearby, a bearded wax figure who resembles Vincent Price bears a placard with the startling inscription, "Lincoln Abramo."

Wild Cats: in ruins and archaeological sites throughout the city.

The real inheritors of the Roman Empire are the city's 150,000 wild, ownerless cats, who have essentially taken over the main Roman ruins. The Coliseum cats are the most famous, but there are just as many prowling all the forums on Palatine Hill, the Domus Aurea, the Baths of Caracalla, and other ruins, parks, and unoccupied areas in the center of Rome. Cats are naturally nocturnal, so they're most active at night. But there are plenty up and about in the early morning and late afternoon too. You can join Rome's cat ladies (*mamme dei gatti*) by bringing some scraps of food or some milk, and paying the furry Romans a visit.

World's Largest Wine Glass: at Trimani Wine Shop, via Goito 20; on display in the window. Visible anytime.

Rome is full of superlatives—the oldest this, the rarest that. It can be overwhelming. The time may come when you feel like seeing a more light-hearted—or, in this case, light-headed—Roman superlative. Made in 1980 in Murano, a city famed for its glassworks, the world's largest wine glass stands an intoxicating four feet tall, and could hold enough *vino* to satisfy the most decadent of emperors.

SANTA MARINELLA
(38 miles west of Rome, on the coast)

Festival of the Sea (Sagra del Mare): August 15. Acotral buses leave for Santa Marinella from Rome's via Lepanto. You can also take a train. For more information, call (0766) 737.376.

Among other seaside activities, this festival features the consumption of hundreds of pounds of very fresh fish, cooked in giant frying pans (ten feet in diameter). While they're showing their gratitude to Neptune, the Santa Marinellans aren't stingy: fried fish are distributed free to all takers.

SARACINESCO
(33 miles east of Rome)

The Men of Saracinesco: Acotral buses run to Saracinesco from Rome's viale Castro Pretorio.

Looking for a few good men? For several hundred years, the Italians have believed that tiny Saracinesco produces the best-looking males in all of Italy. Artists in search of models have traditionally headed for Saracinesco, which is named for the allegedly handsome band of Saracens who founded the town in the ninth century A.D.

TIVOLI
(20 miles east of Rome)

Villa d'Este: at the southern edge of the city. Acotral buses run to Tivoli from Rome's Piazza Cinquecento. You can also take a train. Open Tuesday–Sunday, 9 A.M. to one hour before sunset. April–October, open later at night for illuminated fountain performances. Admission: L 5000. Phone: (0774) 22.070 or (0774) 21.249.

A product of Renaissance brainstorming, Villa d'Este squirts and spurts like a water balloon thrown at a porcupine. Along the Avenue of One Hundred Fountains (*Viale delle Cento Fontane*) stone flowers, animals, and birds squirt cool jets. In the Organ Fountain, water power activates organ music. The Owl Fountain performs birdcalls; another fountain toots like a horn. Rometta, on the top level of Villa d'Este's fountain area, is an abbreviated, watery version of Rome, with miniature ruins and Roman landmarks—and a miniature Tiber, of course.

VITERBO
(40 miles northwest of Rome)

Procession of Santa Rosa's Tower (Macchina di Santa Rosa): yearly on September 3, beginning at 9 P.M. Procession starts at the Roman Gate (Porta Romana) at the southern edge of town and continues to the Church of Santa Rosa. Procession halts en route to rest at Piazza Fontana Grande, at Piazza del Plebiscito, at Suffragio Church, and at Piazza Verdi. For more information, call (0761) 226.666.

Viterbo's tower of Santa Rosa is a sky-scraping 100 feet tall and weighs over four tons, topped with a figure of the saint and studded with lighted candles. Every year, in a ritual so dangerous that the church has disclaimed it, a group of 100 men standing shoulder-to-shoulder lift, carry, and finally run with the towering, ungainly structure. This event is said to recall a medieval procession in which the body of St. Rose was carried through the town.

SOUTH

CALATFINI and SALEMI
(On Sicily, 18 miles east of Trapani and six miles from each other)

Bread Sculpture Festival: every year on the feast day of St. Joseph (San Giuseppe), March 19. For more information, call (0923) 27273.

Food, faith, and folk art merge when these villages honor St. Joseph. Both men and women do the baking and carving. The end result is thousands of loaves of all sizes, not only in the shapes of Mary, the baby Jesus, and Joseph—but also fish, angels, cats, butterflies, flowers, lambs, doves, and many other votive motifs. Some of the loaves weigh nearly 20 pounds. A procession through the streets of town—with the bread—is followed by a full day of festivities.

FAVIGNANA
(An islet 10 miles southwest of Trapani, at the western end of Sicily)

Tuna Massacre (Mattanza): every year, for several days in

late May. For exact dates and directions, call (0923) 27273.

All fantasies about the carefree life of the fish in the sea go right out the porthole when you see the Favignana fishermen in action. For the *mattanza*, they build special tuna corrals. Once the fish become trapped in these labyrinths, the fishermen haul them up by the hundreds while singing ancient chants to their patron saint, Peter. Then the tuna, which are nearly as large as their captors, are pounded and clubbed to death. Italians, who find the bloody *mattanza* a powerfully beautiful event, believe the practice is a legacy of medieval Arab traditions.

MESSINA
(On the eastern tip of Sicily)

Fata Morgana Mirage: across the strait of Messina on hot afternoons.

Mirages are so transient and unpredictable, you wouldn't think it was possible to assign one an address and opening hours. Yet here is a mirage that recurs consistently. Where? You can see it along the Sicilian coast south of the city of Messina, looking across the strait toward the Calabrian coast of mainland Italy. It is best to be on a promontory at sea level—or, even better, in a boat off the Sicilian coast. When? On hot, sunny, cloudless days in the early afternoon. (The hottest days are the best.) What? A shimmering city in the sky, impressive enough to terrify the ancients, become a part of medieval legend, and baffle modern scientists.

Parade of the Giganti: in the streets of Messina on August 15.

As the climax of an annual three-day festival, the Messinians haul out the immense statues of Mata and Grifone, the legendary couple who founded the city, and give them their yearly exercise. The *giganti* are aptly named—so big that they would draw comment were they included in the Macy's Thanksgiving Day Parade.

World's Largest Astronomical Clock: in the Piazza del Duomo. Performances daily at noon, with an abbreviated version hourly, at 15 minutes past the hour.

At the stroke of noon, a golden lion rears up and roars, thus setting in motion one of Italy's most entertaining free shows. A rooster flaps his wings and crows, a dove flies, and a model church rises slowly from the ground. Figures of famous men salute the Virgin Mary, and Jesus pops out of his tomb while golden ladies ring the church bells and "Ave Maria" floats out above the noise of the traffic. As if this were not enough, the right-hand side of the tower provides the date, year, phase of the moon and location of the planets.

PALERMO
(On Sicily)

Catacombs of the Capuchin Monks: under the Cappuccini convent in Piazza Cappuccini, on the southern edge of the city. Open daily, 9 A.M.–noon, and some afternoons in summer. Admission: voluntary donation.

Sure they're famous—but these catacombs are so weird and creepy, we just had to include them. The monks leave you to explore the gloomy corridors by yourself, but you may end up wishing you had a reassuring guide to hide behind. Every turn you take, everywhere you look, are bones, whole skeletons, and robe-wearing mummies, some of which are hanging off the wall. You'll feel like a mole lost in a graveyard.

STROMBOLI
(Aeolian island 35 miles north of Sicily)

Active Volcano: a three-hour walk up to the crater from the Point Labronzo Observatory on the north coast of the island. You can make the walk unaccompanied, but going with a guide is recommended, as the walk down the mountain is generally done at night. Ferries leave for Stromboli from Milazzo and Messina (on Sicily), and from Naples and Vibo Valentia (on mainland Italy).

No need to look for the volcano on Stromboli; Stromboli *is* the volcano: most of it is underwater, and the island is its peak. Etna, the area's only other active volcano, erupts unpredictably once every couple of decades, whereas Stromboli erupts every single day. In fact, it never stops erupting; it is the world's most active volcano. Lava flows, red-hot rocks fly through the air, and steam and smoke billow into the sky 24 hours a day. The fireworks are especially impressive at night, when the River of Lava (*Sciara del Fuoco*) cascades luminously into the sea. Note that the active crater is about 600 feet down the slope from the highest peak.

VULCANO
(Aeolian island 17 miles north of Sicily)

The Vulcanello Peninsula: starting one mile north of the main city, Porto Levante. The walk takes an hour. Ferries leave for Porto Levante from Milazzo and Messina (on Sicily).

Vulcanello is 2,171 years old this year. Roman writers chronicled its emergence from the sea in 183 B.C. The little volcano is now extinct, so you can stroll around the new peninsula in safety. The landscape is barren and strange, with recent erosion exposing suggestive formations and caves with multihued rocks. The whole eastern coast of the island (south of Porto Levante) is alive with fumaroles and macalubes (cracks in the earth and mini-volcanoes) spewing gas and steam. On calm days, the underwater fumaroles a few yards from the beach set the sea to boiling with bubbles, hot water, and sulphurous vapor.

THE NETHERLANDS

Legend:
1. Amsterdam
2. Haarlem
3. Leiden
4. The Hague
5. Rotterdam
6. Eindhoven
7. Nijmegen
8. Utrecht
9. Groningen
10. Leeuwarden
11. Maastricht
12. Zwolle
13. Tilburg

No Dutch child need ever wake up in the middle of the night ashamed of his or her ancestors. In 400 years, the Dutch have never erred; they have the knack of never making fools of themselves. Everything they touch turns to diamonds or cheese. And those Dutch children of a gentler nature, those who shy away from diamonds and cheese, need only recall Rembrandt. Or Vermeer. Or the Amsterdam Sex Museum.

No wonder the Dutch are contented; even their geography inspires a sense of security, for Holland is a land as flat as a ping-pong table.

The Netherlands / 211

Wacky houseboats bob in the canals, sprouting crazy ferns, anarchist flags, and pinwheels, as white swans glide blandly past. Pole vaulting is a championship sport. And confectioners, as hard-working as everyone else in Holland, slave over marzipan, fashioning it into sweet exact replicas of lobsters, clogs, and the Venus de Milo.

AALSMEER
(Ten miles southwest of Amsterdam)

Flower Auction (Bloemenveiling): Legmeerdijk 313. Take bus CN 171 or 172. Open Monday–Friday, 7:30–11 A.M. (Visitors are advised to arrive as early as possible.) Closed Saturday and Sunday. Admission: f2.50; children 14 and under, free. Phone: 02977-3 45 67.

For the Dutch, the flower auction is big business: three billion flowers and 220 million potted plants change hands in this vast complex every year. But for you—strolling out of harm's way on the overhead Visitors' Gallery—it's a psychedelic early-morning dose of color. While the high-tech bidding and buying goes on around you, stand back and drink in those surreal pinks, dazzling yellows, and throbbing purples.

AMSTERDAM

Bible Museum (Bijbels Museum): Herengracht 366. Open May–December, Tuesday–Saturday, 10 A.M.–5 P.M.; Sunday and holidays, 1–5 P.M. Closed January–April. Admission: f3; children under 16, f2. Phone: 020-24 79 49.

In the Exodus Room is a mummified head sprouting brick-red hair. You can get up real close and inspect its still-intact teeth and tongue. Nearby in a glass case is a small mummified girl still wrapped up in her linen. Further on are a mummified cat and human hand. In Room 5, a partly mummified skull rests on a bookshelf. Yes, we *are* talking about the Bible Museum here; it just happens to be full of mummies. Other unusual exhibits include a chunk of the Wailing Wall and a display about the daily life of ancient Jews. Of course, there are bibles all over the place, too; but you didn't come here to see those, did you?

Hash Info Museum: Oude Zijds Achterburgwal 148. Open daily, 10 A.M.–11 P.M. Admission: f4.

In 1987, a worldwide news release reported that a cannabis museum had opened in Amsterdam, and was closed down by police the day after it opened. Readers mourned or snickered. But when the museum opened again a few days later, nobody was there to report it to the papers. So now everybody agrees that the Hash Info Museum would be really great, if only it existed. Even the Amsterdam Tourist Office insists that the museum isn't there. But it *is*: we found it, quietly displaying (among other things) a functional indoor greenhouse, a globe marked with dots indicating places where cannabis is a cash crop, a huge poster and T-shirt collection, and plenty of "info." A mannequin called "Jerry, the U.S. pot grower" presides over all of this. A few cases stand empty, bearing signs that read "Confiscated."

Museum Vrolik: Meibergdreef 15; east side of the AMC medical school. Take the Amsterdam-Gein metro to the Holendrecht stop, in the southeastern part of the city. Open Wednesday and Thursday, 1:30–5 P.M., and by appointment. Admission: free. Phone: 020-566 46 64 or 020-566 46 00.

We still don't know who Vrolik is, but we do know this is an interesting anatomy museum. Embryos, bones, and genetic boo-boos of the last 200 years are intended for the scrutiny of medical students, but amateurs can see them too.

Narrowest House in the City: Kloveniersburgwal 26, at the corner of Bethanienstraat.

A wistful seventeenth-century coachman once mused, "Gee, Boss, I wish I had a house—even one just as wide as your front door." His boss took the comment to heart and in 1696 built the coachman a house exactly as wide as his own front door. The four-story edifice, decorated with big-breasted sphinxes and hourglasses, stands only eight feet wide.

Our Lord in the Attic (Museum Amstelkring, a.k.a. Ons Lieve Heer Op Solder): Oude Zijds Voorburgwal 40. Open Monday–Saturday, 10 A.M.–5 P.M.; Sunday 1–5 P.M. Admission: f3.50; students, seniors, and children, f2. Phone: 020-24 66 04.

Catholics of seventeenth-century Amsterdam would swoon if they saw how liberal the city is today. *They* had to worship in secret, constructing clandestine churches in the most unlikely spaces. This one hides in the joined attics of three houses. Its pews are wide enough to seat only five across; its tiny confessionals look like WCs. But no luxury was spared in decorating the altar: sleek marble columns flank a glorious fresco (tall but narrow), and works of art illuminate the walls. Sneaky. Very sneaky.

Piggybank Museum (Nationaal Spaarpotten Museum): Raadhuisstraat 20, six blocks west of Dam Square. Open Monday–Friday, 1–4 P.M. Admission: f1. Phone: 020-22 10 66.

Pigs aren't the only creatures we appoint to guard our pennies, pesos, and piasters. Consider a coconut bank, rat bank, hedgehog, fish, shoe, Santa Claus, and mechanical rifleman. The 12,000 money boxes in this collection (which does, for the conventional among you, include enough pigs to sicken a synagogue) present a whimsical view of world folk art: check out the extensive Surinam section and the Nigerian mudball banks. Some are grown-up and serious, crafted of gold and silver, but most of the banks are slyly silly, smirking at our attempts to save money; daring us to bash their heads in with a hammer.

Sex Museum Amsterdam (Venus Tempel): Damrak 18. Open daily, 10 A.M.– 11 P.M. Admission: f3.50.

The rumors are true: Amsterdam really does have a museum about sex, even though it's never mentioned in any guidebooks or lists of the city's attractions. The Sex Museum manages to be shocking yet scholarly, sleazy in some parts and respectable in others. The ground floor is mainly about pornography and the urban folklore of sex; the second floor is devoted to erotic art and the history of the sexual image. In the first display area is a mock-up of a typical Amsterdam sex-shop window (X-rated videos, dildos, etc.), watched over by mannequins dressed as a pimp and his prostitute. Passing the naughty postcard collection and the suspect private booths, you come to a sign reading, "Enter of your own free choice, you could be shocked (no complaints please)." The warning is no joke; the room behind it contains totally explicit and uncensored photographs of unnerving sexual proclivities, sexual freaks of nature (big, long,

214 / *The Netherlands*

etc.), and a potpourri of weird pornography. Upstairs are paintings with sexual themes, erotic cookie molds, plates, music boxes, jewelry, and interesting erotic folk art from Africa and Asia. One fascinating display chronicles the history of homemade "naughty photos"—some from as long ago as the 1860s. The museum sells a catalogue that might be Amsterdam's most risqué souvenir.

Tropical Museum (Tropenmuseum): Linnaeusstraat 2. Take tram 9 or 10. Open Monday–Friday, 10 A.M.–5 P.M.; Saturday and Sunday, noon–5 P.M. Admission: f5; seniors and children under 18, f2.50. Phone: 020-568 82 00.

Step into the shops and shanties; it's as if the occupants—modern, urban Africans, southeast Asians, Indians, and Latin Americans—have just gone out for a breath of air and will be returning any minute. Sandals wait expectantly in front of cots; portable TVs flicker and hum beside Hindu shrines. Sounds of barking dogs, arguments, and traffic echo through the walls, deepening the eerie sense of reality. These reconstructed corners of the Third World were assembled with an incredible eye for detail, and are not without humor (for neither is real life). Other exhibits in the museum are equally arresting: for example, the Yaqui Indian toothpick sculptures are intricately detailed and painted—down to the whites of the little figures' eyes—yet they're so small that you can see them only with the aid of a magnifying glass.

APELDOORN
(45 miles east of Amsterdam)

Ape Park (Apenheul): just west of town, at J.C. Wilslaan 21-31. Open April–June, daily, 9:30 A.M.–5 P.M.; July and August, daily, 9:30 A.M.–6 P.M.; September and October, daily, 10 A.M.–5 P.M.; March, Saturday and Sunday only, 10 A.M.–4 P.M. Closed November–February. Admission: f8.50; children 4–11 and seniors, f5; children under 3, free. Phone: 055-55 25 56.

If life in the Netherlands is too civilized, and too tame for your nature, go to Apeldoorn and let beady-eyed little South American monkeys climb all over your children. A large number of the park's 250 primal primates roam free among the visitors. You can kneel down and chat with the apes, who might whisper in your ear: "If you wanted wild life, you should have gone to New York."

BAARLE-NASSAU

See Baarle-Hertog in the Belgium chapter.

BERG EN DAAL
(Just south of Nijmegen)

African Museum (Afrika Museum): Postweg 6. From Nijmegen train station, take bus 5. Open April 1–November 1, Monday–Friday, 10 A.M.–4:30 P.M. and Saturday–Sunday, 11 A.M.–4:30 P.M. Admission: f3.50; seniors f3; children under 12, f2.50. Phone: 08895-4 20 44.

The only things missing are the tsetse flies and amoebic dysentery. Surrounded by a deer park, life-size replicas of dwellings from Ghana, Mali, and other parts of Africa stand shivering in the Dutch air, complete with thatched rooves, gourds in the backyard, and other equatorial amenities. There's a whole village's worth of dwellings. A pair of stilt houses, perched over a lake, are decorated with painted skins and have dugout canoes "parked" alongside. They're especially evocative of that "Wh-where am I?" feeling.

BEST
(Five miles north of Eindhoven)

Clog Museum (Klompenmuseum de Platijn): Broekdijk 16. Open daily, 10 A.M.–5 P.M. Admission: f1.50; children, f1. Phone: 044998-7 12 47.

You can't jog in wooden shoes, but they sure look sweet in Flemish paintings. On display here are sabots ranging in size from Baby's First to the village giant's. The collection of clogmaker's tools shows what a difficult craft this really is. And if *klompen* isn't a glowing example of Dutch onomatopoeia, we'll eat our shoes.

EINDHOVEN

Evoluon: Noord Brabantlaan 1A, west of downtown and next to the Rondweg. Open Monday–Friday, 9:30 A.M.–5:30 P.M. and Saturday–Sunday, 10:30 A.M.–5 P.M. Admission: f12.50; children 6–12, f10; children under 6, free. Phone: 040-51 27 36.

Evoluon is a huge flying-saucer-shaped science museum built by the Philips Corporation. Inside are four ring-shaped floors filled with so many gadgets, hands-on experiments, futuristic games, and scientific displays that we won't even attempt to list them here. However you feel about science, you're sure to find some weird little gewgaw or half-forgotten display to keep you bewildered or fascinated.

GRIJPSKERK
(Ten miles west of Groningen)

Pole Vaulting Championships (Fierljeppen): For current dates and locations of championship bouts (usually in spring), call the Grijpskerk Fierljepcentrum at 09947-1 36 36.

The local sport of choice is a serious one; vaulters go for distance rather than height, often propelling themselves more than 40 feet (over water, no less). Every town stages its own championship, building up to the annual North Holland vault-off. Fiercest of all is the North-vs.-South Holland championship, which gives spectators a certain sympathy for the way a tennis ball must feel.

THE HAGUE
('S GRAVENHAGE; DEN HAAG)

Madurodam: Haringkade 175. From the central train station, take tram 1 or 9 or bus 22 or 88. Open March 26–May 31, 9 A.M.–10 P.M.; June–August, 9 A.M.–10:30 P.M.; September, 9 A.M.–9 P.M.; October 1–October 26, 9 A.M.–6 P.M.; all daily. Admission: f10; children under 13, f5. Phone: 070-55 39 00.

Madurodam is perfection. This miniature city, composed of exact one twenty-fifth-scale replicas of Dutch buildings, boats, trains and canals, is clean, efficient, logical, and crime free. Madurodam never has traffic jams; its model train system always runs on time, and its tiny streets are free of tiny litter. At night, 50,000 little light bulbs illuminate the town. Visiting Madurodam is a little like reading Cliff's Notes: once you've been there, there's no real need to visit the rest of Holland. (Just kidding.) A new show, called Moonlight Miracle, starts every night just after the formal closing time: colored lights and lasers whiz through the town while you listen through headphones to the legends and lore of Madurodam.

Panorama Mesdag: Zeestraat 65B. Take bus 4, 5, 13, or 22. Open Monday–Saturday, 10 A.M.–5 P.M.; Sunday, noon–5

P.M. Admission: f3; children under 14, f1.50. Phone: 070-64 25 63. Ask the cashier to let you hear the English tape.

H. W. Mesdag's panorama of the Scheveningen seaside in 1881 may be the largest painting in the world. To view it, visitors walk down a long hallway and up a spiral staircase to reach a central viewing platform. The painting surrounds the platform on all sides, presenting a striking 360-degree view of the seashore. Real sand rolls all the way from the viewing platform to the edge of the canvas (a distance of 45 feet), where it merges with the painted sand. In the real sand is real nineteenth-century debris: broken wooden shoes, a rusted anchor, bits of rope. The painting, a floor-to-ceiling cylindrical canvas, depicts beached ships in the distance; houses; and promenaders. The perspective is unsettlingly perfect, enhanced by the tape-recorded sea gull cries on the soundtrack, which explains the techniques Mesdag and his wife used in creating this panorama—one of a handful of such paintings left in the world.

Prison Gate Museum (Rijksmuseum Gevangenpoort): Buitenhof 33, across the street from the Binnenhof and the adjacent fountain. Tours Monday–Friday at 10, 11, and 11:30 A.M.; noon; and 12:30, 1, 1:30, 2, 2:30, 3, 3:30, and 4 P.M. Tours Saturday, Sunday, and holidays at 1, 2, 3, and 4 P.M. (From October to March, closed Saturday and Sunday.) Admission: f3.50; people under 18 and over 65, f2; children under 6 not admitted. Phone: 070-46 08 61.

Anything whose name starts out with the word "Rijksmuseum" ought to be a nice place, but the Prison Gate is about as far from nice as a place can get. Used for 400 years as a prison and torture chamber, the Gevangenpoort retains much of its former ghastliness. Chilly, narrow hallways lead to dark cells (beware the practical-jokester guides who occasionally lock people up without warning). A chamber of horrors holds a large collection of torture instruments: execution axes, balls and chains, racks, branding irons, and other cheery toys. Note: if the door is locked when you arrive, that means a tour is going on. Just stand there and wait for the next tour.

HEERLERHEIDE
(Next to Heerlen, 12 miles east of Maastricht)

Fantastico Dream Castle (Droomkasteel Fantastico): Ganzeweide 113-115. Open Easter–September, daily, 10

A.M.–6 P.M. Phone: 045-21 17 67.

A park filled with countless statues and sculptures of every character in every folk tale you ever heard of—and then some. This is what Disneyland would have been like if Walt Disney had been an impoverished Dutchman. If you feel like retreating from reality for a few hours, this is the place.

KAATSHEUVEL
(Ten miles north of Tilburg)

Efteling Fairytale Park: just outside of town, on Europaweg. Open April–July, daily, 10 A.M.–6 P.M.; July and August, 10 A.M.–8 P.M.; September and October, 10 A.M.–5 P.M. Admission: f18; seniors, f15.50; children under 4, free. Phone: 4167-8 05 05.

Long before most *My Little Pony* fans (and their parents) were born, Dutch artist Anton Pieck designed Efteling's Enchanted Forest, peopled with soulful dwarves, dragons, and familiar heroines. This stuff is good in the way most 30-year-old amusement parks are good: the characters lurking among the glades and waterfalls come from folklore, and from one man's imagination. Pay your respects to Long Neck, whose nervous gaze overlooks the whole park. In the Fata Morgana—Forbidden City—costumed automata do scenes from the 1001 Nights.

KAMPEN
(Ten miles west of Zwolle)

Tobacco Museum (Tabaksmuseum): Botermarkt 3. Open by appointment. Admission: f2. Phone: 05202-2 53 53.

The cigar manufacturing tools, machines, boxes, and recipes are just an aperitif compared to this museum's pride and joy: a 15-foot cigar, which they claim is the world's largest.

LEIDEN

Clay Pipe Museum (Museum Voor de Tabakspijp van Klei): Oude Vest 159A. Open Monday–Saturday, 10 A.M.–10 P.M.; Sunday, 1–5 P.M. Admission: f2. Phone: 071-12 13 40.

Over 10,000 specimens make this one a contender for the title of World's Largest Pipe Collection. The emphasis is on long-stemmed local clay pipes, but 50 other countries are represented as well.

MAASTRICHT

Caverns: There are several different cave systems, located south of downtown: Zonneberg (entrance at Slavante 1), Noordelijk (entrance at Luikerweg 71), Canneberg (entrance on Canneweg), and the main cavern, St. Pietersburg (entrance on St. Pieter's Hill). Open Easter–September, daily, 10:45 A.M.–3:45 P.M. Guided tours only. Admission: f3.75; children under 13, f2.25. For more information, call the Maastricht Tourist Office at 043-25 21 21.

These hand-hewn caverns served as limestone quarries for the ancient Romans. More recently they did a stint as air-raid shelters. In between, they have served variously as hiding place, resting place, cooling-off place, and artist's canvas. The one-hour guided tour takes you past diverse drawings and scribblings, as well as other cave dwellers' mementoes.

MIDDELBURG
(Four miles north of Vlissingen, Zeeland)

Miniature Town of Walcheren (Miniatuur Walcheren) Koepoortlaan 1, Molenwater. Open Easter–June, daily, 9:30 A.M.–5 P.M.; July and August, daily, 9:30 A.M.–6 P.M.; September 1–October 19, daily, 9:30 A.M.–5 P.M. Admission: f4.50; children, f2.50. Phone: 01180-1 25 25.

Walcheren—the big one—is a quaint Dutch peninsula that took a beating in WWII. The inhabitants got to work rebuilding as soon as the war was over, and were so pleased with their repair job that in 1954 this miniature Walcheren was constructed to commemorate it. The message is: get back on your feet, dust yourself off, and set things right again. The dikes and windmills, trains and houses are all here, reproduced on a one twenty-fifth scale. The miniature lake is stocked with tiny radio-controlled boats.

NAALDWIJK
(Ten miles south of The Hague)

Westland Flower Auction (Bloemenveiling): Dijkweg 66. From The Hague train station, take yellow ZWN bus 127 or 128. Open Monday–Friday, 8–10 A.M. (Visitors are encouraged to come early.) Admission: f2.50; children under 13, f1.25. Phone: 1740-3 33 33.

Take the signposted walking tour, which wends its way through a half-mile of auction action—including greenhouses and fast-moving electronic bidding. Of course, the best part is the flowers: 30,000 square feet of roses, mums, carnations, begonias, tulips.... Watch them being prepared to serve mankind.

NIEUWOLDA
(15 miles east of Groningen)

Baby Carriage Museum (Het Kinderwagen Museum): Hoofdweg West 25. Open Wednesday, Saturday, and Sunday, 1–6 P.M. Admission: f2; children under 13, f1. Phone: 05964-1941.

Mercifully devoid of babies, these 100 antique baby buggies invite you to inspect them in restful silence. They're parked in a historic eighteenth-century farmhouse, and provide an overview of the way in which grown-ups have sought to make infants as ornamental as possible.

NIJMEGEN

The Holy Land Open Air Bible Museum (Heilig Land Stichting): Mgr. Suyslaan 4, just south of Nijmegen. From Nijmegen train station take the "Groesbeek" bus 84 to the Heilig Land Stichting stop. Open Easter–November 1, daily, 9 A.M.–5:30 P.M. Admission: f7.50; children under 14, f4.50. Phone: 080-22 98 29.

Not simply an open-air museum, The Holy Land is an entire region transported to modern-day Holland from first-century Palestine. Thirteen acres' worth of the ancient Middle East, complete with actors dressed as Bedouins, Arabs, Romans, and Jews—including a Galilean fishing village, a caravan inn, a goat-hair tent encampment, and a couple of reconstructed near-Eastern cities. The only clue that you're really in the Netherlands is the spotlessly clean streets.

OUDEWATER
(12 miles west of Utrecht)

Witches' Weigh House (de Heksenwaag): Leeuweringerstraat 2. From Utrecht, take bus 180. Open April–October, Tuesday–Saturday, 10 A.M.–5 P.M.; Sunday, noon–5 P.M. Closed Monday. Price (including weighing, certificate, and admission to museum): f1.50; children 4–12, f1; children under 4, free. Phone: 03486-34 00.

In sixteenth-century Holland, women accused of witchcraft were literally put on the scales of justice: an official weighmaster decided whether or not the accused was light enough to fly on a broomstick. If you were healthy or hefty, you went free: skinnies were doomed. Emperor Charles V, passing through one village, saw a corrupt weighmaster (who had been bribed) condemning an accused woman by stating that she was almost weightless. Charles ordered a retrial; a new weighmaster from Oudewater proved himself uncorrupt by declaring the woman's true weight, and thereby acquitting her. Charles, convined of the weighmaster's honesty, gave the man the authority to hand out certificates stating that the bearer was of normal weight. Any woman with this certificate was safe from all accusations of witchcraft. Suddenly, Oudewater became a very popular place to visit. Nowadays, you can still get an official certificate stating that you're too heavy to fly: just get on the old-fashioned balance scales and let the weighmaster put you to the test. (Don't worry—he's never condemned anyone yet.) Upstairs from the weighing room is a small museum about the treatment of witches in the old days.

ROTTERDAM

Tax Museum (Belastingmuseum): Parklaan 14, near the park and the harbor. Open Monday–Friday, 9 A.M.–5 P.M. Admission: free. Phone: 010-4 36 63 33.

People have been avoiding the taxman since the day taxes were invented—which was probably the day after the invention of money. The tax museum tells the history of taxes and ways to avoid paying them. The parts about smuggling and cheating are, obviously, the most instructive. Save your entrance ticket and claim the visit as a business expense.

STEENWIJK
(20 miles north of Zwolle)

Circus Museum (Kermis- en Circusmuseum): Markt 64. Enter via Oudheidskamer. Open Tuesday–Friday, 10 A.M.–noon and 2–5 P.M.; in July and August, also open Saturday 2–4 P.M. Admission: f1; children under 17, f0.50. Phone: 05210-1 17 04 or 05210-1 20 10.

If clowns give you the creeps, avoid this museum, for even in miniature, a leering grin is a leering grin. But if you like acrobats, fat ladies, silly balloons, and suicidal trapeze artists, this is the place for you. You'll find here a mini-circus with mechanical merry-go-round, miniature carnival, and other circus and carnival memorabilia.

UTRECHT

"From Music Box to Barrel Organ" Mechanical Music Museum *(National Museum van Speelklok tot Pierement)*: Buurkerkhof 10. Open Tuesday–Saturday, 10 A.M.–5 P.M.; Sunday, 1–5 P.M. Closed Monday. Admission: f4.50; children under 14, f2.25. Phone: 030-31 27 89.

Talk about gilding the lily! You'll see music boxes decorated with golden canaries, hopping hummingbirds, bobbing boats, and dancing waters. Also here are singing clocks, automatic violins, and snuffboxes that just don't know how to keep quiet.

VALKENBURG
(12 miles east of Maastricht)

Town Cave (Gemeentegrot): entrance at Cauberg Straat 2. Open Easter–September, Monday–Saturday, 9 A.M.–5 P.M. and Sunday, 10 A.M.–5 P.M. In summer, walking tours begin every two hours at half past the hour (even-numbered hours). Tram tours begin every two hours at 45 minutes after the hour (odd-numbered hours). October–Easter, daily tours at 3 P.M. only. Admission: walking tours, f4.10; children f2; tram tours, f5; children, f2.95. Phone: 04406-1 22 71 or 04406-1 36 41.

Spooky, kooky, green-and-blue lights; elaborate charcoal drawings of alligators and queens; baroque sculptures posing in niches and archways—this cave is every would-be Tom Sawyer's dream-come-true. First quarried about 2,000 years ago, the labyrinth still bears tantalizing traces of its many human occupants, up until the 1940s. Carved graffiti and artsy bas-reliefs are only part of the fun.

VOLENDAM
(Ten miles northeast of Amsterdam)

Cigar Band "Golden Room" (Goulde Kammer): Oudedraaipad 8. Open daily, 9 A.M.–6 P.M. Admission: f1. Phone: 02993-6 36 73.

A certain Mr. Molenaar chain-smoked cigars for years, and saved the cigar bands from every one. Eventually his collection grew unmanageably large; one fateful day Molenaar decided to make a mosaic on his wall, using his cigar bands. His first design pleased him so much that he went ahead and made another. Thus an obsession was born. Friends and relatives donated their bands, and

Molenaar spent nearly two decades covering the inside of his house with cigar-band mosaics. Now his house is open to the public. Every square inch of the interior is covered in cigar bands; some form geometric patterns, while others depict Big Ben, the Statue of Liberty, windmills and other notable structures.

WIEUWERD
(Between Sneek and Leeuwarden, in Friesland)

Mummy Cellar (Mummiekelder): under the village's one church. Open Monday–Saturday, 9 A.M.–noon and 1–4 P.M. Closed Sunday. Admission: Fl 1.50. Phone: 05104-226.

You'd think those nice clean Dutch people would just bury their dead and leave it at that. Well, in this case they tried, but these four corpses just refused to decompose. Gasses rising from the earth did their stuff and naturally mummified them, so that now these four dead people are local celebrities—as are the tiny mummified birds exhibited alongside the humans in their 1609 tomb.

WOUW
(30 miles west of Tilburg)

Silk Museum (Zijdemuseum ter Zijde): Schoolstraat 3. Open Monday–Saturday, 10 A.M.–5 P.M.; Sunday, 1–5 P.M. Admission: f5; seniors, f4; children, f2.50. Phone: 01658-3690.

Silkworms aren't pretty, as this museum proves. But the stuff they produce is gorgeous, as this museum also proves. Exhibits include antique silk clothing, looms, and a reconstructed dyeworks. Learn all about silk—all, that is, except how to get grape-juice stains out of it.

NORWAY

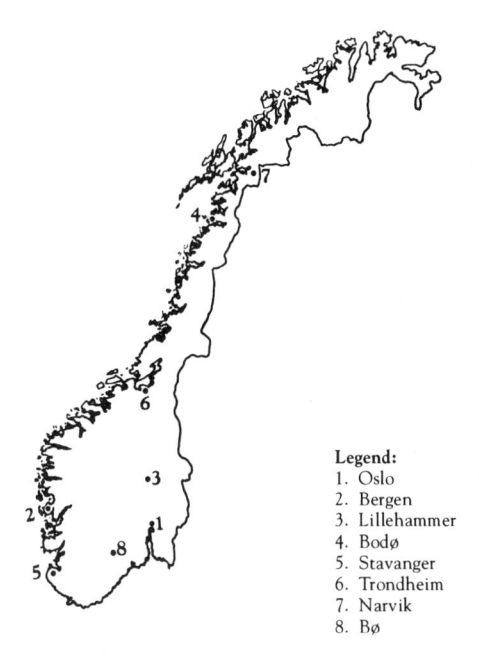

Legend:
1. Oslo
2. Bergen
3. Lillehammer
4. Bodø
5. Stavanger
6. Trondheim
7. Narvik
8. Bø

Trolls still lurk in Norway; they never left. That's the only explanation for the raw, spirited wildness you feel upon entering the country.

Dense forests soar in misty, icy silence. Trolls chortle over the treacherous beauty of primeval fjords; they bask worshipfully in the Midnight Sun. Even in downtown Oslo the trolls dwell, deep under the cellars of the fancy hotels. They drink to old times; they remark gleefully how the woods crouch on one side of the city while the sea teases the other. Nature, in a rare polite moment, lets things like trains and Oslo happen. But the trolls know who's boss in Norway.

The country demands great vigor of Norwegians—and they respond by making games of their jagged, frozen environment. Ice skating becomes an art; the king's babies ski. Give Norwegians a maelstrom and what do they do? They fish in it.

BERGEN

Leprosy Museum: St. George's Hospital, 59 Kong Oscarsgate. Open mid-May to end of August, 11 A.M.–3 P.M. Admission: NOK 10; children, NOK 2. For more information, call the Bergen Tourist Office at (05) 32 14 80.

Maybe you've always associated leprosy with tropical climes, but the disease has figured in Norway's history, and Norwegian doctors have made a name for themselves in ground-breaking leprosy research. The museum, on the site of a medieval lepers' hospital, contains vivid displays relating to one of medicine's most interesting diseases. Free viewings of an explanatory film (in English) are available.

BØ
(35 miles northwest of Skien in the Telemark region)

Telemark Sommarland: in the town of Bø, with no exact address—but once you're there you can't miss it. Open June 12–August 16, 10 A.M.–8 P.M. Admission: NOK 70; children under 14, NOK 55. Phone: (036) 61 699.

This amusement park, practically out in the wilderness, features a 75-foot-tall slide that is almost a straight drop for most of its length, on which you can experience the weightlessness of free-fall. Also check out the Westernland, with cowboy-assisted horse rides, water bumper cars, BRIO toyland, radio-controlled cars, and even a place for relaxing rowboat rides when the frenzy becomes too much.

BODØ
(North of the Arctic Circle, on the coast)

The Midnight Sun (Midnattsol): end of May to middle of July. The upper edge of the sun is visible all day beginning May 30. From June 3 to July 8, the entire sun is continuously visible. The sun sinks after that and is last visible (and even then just a fragment of it) July 12. For more information, call the Bodø Tourist Office at (081) 21 240.

Every bit as mythic as you thought it was, the sun burns for over a month, huge and golden in an amber sky. The nights on which the sun is less than 18 degrees below the horizon are called "light nights." You might lose sleep, but there's no end to the surreal waking dreams that the Midnattsol can inspire.

Saltstraumen Maelstrom: east of Bodø across the Saltfjorden. Accessible by car via Løding and Straumen (approximately 25 miles) or by regularly scheduled buses between May 1 and August 23. Buses depart from the Bodø bus station five times daily, according to the tides. Call (081) 25 025 for current departure times. The ride takes 40 minutes.

"Maelstrom" in Norwegian refers to an odd phenomenon in which tidal waters are squeezed through narrow straits that connect coastal fjords and the open sea. There are maelstroms all up and down the Norwegian coast, but the most remarkable is here just east of Bodø. Edgar Allen Poe's terrifying tale, "A Descent Into the Maelstrom" is a description of the Saltstraumen Maelstrom, a description so memorable that the word "maelstrom" became part of our language because of it. If you want to see the roaring, whirling ferocious tidal rush of up to 80,000 billion gallons of water at its most extreme, go during a new or full moon when the tidal pull is the strongest.

HELL
(20 miles east of Trondheim)

Hell merits mention on the map of Norway only as a key railway junction. For our purposes, though, Hell is an important place to visit, not only for sending heart-stopping postcards, but so that in the future, any time someone tells you to "Go to Hell" you can come back with the cutting retort, "I've been there already."

LILLEHAMMER
(85 miles north of Oslo)

Hunderfossen Lekeland: eight miles north of Lillehammer on Highway E6. Open late May and early June, daily, 10 A.M.–4 P.M.; the rest of June, July, and August, daily,

10 A.M.–7 P.M. Admission: NOK 45; once inside, all activities are free. Phone: (062) 74 222.

This amusement's park's mascot and star attraction is an immense sculpture of a Norwegian troll—over 30 feet tall, even in his sitting position. For a walking stick he uses a tree trunk, while foliage sprouts from his uncombed mane. He keeps guard over the park's other attractions, such as the race course with drivable mini-Mercedes Benzes, the "Surf Hill," which really involves no surfing at all, lots of trampolines, a giant chess game, a miniature golf course, and dozens of other things much bigger or smaller than they're supposed to be.

OSLO

Customs Museum (Norsk Tollmuseum): Tollbugata 1A (downtown near the train station). Open in summer, Tuesday and Thursday, noon–3 P.M.; winter, Thursday only, noon–3 P.M. Admission: Free. Phone: (02) 41 49 60.

What comes in and what goes out of a rich country like Norway is a complicated business, as you can see from the original customs-related materials on display at the museum.

Emanuel Vigeland's Museum: Grimelundsveien 8, in the Slemdal suburb. Take commuter train to the Slemdal stop. Open Sunday, noon–3 P.M. Admission: free. Phone: (02) 1423 28.

You'd think that in liberated Norway, land of naked saunas and sexual liberation, everybody wouldn't be so determinedly close-mouthed about the erotic art museum of Emanuel Vigeland, the unfamous younger brother of Gustav (creator of Oslo's Vigeland Sculpture Park). Among other unabashed artworks on display is Emanuel's masterwork, a series of frescoes called VITA, celebrating the colorful phases of the human life cycle. Just getting an Oslo tourist offical to admit the museum exists is like pulling teeth. But it's there. Trust us.

Freia Chocolate Factory Tours: Johan Throneholsts Pl. 1, northeast of downtown. Tours (available in English) are given Monday–Thursday at 12:30 P.M. For reservations (make them as early as possible), phone (02) 38 14 70.

The employees' dining room of an urban factory is the last place you'd expect to see original Edvard Munch paintings. Not only does the tour of Norway's largest chocolate company offer history, good smells, and even free samples, it also glitters with works of art. Freia's founder, Johan Throneholst, wished to give his workers a break from smokestacks and grimness, so in 1920 he commissioned a group of paintings from Munch. Collectively called the Freia-Frisen, these works are big, bright, and remarkably (for Munch) hopeful. Also in the canteen are Edvard Grieg's piano, a bust of Hadrian, and a view of the garden, which boasts sculptures by Gustav Vigeland and other Scandinavians, as well as copies of Greek and Roman classics.

The International Museum of Children's Art (Det Internasjonale Barnekunstmuseet): Lille Frøens Vei 4, northwest of downtown. Take the Sognsvann Line commuter train from National Theater to Frøen. Open Tuesday, Wednesday, and Friday, 9:30 A.M.–2 P.M.; Saturday and Sunday, noon–4 P.M. Admission: NOK 20; children and seniors, NOK 15. Phone: (02) 46 85 73.

Few art museums are as full of revelations as this one. Nearly 100,000 works of art by youngsters from 130 countries form a startling collection, with themes that range as far as a child's mind—including such images as old people, violence, peace, music, and many fantastic things that adults have long forgotten. Paintings, sculptures, ceramics, weavings, and books (written and illustrated by children) are on exhibit. Many of these, such as the surrealistic works by children in Guatemalan refugee villages, are strangely unsettling. The museum holds workshops for children and adults, and has in its collection some works created by now-famous artists when they were tiny tots.

Kon-Tiki Museum: on Bygdøy Peninsula, at the tip. Take bus 30 from downtown, or, in summer, take the ferry from Pier 3 next to city hall to the Bygdøynes stop. Open November–March, daily, 10:30 A.M.–4 P.M.; April 1–May 16, daily, 10:30 A.M.–5 P.M.; May 18–August 31, daily, 10 A.M.–6 P.M.; September–October, daily, 10:30 A.M.–5 P.M. Closed May 17. Admission: NOK 10; students and children, NOK 5. Phone: (02) 43 80 50.

In 1947 Thor Heyerdahl, a slightly mad Norwegian, built a raft out of balsa wood and floated 5,000 miles across the Pacific to prove some obscure theory about prehistoric population shifts. This museum is devoted to that journey, and contains the original Kon-Tiki raft, models of the undersea life the boat had to contend with (including a shark larger than the boat itself) and weird displays about the gods and secret religions of Easter Island and Polynesia. In 1970 Thor sailed across the Atlantic on a boat of papyrus reeds, and the Ra II, as it was called, is preserved here too.

Skating Museum (Skøytemuseet): at Frogner Stadium, which is at the eastern end of Frogner Park. Entrance on Middelthuns Gate. Take tram 2 to Frogner Station. Open daily, by appointment only. Phone: (02) 55 89 94.

Here in the frozen north, ice skating is a means of transportation and an art form, as well as a midwinter cheer-up for teens in woolen tutus. The museum features a diverse array of skates in all shapes and sizes, including some worn by famous skaters.

Ski Museum (Skimuseet): Kongeveien 5. Take the Holmenkollen train (number 15) from National Theater Station to the Holmenkollen stop. Once you get off the train, follow the signs uphill to the ski jump and museum. Open daily, October–April, 10 A.M.–3 P.M.; May, 10 A.M.–5 P.M.; June, 10 A.M.–7 P.M.; July, 9 A.M.–10 P.M.; August, 10 A.M.–8 P.M.; September, 10 A.M.–5 P.M. Admission: NOK 12; students, NOK 8; children, NOK 6. Phone: (02) 14 16 90.

Even if you don't know a thing about skiing, it's fascinating to learn how people have, over the centuries, managed to get from one place to another in this largely snow-covered country. Skis on display here range from prehistoric ones to royal skis belonging to Norway's King Haakon and Queen Maud. The oldest ones, excavated from bogs and glaciers, employ ingenious materials—for example, fur on the bottom to prevent backsliding. Ancient rock carvings on display pay homage to Ull, the Norse pagan ski god. Athletic mannequins in full ski gear, poles and all, are poised above your head as you inspect the racing memorabilia and dioramas of polar exhibitions, both successful and tragic. The museum, the world's oldest on this subject, was recently installed here next to the huge and legendary Holmenkollen ski jump.

Vigeland Sculpture Park: entrance on Kirkeveien. Park is northwest of downtown. Take tram 2 from the center. Always open. Admission: free.

Grimacing, grinning, caressing, leaping, and embracing their way across every aspect of human relationships, Gustav Vigeland's 650 figures seem more alive than we do. A crone braids a younger woman's hair; a truly furious man beats his son; exhausted lovers rest back to back. The long avenue of bronze sculptures and three circular tiers of granite ones (all of the figures are smooth, strong nudes) are a striking testament to the nearly infinite range of human feelings, including the subtlest, impossible-to-verbalize ones.

STAVANGER
(South of Bergen on the coast)

Kongeparken: 15 miles south of Stavanger on Highway E18, near the town of Ålgård. Open May 1–June 19, noon–8 P.M.; June 20–August 16, 10 A.M.–8 P.M.; August 17–30, 2–8 P.M. Admission: NOK 50; children under 3, free. Phone: (04) 61 71 11.

Should you happen to see a 250-foot-tall Gulliver lying exhausted by the side of the road, you'll know you've found Kongeparken, probably Scandinavia's largest amusement park. Gulliver is actually a building full of crazy games, a maze, and sophisticated toys: around him, human-sized Lilliputians soak up the kitsch of the American Wild West mining town, dig holes with miniature hydraulic cranes, shrink in horror from the clown parades, run red lights at the Lilliput traffic school, and straighten their hair on the bobsled course. The list of things to do here is so long you can find something off-the-wall no matter what your taste.

Old Stavanger Canning Museum: Øvre Strandgate 88A, a few blocks from the waterfront. Open May–August, Wednesday, Friday, Saturday, and Sunday, 11 A.M.–3 P.M.; September–April, Sunday only, 11 A.M.–3 P.M. For more information, call the Stavanger Tourist Office at (04) 52 84 37.

Life on the sardine processing line was and is a reality for many generations of Norwegians. This reconstructed factory-office complex features authentic equipment and furnishings, as well as exhibits of sardiniana. It's all here except the smell—which you can provide yourself with the help of your mind's nose.

TRONDHEIM

Ringve Museum of Music History: east of Trondheim in the suburb of Ringve in Ringve Mansion at Lade. To get there, take tram 1 from downtown east to the Lade stop. Guided tours only. Tours in English given May 20–June 19, daily, noon and 2 P.M.; June 20–August 19, daily, 11 A.M., 1 and 3 P.M. and also at 7:30 P.M. on Tuesday and Wednesday; August 20–September 30, noon and 2 P.M.; October, Monday–Saturday, noon, and Sunday, noon and 2 P.M.; November 1–May 19, Sunday only, 1 and 2 P.M. Admission: NOK 20; children, NOK 10. Phone: 92 24 11.

Most times conducted tours are a bother, but at this museum they're necessary. For not only can you see and learn about old instruments from all over the globe, but you can hear them played, too—by the guides.

PORTUGAL

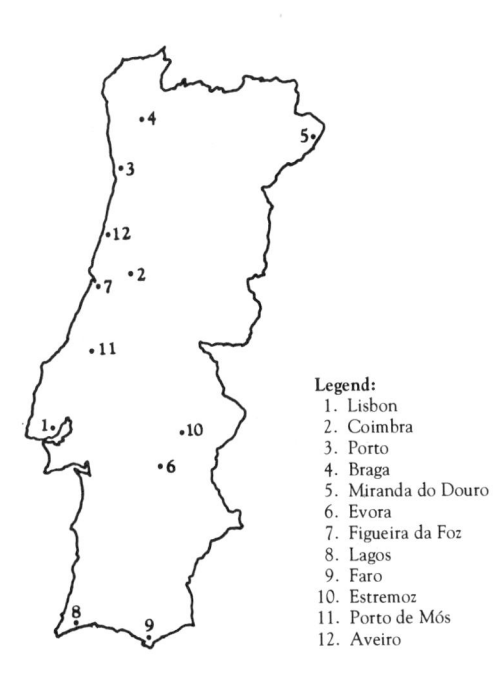

Legend:
1. Lisbon
2. Coimbra
3. Porto
4. Braga
5. Miranda do Douro
6. Evora
7. Figueira da Foz
8. Lagos
9. Faro
10. Estremoz
11. Porto de Mós
12. Aveiro

When you step into Portugal, you step back in time. The country sleeps, curled up in the warm sunshine, with swashbuckling dreams dancing in its head: Vasco da Gama hoists his sails and shoves off past Cabo São Vicente; Moors dash about on horseback. Templars and kings, nuns and fishwives march vividly across Portugal's dreamscape.

What's happening now? Portugal sleeps. It is a well-deserved rest; so much has gone before. The sun bakes Portugal's south and east while rain lashes the north. Wine grapes, wheat, plums, sardines, and tourists thrive while the Portuguese people blink with startling green eyes and do not keep up with fashion or culture.

Turn-of-the-century yellow trolleys clank up and down Lisbon's hills, not because the city has decided to revive them, not because tourists like the trolleys, but because no one ever noticed they were becoming antiques. Photographs in brochures the Tourist Office hands out are 10, 15, 20 years out of date: the people in the pictures wear bell-bottom pants and wide flowered ties. And the part of us that loves nostalgia loves these things about Portugal.

Despite its small size, Portugal harbors immense variety—in architecture, cuisine, terrain, and lifestyle. A quaint chapel built of bones stands an hour's drive from a stunning modernistic bridge. Peculiar folkloric customs, geographical extremes, and religious oddities abound. Portugal may be sleeping, but it has had the strangest dreams.

ALCOCHETE
(Ten miles east of Lisbon, across the Tagus River)

Bull Run and Green Cap Festival (Largadas de Touros and Festas do Barrete Verde e das Salinas): second Saturday in August. Festival lasts three days. For directions and more information, call 2 42 84 or 2 95 07.

Bull herders in this area traditionally wear tasseled green caps, and the tassels really fly when bulls are released into the streets of town and the men dart in and out among them. This is Portugal's answer to Pamplona, and is far less crowded. The local bulls are lean but powerful, and while townspeople make a great show of alternately chasing the animals and escaping them, visitors are usually advised to maintain a safe distance. The festival also involves a religious procession, folk music, and lots of fish.

BRAGA

The Stairway to Bom Jesus do Monte de Santa Marta

Sanctuary: three miles southeast of town. Take a city bus (sign in front reads "Bom Jesus") from the square facing the old Hospital São Marcos. Buses leave every half hour at 10 after the hour and 40 after the hour. Last bus back to downtown Braga leaves Bom Jesus at 9 P.M.

As wide as the church itself, and proceeding grandly down the mountainside, the stairs zig and zag with precision. All the way up, chapels house life-size full-color recreations of scenes from the Passion; baroque statues crown the bannisters; squat topiary bushes guard the sides like conical sentinels. But the real reason for climbing the stairs is to experience its top level, "The Stairway of the Five Senses," where sculptured fountains dedicated to the senses squirt water from various surprising orifices: a man's nose pours a continual stream, another figure spits, a punctured heart bleeds crystal-clear jets, a pair of ears sends forth incongruous cascades. The young girl's head whose bulging eyes squirt water in two horizontal jets is most disturbing. Our tip: while the general practice is to start at the bottom and climb up the stairs, we recommend taking the funicular to the top (30$00) and walking down. Sure, you see Jesus' Passion backwards this way, but it's easier on the legs.

Dom Lourenço Vicente's Mummy: in the Capela dos Reis, behind the Cathedral (called the Sé), in the center of town, three blocks west of the Tourist Office. Signs point the way from all directions. The required guided tour includes Capela dos Reis and another chapel (collectively called As Capelas Tumulares) and the Cathedral Treasury Museum. Open daily during normal business hours. Admission: 75$00.

At the far end of the right-hand wall stands the glass case containing Dom Lourenço Vicente. He's a mummy, and he's been in that condition since the Middle Ages. The former Braga bishop, clad in his shining vestments, looks polished. His ears are uncorrupted, and from the ankles up, he's a testament to the embalmers of his day. Beware, however, the bishop's defiantly decomposing feet and their fierce nails.

CABO DA ROCA
(Six miles west of Sintra, north of Lisbon)

Europe's Westernmost Point, and Certificate: buses run from both Sintra and Cascais to Cabo da Roca, although some of the buses from Sintra only go to about one mile from the actual cape. Certificates are available at the Cabo da Roca Tourist Office (you can't miss it): regular paper version, 175$00; parchment version, 350$00. Tourist office open daily, 9 A.M.–8 P.M. Phone: 9 29 09 81.

On the map it looks like just another bulge on just another coastline, but this bulge is something special: the westernmost point of the Eurasian land mass. Here starts the world's longest hike—you can, if you plan your route carefully, walk 7,000 miles to the eastern tip of Siberia on the Bering Strait and never cross a single body of water. The best part of the trip to the cape is the great certificate available at the tourist office (and nowhere else), which certifies you as an authentic explorer of the ends of the earth, and which is elegant enough to make Columbus and Vasco da Gama jealous.

CABO DE SÃO VICENTE
(3½ miles west of Sagres)

The End of the World (O Fim do Mundo): infrequent buses run from Sagres to the cape; otherwise you must walk, hitchhike, take a taxi, or rent a car or bicycle. Open until sunset. Admission: free.

Though parts of Spain are further south and Cabo da Roca is further west, the ominous Cabo de São Vicente ranks as the most southwesterly point in Europe. Up until the 1490s, this was considered to be, literally, the end of the world, and if you visit it, you'll be convinced. The whole promontory seems forbidding and final; once you reach the lighthouse (one of the most powerful in the world) the view will make you see why most sailors thought twice befor heading off into the void. On windy or stormy days, the surf can be ferocious. On clear days it seems possible to actually see the curvature of the earth as you scan the endless ocean. Either way, there is a certain indescribable sense of satisfaction in knowing that you've reached the end of the road and that you couldn't go any further, even if you wanted to.

COIMBRA

Portugal dos Pequenitos: across the bridge from the old town at the corner of Avenida João das Regras and Rua Antonio Augusto Gonçalves. Open daily, 9 A.M.–8 P.M.

(earlier closing times in winter). Admission: 150$00; children, 50$00. Phone: 28829.

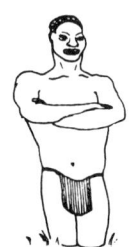

The Portuguese world in miniature, with buildings, statues, and exhibits, representing every region in Portugal and every country from Portugal's once far-flung empire. Twenty-foot-tall Angolan warriors, intricately hand-carved chess sets representing nineteenth-century politicians from the Azores, and other exotica vie with quaint model houses and gardens to make an entertaining crash course in Portuguese history and architecture. Designed to please children, this open-air park affords a walk from one end of the world to the other.

ESTREMOZ

Museum of Crucified Christs (Museu dos Cristos): $5\frac{1}{2}$ miles east of Estremoz, between the towns of Arcos and Borba, to the right side of National Road 4. The nearest train station is at Borba, two miles away. Open 9 A.M.–9 P.M. For more information call the Vila Viçosa Tourist Office at 4 21 40 or 4 23 05.

Here is Catholicism at its most macabre: a museum of nothing but statues of Jesus being crucified. Countless hundreds of intricate crucifixes line the walls and rooms. Jesus dies over and over again, grimacing, bleeding, sagging, crying, writhing, and in general not having a very good time. The curators claim that this museum is unique in the world—for Jesus' sake, we hope they're right.

EVORA

Chapel of Bones (Capela dos Ossos): in the church of São Francisco, on the Praça 28 de Maio. Open 9 A.M.–12:30 P.M. and 2:30–5:30 P.M. Admission: 20$00.

Some of Europe's most patient and unrattlable bone architects produced this chapel, the repository for the remains of 5,000 persons. The walls are tightly paneled with bones in a way that is as economical and meticulous as it is creepy—not a bone out of place. Just in case the architects' message has managed to elude you during the visit, a sign accosts you at the exit: "Here are our bones—waiting for your bones." A collection of human braids hangs near the chapel door, left there by local women about to be married.

FARO

Chapel of Bones (Capela dos Ossos): behind the Church of Carmo, on Largo do Carmo, on the north side of town near the main post office. Open daily, 4 P.M.–6 P.M. Admission: free. Ask the church sacristan to unlock the chapel door for you.

It's a small chapel, simple and boxlike. But what sets it apart from other chapels are the many rows of eyes staring at you from its four walls—well, rows of eye sockets, at least. When the neighboring churchyard became overpopulated some years ago, skeletons were dug up, pulled apart, and used as floor-to-ceiling paneling in this chapel. The effect is, somehow, understated and serene.

FÁTIMA
(65 miles north of Lisbon)

Wax Museum (Museu de Cere): on rua Jacinta Marto. Open daily, 9 A.M.–8 P.M. Phone: (049) 52 1 02.

The museum focuses on "the story of Fátima," meaning, of course, the history of this former village since a fateful day in May 1917, when three peasant children first saw an apparition of the Virgin Mary, who gave the children messages and instructions concerning world peace. The annual pilgrimages to Fátima on May 13 and October 13 attract cascades of humanity numbering in the hundreds of thousands; the wax museum is a comparatively quiet way to observe Fátima's story. The fact that the museum has but 28 figures and was constructed as recently as 1984—yet is Portugal's first wax museum—is testament to this country's endearingly sleepy quality.

FIGUEIRA DA FOZ

Semi-Permanent Rainbow: on the city beach, in the late afternoon, on sunny days only.

The relentless Atlantic waves have, over the millennia, pounded out one of the most enormous beaches you'll ever see, a beach so wide (over $\frac{3}{4}$ of a mile in places) that it once had its own railroad to transport bathers to the ocean. Now you must walk, but when you get to the actual shore you will, more often than not, be treated to an unusual sight. The crashing surf produces a fine mist that hangs over the portion of the beach next to the water; if you stand with your back to the waves on a sunny afternoon when the sun is lower than 40 degrees above the horizon (anytime after about 4 P.M.), you'll observe a bright rainbow in the mist above you. And because the mist runs along the shore, the rainbow follows you as you stroll down the beach.

LISBON

Bullfighting Museum (Museu Tauromaquico): in the Lisbon bull ring (Praça de Touros), on Avenida da Republica. The metro stop Camp Pequeno is right next to the bullring. Call 76 61 61 or the Lisbon Tourist Office at 36 36 24 for current hours and prices.

Some people find Spanish-style bullfighting exciting. Others are horrified by it. If you, like us, can't stand to see an animal being killed, you'll be happy to know that in Portuguese-style bullfighting the bull is never killed. Portuguese bulls, instead of battling it out with sword-wielding matadors, must fend off eight "moços de forcados"—unarmed daredevils who literally try to grab the bull by the horns. The victory is in outwitting the bull, not killing it. Lisbon's unique bullfighting museum documents this unusual spectacle.

Golden Gate Bridge Twin (25 de Abril Bridge): crossing Rio Tejo (Tagus River) from the western side of the city. The best views of the bridge are from the harbor or from one of the city's hills.

What famous city stands at the western edge of a continent, was once destroyed by an earthquake, has cable cars that go up and down its many hills, and has a famous orange-colored suspension bridge with two towers connecting the city with a nearby peninsula? San Francisco? Wrong. Guess again. It's Lisbon. Unsuspecting San Franciscans visiting Lisbon have been known to faint at their first sight of the 25 de Abril Bridge. It doesn't merely resemble the Golden Gate Bridge: it practically *is* the Golden Gate Bridge. Only an expert eye can notice the differences: the 25 de Abril's towers are slightly shorter and wider, and both of its foundations are in the water. (The Golden Gate only has one foundation in the water.) Americans are shocked to learn that the 25 de Abril Bridge is actually the longer of the two, and is in fact the second longest suspension bridge in the world. A great practical joke is to buy a convincing 25 de Abril Bridge postcard, scribble out the name of the city printed on the back, and mail it home, explaining that you've changed your travel plans and are now in San Francisco. You may not fool anybody, but it's a good way to keep 'em guessing.

The House of Cork (a.k.a. "Mr. Cork"): Rua da Escola Politécnico 4–6. Open 10 A.M.–1 P.M. and 3–5 P.M. Phone: 25 85 8.

Signs in this store proclaim: "Portugal grows the MOST and the BEST cork in the world." This is the truth. Portugal is one country that does not need to import corks to stick in its wine bottles. And for several decades, the man who calls himself Mr. Cork (not "Senhor Cork"— *Mister* Cork) has been purveying all sorts of unlikely items made out of his country's porous pride and joy. Cork postcards (amazingly thin but durable) are here, as well as cork dice; chess sets, checkerboards and checkers; letter openers; nativity scenes; and ships in glass bottles. Don't miss the most patriotic souvenir of all—a colorful map of Portugal printed on a sheet of cork.

Illuminated Fountain Show (Fonte Luminosa): in Império Square, which is in front of the Jerónimos Monastery (officially named Santa Maria Church and Monastery), one block from the river, between Avenida da India and Rua Bartolomeu Dias, in Lisbon's Belém suburb, which is at the southwestern end of the city. Performances on weekend evenings. Admission: free. For more information, call 36 36 24 or 57 59 81.

As if to prove that a palatial monastery need not be all pomp and circumstance, Lisbon offers the Fonte Luminosa right in front of its own favorite sixteenth-century building. When the show gets going, the fountains become great soft plumes shooting deliciously improbable colors against the black sky: caramel gold, bubblegum purple, shamrock green. And for one small part of the day, at least, colossal Jerónimos must take a passive back seat.

Pet Cemetery: in the city zoo (Jardim Zoológico) on Estrada de Benfica in the northwest part of the city. The metro stop Sete Rios is right outside the zoo's entrance. The cemetery is at the back of the zoo, on the hill. Signs point the way. Admission: 250$00; students, 200$00; children aged 7–10, 125$00; children under 6, free. Open 9 A.M.–7 P.M.

Any old zoo has live animals, but only the Lisbon zoo has dead animals as well. Oddly, though, the zoo's cemetery only has graves of household pets, and none for any zoo animals that have gone to that great cage in the sky. In theory, only former pet owners are allowed in, but the gardener generally admits anybody who shows an interest. Some graves have little doggie statuettes on them, others have ceramic photographs of "the loved one," and some are even decorated with traditional Portuguese "azulejo" tiles depicting dogs and cats. Canine names here also are interesting: a quick search of the gravestones turned up Tarzan, Snoppy, Kaiser, Führer, Nikita, Lord, John and Ringo (right next to each other), and even Spot and Fido.

MIRANDA DO DOURO
(Northeast corner of Portugal, on Spanish border)

Jesus in a Top Hat (Menino Jesus da Cartolinha): on permanent display in the south side of the Miranda Cathedral, in the center of town. Open 8:30 A.M.–6 P.M. in summer; 9 A.M.–5 P.M. in winter. Closed Mondays. For more information, call (073) 22271 or (073) 22273.

Miranda's prized possession is a statue of the baby Jesus. Swaddling clothes, you say? Never jump to conclusions on the Iberian Peninsula. Miranda's Jesus sports a top hat, white necktie, and complete 19th-century suit. The church has several different outfits for the statue to wear on special occasions, but his workaday wear is the suit and top hat. He's lucky the faithful of Miranda didn't give him a handlebar moustache to go with it.

MONTE
(On the island of Madeira, $1\frac{1}{2}$ miles north of Funchal)

Toboggan Rides (Carros de Cesto): running from the town of Monte down the hill to Funchal; also shorter rides from the town of Terreiro da Luta (one mile north of Monte) down to Monte. Toboggans are owned and operated individually, so there is no set price, address, or phone number. Both Monte and Terreiro da Luta are small, and toboggan drivers can easily be found in the center of town. Monte and Terreiro da Luta are both accessible from Funchal by bus or funicular, or on foot. Madeira has frequent airplane connections to Lisbon.

For more information, call the Funchal Tourist Office at 25658 or 29057.

Back before Madeira was civilized by the automobile, farmers used to bring their produce down the hills to Funchal on wicker sleds that slid crazily down the cobblestone streets to the market. In the evening they would carry the then-empty sleds back up the hill. All that is a distant memory now; the streets are worn smooth and modern farmers use trucks. The sleds remain, but they now carry tourists instead of vegetables. The hair-raising ride can be arranged with any number of professional toboggan drivers, unmistakable in their straw hats and all-white outfits. Two drivers run along behind each sled, guiding and steadying it with rope leads as they rocket down slopes and around corners. They leave you weak-kneed at the bottom as they jump, tobaggan and all, into a taxi for a quick ride back to the top.

OPORTO (PORTO)

Paper-Costume Parade and Holy Bath (Cortejo de Papel e Banho Santo): Annually on August 23. Procession begins in the Foz do Douro suburb, in the New Quarter of the city, and ends up at Ourigo Beach. Date varies slightly some years. Call (02) 31 2 740 for current date and time.

A suit made of paper is inappropriate beachwear. It makes even worse swimwear, but don't tell that to the people of Foz do Douro, who happily don their colorful paper outfits and swarm in vast numbers down to the beach. One costumed man, designated Neptune-for-a-day, presides over a sprawling mock battle between paper-clad "pirates" and "landlubbers," after which Neptune rides his carriage into the ocean and everybody else piles in after him. What all this could possibly have to do with St. Bartholomew (whose feast day this celebrates) is unknown even to the participants, who maintain in spite of the frat-party-ish paper-suit antics (which are allegedly of ancient origin) that the communal sea bath taken on this day is a "holy bath," worth seven ordinary baths in its power to protect the bather from evil.

PORTO DE MÓS
(14 miles south of Leiria)

Santo Antonio Caves (Grutas de Santo Antonio), Alvados Caves (Grutas de Alvados), and Mira de Aire Caves

(*Grutas de Mira de Aire*): nine miles southwest of Porto de Mós. Buses run to the caves from Fátima, which is 15 miles northeast, and from Porto de Mós. Open daily, 9 A.M.–9 P.M. Admission: 200$00 each. Phone: (049) 23389, (049) 84876, or (049) 84306.

All three of these caves were accidentally discovered, one by one, within the last 40 years. All are absolutely spectacular, and each has its own personality. The Santo Antonio caves, furthest south, have forests of stalactites and stalagmites and great oozing blobs of mineral excretions that look like the set of *Aliens III*. The unnecessary piped-in music is only slightly distracting. Just one mile north, the Alvados caves offer incredible vistas of interconnected underground rooms, filled with strange natural columns, phallic stalagmites, and an excellent lighting system that heightens the overall effect. Separated from the other caves by several miles, the Mira de Aire caves are different altogether. Rivers, lakes, and waterfalls combined with opalescent, colorful rocks make for a more hallucinatory experience. At all three caves you must follow a tour guide (included in the admission price).

REGUENGO DO FETAL
(10 miles east of Batalha; 70 miles north of Lisbon)

Festival of the Snails (Festa dos Caracóis): traditionally held the last weekend in September or the first weekend in October. Festivities last all night; lantern procession starts at 10 P.M. Saturday. For directions and date, call (044) 9 61 80.

This tiny village's patron saint is Our Lady of Fetal (Senhora do Fetal), and we hope she appreciates the villagers' ingenuity in fashioning thousands of lamps out of large snail shells to light the way for her annual procession. Participants in the procession carry the lanterns as they go; and families line their homes, windowsills, doorways, and paths with many more snail lanterns, which burn all through the night. On Sunday, the feast features elongated white egg cakes, dusted liberally with sugar, which are traditionally associated with this festival.

SANTA MARIA DA FEIRA
(20 miles north of Aveiro)

Bread Basket Festival (Festa das Fogaçeiras): Annually on January 20. For more information, call (02) 32611 or (056) 23680.

Innocent youth as the bringer of hope and abundance: that has been the theme of Santa Maria da Feira's annual festival for 400 years. To thank St. Sebastian for rescuing the town from a plague in the sixteenth century, villagers dress up several hundred little girls all in white, and place on their heads beribboned baskets. Into each basket, flowers and loaves of bread are piled in such numbers as to make the burdens far out of proportion with the children's size. The sweet loaves are called "fogaças"; the girls are, for the occasion, called "fogaçeiras," and they proceed through the streets of town maintaining incredible poise as they balance their unwieldy burdens. Villagers come from all over the surrounding area to cheer the girls on and join in the procession.

SPAIN

Legend:
1. Madrid
2. Segovia
3. Santiago
4. Oviedo
5. Bilbao
6. Pamplona
7. Barcelona
8. Valencia
9. Alicante
10. Granada
11. Seville
12. Cordoba
13. Toledo
14. Salamanca
15. Burgos
16. Zaragoza
17. León

If you've been wondering whether 40 years of totalitarian government left a dent in the Spaniards' need for rugged individualism, just try ordering gazpacho in a restaurant.

Gazpacho, one of Spain's national dishes, is a summer vegetable soup, traditionally served cold with bread crumbs as a thickener. Every Spanish chef will swear on ten copies of *Don Quixote* that he or she is using the most authentic gazpacho recipe in all of Spain; but you, upon ordering it, will never find the soup prepared the same way twice. Sometimes it is ice-cold; sometimes it arrives so decidedly lukewarm that you'd swear that was part of the recipe. Some cooks serve a water-thin broth with chopped onions floating on top; others hurl vegetables, bread crumbs and all into the blender, serving you a thick, orange-colored

Spain / 245

brew the consistency of buttermilk. That's how it is in Spain.

Imagine yourself lost in a city, looking for the train station. Ask a stranger on the street for directions, and your savior will be solicitous and verbose, repeating the directions several times in rapid-fire Spanish to make sure that you understand completely. A few blocks farther on, ask another stranger the same question. You'll get the same helpful treatment, but an absolutely different answer. No overlap at all. Ask a third stranger. Get a third answer. Every man, woman and child in Spain has a unique opinion about where things are located and how to get there.

And a beloved Spanish form of debate—a showcase for personal philosophy, clairvoyance, superstition, and idiosyncrasy—is a discussion regarding what time a certain train will arrive, the posted timetable, if any, notwithstanding. A gushing *Turismo* brochure might translate all this into one sentence: "Spain is a country full of surprises."

Yup. Sure is. Folk festivals, whose roots could be Moorish, could be Celtic, or could be Catholic, involving such unnerving elements as living people in coffins—and dancing eggs—are a dime a dozen in surprising Spain.

CATALUNYA

ARGENTONA
(15 miles northeast of Barcelona)

Water Receptacle Museum (Museu Municipal del Cántir Joan Rectoret i Rigola): Placa de L'Església 3. Open in summer, Saturday, 6–8 P.M.; Sunday, 11 A.M.–2 P.M. and 6–8 P.M. In winter, Saturday, 5–8 P.M.; Sunday 10 A.M.–2 P.M. Admission: 25 Pta. Phone: (93) 797 07 11.

The Spanish people could write epics on the subject of thirst. This museum celebrates the great variety of vessels used in connection with water—vessels made of every imaginable substance, designed for guarding, transporting, serving, conserving, and drinking water. If you can manage to leave here without feeling thirsty, then you must be a fish.

BARCELONA

Aerial Tramway (Transbordador Aeri del Port): connecting Montjuic and the port. Boarding stations at the southeast corner of Montjuic off Plaça Armada and at the port next to the aquarium (you can't miss it). Open daily, noon–8 P.M. Round-trip ticket: 500 Pta; one-way, 400 Pta. A round-trip ticket to and from the halfway point, called Jaime I, is 450 Pta. Children under 3, free.

If you have acrophobia, stay away. Far away. Even the view from the balcony of the boarding station is dizzying. When the cable cars launch out over the port, the sea stretches out in one direction, Barcelona in the other, both far, far below you. The ride is either exhilarating or terrifying, depending on your point of view.

Automaton Museum (Museu dels Autómates): in the Tibidabo Amusement Park. Open Monday–Friday, noon–2 P.M. and 3–5:45 P.M.; Saturday, Sunday, and public holidays, noon–3 P.M. and 4–5:45 P.M. Admission: 40 Pta. Phone: (93) 211 79 42.

These are the kinds of dolls you've had nightmares about since childhood: big, almost life-like, and able to move by themselves. The collection of antique automatons, most of which were made in Barcelona, would be interesting even if the dolls didn't move—the details in their construction is incredible: pearly teeth, rings on fingers, blushes on cheeks. But they *do* move; museum workers operate them for the visitors' enjoyment.

Bullfight Museum (Museu Tauri de la Monumental): in the Monumental Bullring (Praça de Braus Monumental), Gran Vía de les Corts Catalanes 749, northeastern part of town. Bullring is halfway between the Sagrada Familia and Marina metro stops. Open daily, 10 A.M.–1 P.M. and 3:30–7:30 P.M.; on bullfight days, open 10 A.M.–1 P.M. only. Admission: 200 Pta; children: 100 Pta. Phone: (93) 225 65 07.

No matter how you feel about bullfighting, about the one-eared bulls' heads lining the walls, about the enshrined ticket to the Aug. 28, 1947 bullfight at which Spain's beloved matador, Manolete, was fatally wounded—the dozen or so mannequins here are guaranteed to please. Not only do they serve their intended purpose of exhibiting several centuries' worth of exquisite matadors' costumes, appropriately called *trajes de luces* (suits of lights), but also the mannequins themselves are treasures of well-meaning kitsch: bronze-skinned; with the kind of shamelessly shapely buttocks for which *trajes de luces* were designed. And their generously sideburned wigs, placed lightly askew on their heads, are a dubious blend of 1776 and 1976, ranging in color from raven to coral. Why visit Michelangelo's David? Why fall in love with a flesh-and-blood man?

Criminology Museum (Museu de L'Institut de Criminologia): Located in the Criminology Department of the university's law school (on Avinguda Diagonal). Open during school hours. Admission: free. To arrange an off-season visit, call the faculty at (93) 205 11 12 or (93) 203 75 09.

This stuff is university property and not some sleazy sideshow, but you still get to see an array of murder weapons, objects used by terrorists, various guns, and other crime-related relics. It's a small collection, but it packs an emotional wallop.

The Dancing Egg (L'Ou Com Balla): performed every year on the eighth day of Corpus Christi (usually early to mid-June) in the cathedral's cloister fountain. The cloister is reached through the door in the rear wall of the cathedral; the cathedral is located in the Gothic Quarter on Plaça Catedral. For date, call (93) 301 74 43.

Locals gather 'round and watch as an egg is placed in the vertical fountain jet early in the morning. The water supports the egg, which jumps, twirls and bounces around— "dancing" to the musical splash of the cloister fountain. All day long the egg is left to perform—a simple white egg—and in the evening it is taken out and laid to rest. No one knows why the ritual is performed, when it began, or what the egg is supposed to symbolize.

Dentistry Exhibition (Exposició Permanent d'Odontologia): Carrer de Tapineria. Open Monday–Friday, 10 A.M.–1 P.M. Admission: free. Phone: (93) 310 15 55.

As long as you're not lying in the dentist's chair with your mouth wide open, the world of dentistry can be pretty interesting. This permanent exhibition traces the history of the profession, with instruments, pictures, and teeth. Persons with a dentist phobia might find the collection a bit too strenuous for a morning's entertainment, but those with a scientific—or macabre—inclination will eat it up.

Gaudí

Antonio Gaudí (1852–1926), was a Catalunyan architect of fantastic imagination. Famed for designing some of the most unusual buildings in Europe, Gaudí made each of his works daringly personal. Many of them are downright startling. A description of some of his structures in Barcelona follows.

Bellesguard Villa (Casa Figueres): Carrer Bellesguard 46, on Tibidabo Hill.

A skinny spire topped with a pinwheel-like ornament lends a churchly look to this palm-fronted house. Elongated windows add to the gothic effect. Irrepressibly cheery colors and shapes in the stained-glass windows make the building unmistakably Gaudí. And the whimsical part is, it's *not* a church: it's a private residence.

Casa Batlló: Passeig de Grácia 43.

The house drips and swells like unbaked cake batter. Balconies are abstract, bottom-floor windows undulate, and mosaics splash across the façade, while the fantastic roof defies every straightedge in the world, heaving and rippling like some wild animal's back.

Casa Calvet: Carrer de Casp 48, near the Urquinaona metro stop.

The balconies, walls, and windows are normally shaped—not a warp or a blob to be seen. But the baldheaded humanoid gargoyles lurking on the top floor are shiveringly weird. City Hall awarded Gaudí an architectural first prize for this one in 1901.

Casa Mila: Passeig de Grácia 92. Roof visits available Tuesdays, 10 A.M.–noon.

Gaudí's legendary apartment house squats on a corner, its surface rolling like shaken gelatin. Balconies are a riot of twisted metal, perhaps the architect's homage to his coppersmith forebears. Chimneys are vast concrete perfume bottles and masked marauders. The interior courtyards, shaped as irregularly as if nature herself had made them, provide views of cavernous stairways. Barcelonans call this house *"La Pedrera"* (the Quarry).

Casa Vicens: Carrer de les Carolines 24 and 26, in the Grácia neighborhood, north of downtown. House is a few blocks west of the Fontana metro stop.

Gaudí at his gaudiest: a Moorish fantasy, a patchwork quilt of tiles in a variety of colors and patterns.

Finca Güell: on Avinguda de Pedralbes, across from Carrer Toquio, near the university.

Guadí was in an oriental mood when he designed these entrance buildings for the property of his staunch patron, Don Eusebio Güell. A domed tower, monolith, scalloped wall, and green tilework are mere background for the entrance gate, which bears the jeering metal dragon that has come to be an emblem of the architect.

Güell Palace (Palau Güell): Nou Ramblas 3, just off the Ramblas dels Caputxins. A theater arts library housed in the building is open Monday–Friday, 9:30 A.M.–1:30 P.M. and 4–8 P.M. Theater Arts Museum is open Monday–Saturday, 11 A.M.–2 P.M. and 5–8 P.M. Closed holidays.

A scary, phoenix-like bird glowers among the twisted metal hanging over the entrance. This is one of the few Gaudí edifices in Barcelona whose interior is open to the public: visit the library and museum if you want to see Gaudí from the inside out.

Güell Park (Parc Güell): at the northern edge of town, near the Vallcarca metro stop. Open daylight hours. Admission: free. The Gaudí House-Museum (*Casa-Museu Gaudí*), inside the park on Carrer d'Olot, is open Sunday and holidays, 10 A.M.–2 P.M. and 4–6 P.M. Admission: 20 Pta. Phone: (93) 214 64 46.

For Gaudí fans, this is better than Disneyland. All the benches, fountains, walls, and buildings were designed by Gaudí as a commissioned city-planning experiment. You'll see a surrealistic Doric temple; a zigzagging bench done in screamingly bright mosaics; a little lodge that is half-cathedral, half wicked witch's cottage. All over the park are glass-and-tile collages, mosaic reptiles, and undulating forms. On the grounds are 60 lots originally intended for houses, but as only two lots were ever sold, the project was considered—believe it or not—a failure.

Holy Family Cathedral (Templo Expiatori de la Sagrada Familia): On Carrer de Marina, between Carrer de Mallorca and Carrer de Provençá, right next to the Sagrada Familia metro stop. Open daily, 8 A.M.–9 P.M. Admission: 250 Pta (including slide show).

A dozen perforated spires race toward the sky, encrusted with concrete lizards, turtles, donkeys, bull heads, frogs, flowers, turkeys, and the Holy Family itself. This unfinished spectacle absorbed Gaudí's attention for the last 40 years of his life, and the architect said it would take 200 years to complete. The words "Sanctus," "Excelsis," and "Hosanna" march up and down the tassel-topped spires, and so can you—on a spiral staircase. Construction materials litter the complex as work continues, ever so slowly, to finish the cathedral.

Lampposts: in the Plaça Reial, off the Ramblas dels Caputxins.

Gaudí didn't limit himself to designing houses. Here in the Plaça Reial, you can see the lampposts that the city commissioned from him in 1878: full of serpentine and wing-like ornaments, the lampposts look ready to take off at any moment.

St. Theresa's School (Col•legi de les Teresinas): Carrer Ganduxer 41, west of downtown.

This vast and comparatively severe building has ornamental concrete spikes marching across the tops of all four walls. A cast-iron fence is another spike fiesta. The hundreds of lofty, tall windows lend a spiritual touch.

* * * *

Hearse Museum (Museu de Pompes Funebres): Sancho de Avila 2, north of downtown. Open Monday–Friday, 9:30 A.M.–1:30 P.M. and 4–6:30 P.M. Admission: free. Phone: (93) 300 50 61.

Not your standard antique car collection, this small but choice selection (owned by Barcelona's municipal hearse service) includes elegant, obscure, and obsolete hearses. You don't have to be a car enthusiast to appreciate this one.

Illuminated Fountain Show (Fuente Monumental de Montjuic): May–September, Saturday, and Sunday, 8–11 P.M. Live music from 8–9 P.M. Fountains are located below the National Palace (Palau Nacional), on Montjuic, just up from Avinguda Rius i Taulet.

Several dozen spouts in a fountain the size of a baseball diamond make for a multitude of color combinations, shapes, and angles. When the fountain gets going, it's a shimmering Niagara of rainbow-sherbet colors, with live music adding to the psychedelic effect.

Perfume Museum (Museu del Perfum): Passeig de Grácia 39. Museum is located at the rear of the Regia Perfumeria Store. Open Monday–Friday, 10 A.M.–1 P.M. and 4–7 P.M. Admission: free. Phone: (93) 216 01 46.

The only thing missing is the scent itself. Louis XV flasks; a rare bottle designed by local boy Salvador Dalí; and exotic bottles from Rumania, Thailand, Israel, Japan, Morocco, Poland, and Russia are all displayed here. You'll see social history represented through the changing shapes and names of the world's perfumes. Don't miss the Parisian atomizer shaped like a naked little boy. Guess which orifice squirts the perfume.

Snowflake (Floquet de Neu): in the Barcelona Zoo (Parc Zoologic): southeastern area of the city, in Parc de la Ciutadella, off Passeig de Circumvallacio. Open daily, 9 A.M.–7 P.M. Admission: 300 Pta. Signs point the way to Snowflake. Phone: (93) 309 25 00.

Every gorilla on this planet has black or brown fur. Except one: Barcelona's treasured Snowflake. This unique genetic faux pas attracts curiosity seekers and scientists alike. Snowflake's intelligence and antics, combined with the disorienting white fur and pink skin, make for quite an entertaining sight.

FIGUERES
(80 miles north of Barcelona)

Salvador Dalí's Own Museum (Teatre-Museu Dalí): on the Plaça Salvador Dalí i Gala. Open Monday–Friday, 11 A.M.–12:30 P.M. and 4:30–7:30 P.M.; Sunday and holidays, 11 A.M.–1:30 P.M. and 4:30–7:30 P.M. Admission: 250 Pta. Phone: (972) 50 56 97.

Maybe you've never heard of Figueres, but it's Dalí's hometown, and the artist chose it as the site of his own personal museum. Housed in an old theater, the collection is full of Dalí-esque surprises, such as a room that turns into a 3D portrait of Mae West when you take a few steps backwards out the door. Perspective tricks and optical illusions abound: the ceiling looks like a glass plate with Dalí himself standing over your head painting yet another, higher ceiling.

LLIVIA

The border between France and Spain is not quite as

simple as it appears at first glance. Andorra, a tiny independent nation, nestles between its larger neighbors; and just east of Andorra is another strange cartographical irregularity. The city of Llivia, legally a part of Spain, is entirely surrounded by French territory. It looks like a piece of Spain that has broken off and floated up into France: actually, Llivia's odd fate is the result of a mistake in a 1659 treaty in which the name "Llivia" was accidentally left off a list of territories Spain was giving to France. No one has ever bothered to correct the booboo. The Spanish-speaking Llivians are loyal to Madrid, and France isn't about to change its national boundary just to reconnect this pesky city with its homeland, so Spain's island inside France is a permanent international quirk. (Llivia is accessible by bus or car from Puigcerda in Spain.)

SANT VICENÇ DELS HORTS
(15 miles west of Barcelona)

Maternity Art Museum (Museu d'Art Matern): Barcelona 302. Open by appointment. Admission: free. To arrange a visit, call 656 00 57 or 656 04 06.

Motherhood is a powerful subject, and this museum—one woman's private collection—is unique in the world. Maternity clothes and obstetrical implements are supplemented by sculptures, paintings, and curios from various eras, all of which deal with birth and maternity.

VILANOVA DEL CAMI
(30 miles northwest of Barcelona)

Museum of Water (Museu de l'Aigua): in Moli de Rigat. Open by appointment, generally on Saturdays. Admission: free. Phone: (93) 803 14 83.

This private collection isn't about water itself, but rather about every type of object related to water—jugs, cups, fountains, waterwheels—ranging from the essential to the frivolous.

VILANOVA I LA GELTRÚ
(25 miles south of Barcelona)

Museum of Sea Curiosities (Museu de Curiositats Marineres Roig Toqués): Almirall Cervera 2. Open Monday–Friday,

5–8 P.M.; Saturday, Sunday, and holidays, noon–2 P.M. and 5–8 P.M. Admission: free. Phone: (93) 815 42 63.

A sailor displays a lifetime of souvenirs gathered on or about the rolling sea. His private collection includes shells, bells, model ships, fishes, and curios—all of it oozing that aura of strangeness associated with exotic ports and fish stories. The star attraction is a carp in a tank that visitors can feed with a tiny *porrón* (a long-nosed Catalunyan pitcher). The fish tilts its head up and begs for a sip.

MADRID AND THE SOUTH

ALICANTE

Piece of St. Veronica's Veil: in the Monastery of Santa Faz (Monastery of the Holy Face), three miles north of Alicante on the road to Alcoy. Chapel containing the veil open 8:30 A.M.–1:30 P.M. and during mass. Admission: free. For more information, call 21 22 85.

When St. Veronica wiped Jesus's brow, his face is said to have miraculously imprinted itself on her handkerchief. This parting snapshot has had a rough history, but part of it has ended up here at the monastery named in its honor. This and the Shroud of Turin are the only known "photographs" of Jesus.

CEUTA

The British seized Gibraltar from Spain long ago and never gave it back; the Spanish still wince in pain at the thought of their missing southern promontory. But don't pity them too much. Just across the strait of Gibraltar is the city of Ceuta, which the Spanish seized form the Moors long ago and never gave back. So now Gibraltar, almost the southernmost point in Spain, is legally British, and Ceuta, the northernmost point in Morocco, is legally Spanish. Now, if only the British would give Land's End, their southwesternmost point, to Morocco, everything would be even. Ceuta is a favorite exotic shopping excursion for Spaniards. (Frequent ferries connect Ceuta and Algeciras on the Spanish mainland.)

CORDOBA

Municipal Museum of Cordoban Art and Bullfighting (Museo Municipal de Arte Cordobés y Taurino): on Plaza de Maimonides, on the southwest side of the city. Open Tuesday–Sunday, 9:30 A.M.–1:30 P.M. and 5–8 P.M. Closed Monday. Admission: 200 Pta.

Despite the title, this is primarily a bullfighting museum, and has more stuffed bull heads than any other museum—bullfighting or otherwise—in the world. Many of the bulls on display defeated their matador opponents, though just as many are now losing the battle with mildew. Also on display is the hide of the revered/reviled bull that killed the famous matador Manolete, and a miniature Manolete coffin, among all the bullfighting trinkets and trivia.

JAEN
(58 miles north of Granada)

St. Veronica's Veil: in the Jaen Cathedral, in the main chapel, on Plaza de Santa María. Chapel is open normal church hours. Admission: free. For more information, call 22 27 37.

St. Veronica's veil, which supposedly bears an image of Jesus' face, is enshrined here in a fancy gold reliquary, and can be visited whenever the church is open. By an odd coincidence, the Monastery of Santa Faz (see Alicante), just 250 miles away, has a piece of the veil—even though the whole thing is supposed to be here in Jaen. Rarely are two such conflicting claims so close together. You can see both in one day and decide for yourself who's right.

JIJONA
(15 miles north of Alicante)

Nougat Factory Tour: El Lobo Nougat Company (Fabrica Lobo), Avenida de Alcoy 62, number 17. Closed Sunday and holidays. To find out about current schedule of guided tours, call (965) 61 02 25 or (965) 61 02 50.

Jijona is Nougatville. Generations of Spaniards and their dentists have enjoyed this city's nutty, sticky specialty. The El Lobo company has been making nougat (*turrón*) since 1725; guided tours of the factory tell you about nougat from the inside out. Watching all that

Madrid and the South / 255

candy in action is enough to make your mouth water as shamelessly as the mouth of the wolf on the El Lobo package. Luckily, free samples are provided as part of the tour, to round out your *turrón* education.

MADRID

Aerial Tramway (Teleférico): connecting Casa de Campo Park and Parque del Oeste. Boarding point is near Paseo Pintor Rosales and Calle Buen Suceso, on the western edge of the city. Open daily, 10 A.M.–2 P.M. and 4:30–7 P.M. Round-trip ticket: 260 Pta; one-way ticket: 185 Pta; children 5 and under, free.

This soaring funicular ride connects two of Madrid's largest and most beautiful open spaces. If you're tired of tunneling your way through the city on the metro or sweating it out in the traffic, then treat yourself to Madrid's most pleasant mode of transportation. The view from the cars is vast, and either way your destination is a verdant park.

Aquarium (Aquarium de Madrid): Calle Maestro Vitoria 8, a few blocks west of the Puerta del Sol. Open daily, noon–2 P.M. and 5–8:30 P.M. Admission: 250 Pta; children, 150 Pta. Phone: 231 81 72.

In the States, this goofy aquarium would be at home in a small-town circus. Psychedelic Asian tarantulas, wild-eyed piranhas, and frogs that look like mud cavort in a delightfully unscientific atmosphere. Someone obviously had a lot of fun building the fake Mayan temple that houses the Mississippi alligator, and the fake Egyptian sarcophagus that serves as the desert tortoise's sole companion. There are few explanatory signs to distract the visitor, just a maze of beasts that are surprisingly lively and satisfyingly large.

Bullfight Museum (Museo Taurino): located in the Las Ventas Bullring (Plaza de Toros de Las Ventas), northeast of downtown, right next to the Ventas metro stop. Open Tuesday–Friday and Sunday, 10 A.M.–1 P.M. Admission: free. Phone: 255 18 57.

The museum's pride and joy is the suit the famed toreador Manolete was wearing when a bull fatally gored him. Generations of Madrileños have come here to grieve over the blood-encrusted pants, vest, jacket, socks, and shoes of their favorite matador, never again to be taken to the laundry. The large and evocative museum also features a photo essay on bullfighting's emotional side. Many slain *toreros'* death masks are here, including one grisly rubber specimen complete with hair, eyelashes, makeup, and collar. Note also the exhibit on Juanita Cruz, one of Spain's few female bullfighters. From the museum's windows you can watch workmen preparing sturdy horses for the ring.

Cork Store (Corchera Castellana): Calle Colegiata 4, behind Plaza Mayor. Open Monday–Friday, 9:30 A.M.–1:30 P.M. and 4:30–8 P.M.; Saturday 9:30 A.M.–1:30 P.M. Closed Sunday. Phone: 227 91 78 or 227 47 19.

For 100 years, Corchera Castellana has been supplying Madrileños with all the cork they need. In addition to normal cork items—bottle stoppers, pool floats, wall paneling, bulletin boards—they have a selection of unusual items, all made entirely of cork: wallets, purses, business cards, model houses, checkbook covers, cigarette holders, ice chests, spindles, and even cork carvings and paintings.

The Encarnación Monastery (Monasterio de la Encarnación): Plaza de la Encarnación 1, near the Opera metro stop. Open Tuesday, Wednesday, Thursday, and Saturday, 10:30 A.M.–12:45 P.M. and 4–5:15 P.M.; Friday, 10:30 A.M.–12:45 P.M. only; Sunday and holidays, 11 A.M.–1:15 P.M. Closed Monday. Guided tours only (in Spanish). Admission (including tour): 100 Pta. Phone: 247 05 10. (Monastery is also closed to public January 6, March 19, March 25, May 1, June 18, July 27, August 28, and October 12.)

They call it a monastery; we call it a museum of the strange art of the religious relic. One room houses 1,500 elaborately decorated bits of saints' bodies: bone fragments, skulls, twists of flesh, and mounds of powdered protoplasm, neatly tagged with saints' names. The relics peep out through windows in silver boxes, gold hearts, candlesticks, columns, jars, miniature houses, dioramas, and statues. Gold-and-glass arms have real armbones encased inside. Just to the right of the door as you enter is a tiny apothecary jar bearing the powdered blood of Saint Pantaleon, said to miraculously liquefy every year on July 27. The monastery is closed to the public on that day, so you'll never know for sure.

Monument to the Fallen Angel (Angel Caído): in Retiro Park, at the intersection of Paseo del Uruguay and Paseo del Ecuador.

The fallen angel in the title is Lucifer—better known as Satan—and this is said to be the world's only public monument in his honor. Lucifer is given a kindly treatment: at the top of the fountain, the handsome young angel grapples with a serpent and tumbles from heaven. Below, grinning maniacal demons squirt water while gripping writhing alligators. The monument's nineteenth-century sculptor, Ricardo Bellver, had as much sympathy for the devil as does Mick Jagger.

Temple of Debod: in Parque del Oeste, near intersection of Calle de Ferraz and Calle Luisa Fernanda, on the western edge of the city. Nearest metro stop: Plaza de España.

When the Aswan Dam was built, the waters of the Nile started backing up and threatened many ancient Egyptian monuments with inundation. Several were saved and moved to high ground. This temple, built in the fourth century B.C., was instead moved stone by stone to a park in Madrid where it now stands, an architectural anomaly. Though a youngster by Egyptian standards, it has acquired the new status of being one of the oldest buildings in Spain.

Wax Museum (Museo de Cera "Colón"): Paseo de Recoletos 41, off the Plaza de Colón. Nearest metro stop: Colón. Open daily, 10 A.M.–2 P.M. and 4–9 P.M., although no entry is allowed after 1:30 and 8:30 P.M. Admission: 500 Pta; children, 300 Pta. Phone: 419 22 82.

A twisted waxen stroll through history. This museum's combination of grotesquery and accuracy has earned it a reputation as Europe's most enjoyable wax museum. See an authentic Spanish bullfight in which the bull is goring the matador in the eye. Nixon, Mao, Hitler, Eisenhower, and Stalin all chat around the dinner table. Dracula shares the Gallery of Criminals with Charles Manson. Laurel and Hardy, Inca priests, brawling cowboys, execution scenes ... the curator's gruesome sense of humor is omnipresent.

MELILLA

Spain is in Europe, and Melilla is part of Spain, so Melilla is in Europe—right? Any logician could tell you that. Unfortunately, politics has little to do with logic, so the correct answer is actually: Melilla is in Africa. Like Ceuta, it's a remnant of Spanish colonialism. You can take a ferry to Melilla and back from Malaga or Almeria; then, years later, when discussing your travels with a new friend, you can say inscrutably, "Yes, I've been to the African continent, but I've never been to any African country." Let them try to figure *that* one out.

PORTO CRISTO
(Eastern coast of the island of Mallorca)

Dragon Caves (Cuevas del Drach): one mile southwest of Porto Cristo. Hours and prices scheduled to change. Call 21 22 16 for new information.

These caves are dreamlike, containing a huge underground lake (one of several claiming to be Europe's largest). As the water shimmers with colored lights, local musicians drift about the lake dubbed "the Amphitheater," hamming it up on harmoniums to entertain cave visitors. The blend of nature and artifice is deliciously surreal.

TABERNAS
(15 miles north of Almeria)

Yucca City Film Towns (Poblados Cinematograficos): in the hills around Tabernas. Signs point the way to the various sets. Visit the Tourist Office in Almeria for a map of the area.

This appropriately dusty replica of the Wild West is where many a familiar movie was filmed, including *A Fistful of Dollars*, *Lawrence of Arabia*, *The Centurions*, and dozens of "Paella Westerns." Among the scattered sets you'll find a fully functional old western saloon, the occasional mock bank raid, and a place to have your picture taken in cowboy duds.

VALENCIA

Bullfight Museum (Museo Taurino): Pasaje del Dr. Serra 18. Entrance to the museum is on the east side of the bullring. Bullring is on the right side as you exit the train station, on Calle Jativa. Open Monday–Friday, 11 A.M.– 1 P.M. Admission: free. Phone: 351 18 50.

This relatively tasteful collection, established in 1929, was Spain's first bullfighting museum—and thus was probably the world's first. A selection of bone fragments from unlucky *picadors* (horsemen who weaken the bull by pricking its neck with a lance) rounds out the five-room array of matador outfits, mounted bull heads, shiny weapons, and portraits. The stairway is dedicated to art: six Goya drawings (all bullfight-related) are an exciting discovery, as is a 12-by-5-foot tapestry, made in Seville in 1896 to advertise a bullfight. Also worth noting here: Manolete's death mask, a photo of a bull in the act of mortally goring a matador, a photo of a matador kissing a bull on the lips, and a photo of a female matador fighting a bull while wearing a tight skirt and high heels.

Fallas Festival: March 12–19, all over the city: bonfires at midnight on March 19.

Valencia's Las Fallas ranks as one of Europe's most creative municipal celebrations. Sure, there are parades, musicians in the street, people in costume, bullfights, and fireworks, but what people really get excited about are the *ninots*, humorous papier-maché statues found throughout the city. Artists and neighborhoods spend months designing their *ninots* in secret, and the competition is fierce, since only one *ninot* each year is chosen to be saved. Throughout the festival, hundreds of fantastically intricate, three-dimensional, cartoon-like *ninots* are displayed in every part of the city, some on stationary platforms, others on rolling floats. The crazy *ninots*, which can be as tall as 40 feet and have up to 25 separate figures, usually satirize some allegorical theme. Each one is rightfully considered a work of art, but no matter: on March 19 at midnight, the festival is brought to a fiery climax when all the *ninots* are put to the torch (*falla* means bonfire in the Valencian dialect). It's exciting—but also sad—finale.

Fallas Museum (Museu Faller): Plaza Monteolivete 4. Take bus 13 from the south side of Plaza País Valenciano, heading east. Open daily, 10 A.M.–2 P.M. Admission: 50 Pta. For more information, call 351 76 90.

Valencia saves its favorite *ninot* (see Fallas Festival) from the flames every year and adds it to the collection of hilarious works of art at the Fallas Museum. Sexy walruses, cupids climbing a pigsty, babies in gas masks—such are the themes represented in 50 years' worth of salvaged *ninots*. It's hard to believe the figures were made by ordinary minds and hands, so insistently grotesque, expressive, and detailed are they.

Holy Grail: in the Valencia Cathedral, on Plaza de

Zaragoza, in the Old Town. It is in the Chapel of the Holy Grail, on the right side of the cathedral, near, but not in, the Cathedral Museum. Open 7:30 A.M.–1 P.M. and 4:30–8:50 P.M. Admission: free.

Of all the Holy Grails floating around Europe, this one might have the strongest claim for being *the* Holy Grail. Its history can be traced back to the third century A.D., at least. Archaeologists and art experts concede that it could be about 2,000 years old. As is common with relics, it has been altered and embellished over the centuries, and we're not quite sure how it looked originally. Now it is an agate bowl on top of an ornate, bejeweled gold stand with two curved handles. Visitors to the chapel can get no closer than about 15 feet, but there are plenty of good pictures of it in the cathedral's gift shop.

VILLANUEVA DE LA CAÑADA
(15 miles west of Madrid)

Aquopolis: Free buses run from Plaza España in central Madrid to Aquopolis daily at 10 A.M., 11 A.M., and noon. Free buses return to Madrid at 5 P.M., 6 P.M., and 7 P.M. Open daily, 10 A.M.–8 P.M. Admission: 1200 Pta; children under 12, 800 Pta. On holidays, 1300 Pta; children under 12, 900 Pta. Phone: 8156911.

"Madrid's a lonely town, when you're the only surfer boy around...." And that goes double when the nearest beach is 200 miles away. But if that sweltering Madrid heat makes you ache for that surfboard in your closet back home, then it's time to head out to Aquopolis, Madrid's brand-new water city. Not only do they have a surf pool with a wave-making machine and complimentary surfboards, but a dozen other theme pools as well: the waterfall pool, the maze pool, the diving pool, the jungle-gym pool, the waterslide pool, the octopus pool, and even a plain old swimming pool for serious swimmers. (Aquopolis opened in the summer of 1987; call ahead to make sure it's still in business.)

THE NORTH

ASTORGA
(27 miles west of León)

Bishop's Palace (Palacio Episcopal): directly behind the Astorga Cathedral, off Puerta de Hierro.

Antonio Gaudí (see Barcelona section), after designing and half-constructing this palace, abandoned the project and let another architect finish the job. Though it was supposed to be a bishop's residence, no bishop ever lived in it. And no other Gaudí building is farther away from Barcelona. Despite all these handicaps, this is one of Gaudí's most satisfying and impressive works. A futuristic porch, ancient-looking towers, smooth white masonry, and black pointed roof—only Gaudí could blend them so convincingly. You can see the inside, also, since the palace now houses a museum.

CATOIRA
(25 miles south of Santiago de Compostela)

Viking Festival (Romería Wikinga): first Sunday in August. Catoira has both a train and a bus station. For more information, call 853 716 or 851 048.

One of northern Spain's biggest surprises—apart from bagpipes and rain—is its number of red-haired, blue-eyed natives. Viking explorations in this area a millennium ago left their mark, and the village of Catoira remembers the Nordic visitors every year. The locals dress in an approximation of Viking costume, float "Viking" ships in their waterways, and make merry. You won't see bullfights in Denmark, but you *can* see Viking ships in Spain, at least one day out of the year.

CELORIO
(36 miles west of Santander)

Face in the Rocks (El Cristo): visible from the village of Celorio, which is just west of Llanes, on the coast. For more information, call 40 01 64.

When Mother Nature puts on a smock and dabbles in sculpture, huge things happen. Ask anyone in Celorio where to see "El Cristo," and they'll point you toward two cliffs, which, seen from a distance, form a dazzling sky-to-sea profile of Jesus' head—beard, crown of thorns, and all. Locals are especially delighted to point out that it takes *two* cliffs, not one, to form the image: Nature, in other words, put extra effort into this œuvre.

ESCATRÓN
(A suburb of Zaragoza)

Mayoress's Festival (Fiesta de la Alcaldesa): held every year on St. Agatha's Day, February 5.

This Aragonese version of the "Women's Day" Festival finds local girls in rustic peasant (laboradora) costumes carrying baskets of bread on their heads in a "Blessed Loaves" procession. (See Zamarramala.)

ESTELLA
(75 miles southwest of Pamplona)

Coed Bull Run (Encierro): held during the annual city festival week, July 31–August 6. For more information, call 55 02 76.

Sick and tired of watching the Pamplona bull run on TV and seeing only men? Men being gored, men being trampled, men hurtling down the street in a drunken clamor? Estella offers a fresh alternative, as this town is one of a handful in Spain that has no ban against women joining its encierros. The women share the action with the men, and have the opportunity to roister and be mortally wounded alongside their masculine counterparts.

LA CORUÑA

Tower of Hercules (Torre de Hercules): about one mile north of downtown, at the tip of the city's promontory (Punta del Orzan). Take bus 9 or 13. Open Monday–Friday, 10 A.M.–1:30 P.M. and 4 P.M.–sunset. Closed weekends and holidays. Admission: free. Phone: 202 759.

The Tower of Hercules is actually a lighthouse built by the Romans in the second century A.D. What makes it different from other Roman ruins is that it's not a ruin at all: to this day it is still used as a lighthouse, and is in fact the only still-functioning Roman lighthouse in the world, and one of a very few Roman buildings still used for its original purpose.

LAS NIEVES
(20 miles southeast of Vigo, on the Portuguese border)

Coffin Pilgrimage (Santa Marta de Ribarteme): every year

on July 29. For more information, call 853716 or 851048.

It's sobering enough to watch a procession in which coffin after coffin is carried through the streets of town. But what if you knew that many of the caskets held living people? People of this region who believe they are about to die have the option of making this vow to Saint Martha: if she can save them from the jaws of death, they will climb into a coffin and be carried therein through the streets on July 29. Apparently the bargain is agreeable to the saint, because every year finds a new crop of grateful people only too willing to take the short ride in a coffin. At the end of the procession they climb out with a new lease on life.

LEÓN

Casa de Botines: between Plaza de Santo Domingo and Plaza de Marcelo.

This building is one of the very few designed by Antonio Gaudí (see Barcelona section) outside of his native Catalunya. Its four towering, sharply pointed spires, tall thin windows, and rough-hewn granite blocks all add to Casa de Botines' castle-like appearance. A waterless moat surrounds the sunken bottom floor, and thousands of mean black spikes fend off the invaders. Yet oddly (though luckily for us), this is now a bank and not a castle, so you can inspect the inside, too. Note the startling St. George and the Dragon sculpture over the door.

MIRANDA DEL CASTAÑAR
(Near Salamanca)

Mayoress's Festival (Fiesta de la Alcaldesa): held every year on St. Agatha's Day, February 5. For more information, call 24 37 30.

In this variation on the "Women's Day" theme, it is the church wardens' wives who rule the day's festivities. (See Zamarramala.)

POTES
(50 miles southwest of Santander)

Pieces of the True Cross: in Santo Toribio de Liébana Monastery, $1\frac{1}{2}$ miles southwest of Potes. Signs point the way. For more information, call 21 14 17.

Though this monastery has the largest single piece of the True Cross left anywhere, it rarely advertises this fact. Instead, its reputation rests on its immense collection of illuminated medieval manuscripts. The Lignum Crucis (wood of the cross) must take a back seat to the manuscripts, but it is still available for public viewing.

SAN PEDRO MANRIQUE
(20 miles northeast of Soria)

Firewalking (El Paso del Fuego): June 24, in the evening. San Pedro Manrique is a very small village, so the festivities are easy to find. For directions and exact time of ritual, call 21 20 05 or 21 20 52.

They almost make it look easy, but they sure don't make it look like fun. To mark St. John's Eve (which is celebrated with bonfires and other fire-related rituals all over Europe), the men of San Pedro Manrique walk barefoot, repeatedly, across a mound of live coals (6 feet long, $2\frac{1}{2}$ feet wide, and 6 inches tall). As crowds of celebrants look on, the men step lively—often carrying passengers on their backs to make the trial appear even more spectacular.

SANTIAGO DE COMPOSTELA

Leaning Church (Colegiata de Santa María de Sar): on southeast edge of town: go down Calle de Sar de Afuera under the railroad tracks, and turn right after one block—it's hard to miss. Open Monday–Saturday, 10 A.M.–1:30 P.M. and 4–6:30 P.M. Closed Sunday and holidays. Admission: 50 Pta.

The church is noted for its outstanding design—outstandingly bad, that is. The anonymous twelfth-century architect who built this church apparently wasn't convinced that buildings need a foundation, nor did he realize that this low-lying area's soil lacked a certain firmness. So, over the centuries, the Santa María de Sar Church started sinking and tilting. It's still standing and still used for services, but the inside is like a funhouse: columns lean at odd angles, arches are lopsided and distorted, and the floor isn't quite flat. Even the outside walls are leaning sideways. One theory claims that the church was built this way on purpose.

Medical Museum (Museo Médico Compostelano): Calle San Pedro de Mezonzo 41 (*not* 39, as the pamphlets indicate) in Colegio Médico. Ask at front desk to see the museum, and they will open it for you. Open 10 A.M.–3 P.M. Admission: free. Phone: 595 562.

This museum's specialty is anesthesiology: iron lungs, inhalers, bottles of chloroform, and plenty of disturbing medical implements are on display. There is also a proud exhibit about how doctors in Santiago started anesthetizing their patients within a month of anesthesia's first medical use in 1847—the first place in the world outside of England to use it.

SOTOSALBOS
(12 miles from Segovia)

Mayoress's Festival (Fiesta de la Alcaldesa): held every year on St. Agatha's Day, February 5. For more information, call 43 03 28.

A woman serves as "mayoress"-for-a-day, advised by a phalanx of female counselors-for-a-day, all dressed in rich old-fashioned costume. Other women-oriented festivities round out the day, which is meant to honor the patron saint of wives and nursing mothers. (See Zamarramala.)

ZAMARRAMALA
(A suburb of Segovia)

Mayoress's Festival (Fiesta de la Alcaldesa): held the Sunday immediately following St. Agatha's Day, which is February 5. For more information, call 43 03 28.

Two matrons, elected co-mayoresses-for-a-day, enjoy blustering regally about the town, laying down the law, advised by other townswomen. The mayoresses *(Alcaldesas)* wear lavish black-and-red costumes, hung with silver ornaments. Meanwhile, the men of Zamarramala are banished to their homes, where they must perform domestic chores. The mayoresses read proclamations, give orders, and control the city all day, in honor of St. Agatha, the martyred patron saint of married women and nursing mothers. Despite the fact that St. Agatha met a tragic and bloody end, this festival is full of laughs and satire.

SWEDEN

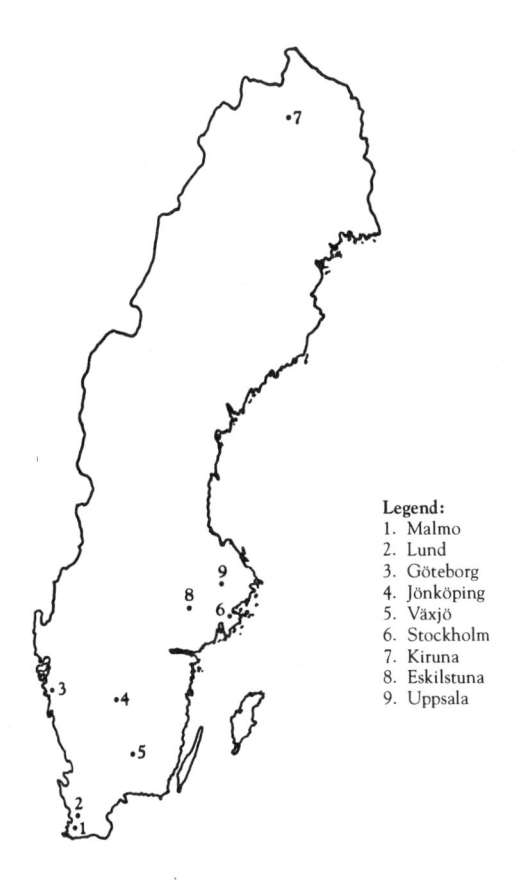

Legend:
1. Malmo
2. Lund
3. Göteborg
4. Jönköping
5. Växjö
6. Stockholm
7. Kiruna
8. Eskilstuna
9. Uppsala

Let's play a game: I'll say a word, and you tell me the first thing that comes into your head. Ready? Here it is: Sweden. Now, what did you just think of? No, don't tell me, I already know. When you hear Sweden, you think big. Large.

Everything about Sweden is big. The people are big, the countryside is big, even the meatballs are big. Swedes stride around like they've got plenty of elbow room; and, by Thor, they *do* have elbow room, all over the place. Leg room too. Ever driven a Volvo? I haven't, but I rode in the back seat once and boy, was there a lot of leg room.

Sweden / 267

A country that big has space for strange things, and Sweden has its share of oddities. Sweden has interesting cities, a varied landscape, a unique history, an alcohol problem, and a lot of smart people: a combination like that is prime breeding territory for off-the-wall attractions. Big off-the-wall attractions. Come and see for yourself.

ÄDELFORS
(Ten miles east of Vetlanda)

Gold Panning (Ädelfors Guldgruva): on the river. Open daily, 10 A.M.–6 P.M. Price for gold-panning instruction and use of pan: 24 Kr. For more information, call the Tourist Office at (0383) 974 14 or (0383) 974 08.

On the site of an abandoned gold mine, you can rent a pan and become a prospector for a day—dipping, sloshing, searching hopefully for yellow sparkles—on the banks of a cold river. You get to keep what you find, and for free you can visit the nearby abandoned nickel mine. Maybe you'll set off the next Swedish gold rush.

ESKILSTUNA
(55 miles west of Stockholm)

Phantomland: part of the Parkenzoo complex. A 15-minute walk (or five-minute drive) west of Eskilstuna. Open May 1–September 6, daily, noon–6 P.M. Admission: 44 Kr; children 4–14, 20 Kr; children under 4, free. Phone: (016) 14 73 80.

Several generations of vicarious superheroes can indulge in bloodcurdling fantasies at this theme park, based on American comic artist Lee Falk's purple-clad character, The Phantom. His comic-book adventures usually took place in steamy, danger-filled jungles, and Phantomland accordingly offers vine swings, hollow trees, suspension bridges, waterfalls, a Skull Cave, Phantom Lake, Mysterious Well, and scenarios based on the comic-book adventures. You might even see the Phantom himself.

HILLERSTORP
(11 miles northwest of Varnamo, in Jönköping County)

High Chaparral: four miles southwest of Hillerstorp, just outside the town of Viborg. Open May–September, daily, during daylight hours. Admission prices scheduled to change. For new prices and more information call (0370) 822 20.

Europe's most sophisticated Wild West town is a dusty hunk of Texas in the middle of Sweden. Millionaire businessman Bengt Erlandsson lived out a childhood fantasy by building the city; he changed his name to Big Bengt, and now he watches over the place as self-appointed sheriff. Every day in summer there are stunt horseback-riding Swedes in western duds, masked raids on the town's steam train, country music performances by locals, and tons of quasi-authentic atmosphere. The town has everything you'd ever want from a frontier town and more, including a saloon, walled fort, stagecoach rides, an Indian reservation, a corral, and even a real hotel and campground. Except for the occasional comic blunder, the recreation of the American West is pretty impressive.

HÖÖR
(18 miles northeast of Lund)

Stone Age Village (Stenåldersbyn): part of Skånes Djurpark, located $2\frac{1}{2}$ miles north of town. From Lund, Helsingborg, or Malmo, take the Pågatågan commuter train to the Höör stop. Open in summer daily, 9 A.M.–5 P.M.; in winter, 10 A.M.–3 P.M. Admission: 35 Kr; children 6–16, 10 Kr. Phone: (0413) 220 60.

Wielding forked sticks, stone mortars, and even primitive musical instruments, the Stone Age families frolic in their tunics at the southern end of Skånes Djurpark. Thatched huts are home to their rustic activities. Ancient animal breeds, such as boars, add even more savagery to the scene. Elsewhere in the park are a labyrinth and a reconstructed dolmen. Summertime activities include solstice festivals, weaving workshops, and a Viking festival.

HUSKVARNA
(Just east of Jönköping)

Dr. Skoras' Wax Museum (Vaxkabinett): Grännavägen 24, northeast of downtown. Open March, April, September, and October, daily, 11 A.M.–5 P.M.; May–August, daily, 10 A.M.–7 P.M.; November, Friday–Sunday, 11 A.M.–5 P.M. Admission: 30 Kr; children under 14, 10 Kr; children under 7, free. Phone: (036) 14 20 80.

Sweden's royal couple stare fixedly at visitors, looking for all the world like aliens: with toothy smiles, and arms held out in identical positions. But it gets even better: at the push of a button, the wax king and queen put on a show. Dr. Skoras' renditions of Swedish heroes Bjorn Borg and ABBA mug alongside their American counterparts, Elvis Presley, Barbra Streisand, and the Muppets. Several of the figures put on mechanical acts.

JÖNKÖPING

Bird Museum (Fågelmuseet): in the City Park (Stadsparken), west of downtown. Open May–August, 10 A.M.–1 P.M. and 1:30–5 P.M. Admission: 5 Kr; children, 2 Kr. Phone: (036) 12 99 83.

You don't need to put salt on their tails in order to get a closer look; these birds won't fly away. They're stuffed, all 1,400 of them. Every Scandinavian species is represented, as are a large number of European ones. Also on display is a large collection of eggs.

Giant Sculptures: three miles from Jönköping, in Riddersburg (on the road to Nässjö). Open daily. Admission: free. For more information call the Jönköping Tourist Office at (036) 10 50 50.

The world's tallest sculpture is right here in Sweden—in the sculptor's own backyard, no less. The sculptor is Calle Örnemark, and his tall masterpiece is "The Indian Rope Trick"—a giant of a man climbing a 310-foot "rope" up to the sky. It is constructed entirely of wood, as are the other gargantuan statues dotting the property. Örnemark really does live here, and often gives visitors a personal tour of his works. Don't miss "Mutiny on the Bounty," a life-size sculpture of a sailing ship, complete with masts and vast interlacings of rope, resting serenely on the shore of Lake Vättern.

Matchstick Museum (Tändstickmuseet): Västra Storgatan 18, on the lakefront. Open Monday–Friday, 11 A.M.–5 P.M.; Saturday, 11 A.M.–1 P.M.; Sunday 1–5 P.M. Admission: 10 Kr; children under 15, free. Phone: (036) 10 55 43.

A matchstick museum in the middle of Sweden is not as crazy as it seems at first sight, for Jönköping is the very place where safety matches were invented over 100 years ago. The museum, housed in the original match factory, has two basic sections. One illustrates the history of man's attempts to create fire, culminating in the invention of the safety match; the other is an amazing collection of matchbox labels from all eras and all countries.

KIRUNA
(North of the Arctic Circle)

What's the biggest city in the world? New York? London? Mexico City? Wrong. The biggest city in the world—geographically speaking, that is—is Kiruna, Sweden, population 27,000. A few years back the city council decided, in order to make administration easier, to extend the city's boundaries all the way to the edges of the province. So now Kiruna has an area of almost 7,200 square miles. In most of the city, reindeer far outnumber people, and there is nary a parking meter to be seen. To make things even stranger, the sun never sets in Kiruna during the entire month of June and the first two weeks in July.

KLIPPAN
(17 miles east of Helsingborg)

Dino World: five miles north of Klippan off Highway E4, adjacent to the town of Stidsvig. Open June–August, daily, 10 A.M.–6 P.M. Admission: 20 Kr; children 4–11, 15 Kr; children under 4, free. Phone: (0435) 220 52.

Dino World is all you'd expect from a place called Dino World: dinosaurs, dinosaurs, and a few prehistoric mammals thrown in for seasoning. The saurian sculptures in this kitschy outdoor museum are "life size," which means a lot bigger than us. And since the park opened its doors for the first time in June 1987, all the dinosaurs are still new and glistening. We're still trying to puzzle out why places like this, no matter where they are, always have English names.

LUND

Gambro Tours: the plant is on Magistratsvägen, north of downtown. Take bus 4. Tours by prior arrangement. Admission: free. Phone: (046) 16 90 00.

How many times have you scratched your head and wondered, "How *do* they make artificial kidneys, anyway?" Or "What *happens* to human blood between the time someone donates it and someone else receives it?" A guided tour of Gambro, one of the world's largest medical technology plants, provides the answers, touching on dialysis machines, heart–lung machines, extracorporeal blood—the works. Just be glad they don't offer free samples.

Medical History Museum (Medicinhistoriska Museet i Lund): on Getingevägen, north of downtown. Open by appointment only, Wednesday, 5–7 P.M. and Thursday, noon–2 P.M. Phone: (046) 10 22 90.

The city of Lund has long been associated with medical progress. This collection, with its many rare implements, provides a glimpse into the ways in which Swedes have been prodded, tweaked, pierced, stitched, and otherwise repaired for the last several centuries.

Medieval Mechanical Clock: on the cathedral, in the exact center of town on Kyrkogatan, just north of the main door. Performances daily at noon and 3 P.M., and on Sundays at 1 and 3 P.M. Free.

This ancient clock is so classy it even has a Latin name: Horologium Mirabile Lundense. It shows the minute, hour, day, week, month, and year, the positions of the sun and moon, and the sign of the zodiac. At noon and 3 the Three Wise Men troop out to the hymn "In Dulci Jubilo" and offer presents to Jesus and Mary; knights emerge to joust and then strike the hour; two heralds raise their trumpets to play. A Timex this is not.

Mental Hospital Museum (Museet Sankt Lars Sjukhus): Sankt Larssjukhusområde 7, south of downtown. Open Monday–Friday, 10 A.M.–2 P.M. Phone: (046) 16 48 15 during office hours; at other times call (046) 16 47 40.

One of Europe's earliest psychiatric hospitals is the source of this museum. On display are former patients' quarters, including a turn-of-the-century isolation room (frighteningly symmetrical and narrow), and a first-class patient's room (with elegant furniture and candlesticks). Also here are bathtubs and other treatment equipment. Patients' handicrafts and artwork provide a more intimate glimpse of life on the verge.

SKARA
(45 miles northwest of Jönköping)

Skara Sommarland: five miles east of town. Buses travel regularly between Skara and Sommarland. Open May 15–June 5, daily, 10 A.M.–5 P.M.; June 6–21, daily, 10 A.M.–6 P.M.; June 22–August 16, daily, 10 A.M.–7 P.M.; August 17–30, daily, 10 A.M.–5 P.M. Admission: 60 Kr

(65 Kr between June 19 and August 16); seniors, 30 Kr; children under 4, free. Phone: (0511) 62245.

Kooky amusements here include a stunning specimen of that European standby: an Indian Village with teepees and totem poles standing blithely side by side. Also available in the park are a Smurf House (complete with Smurfs) and a Mad House (with crazy angles and pictures of Alfred E. Neuman). For adults who want to feel small again, the Dinosaur Park has a luridly colored tyrannosaurus and brontosaurus glaring from above the treetops.

STOCKHOLM

Brewery Museum Pripporama: Voltavägen 30. Take the metro to the Alvik stop and then bus 110, 111, or 112 to Voltavägen. Open June 15–August 14, Monday–Friday; two-hour tours given at 10 A.M. and 1 P.M.

The brewery and bottling company Pripporama gives extensive tours of its plant: see movies, check out the bottling rooms, and get a visual and verbal (in English) explanation of how the drinks are made and packaged. At the end of the tour is a visit to the brewery museum, dedicated to beer-making (which is only a part of the goings-on here). The best part of all is the free samples of beer, soft drinks, and whatever else is rolling off the line that day.

Giant Chess Game: at the southern end of Kungsträdgården, in the center of town near the corner of Kungsträdgårdsgatan and Arsenalsgatan. This extralarge giant chess game has wooden Swedish modern pieces. They take a little getting used to, but they are nice to look at, and each game is like a moving sculpture garden.

Kaknäs Tower Elevator: inside Kaknäs Tower (Kaknästornet), in Ladugårdsgärdet Park, north of Djurgarden, east of downtown. Take bus 69 from Karlaplan (take bus 47 from the city center to get to Karlaplan); during the summer, bus 68 goes directly from the city center to the tower. Open May–August, daily, 9 A.M.–midnight; April and September, daily 9 A.M.–10 P.M.; October–March, daily, 9 A.M.–6 P.M. Admission: 12 Kr; students and children, 6 Kr. Phone: (08) 67 80 30.

Kaknäs Tower (which, at 508 feet, is Scandinavia's tallest building) has many remarkable features, not the least of which are its elevators. Among the fastest in the world, they rocket up and down at over 15 feet per second (some brochures claim 18 feet per second), but they go so smoothly and are so well designed that you hardly notice any motion. You enter the elevator on the ground floor, the doors close, your ears pop, the doors open and you're at the top. On the way down, the pressure change and acceleration are, for some reason, even less noticeable. When you first exit after the 450-foot descent your body thinks you're still on the top floor; your knees go weak and you start to feel a little tipsy. After a minute your sense of balance catches up with you.

Museum of the Dance (Dansmuseet): Laboratoriegatan 10. Take bus 69 to Ambassaderna, or bus 44 or 47 to Djurgårdsbron. Open Tuesday–Sunday, noon–4 P.M. Closed Monday. Admission: 10 Kr; children and students, 5 Kr. Phone: (08) 67 85 12.

This museum, with its diverse array of costumes and masks, celebrates the human body as musical instrument, ritual object, and plaything. Items in the collection come from all over the world and include set designers' sketches and pictures as well as dazzling dancewear. Films and videos add the necessary dimension of motion. Ranging from trance-dance to classical ballet, the museum whispers: "Let your backbone slip!"

Music Museum (Musikmuseet): Sibyllegatan 2. Take the metro to Östermalmstorg. Open Tuesday–Sunday, 11 A.M.–4 P.M. Closed Monday. Admission: 8 Kr; students and children, 5 Kr. Phone: (08) 63 36 71.

This music collection (over 45,000 instruments in all) might be Europe's most up-to-date: it covers punk as well as more antiquated forms of rock, displaying synthesizers and guitars of all shapes and descriptions. For those visitors too unhip to appreciate such things, the museum also offers lutes, viols, and hurdy-gurdies.

Royal Armory Museum (Livrustkammeren): Slottsbacken 3. Take the metro to Gamla Stan, or bus 43, 46, 55, 59 or 76 to Slottet. Open Tuesday–Friday, 10 A.M.–4 P.M.; Saturday and Sunday, 11 A.M.–4 P.M. Admission: 10 Kr; students and children, 5 Kr. Phone: (08) 20 95 69.

At a masked ball in 1792, Sweden's King Gustav III was enjoying himself mightily when a party-pooper suddenly shot him in the head. The Armory Museum has the king's bloody costume. Bloody costume lovers will also appreciate the gory jerkin King Gustavus Adolphus was wearing when killed in 1632.

Telemuseum: Museivägen 7, north of Djurgarden, near Kaknäs Tower. Take bus 69 from Karlaplan or, during summer, bus 68 from the city center. Open Monday–Friday 10 A.M.–4 P.M.; Saturday and Sunday, noon–4 P.M. Admission: 15 Kr; students and children 7–16, 5 Kr; children under 7, free. Phone: (08) 63 10 85.

The Telemuseum, which you enter through the Swedish Technical Museum, is devoted to communications of all kinds. Television-fanatic Couch Potatoes won't even make it past the first exhibit, which consists of 6 TVs, all on different channels, going simultaneously for your viewing pleasure. Another exhibit explains naval flag language; nearby is a mockup of an ancient Roman torch-lamp communication network. A few steps down is an oscillator that responds to your voice. (Be careful here: people might think you're talking to yourself.) The most remarkable among the dozens of other displays are the great home radio collection and the flight simulator on the second floor.

STRÄNGNÄS
(35 miles west of Stockholm)

Sioux Indian Club: Indian Village is 3 miles east of town on the E3 road. Open three weeks out of every year, usually in July, daily, noon–4 P.M. Admission: 10 Kr. For more information call (0152) 177 72 or (0152) 253 17.

The Sioux Indian Club is a regular bunch of Swedes—housewives, families, working stiffs—who balked at American Indians' Hollywood-movie image (which is many Europeans' sole information source about Indians). They decided to build their own Indian village—a really accurate one, based on real facts about Plains Indian life. Now in its eleventh year, the village has 11 teepees, inhabited by costumed Swedish "Indians" who perform Sioux dances and work on Plains handicrafts under the Nordic sun. Club members will gladly show you around and explain how they got so absorbed in this subject and how they ensure their village's accuracy. Overlook, if you will, that Viking-blonde hair.

VÄXJÖ

The Emigrants' House and Research Institute (Emigrantinstitutet): on Södra Järnvägsgatan, near the northwest corner of the Växjösjön Lake. Open Monday–Friday, 9 A.M.–4 P.M.; Saturday, 11 A.M.–3 P.M.; Sunday, 1–5 P.M. Phone: (0470) 201 20 or (0470) 414 10.

Does Swedish blood run in your veins, making you crave herring and Ingmar Bergman films? If so, you can research your roots here. One whole floor is stocked with microfilm, archives, and documents regarding local emigration. (Most of the Swedes who left for North America in the nineteenth century came from this boulder-studded, nonarable part of the country.) An Emigration Museum in the building has some original Vilhelm Moberg manuscripts; and the annual "Minnesota Day" (held in early August) is a big event, drawing thousands of Swedish-Americans who come to hear speeches, folk music, and lectures, and to lament the difficulties of obtaining smoked herring in Oklahoma.

Temple of Echoes: Just south of Växjö in the suburb of Teleborg. To reach it, go down Teleborgsvägen, go past the Teleborg tract houses, and look for a tall water tower on the left side of the road. For more information, call the Växjö Tourist Office at (0470) 414 10.

If it looks like a water tower, that's because it *is* a water tower. Yet it is the most unusual and least-known tourist attraction in all of Sweden. The "Temple of Echoes" (actually an unofficial local nickname) looks totally unremarkable, even from a few feet away. But try this: walk to the center point underneath the 100-foot-tall tower and say "hello." For the next 30 seconds you'll hear that same "hello" over and over again countless times. The underside of the water tank is a perfect parabolic curve, and the focal point just happens to be at ground level right below it. Any sound you make there will bounce off the tank and come right back, where it will bounce off the ground up to the tank, and so on and so on. Even though it's an absolutely perfect acoustic echo chamber, the effect was apparently unintentional. Be warned that although the temple sparks uncontrollable laughter in some people, others are terrified by the crazily repeated sound. Go at your own risk.

VIMMERBY
(60 miles east of Jönköping)

Saga Town (Sagobyn): half a mile north of town; follow the signs. Open daily in summer. Admission: 25 Kr; children 6–14, 10 Kr; children under 6, free. Phone: (0492) 113 85.

Pippi Longstocking is literature's littlest feminist: strong as an ox, and determined to keep her life from getting in a rut. Writer Astrid Lindgren, creator of Pippi (and her giant shoes and her monkey), was born in Vimmerby. Saga Town commemorates her works: the collection of little houses based on various Lindgren works is inhabited by costumed Lindgren characters. Emil—Pippi's mischievous male counterpart—is a star attraction here.

VISBY
(On Gotland Island, off Sweden's east coast)

Medieval Week: all over the town center, usually the first full week in August. For current dates, call the Visby Tourist Office at (0498) 109 82.

For one whole week the center of Visby sheds 600 years and becomes a medieval village. The first and second Sundays of the month see the liveliest action, with the majority of the town's population in medieval costume, performing medieval plays, selling authentic crafts, playing ancient melodies. Beggars, executioners, hawkers, and jesters throng the streets. Tourists get caught up in the spirit—even if they had intended to stay in the twentieth century.

Villa Villekulla: $2\frac{1}{2}$ miles from downtown. A free double-decker bus travels from Visby to Villa Villekulla regularly. Open in summer, daily, 10 A.M.–6 P.M. Admission: 45 Kr. Phone: (0498) 643 65.

Some of Pippi Longstocking's most outrageous adventures began in her candy-colored ramshackle house, Villa Villekulla. The mansion itself—at least, the one used in all the *Pippi* movies—is here in Gotland. You can ramble around its pink-and-green expanses; on the grounds are Pippi's makeshift airplane and her father's boat. Other amusements here continue the Pippi theme: for example, you can hunt for her father's gold coins on a sandy mini-island. Finders keepers.

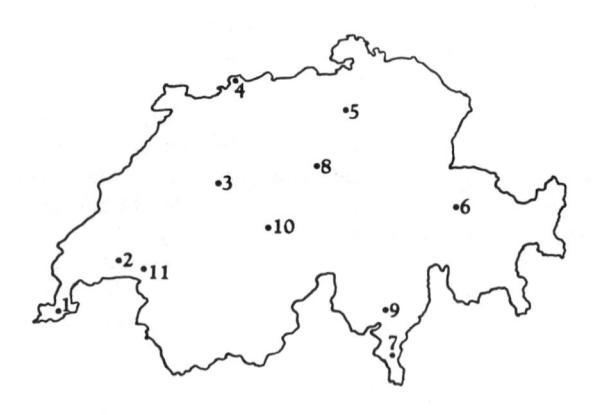

SWITZERLAND

Legend:
1. Geneva
2. Lausanne
3. Bern
4. Basel
5. Zurich
6. Chur
7. Lugano
8. Lucerne (Luzern)
9. Bellinzona
10. Interlaken
11. Montreux

Tick, tock, tick, tock ... that's what you hear the moment you cross the Swiss border. You don't necessarily hear it with your ears; you hear it with your psyche. The Swiss view time as an entity, an entity that they have captured, tamed, and studied. Yet little do the Swiss know, they have brought an irreversible curse upon themselves: punctuality. Swiss clocks are always correct, and have surreptitiously seized total control of the country: stores always open and close when they're supposed to; trains are never late; eight seconds after the Zurich Stock Exchange opens in the morning, the average businessman has completed three transactions and made half a million francs; no one in Switzerland has ever missed an appointment; antique clock towers have been striking the hour with bone-chilling accuracy without fail for 500 years. Obsessive Swiss watchmakers churn out precious, flawless watches at a furious pace; eventually every one ends up in a museum, so now Switzerland has five times as many clock museums as do the rest of the countries in the world put together.

In spite of, or perhaps because of, this temporal tyranny, Switzerland has retained its natural beauty: lush valleys, soaring mountains, untouched forests. The wild Switzerland goes by a different—though just as reliable—schedule: the seasons. Long before the invention of clocks, the ancient mountain tribes marked time with festivals heralding the end of winter or the completion of a successful harvest. Even in modern Switzerland, the people understand this need to appreciate the passage of time on a grander scale, so many of the old festivals and customs survive to this day.

BASEL

Anatomy Museum (Anatomisch Sammlung): Pestalozzistrasse 20, north of the center. Open Sunday, 10 A.M.–noon. Admission: Fr. 2. Phone: 061-57 05 55.

We won't say this is an anatomy museum with pretentions, but there *is* something of the art museum in the way they display their fetuses and skull-tops. The human skeletons here are among the world's oldest prepared-for-science specimens. One of these has a conspicuous lack: it used to belong to a prisoner who was beheaded in 1573.

Basel Paper Mill and Museum of Paper, Writing, and Printing (Basler Papiermühle/Schweizer Papiermuseum und Museum für Schrift und Druck): St-Alban-Tal 35-37, east of the center. Open Tuesday–Sunday, 2–5 P.M. Closed Monday. Admission: Fr. 5; students, Fr. 3.

You may never again throw away a piece of paper after seeing what our medieval ancestors had to go through just to obtain a single sheet. Paper-making equipment on display here dates back several hundred years, and includeds such hefties as a paper mill, printing office, bookbindery, and book press. Craftspeople periodically demonstrate these for visitors' enlightenment.

Caricature and Cartoon Collection (Sammlung Karikaturen und Cartoons): St-Alban-Vorstadt 9, just east of the

Wettstein Bridge. Open Wednesday and Saturday, 4–6:30 P.M.; Sunday, 2–5 P.M. Closed July. Admission: Fr. 5; students, Fr. 2.50; children under 11, free. Phone: 061-22 13 36 or 061-22 12 88.

Here's further proof that Swiss people occasionally laugh. Seventeen hundred originals make up this collection; changing exhibits highlight the works of cartoonists and caricaturists of various countries.

Cat Museum (Katzenmuseum): Baselstrasse 101, in the suburb of Riehen. Take tram 6 from downtown Basel. Open Sunday, 10 A.M.–noon and 2–5 P.M., and by appointment. Phone: 061-67 26 94.

You could spend nine lives inspecting the 10,000 kitty-related items that decorate this museum inside and out: statues and paintings, of course, but more eclectic cat-cult objects as well: cat jewelry, dishes, postage stamps, teapots, ashtrays, toys, sheet music, and more. A cat skeleton and ancient cat mummy will satisfy the scientists and latent cat-haters among you.

Coach and Sleigh Collection (Kutschen- und Schlittensammlung): in the barn near Villa Merian in St. Jakob's Botanical Garden. Open Wednesday, Saturday, and Sunday, 2–5 P.M. Admission: Fr. 2; children, free. Phone: 061-22 05 05.

Sleighs are to the Swiss what dune buggies are to Southern Californians. This collection includes many sleek historical vehicles, which must have seen many a great day dashing through the snow.

Collection of Ancient Musical Instruments: Leonhardstrasse 8. Open Wednesday and Friday, 2–5 P.M.; Sunday, 10 A.M.–noon and 2–5 P.M. Admission: Fr. 3; free on Sundays. Phone: 061-25 57 22.

Three hundred years' worth of the most elegant classical musical instruments form the major part of this museum. Another section focuses on Swiss and European folk instruments: drums, tin flutes and many other folkloric curiosities.

Crazy Music Night (Guggemuusige): the Tuesday following Ash Wednesday.. For more information call the Basel Tourist Office at 061-25 50 50.

The days surrounding Crazy Music Night make up Carnival Week (Fasnacht) in Basel—Switzerland's biggest Gestalt therapy session, full of costumed hijinks, 4 A.M.

parades, and other antirepression devices. Crazy Music Night features drummers and other musicians clad in grotesque masks (tongues hanging out; noses like sweet potatoes), playing as badly and as loudly as they possibly can. They play badly on purpose, mind you, sending the other 15,000 Fasnacht participants howling and covering their ears, and loving every cacophonous minute. Chamber music fans, take flight.

Life-Size Dinosaur: in St. Jakob's Park.

It looks *very* real. This baggy-legged brontosaurus, king of the hillock, was built for a landscaping exhibition in 1980, and now Basel's got him for keeps.

Swiss Museum of Pharmaceutical History: Totengässlein 3. Open Monday–Friday, 9 A.M.–noon and 2–5 P.M. Admission: free. Phone: 061-25 79 40.

The two reconstructed pharmacies—from the eighteenth and nineteenth centuries—provide a shivery look at pharmaceuticals in the golden days of chloroform and leeches.

Swiss Museum of Sport (Schweizerisches Sportmuseum): Missionsstrasse 28. Open Monday–Saturday, 2–5 P.M.; Sunday, 10 A.M.–noon and 2–5 P.M. Admission: free. Phone 061-25 12 21.

This museum is faced with the tragic dilemma of having only enough space to show 1 percent of its gigantic collection. Because of this, many of the exhibits are rotated periodically. On permanent display are nineteenth-century bicycles, a tricycle with no handlebars, a primitive bicycle from 1818, a bicycle built for four, and funny pictures of people falling off bicycles. Upstairs are a section on Swiss winter sports and an excellent collection of circus posters about a trick cycling troupe. Obscure sports are covered, too: Persian-style wrestling, professional stone-throwing (*steinstossen*), pelota, and ping-pong.

Three Countries' Corner (Dreiländereck): one a promontory jutting out into the Rhine north of the city center.

The tall pylon, visible from all around, represents the point where the borders of France, Germany, and Switzerland meet. Technically, the real meeting point is in the middle of the river, but this is as close as you can get without a boat. By wrapping your arms around the pylon, you could—symbolically, at least—embrace three countries at once.

Winter's End (Vogel Gryff): held alternately on January 13, 20, and 27. For the current date, call the Basel Tourist Office at 061-25 50 50.

In the misty, frosty morning, a raft floats down the Rhine bearing the ivy-wreathed Savage—the Wilde Mann—who shakes an uprooted pine tree in the direction of Kleinbasel (the Rhine's right bank). On the Mittlere Brücke, the Savage is joined by two fearsome companions: a shaggy lion and a green-winged griffin. At noon the three dance together as they have done for 400 years, chasing away the winter with their dance, and always taking care never to face the left bank.

BELLINZONA
(In Italian Switzerland)

Rice Feast (Risotto a Carnevale): every year on Shrove Tuesday (in February). Some other towns in the Ticino also have risotto feasts. For more information, call the Bellinzona Tourist Office at 092-25 70 56.

A hundred years ago, this custom ensured that even the poorest members of the community would eat a satisfying pre-Lenten meal. Now, as then, chefs prepare an enormous vat of rice outdoors, and everyone present gets a free serving. This includes tourists. Bellinzona traditionally prefers sauced, spiced rice (*risotto*); other Ticino villages mark the day with huge open-air feasts of dumplings or polenta.

BERN

Child-Eater Fountain (Kindlifresserbrunnen): on Kornhausplatz, near Marktgasse.

"Mommy! Save me! Mommy, save..." Gulp. Also known as the Ogre Fountain, this brightly painted sixteenth-century statue, whose origins remain a mystery, depicts a giant busily stuffing a baby into his mouth. There's nothing cute about it, but it sure is funny, especially if you've ever been trapped on a train full of Boy Scouts. Several more infants writhe unhappily in the giant's arms, but he isn't about to let go. *You* wouldn't let your dessert run away, would you?

Clock Tower (Zytgloggenturm): on Theaterplatz, at Kramgasse. Mechanical figures perform at four minutes before the hour. Guided tours between May 1 and October 31, daily, at 4:30. Price of tour: Fr. 3. For more information call the Bern Tourist Office at 031-22 76 76.

Since bears are the city's mascot, it's no wonder that the mechanical figures On Bern's clock tower include a procession of crown-wearing, drum-beating, gun-toting bears. An astrolabe displays the exact time, date, sign of the zodiac, and phase of the moon. And the hourly mechanical show finds Father Time mumbling to himself and flipping an hourglass; a rooster crows; a lion roars; the adorable bears lumber past. A larger-than-life golden knight—by the name of Hans—strikes the hour.

Feeding the Bears: bear pits (Bärengraben) are located east of the center, across Nydeggbrücke. Take bus 18. Pits are open April–September 7 A.M.–6 P.M.; October–March, 8:30 A.M. to 4 P.M. For more information call the Bern Tourist Office at 031-22 76 76.

Long ago, Duke Berchtold V vowed that he'd name this city after the first animal he killed on his next hunt. Some unfortunate bruin did him the honor. The town was named Bern, and live bears have been permanent guests of honor here ever since. About a dozen of them cavort in the pit; in late spring you can often see some cubs as well. Unlike Duke Berchtold, the bears are strict vegetarians. The city feeds them bread and vegetables, but visitors are encouraged to feed the bears such snacks as fruit and muffins. To the bears, this is as much fun as a buffet brunch, and they'll willingly roll over and do tricks in exchange for the treats.

Justice Fountain (Gerechtigkeitsbrunnen): on Gerechtigkeitsgasse, east of the Clock Tower, on the way to Nydeggbrücke.

"...And if you don't untie this damned blindfold, I'll do it again!" Four severed heads loll balefully at Madam Justice's feet, but she feels no regrets. She's gripping her sword with appropriate zeal; she's another of Bern's bloodthirsty sixteenth-century fountain statues. The heads belong (belonged) to an emperor, a sultan, a mayor, and a pope. No, nothing's sacred.

BEX
(15 miles south of Montreux)

Salt Mine and Museum: Le Bouillet, in Bex. Open April 1–November 15, daily; tours at 9 A.M. and 2 and 3 P.M. Reservations are necessary. Phone: 025-63 24 62.

The two-hour tour starts in the museum, where a slide show outlines the mine's 300-year history, and where artifacts suggest what life was like for the salt miners of old. Then, the juicy part: hop onto an underground train and chug your way deep into the heart of the mountain. Once out of the train, the guide leads on foot back through a bewildering maze carved out of salt. The tunnels and chambers actually go on for 30 miles, but the tour group would be lost for days even if you only visited half of them. As it is, you get to see some of the best parts, including underground lakes, salt columns, stairways carved out of salt, and ancient, salt-encrusted wheels and walkways.

BÜRGLEN
(20 miles southeast of Lucerne)

William Tell Museum: in the Wattigwiler Tower. Open June–October, daily 10–11:30 A.M. and 2–5 P.M. Phone: 044-2 10 10 or 044-2 24 75.

How do you pronounce "Robin Hood" in Swiss-German? "Wilhelm Tell," that's how. It's a rough translation, but the Swiss folk hero's daring archery won him a similarly honored place in his people's hearts. In the thirteenth century, Tell refused to salute a cruel governor, and thus was sentenced to shoot an apple off his son's head, or die. He succeeded, and went on to spend the rest of his life insulting cruel governors. The museum displays Tell-related works of art, documents, handicrafts, and relics. (Bürglen, William Tell's alleged hometown, also has a Tell chapel.)

CAMPIONE D'ITALIA
(Just across Lake Lugano from Lugano)

The official name of this place serves also as a reminder to the Swiss: this is an Italian city, even though it is in Switzerland. And it's not simply Italian in customs and language. It's legally and politically Italian, and is indicated as such on the map. How a city within Switzerland's borders became an official part of Italy is a story too long to tell here, but it looks like this cartographical anomaly will be a permanent feature of the landscape.

CANTINE DI GANDRIA
(Ten miles south of Bellinzona)

Smugglers' Museum (Museo Doganale Svizzero): in the old

Customs House, reachable only by boat. Open April–September, daily, 2:30–5:30 P.M. Admission: free. Phone: 091-23 98 43.

Italy is on the opposite shore of Lake Lugano, and if those blue waters could talk! Many a would-be smuggler has ventured across the lake laden with ingeniously hidden contraband, only to have their ruses defused by sharp-eyed Swiss border guards. Would *you* have been able to detect the hidden compartment in those innocent-looking shoe heels? Would *you* have had the nerve to wear them? Other hidden compartments and smuggling devices on display here are masterworks of bravado, foolhardiness, and cunning.

DORNACH
(Five miles south of Basel)

The Goetheanum: on a hill next to the town (no specific street address). It's visible from almost everywhere in Dornach, and is unmistakable. Open daily, 10 A.M.–noon and 2:30–4 P.M. Admission: Fr. 2. Phone: 061-72 42 42 or 061-72 40 41.

The Goetheanum is not simply a building—it's a philosophical statement. Designed by Rudolph Steiner, founder of the anthroposophical movement, the Goetheanum serves both as headquarters for the society and as a physical expression of its belief system, which, in a phrase, states that man is the center of the universe and that education of the soul leads to spiritual freedom (am I a philosopher yet?). The building, finished in 1928, is half-geometric and half-organic: odd angles, curves, rounded surfaces, and strangely shaped windows and doors all draw you to the interior, parts of which are supposed to represent (symbolically, at least) various human internal organs. During the tour, the guide explains it clearly and tells you all you need to know about anthroposophism. A building? A sculpture? A philosophy? You decide.

GENEVA

Giant Chess Games: in the northwest corner of Promenade de Bastions Park, near the entrance of Place Neuve.

This park has three eight-foot-square chessboards in a row, all sporting knee-high plastic pieces.

Museum of Ancient Musical Instruments: rue François Le-Fort 23. Open Tuesday, 3–6 P.M.; Thursday, 10 A.M.–noon and 3–6 P.M.; Friday, 8–10 P.M. and by appointment. Admission: Fr. 1; students and children, free. Phone: 022-46 95 65 or 022-21 56 70.

The 300 antique instruments here are all still in playable condition, so you can hear them as well as see them. Once a month the museum stages chamber music concerts in which the instruments are used.

GOLDAU
(Ten miles east of Lucerne)

Avalanche Museum (Bergsturzmuseum): Parkstrasse 46. Open April 15–November 1, daily, 1:30–6 P.M. Admission: Fr. 1; children under 16, Fr. 0.50. Phone: 041-82 19 39.

The whole city of Goldau was buried in an avalanche in 1806. Now "new" Goldau is home to this museum, which is stocked with objects salvaged from the 1806 disaster, as well as Swiss avalanche warning devices.

INTERLAKEN

Jungfraujoch Ice Palace: From Interlaken Ost Train Station, take train through Lauterbrünnen or Grindelwald to Kleine Scheidegg. From there take the private rail line up to Jungfraujoch (price varies according to what time you go and what type of railpass, if any, you have). Once you're at Jungfraujoch, the ice palace is free: take the elevator behind the post office up to Ice Palace Corridor. Open whenever trains arrive. The round trip takes most of the day. For more information call 036-22 26 21.

Up up up you go through tunnels blasted out of two mountain peaks to the world's highest train station, Jungfraujoch. Walk to the elevator and ride up to what is the most inaccessible off-the-wall place in Europe. The Jungfraujoch Ice Palace is a series of tunnels and caves carved straight out of a glacier: everything, including the floor, ceiling, and walls, is pure ice. In the tunnels are ice sculptures of furniture, Mickey Mouse, an entire car, and many other things—all carved out of solid ice and permanently frozen. As you're admiring the huge caverns and funny sculptures, remember that the floor can be very slippery.

St. Beatus Caves (St-Beatus-Höhlen): four miles east of town, along the cliff bottom road. Buses travel regularly between Interlaken and the caves; caves can also be reached on foot. Open Palm Sunday–October 18, daily, 9:30 A.M.–5 P.M. Admission: Fr. 6; children, Fr. 2.50. Phone: 036-41 16 43.

Pay your respects to the cowled wax figure of St. Beatus, the sixth-century monk who moved into the cavern after forcibly evicting its previous occupant, a dragon. Other life-size waxen denizens in the cave today include a fair-haired prehistoric family—reminders that the place was inhabited several thousand years ago. Electrically lit grottoes and passageways feature stalagmites, waterfalls, underground streams, and reflecting pools.

KIESEN
(Ten miles south of Bern)

National Dairy Museum (Milchwirtschaftliches Museum): museum is easy to find in the tiny village: from the train station, walk two blocks to the main street and turn left. Open April–October, daily 2–5 P.M.; other times by appointment. Admission: free. Phone: 031-45 33 31.

Life-size flat Swiss people made of plywood serve as the mannequins in the reconstructed cheesemakers' kitchen. Athe the push of a button you can hear the cheesemakers' casual, yet instructive, conversation (in English, no less). Other exhibits and a slide show tell you even more about cheese. We're talking Swiss cheese here, remember, so one of the questions the museum tackles is "Where do the holes come from?" How the Swiss cheesemakers managed to create the moon and put it up in the sky is not discussed, however.

KILCHBERG
(Three miles south of Zurich)

Lindt Chocolate Factory Tours: Seestrasse 204. Tours by appointment only, from May–October, on Thursdays. (English tour given at 1:15 P.M.) Admission: free. Call 01-716 22 23 to get on a tour.

Switzerland's most famous chocolate company offers a luscious free tour. After watching a film on how chocolate is produced, you are led through the factory. Only a single type of chocolate bar is manufactured on the premises each day, and you'll get plenty of samples of whatever the day's product might be. At the end, after a final round of samples, visitors even get some chocolate to take home. Now *that's* a chocolate factory tour.

KÜSSNACHT AM RIGI
(Six miles northeast of Lucerne, on the northern prong of Lake Lucerne)

Chasing Santa Claus (Klausjagen): every year on December 5 (the eve of St. Nicholas' feast day), in the evening. For more information, call the regional Tourist Office in Lucerne: 041-51 18 91.

In the black country darkness, 200 white-robed men and women stream down the street wearing illuminated bishops' mitres. The cardboard headdresses, about as tall as the people wearing them, are resplendent, with intricate cutouts and colored-paper "windows." A candle lights the headdresses from within. These glowing, spectacular figures "chase" St. Nicholas as he makes his rounds through the village. Sure, St. Nick is there; sure, these are mitres—but local anthropologists guess this festival dates back to a pre-Christian light-in-winter rite.

LA CHAUX-DE-FONDS
(30 miles west of Bern near the French border)

International Clock Museum (Musée International d'Horlogerie): rue des Musées 29. Open Tuesday–Sunday, 10 A.M.–noon, and 2–5 P.M. Closed Monday. Admission: Fr. 6; students and children, Fr. 3. Phone: 039-23 62 63.

Despite all competing claims, this is probably the finest collection of clocks and watches in Europe. More than 3,000 timepieces are displayed, each of which is remarkable in some way. The museum, subtitled "Man and Time," and built mostly underground, also has a theater and restoration center.

LA TOUR-DE-PEILZ
(15 miles east of Lausanne)

Swiss Museum of Games (Musée Suisse de Jeu): in the castle. Open Tuesday–Sunday, 2–6 P.M. Closed Monday. Admission: Fr. 3; children under 17, free. Phone: 021-944 40 50.

This collection has an enticing hands-on focus, and is

organized into five sections: educational games, and games of strategy, skill, role-playing, and chance. Puzzles, playing cards, chess sets, casino games, and tarot cards are here, as are some dizzying action games from bygone days. Even cheaters and swindlers are part of the subject matter. If the museum leaves you with an insatiable competitive urge, scurry out to the castle courtyard, where two giant chessboards beckon: knee-high pieces; mellow ambience.

LAUSANNE

Collection of "Art Brut": in the Chateau de Beaulieu, Avenue des Bergières 11, northwest of downtown. Open Tuesday–Friday, 10 A.M.–noon and 2–6 P.M.; Saturday and Sunday, 2–6 P.M. Closed Monday. Admission: Fr. 5; students, Fr. 3. Phone: 021-37 54 35.

"Art Brut" (which translates literally to "crude art" or "rough art") refers to art made by non-artists. In this case, the creators are not only from outside the art world, but also from the fringes of society: insane-asylum inmates, criminals, hermits, eccentrics. The collection is based on the idea that art is at its most creative when it is not intended to be art. The exhibits in the museum are mostly temporary showings culled from the museum's vast collection of shocking, creative, original, and even disorienting works, in the form of collages, drawings, masks, and creations that defy classification, on themes you had never imagined.

Museum of Pipes and Tobacco: rue de l'Academie 7, in the old city. Take bus 1, 5, or 6 from the train station. Open Monday–Saturday, 9 A.M.–noon and 2–6 P.M. Closed Sunday. Admission: Fr. 3.50; children free when accompanied by an adult. Phone: 021-23 43 23.

Smoking's not such a simple pleasure, after all, as you can see from some of the elaborate, precision-crafted pipes in this museum. These are a far cry from the primitive wood and clay specimens found elsewhere in the collection—which contains 2,500 items in all, and spans five continents and five centuries.

LUCENS
(20 miles north of Lausanne)

Sherlock Holmes Museum: in the Chateau de Lucens.

Open April–October, Tuesday–Sunday, 10 A.M.–6 P.M.; March and November 1–December 15, Tuesday–Sunday, 10 A.M.–5 P.M. Closed December 16–February 28, and Monday. Admission: Fr. 4.40; students, Fr. 3.30; children, Fr. 2.20. Phone: 021-95 80 32.

You could always count on Holmes to show up in the most unexpected places. So don't be too surprised when you find him in the cellar of this old Swiss castle, surrounded by exact replicas of his own living-room furniture, memorabilia, photos, and other Doyleiana. An explanatory cassette is available in English.

LUCERNE (LUZERN)

Glacier Garden (Gletschergarten): Denkmalstrasse 4, north of the center. Open May 1–October 15, daily, 8 A.M.–6 P.M.; March–April and mid-October to mid-November, daily, 9 A.M.–5 P.M.; mid-November–February, Tuesday–Sunday, 10:30 A.M.–4:30 P.M. Admission: Fr. 4.50; students, Fr. 3; children, Fr. 2.50. Phone: 041-51 43 40.

The site Lucerne occupies used to be buried in glacial ice. That was 20 million years ago, so you can't make snow-cones, but you can stroll around the weird "garden" of holes, bowls, and craters that millions of years' worth of water carved in the stone hereabouts. The on-site museum explains the glacial miracles, and also has—of all things—a crazy hall of mirrors, a copy of one owned by a maharajah.

MELIDE
(Four miles south of Lugano)

Miniature Switzerland (Swissminiatur): on the lakefront. Follow the signs. Open March 15–October 31, daily, 8 A.M.–6 P.M. Admission: Fr. 7; children, Fr. 3.50. Phone: 091-68 79 51.

Switzerland may already be small enough, but here they squeeze it down into a couple of acres. All things typically Swiss are represented at one twenty-fifth their normal size: chalets, castles, churches, trains, statues, and even a mock-up of locals dancing in the park. For that touch of realism, 20-foot snow-capped mountains loom in the background.

NEUCHATEL

Suchard-Tobler Chocolate Factory Tours: rue de Tivoli 5, west of downtown. To reserve space on a Tuesday-afternoon tour, call Tuesday morning or earlier. Reservations necessary. Admission: free. Phone: 038-21 21 91.

Sadly, the chocolate museum in the factory is now closed. But as a consolation prize, you can take a free factory tour and fatten yourself on the samples provided. Suchard-Tobler is not as well known in America as other brands, but nine out of ten chocoholics agree that Suchard bittersweet is about the best chocolate made anywhere.

ROCHE
(Six miles south of Montreux)

Swiss Museum of the Organ (Musée Suisse de l'Orgue): in the Roche St-Bernard Monastery barn, one-third of a mile from the train station. Open May–October, Tuesday–Sunday, 10 A.M.–noon and 2–5 P.M. Closed Monday. Admission: free. Phone: 021-9 6 22 00.

This is a collection of rare musical instruments all based on the principle of air passing through pipes of varying lengths. Housed in a huge, restored, fifteenth-century barn, the museum includes huge church organs, home organs from the seventeenth century, an organ whose keyboard is operated by pedals, an incredibly ornate organ case from the reign of Louis XVI, little panpipes, and an array of photos. The tour wouldn't be satisfying if you didn't get to hear the organs, so the guide obliges with some thunderous performances.

SAINTE CROIX
(25 miles north of Lausanne)

International Center of Mechanical Art (CIMA Museum): rue de l'Industrie 2. Open Tuesday–Saturday, 1:30–6:30 P.M. and Sunday, 9 A.M.–6:30 P.M. (last tour begins at 5:15 P.M.). Phone: 024-61 44 77. Guided tours last one hour and 15 minutes.

This region of Switzerland is devoted to the manufacture of mechanical frivolities, and this museum is the industry's showcase. Automated mimes and tweeting birds, music boxes, mechanical musical instruments, moving sculptures, and tricky clocks all get equal attention here. Besides being able to admire these things from the front, you'll also get a short behind-the-scenes peek at how they are made.

SCHÖNENWERD
(25 miles southeast of Basel)

Bally Shoe Museum: Gösgerstrasse 15. Open by appointment only. Phone: 064-40 26 82.

Oh, the beautiful, painful, ridiculous things we have been doing to our feet for the past 2,000 years! This extensive collection includes footwear in straw, leather, gold leaf, silk, and more—originally worn by popes, lords, fops, and peasants. Emphasis is also placed on shoes as symbols: note the shoe-shaped Persian burial vessels and boot-shaped Roman wine jars.

SCUOL
(55 miles east of Chur in far eastern Switzerland)

Hom Strom Straw Man Burning: first Saturday in February. Fire is lit at 8 P.M. in the village square.

This prehistoric custom has survived unchanged to the present day. The children spend the morning building a crude six-foot-wide "man" out of rye, which is then stuck on a telephone pole and set up in the village square. In the evening, people strike up flaming balls of gas-soaked rags and twirl them around on chains; at the stroke of 8, they fling the balls at the Hom Strom, who goes up in a blaze of fire. The obvious folkloric explanation for this is that the Hom Strom is the spirit of winter being banished—an understandable concept in Switzerland.

SURSEE
(15 miles northwest of Lucerne)

Knocking Down the Goose (Gansabhauet): November 11 (Martinmas). Takes place in front of the town hall. For more information, call the regional Tourist Office in Lucerne: 041-51 18 91.

This Swiss version of a piñata party uses a flesh-and-blood piñata. Every little boy in town takes a turn trying to knock down a dead goose that is hung from a string; as if that weren't enough, the boys wear a startling, hollow-eyed, golden mask in the shape of the sun, underneath which the boys are blindfolded. Whew. Sursee's children—for this is a children's festival—punctuate the day with sack races, tree-climbing contests, and our favorite European party game: ugly face-making contests.

VALAIS CANTON
(Southwest Switzerland)

Cow Battles: throughout the spring, climaxing in June. For information on organized cow battles, call the regional Tourist Office in Sion at 027-22 31 61.

If you're the type who likes to watch females fighting, consider the cow battles. The Herens is a sturdy breed of cow raised only in the Valais, and this breed has retained the wild primitive instinct to organize into social hierarchies. Every spring they choose a queen who leads the herd. Female cows, of their own accord, battle it out spontaneously all up and down the valley when spring arrives; the local humans love to gather 'round and watch the strong, short-legged black females pawing the ground, snorting, and literally locking horns as their quaint Swiss cowbells clang riotously. The humans love this spectacle so much, in fact, that they give Nature a nudge by organizing regional cow-queen championships. The animals participate in these only too gladly. At least they don't resort to scratching and hair-pulling.

VEVEY
(12 miles east of Lausanne)

Food Museum (Alimentarium): rue du Léman 1, on the lake. Open Tuesday–Sunday, 10 A.M.–noon and 2–5 P.M. Closed Monday. Admission: Fr. 3; students and children, Fr. 1. Phone: 021-52 77 33.

This large modernistic museum tackles food from every conceivable angle. The first section is about how nutrition and energy make their way from the evironment into plants, then into our mouths, and finally into our cells. The other half of the ground floor deals with food from an anthropological viewpoint, showing the connections between diet and lifestyle in cultures around the world. The upper floor is dedicated to food history, starting with hunting and gathering and ending with the twentieth century. Keep an eye out for the combo-animal, a Noah's nightmare that is part chicken, part fish, part sheep, part pig, and part cow. Nearby, a huge mouth houses a theater, in which you can watch a movie about teeth. And if the museum makes its point too convincingly, you can assuage your hunger pangs in the cafeteria.

WILER
(20 miles north of Brig, in Valais Canton)

Ugly Mask Parade: the Saturday preceding Mardi Gras (in February). Held throughout the village, in the afternoon. For more information, call the regional Tourist Office at 027-22 31 61.

You'd expect masks this ugly to come from somewhere like New Guinea. Throughout the Lötschental Valley (wherein are the villages of Ferden, Kippel, Wiler, Ried, Blatten, and Fafleralp), what was once a local folkloric custom of making deliberately ugly masks has now become an export industry. The masks, which were (and are) intended to scare off evil spirits, are displayed throughout the year in the villages, and are used as disguises in parades during Carnival. Made of wood, animal hair, and teeth, each mask is uniquely repulsive, usually elongated and grimacing. Groups of young men (known as Roitschäggätä), wearing the masks and full-body disguises roam around during the days before Shrove Tuesday—especially "Dirty Thursday" and Saturday. A parade with a competition for the most horrifying mask is held regularly in Wiler, and is the high point of the mask year.

YVERDON-LES-BAINS
(20 miles north of Lausanne)

Museum of Utopia, Extraordinary Voyages, and Science Fiction (Maison d'Ailleurs): rue du Four 5. Open by appointment. Admission: Fr. 2. Phone: 024-21 64 38 or 024-21 99 22.

If you lived in a pin-neat Swiss village that ran like clockwork, you'd dream of monsters and amazing voyages, too. The 70,000 items in this collection include postage stamps, fantastic toys, original manuscripts, books dating back as far as 1504, poster, drawings, and even some way-out foods.

ZURICH

Beyer Museum of Time Measurement (Museum der Zeitmessung Beyer): Bahnhofstrasse 31, downstairs. Open Monday–Friday, 10 A.M.–noon and 2–4 P.M.; Saturday, 10 A.M.–noon. Closed Sunday. Admission: free. Phone: 01-221 10 80.

The original owner of the world's smallest wristwatch must have had very good eyesight indeed. Other marvels on display here include a functioning pocket watch with works made entirely of ivory, a clock that automatically lights a candle, and the incredible eyeball watch.

Burning Böögg (Sechseläuten): usually the third Monday in April. Parade begins in front of the train station, travels down Bahnhofstrasse, across Rudolf Brun-Brücke, around the Grossmünster Church. Böögg is finally burned at 6 P.M. at Sechseläutenplatz, adjacent to Bellevue on the shore of Lake Zurich. For exact current date, call the Zurich Tourist Office at 01-211 40 00.

Every year, all of Zurich turns out to see winter burned in effigy—in the form of a towering cotton snowman. Preceding the burning, a parade of guild members in exaggerated costumes winds through the streets (the tailor, for example, wields a huge scissors). At Sechseläutenplatz, precisely at 6, the pyre is lit under the snowman (Böögg), who is mounted on a pole. The snowman is loaded with explosives. He is, in effect, a giant fuse. Everyone waits breathlessly to see how long Böögg will last before his loud and fiery finale occurs. The moisture in the air determines Böögg's life span; Zurichers say that if the snowman lasts a long time, summer is still far away.

Jacobs Suchard Museum of the Cultural History of Coffee: Seefeldquai 17, at the corner of Feldeggstrasse. Take tram 2 or 4. Open Friday, 3–6 P.M.; Saturday, 10 A.M.–4 P.M. Admission: free. Phone: 01-385 12 83.

In Switzerland, they take coffee seriously. This museum is the only one of its kind in the world, maintaining a vast collection of paintings, sculpture, and other art that depicts humans interacting with coffee: serving, drinking, preparing. Several hundred years' worth of European coffee customs are represented here in silver, porcelain, and ink. American worshippers of the caffeine-bean will feel right at home.

Kulturama: Espenhofweg 60 (Schulanlage Letzi). Take tram 9 or 14 to the end of the line; from there, follow the signs to the Kulturama. Open every Monday–Friday, and the first Sunday of every month, 10 A.M.–5 P.M. Admission: Fr. 5; students and children, Fr. 3. Phone: 01-493 25 25 or 01-463 90 09.

In theory this is supposed to be an educational museum about biology and evolution, but it's so much fun that it could pass for a kooky traveling side show. Crazily painted animal and human skeletons pose across from a seamy stuffed crocodile. In one corner, a family of real human skeletons readies itself for a busy day: Mama and Daddy Bone lovingly admire their skeletal infant, which lies curled up in a basket; meanwhile their teenage son, Tad Bone, hurries off to school carrying his bookbag. Another room features a birth control display, decorated with armies of identical little plastic babies (as a warning?); there's also a hilarious skull smoking a cigarette, jars of preserved embryos and preserved organs, and an incongruous array of cultural and medical artifacts.

Medicine History Museum (Medezinhistorisches Museum): Ramistrasse 17, at the university. Entrance is at Künstlergasse 16. Fourth floor. Take tram 6 or 9. Open Wednesday and Thursday, 2–5 P.M. Admission: free. Phone: 01-257 23 77 or 01-257 22 98.

The emphasis is on the doctor's role as magical medicine man, shaman, and high-tech diagnostician. Some of the tools, pictures, and documents on display here date back 2,000 years.

Museum of Ugly Masks (Bundnermasken-Keller): the museum's door (unnumbered) is opposite Obere Waidstrasse 9, west of downtown in the Käferberg neighborhood. Take tram 11 or 15 to Bucheggplatz. Door is open (and thus easy to locate) when museum is open, which is the first Sunday of every month, 10 A.M.–noon. Admission: free. Phone: 01-492 17 09.

Intentionally ugly masks are a less famous Swiss handicraft than, say, cuckoo clocks. But they're every bit as unnerving. It takes a highly skilled carver to create the kind of masks used in Wiler's Ugly Mask Parade (see Wiler); Zurich's Paul Strassmann is one of these, and the 250 scowling, leering wooden faces on display in this cellar are all Strassmann's creations. The oldest dates from 1938; but it's impossible to say which of the stragglehaired, snaggle-toothed creatures is the ugliest.

North American Indian Museum (Indianer-Museum): Schulhaus Feldstrasse, at Feldstrasse 89, west of the center. Take tram 8 or bus 31. Open Saturday, 2–5 P.M. and Sunday, 10 A.M.–noon (hours vary during school holidays). Admission: free. Phone: 01-241 00 50 (recorded message).

Teepees in Zurich? Yup. And Navajo blankets, buffalo skulls, and colorful corn, not to mention some compelling ritual objects—1,400 specimens in all. This is Europe's only museum dedicated to American Indians and their culture, and a lovingly-put-together collection it is. We may see the Swiss abandoning those clumsy alpenhorns for compact gourd rattles someday soon.

YUGOSLAVIA

Legend:
1. Ptuj
2. Zagreb
3. Ljubljana
4. Sarajevo
5. Belgrade
6. Skopje
7. Dubrovnik
8. Split
9. Niš

This chapter should be called Europe Off the Iron Curtain; for although Yugoslavia is communist, they hate the Russians more than they hate the Americans. As a result, Yugoslavia is neither an Iron Curtain nation nor a Western nation, and it now finds itself in political No-Man's-Land. But what do you expect from a country that has six different languages; three different alphabets; four different religions; 13 different ethnic groups; 142 different useless tourist agencies; 3,627 different gun-wielding border guards; and 2.5 million drunken 18-year-old boys, all indistinguishable? Gad, what a place.

BELGRADE (BEOGRAD)

Museum of the Illegal Party Presses (Muzej Ilegalnih Partijskih Stamparija): Banjički Venac 12.

A place of total mystery. We list it as an off-the-wall place to visit, but merely because attempting to visit it is an off-the-wall experience. Locals admit to its existence, but will offer no other information, giving the impression that discussing the place may be a criminal offense. There are a couple of signs in the neighborhood pointing the way to the museum, but when you arrive at Banjički Venac 12, the inhabitants treat you the way they would treat a visiting KGB agent. Does the museum exist? Maybe. When is it open? We don't know. The question, "Can we see the museum now?" sparks a bitter argument in Serbo-Croatian. All the while, the guard dog growls at you menacingly. Possibly the Yugoslav government does not approve of a museum about subversive underground newspapers. Too many dangerous ideas. This is probably the most interesting place in Belgrade. If you feel adventurous, give it a try.

Nikola Tesla Museum: Proleterskih brigada 51, at the corner of Proleterskih brigada and Prote Mateje streets. Monday–Friday, 10 A.M.–noon and 4–6 P.M.; Saturday, 10 A.M.–1 P.M. Admission: D 100.

Nikola Tesla, inventor, genius, and practical joker, was Yugoslavia's one great contribution to the scientific world. Without him there would be no alternating current (the AC part of AC/DC), no dynamos, no induction motors, and no high-voltage current. Basically, he is responsible, more than any other single person, for bringing safe electricity to the world. As a sideline, he came up with the ideas of remote control and radio transmission towers. Yet he remains fairly obscure. This museum deals with every aspect of Tesla's life: weird personal documents (check-out slips from the New York City Public Library; debt notices from J. P. Morgan), copies of his patents, interesting miniature versions of his equipment that you can operate, including his infamous spinning egg and artificial lightning machines. Here also are his ashes, in a bronzed urn, and a gruesome death mask. Unfortunately, there is no documentation here on any of Tesla's amazing practical jokes. Alas.

KRUŠEVO
(30 miles south of Skopje)

The "Ilinden" Monument: on the outskirts of the town of

Kruševo. Open during daylight hours. Admission: free.

They claim this monument is a World War II memorial. We know better. It is actually an extraterrestrial alien probe that crash-landed in southern Yugoslavia. At least it looks like one: a large white soccer ball with wart-like windows protruding in all directions. An opening on one side allows the naturally curious Earthlings to enter the Molecular Analyzation Chamber. A field of knee-high synthetic mushrooms grows in front. You can't fool us. World War II was never like this.

NIŠ

Tower of the Skulls (Ćele Kula): one mile east of the center of town, on Braće Taskovića, which becomes the main road to Sophia. Admission: free.

When the Serbian revolutionaries realized they were losing the battle against the dominant Turks in 1809, they committed mass suicide. The Turkish Pasha, gloating, collected nearly 1,000 of their skulls and used them to adorn a tower he built as a warning to would-be rebels. The Serbs, however, see their Ćele Kula as a war memorial rather than an object of shame. Housed in a cream-colored octagonal building, the silent skulls peer out from amidst the brickwork, looking raw and grotesque.

PTUJ
(40 miles north of Zagreb)

Bird-mask Procession (Kurent): Ash Wednesday morning.

From the nearby village of Markovci comes a procession of men in startling costumes: suits of shaggy fur, wooden face masks with bird-beaks and beady eyes, feathered "wings" on either side of the head, and, incongruously, a foot-long red flap of a tongue and slender horns festooned with crepe paper. They wind through the streets of Ptuj early in the morning, using a birdlike hopping step. Everyone around here knows this is an ancient ritual, that is has something to do with fertility and perhaps death—but beyond that, Kurent is shrouded in mystery.

SKOPJE

Skopje Town Museum: Mito Hadživasilev Jasmin Street. Call 238-122 for current hours and admission price.

On July 26, 1963, Skopje was flattened by an earthquake. One of the few structures left standing was about one-fourth of the old train station. In a dubious stroke of sentimental genius, the inhabitants decided to convert the remnants of the train station into the town museum as a memorial. It's still there, a sight to behold; ready for the wrecking ball, bricks falling off here and there, amidst a city of new buildings. If you dare go inside, they usually have on display an amusing collection of caricatures.

ZAGREB

Museum of the Blind (Tifloški Musej): Draškovićeva 80, six blocks from both the train and bus stations. Open Tuesday–Friday, 9 A.M.–1 P.M. and 4–7 P.M.; Saturday, 10 A.M.–noon. Closed Sunday and Monday. Admission: free. Phone: 433-351.

This museum provides a survey of technologies and ingenuities through which blind people can be creative: Braille typewriters, tape measures, maps, etc. Note the Braille anatomy textbook with raised body parts. Also here are musical instruments played by blind musicians, the works of blind sculptors, photos of famous blind people, and a photo exhibit of blind people in many jobs and occupations.

THE SMALL COUNTRIES

The map of Europe is neither logical nor tidy. Here and there, squeezed into unlikely corners or resting on forgotten mountaintops, are a sprinkling of strange, anachronistic countries that have managed to maintain their identity because no one pays them any attention. Small and secure, they watch serenely as the rest of Europe slugs it out in the political ring.

Andorra (which is, despite its size, one of the oldest sovereign states in the world) has survived for centuries on a diet of smuggling, sheep herding, skiing, and shopping, and shows no sign of letting up.

Liechtenstein, a country whose *raison d'être* has never been clearly explained, consists of little more than a few pastures and vineyards with an occasional building here and there.

Luxembourg tries its best to act like a normal-sized country, and sends tall ambassadors to the United Nations who murmur challengingly, "Size? What's so remarkable about my *size?*"

Monaco, which is smaller than the parking lot of the Omaha Woolworth's, caters mainly to poodles and bleary-eyed gamblers.

San Marino, like a stubborn child, stopped aging about 500 years ago and still lives in a self-construed fantasy world.

Vatican City has the highest Influence-per-Square-Foot rating of any country in the world: its head of state has a hotline to heaven, and its post office dominates the philatelic scene.

ANDORRA

ANDORRA LA VELLA

Aleix (store): at the corner of Avinguda Meritxell and Carrer de la Unio. Open 9 A.M.–1 P.M. and 3–8 P.M.

This is your typical Andorran corner store, stocking a ready supply of cheese, toys, watches, and Donald Duck umbrellas. But Aleix stands apart from its neighbors because it sells giant cigars. Ranging from foot-long knockwurst-like specimens to their two-foot-long cousins, reminiscent of pudgy baguettes, the cigars are allegedly smokable—if you've got the maw for it. They're made in Andorra, of course.

Pyrenees Department Store: at the lower end of Avinguda Meritxell in the center of town. Open normal business hours.

It's hard to believe a store this size could even fit in a country as small as Andorra. Gargantuan Pyrenees is practically a city under one roof, dispensing goods in a quantity and diversity that is both overwhelming and puzzling. Here is a random sampling: hookahs, chocolate, underwater cigarette holders, designer tennis shoes, pickled peppers (in bulk), squid, economy size detergent, car parts, miniature cameras, caviar, marzipan, soccer balls, perfume, pet food, hams, "Ye Whiskey of Ye Monks," mushrooms, and barnacles (for eating). Whole departments are given over to men's umbrellas, women's umbrellas, children's umbrellas, and cheese. The butter department is bigger than the city's bus depot.

ENCAMP
(Three miles up from Andorra la Vella on the main road)

The Smugglers' Play (Los Contrabandistes): date varies. Call the Encamp Tourist Office for exact time and location: 31 4 05.

Until very recently, Andorra's national industry was smuggling. So it makes sense that one of their few folkloric customs centers on smuggling. The traditional play is a reenactment of the trial of a smuggler in the days before the Spanish Civil War. The action is colorful, but a good knowledge of Catalan or Spanish helps considerably if you're trying to follow the plot.

LUXEMBOURG

BEAUFORT
(20 miles northeast of Luxembourg City)

Castle Torture Chamber: in Beaufort Castle. Open April 1–October 15, daily, 9 A.M.–6 P.M. Admission: 40LF; children under 15, 15LF. For more information, call 860 81.

Yes, even in a cute little place like Luxembourg they used to torture people. The country's only remaining torture chamber is in the dungeon of Beaufort Castle, underneath the ground floor. Thumbscrews, a rack, and several other unsavory playthings are exhibited. Free, mandatory demonstrations are given. Okay, okay—just thought we'd give you a scare.

BOUR
(Seven miles northwest of Luxembourg City)

Transportation Blessing: Easter morning, in front of the town chapel.

If it gets you from here to there, the priest of Bour will bless it for you. Horses, cars, tractors, donkeys, trucks—all of these get the treatment to ensure their well-being during the following year. Even if you don't want your skateboard sanctified, this ancient ritual is a compelling sight.

ECHTERNACH
(On the German border, 20 miles northeast of Luxembourg City)

The Hopping Procession of St. Willibrord: held every year on Whit Tuesday (usually in May or June). Begins at 9 A.M. on the bridge that crosses the River Sûre. After winding through the town, the procession ends up at the Shrine of St. Willibrord in the Basilica. For more information, call 72 230.

After an early-morning mass in the Basilica, residents and pilgrims assemble on a bridge in a long procession, usually four or five abreast. Musicians strike up what sounds like an old English folk tune, and the participants hop five steps forward; then they hop three steps back, moving alternately slightly to the left or to the right each time. The melody and the hopping are repeated over and over and over until finally, the exhausted people reach the Basilica, where another service is held. As it turns out, the music really is an old English folk tune, which St. Willibrord brought to Echternach in the seventh century. The saint supposedly worked a miracle, ending an epidemic of the disease called St. Vitus' dance. Willibrord ordered afflicted persons to hop up and down until they dropped from exhaustion; and this prescription worked. Despite the legends, it is probably not the direct inspiration for the procession, which didn't take its present form until many centuries after Willibrord's "miracle."

LUXEMBOURG CITY

Bock-Casemate Tours: entrances on Place de la Constitution and Montée de Clausen. Open March–October, daily, 10 A.M.–5 P.M. Admission: 30LF; children under 15, 10LF. For more information, call the Tourist Office at 2 28 09.

To modern Americans, Luxembourg may seem like an inconsequential little country, but throughout the ages it has played a crucial role in the military history of central Europe, even as recently as WWII. Luxembourg City was one of the most extensively fortified sites in Europe, and as a result, the rock on which the city rests is honeycombed with passages, chambers, "casemates" (fortified rooms with windows for shooting out of) and secret tunnels. The "Bock" in the title is the name of the rock out of which the casemates are carved. You only see a small part of the over 13 miles of passages during the tour, but it's still grim and spooky—and disorienting when you peek out of a firing slot in an underground room and see a panorama of the valley below you.

RUMELANGE
(Ten miles south of Luxembourg City on the French border)

National Mine Museum: no street address, but the town is small and signs point the way. Open Easter–October, daily, 2–6 P.M. (but last guided tour starts at 5 P.M.); from November 1–Easter, open only the second Saturday and Sunday of each month, from 2–6 P.M. Admission: 60LF; children under 15, 30LF. Phone: 56 54 71.

The most convincing display here is not what's in the museum—but what the museum is in: an actual mine. Other mining museums try to describe what life is like underground; at this museum you experience it. And for kicks, you can even take a ride on a mining car.

MONACO

MONTE CARLO

The National Museum and Collections of Dolls and Automats of Yesteryear: 17 Avenue Princesse Grace (east of the casino—walk or take bus 4). Open daily, 10 A.M.–12:15 P.M. and 2:30–6:30 P.M. Admission: 22F; children 5–14, 12F: children under 5, free. Phone: 93.30.91.26.

Small country, long museum title. As with just about everything else in Monte Carlo, the accent here is on elegance. These dolls are swank, suave, and dressed to the nines. The "automats" are moving mechanical figures popular a century ago as fortune-telling gimmicks and carnival attractions. To be honest, some of these look more alive than half the people in the Monte Carlo casino.

VATICAN CITY

Papal Souvenir Blessing: in St. Peter's Square (Piazza San Pietro) and Pius XII Square (Piazza Pio XII), in Vatican City. Free.

Is your living-room decor incomplete without a Clark Gable poster blessed personally by the Pope? At the gift shops in front of St. Peter's, you can arrange to have any purchase sanctified by *Il Papa* himself—at no extra charge. The process is simple: if you arrive in the morning, leave your purchase with the shop; return at 5 P.M. and—a miracle!—your item has been blessed by the Pope. It is not exactly clear how this daily blessing is arranged, but everyone, including the Vatican officials, assures us that it is legitimate. (Remember, of course, that this only holds true when the Pope is in town, and that only some shops perform the service; ask before you buy.) If you arrive in the afternoon, you'll have to leave your stuff at the shop and come back the next day. And if you're too rushed to be shuttling back and forth to the Vatican, you can, for a small fee, have the shop mail the purchase to your home. The best part is the vast selection of souvenirs you can buy in Vatican City and have blessed. Should crucifixes or Clark Gable posters not run to your taste, you can try switchblades, tarot cards, backgammon sets, statuettes of poker players or Cyrano de Bergerac, Smurfs, drunken satyrs, beer steins, ashtrays in the shape of toilets, chewing tobacco, corkscrews and thermometers with the Pope's face on them, Manitoba license plates, toy guns, ankhs, Stars of David, octopus lamps, and countless other devotional items.

GENERAL INDEX

Note: This is a complete listing, by country and region (in **boldface type**), of the cities that appear in this Guide. Items in italics represent special interest topics within a particular country or region. The specialized indexes that follow will guide you to places and events by subject matter.

AUSTRIA, 1–16
Graz, 2
Hallein, 2–3
Hallstatt, 3
Hinterbrühl, 3–4
Innsbruck, 4
Kaag, 4–5
Klagenfurt, 5
Pottenbrunn, 5–6
Rust, 6
Salzburg, 6–8
Stadl Paura, 9
Vienna (Wien), 9–15
Werfen, 15–16

BELGIUM, 17–36
Anseremme, 18
Antwerp, 18–19
Baarle–Hertog and Baarle–Nassau, 19
Binche, 20–21
Brugge (Bruges), 21
Brussels (Bruxelles), 22–26
Brussels Art Nouveau Houses, 25
Chaudfontaine, 26
Couvin, 26
Drongen, 26–27
Geer, 27
Gheel (Geel), 27
Ghent (Gent), 28
Han-sur-Lesse, 28
Hoeselt, 28–29
Hotton, 29
Hulste, 29
Ieper (Ypres), 29–30
Kalmthout, 30
Kanne, 30
Knokke–Heist, 30–31
Leuven (Louvain), 31
Liège, 31
Lier (Lierre), 31–32
Mechelen, 32
Mons, 32–33
Morkhoven, 33
Oostende, 33
Peer, 33–34
St-Hubert, 34
St-Truiden, 34
Silly, 34
Sougné–Remouchamps, 35
Tilff, 35
Turnhout, 35–36
Vielsalm, 36
Wezemaal, 36

DENMARK, 37–48
Aabenraa, 38
Aalestrup, 39
Aerøskøbing, 39
Billund, 39–40
Copenhagen (København), 40–41
Frederikshavn, 41–42
Hillerød, 42
Hobro, 42–43
Højer Sluse, 43
Mønsted, 43
Odense, 44
Ribe, 44
Roskilde, 45–46
Rudkøping, 47
Ry, 47
Vinderup, 47–48

FINLAND, 49–56
Alahärmä, 50
Helsinki, 50–51
Iisalmi, 52
Jyväskylä, 52
Mikkeli, 52–53
Naantali, 53–54
Rovaniemi, 54
Salo, 54
Tampere, 54–55
Tankavaara, 55
Turku, 55–56
Tuusniemi, 56

FRANCE, 57–104
Paris, 58–67
Paris Environs, 67–68
Chartres, 67
Conflans–Sainte–Honorine, 67
Coupvray, 67–68
Thoiry, 68

Brittany and Normandy, 68–76
Balleroy, 68
Carnac, 68–69
Cossé–le–Vivien, 69
Fécamp, 69–70
Granville, 70
Île d'Ouessant, 70
Lisieux, 71
Louviers, 71
Morlaix, 71–72
Paimpont Forest, 72
Plouharnel, 73
Ry, 73
St-Malo, 73–74
St-Michel-de-Montjoie, 74

General Index / 307

FRANCE (cont.)
St-Pierre-sur-Dives, 74–75
Le Tertre Rouge, 75
Trégastel, 75
Tréhorenteuc, 75–76
Villedieu-les-Pôeles, 76

Loire Valley, 77–83
Amboise, 77
Blois, 77
Cheillé, 78
Cheverny, 78
Chinon, 78–79
Dénezé-sous-Doué, 79
La Fosse, 79
Montpoupon, 80
Nantes, 80
Nevers, 80–81
Plessis-Bourré, 81
Rochemenier, 81
Saumur, 81–82
Savonnières, 82
Tours, 82–83
Trélazé, 83
Ussé, 83

Southwest, 84–91
Agde, 84
Amplepuis, 84
Andouze, 84–85
Bordeaux, 85
Cap d'Agde, 85
La Chaise-Dieu, 85–86
Clermont-Ferrand, 86
Condom, 86
Foix, 86–87
Ganges, 87
La Grande Motte, 87–88
Montpellier, 88
Oradour-sur-Glane, 88
Orgnac, 88
Palavas, 89
Poitiers, 89
St-Ambroix, 89
St-Emilion, 90
St-Guilhem le Désert, 90
Sète, 90–91
Sorges, 91
La Villedieu, 91

Provence and the Riviera, 92–95
Ansouis, 92
Chateauneuf-les-Martigues, 92
Cuges-les-Pins, 92–93
Grasse, 93
Tarascon, 94
Vence, 94
Villefranche-sur-Mer, 94–95
Villeneuve-Loubet, 95

The Rhone and The Alps, 95–99
Annecy, 95
Bois d'Amont, 95–96
Chamonix, 96
Hauteriues, 96
Lyon, 96–97
Nyons, 97
Oyonnax, 97–98
Romans-sur-Isère, 98
Les Rousses, 98
St-Claude, 98–99
St-Paul-Trois-Chateaux, 99
Seyssel, 99

North And East, 99–104
Alsatian St. John Fires, 103
Arnay-le-Duc, 99–100
Bèze, 100
Chalon-sur-Saône, 100
Dijon, 100–101
Mulhouse, 101
Ornans, 101–102
Prez-sous-Lafauche, 102
Ronchamp, 102
St-Dizier, 102–103
Strasbourg, 103–104
Turckheim, 104

WEST GERMANY, 105–121
Augsburg, 106–107
Bad Homburg, 107
Buende, 107–108
Cologne (Köln), 108
Duisburg, 108
Düsseldorf, 109
Essen, 109
Frankfurt, 109–110
Garmisch-Partenkirchen, 110
Gersthofen, 110–111
Hassloch, 111
Heidelberg, 111–112
Heroldsbach, 112
Hockenheim, 112–113
Kassel, 113
Knittlingen, 113
Mittenwald, 113–114
Munich (München), 114–116
Nuremberg (Nürnberg), 116–117
Pirmasens, 117
Rothenburg ob der Tauber, 117–119
Rüdesheim am Rhein, 119
Schwetzingen, 119–120
Solingen, 120
Speyer, 120
Stuttgart, 120–121
Ulm, 121
Wank, 121

GREAT BRITAIN, 122–171
London, 123–134
Walking Tours, 131–134
Ghosts, 133
Jack the Ripper, 132–133
Miscellaneous, 133–134
Sherlock Holmes, 131–132

South of London, 134–136
Bramber, 134
Godshill, 135
Maidstone, 135
Tonbridge, 135
Wilmington, 136

Southwest England, 136–144
Bolventor, 136
Buckland-in-the-Moor, 136–137
Cerne Abbas, 137
Christchurch, 137
Combe Martin, 137–138
Dartmoor, 138
Dorchester, 138
Exmouth, 138–139
Goonhavern, 139
Looe, 139
Minehead, 139–140
Newquay, 140
Padstow, 140–141
Sark, 141
Shebbear, 141
Sidmouth, 141–142
South Molton, 142
Street, 142–143
Wells, 143
West Putford, 143–144
Yelverton, 144

308 / *General Index*

GREAT BRITAIN (cont.)

Wales, 144–148
Abercraf, 144
Beaumaris, 145
Caldicot, 145
Cardiff, 145
Hay-on-Wye, 145–147
King Arthur, 146
Llanfair P.G., 147
Pembroke, 147
Portmeirion, 147–148
Ruthin, 148

Central England, 148–159
Abbots Bromley, 148–149
Bath, 149
Bristol, 149
Brockworth, 150
Chipping Campden, 150
Gloucester, 150–151
Hallaton, 151–152
Ilkeston, 152
Kilpeck, 152–153
Mow Cop, 153
Northampton, 153
Norwich, 153
Nottingham, 154
Olney, 154
Randwick, 154–155
Redditch, 155
Rushton, 155
Stansted, 157
Stone Circles, 156–157
Stratford–Upon–Avon, 158
Stroud, 158
Symonds Yat West, 158–159
West Wycombe, 159

Northern England, 159–166
Bradford, 159–160
Castleton, 160
Cragg Vale, 160–161
Egremont, 161
Holmfirth, 161
Kendal, 162
Keswick, 162
Knaresborough, 162–163
Liverpool, 163–164
Malton, 164
Masham, 164
Morpeth, 165
Northwich, 165
Ripon, 165–166
West Witton, 166

Scotland, 166–171
Ayr, 166–167
Blantyre, 167–168
Comrie, 168
Dunmore, 168
Edinburgh, 169
Lamb Holm Island, 169
Largs, 169–170
Lerwick (Shetland Island), 170
Oban, 170
Paisley, 170–171
Perth, 171
Postcard Towns, 167
South Queensferry, 171

GREECE, 172–179
Athens, 173–174
Ayia Elini, 174
Kalimnos, 174
Langadas, 174–175
Lesbos, 175
Markopoulo, 175–176
Monoklisia, 176
Nea Petra, 176–177
Panagia, 177
Parikia, 177
Perama, 177–178
Philippi (Filipi), 178
Piraeus, 178
Pirgos Dirou, 178–179
Rhodes (Rodos), 179
Vaï, 179

IRELAND, 180–188
Bunratty, 181
Cork, 181–182
Dublin, 182–183
Galway, 183–184
Glenealy, 184
Gort, 184
Killarney, 184–185
Kilcullen, 185
Killinaboy, 185
Killorglin, 185–186
Kinvara, 186
Lisdoonvarna, 186
Lough Gur, 186–187
Murrisk, 187
Quin, 187–188
Thurles, 188
Tralee, 188

ITALY, 189–210

North, 191–196
Arezzo, 191
Ascoli Piceno, 191
Collodi, 191–192
Florence (Firenze), 192–193
Gubbio, 193
Lucca, 193–194
Perugia, 194
Pescia, 194
Pisa, 194–195
Pontedassio, 195
Sarzana, 195
Siena, 196
Viareggio, 196

Rome and Environs, 197–207
Anzio, 197
Bolsena, 197
Bomarzo, 197–198
Capranica Prenestina, 198
Frascati, 198
Genzano, 199
Ice Cream, 202
Montecompatri, 199
Nettuno, 199–200
Rome, 200–205
Santa Marinella, 206
Saracinesco, 206
Tivoli, 206
Viterbo, 207

South, 207–210
Calatfini and Salemi, 207
Favignana, 207–208
Messina, 208–209
Palermo, 209
Stromboli, 209–210
Vulcano, 210

THE NETHERLANDS, 211–224
Aalsmeer, 212
Amsterdam, 212–215
Apeldoorn, 215–216
Baarle–Nassau, 216
Berg en Daal, 216
Best, 216
Eindhoven, 216–217
Grijpskerk, 217
The Hague, 217–218
Heerlerheide, 218–219
Kaatsheuvel, 219
Kampen, 219
Leiden, 219
Maastricht, 220
Middelburg, 220
Naaldwijk, 220–221
Nieuwolda, 221
Nijmegen, 221
Oudewater, 221–222
Rotterdam, 222
Steenwijk, 222
Utrecht, 223
Valkenburg, 223

General Index / 309

THE NETHERLANDS (cont.)
Volendam, 223–224
Wieuwerd, 224
Wouw, 224

NORWAY, 225–232
Bergen, 226
Bø, 226
Bodø, 226–227
Hell, 227
Lillehammer, 227–228
Oslo, 228–231
Stavanger, 231
Trondheim, 232

PORTUGAL, 233–244
Alcochete, 234
Braga, 234–235
Cabo da Roca, 235–236
Cabo de São Vicente, 236
Coimbra, 236–237
Estremoz, 237
Evora, 237
Faro, 238
Fátima, 238
Figueira da Foz, 238–239
Lisbon, 239–241
Miranda do Douro, 241
Monte, 241–242
Oporto (Porto), 242
Porto de Mós, 242–243
Reguengo do Fetal, 243
Santa Maria da Feira, 244

SPAIN, 245–266

Catalunya, 246–254
Argentona, 246–247
Barcelona, 247–252
Figueres, 252
Gaudí, 249–251
Llivia, 252–253
Sant Vicenç dels Horts, 253
Vilanova del Cami, 253
Vilanova I la Geltrú, 253–254

Madrid and the South, 254–261
Alicante, 254
Ceuta, 254
Cordoba, 255
Jaen, 255
Jijona, 255–256
Madrid, 256–258
Melilla, 258–259
Porto Cristo, 259
Tabernas, 259
Valencia, 259–261
Villanueva de la Cañada, 261

The North, 261–266
Astorga, 261–262
Catoira, 261–262
Celorio, 262
Escatrón, 263
Estella, 263
La Coruña, 263
Las Nieves, 263–264
León, 264
Miranda del Castañar, 264
Potes, 264–265
San Pedro Manrique, 265
Santiago de Compostela, 265–266
Sotosalbos, 266
Zamarramala, 266

SWEDEN, 267–277
Ådelfors, 268
Eskilstuna, 268
Hillerstorp, 268–269
Höör, 269
Huskvarna, 269–270
Jönköping, 270–271
Kiruna, 271
Klippan, 271
Lund, 271–272
Skara, 272–273
Stockholm, 273–275
Strängnäs, 275
Växjö, 275–276
Vimmerby, 276–277
Visby, 277

SWITZERLAND, 278–297
Basel, 279–282
Bellinzona, 282
Bern, 282–283
Bex, 283–284
Bürglen, 284
Campione d'-Italia, 284

Cantine di Gandria, 284–285
Dornach, 285
Geneva, 285–286
Goldau, 286
Interlaken, 286–287
Kiesen, 287
Kilchberg, 287–288
Küssnacht am Rigi, 288
La Chaux–de–Fonds, 288
La Tour–de–Peilz, 288–289
Lausanne, 289
Lucens, 289–290
Lucerne, 290
Melide, 290
Neuchatel, 291
Roche, 291
Sainte Croix, 291–292
Schönenwerd, 292
Scuol, 292
Sursee, 292–293
Valais Canton, 293
Vevey, 293–294
Wiler, 294
Yverdon–les–Bains, 294–295
Zurich, 295–297

YUGOSLAVIA, 298–301
Belgrade (Beograd), 299
Kruševo, 299–300
Niš, 300
Ptuj, 300
Skopje, 301
Zagreb, 301

THE SMALL COUNTRIES, 302–306

Andorra, 303
Andorra la Vella, 303
Encamp, 303

Luxembourg, 304–305
Beaufort, 304
Bour, 304
Echternach, 304–305
Luxembourg City, 305
Rumelange, 305

Monaco, 306

Vatican City, 306

310 / General Index

SPECIALIZED INDEXES

Note: The indexes that follow are alphabetically arranged by topic. Entries are listed below the country and city in which they appear.

ANATOMY MUSEUMS
Austria, Salzburg,
House of Nature, 7
Austria, Vienna,
Museum of Horseshoeing, Harnessing and Saddling, and Hoof and Claw Orthopedics, 12
Finland, Helsinki,
Veterinary Medicine Museum, 51
France, Paris,
Medical History Museum, 62
France, Montpellier,
Anatomy Museum, 88
Great Britian, London,
Hunterian Museum, 126
Great Britain, London,
The Wellcome Tropical Institute Museum, 130
The Netherlands, Amsterdam,
Museum Vrolik, 213
Switzerland, Basel,
Anatomy Museum, 279
Switzerland, Zurich,
Kulturama, 296

"AMERICAN" WILD WEST TOWNS
Belgium, Chaudfontaine,
Western City Recreation Center, 26
Denmark, Billund,
Legoland, 39–40
Denmark, Roskilde,
Roskilde Sommerland, 46
France, Chateauneuf-Les-Martigues,
El Dorado City, 92
France, Cuges-Les-Pins,
OK Corral, 92–93
West Germany, Augsburg,
Fred Rai Western City, 106–107
West Germany, Heroldsbach,
Erlebnispark Schloss Thurn, 112
Great Britain, Ilkeston,
The American Adventure, 152
Norway, Bø,
Telemark Sommarland, 226

Norway, Stavanger,
Kongeparken, 231
Spain, Tabernas,
Yucca City Film Towns, 259
Sweden, Hillerstorp,
High Chaparral, 268–269
Sweden, Skara,
Skara Sommarland, 272–273
Sweden, Strängnäs,
Sioux Indian Club, 275

ECCENTRIC ARCHITECTURE
Belgium, Brussels,
Atomium, 22
France, Chartres,
Mosaic House, 67
France, Cossé-le-Vivien,
The Strange Museum of Robert Tatin, 69
France, Louviers,
Robert Vasseur's Mosaic House, 71
France, La Fosse,
Troglodyte Hamlet, 79
France, Rochemenier,
Troglodyte Village, 81
France, La Chaise-Dieu,
Echo Room, 85–86
France, La Grande Motte,
Unusual Architecture, 87–88
France, Hauterives,
The Ideal Palace, 96
France, St-Dizier,
Marcel Dhièvre's Petit Paris, 102–103
West Germany, Garmisch-Partenkirchen,
Linderhof Castle, 110
West Germany, Garmisch-Partenkirchen,
Neuschwanstein Castle, 110
West Germany, Schwetzingen,
Schwetzingen Castle Gardens, 119–120
Great Britain, Buckland-in-the-Moor,
"My Dear Mother" Clock, 136–137
Great Britain, Combe Martin,
The Pack of Cards Inn, 137–138

Specialized Indexes / 311

ECCENTRIC ARCHITECTURE (cont.)
Great Britain, Exmouth,
  A la Ronde, 138–139
Great Britain, Portmeirion,
  147–148
Great Britain, Mow Cop,
  Mow Cop Folly, 153
Great Britain, Rushton,
  Rushton Hall, 155
Great Britain, Masham,
  Fake Stonehenge, 164
Great Britain, Dunmore,
  The Dunmore Pineapple, 168
Great Britain, Oban,
  McCaig's Folly, 170
Italy, Perugia,
  Underground City, 194
The Netherlands, Amsterdam,
  Narrowest House in the City, 213
The Netherlands, Eindhoven,
  Evoluon, 216–217
Norway, Stavanger,
  Kongeparken, 231
Spain, Barcelona,
  Gaudí, 249–251
Spain, Astorga,
  Bishop's Palace, 261–262
Spain, León,
  Casa de Botines, 264
Switzerland, Dornach,
  The Goetheanum, 285
Yugoslavia, Kruševo,
  The "Ilinden" Monument, 299–300
Yugoslavia, Niš,
  Tower of the Skulls, 300

FACTORY TOURS
Belgium, Leuven,
  Artois Brewery Tours, 31
France, Fécamp,
  Benedictine Museum and Distillery, 69
France, Blois,
  Poulain Chocolate Factory Tours, 77
France, Trélazé,
  Cointreau Tours, 83
France, Grasse,
  Fragonard Perfume Factory Tours, 93
France, Grasse,
  Galimard Perfume Factory Tours, 93
France, Grasse,
  Molinard Perfume Factory Tours, 93
Norway, Oslo,
  Freia Chocolate Factory Tours, 228–229
Spain, Jijona,
  Nougat Factory Tours, 255–256
Sweden, Lund,
  Gambro Tours, 271–272
Sweden, Stockholm,
  Brewery Museum Pripporama, 273
Switzerland, Kilchberg,
  Lindt Chocolate Factory Tours, 287–288
Switzerland, Neuchatel,
  Suchard-Tobler Chocolate Factory Tours, 291

FUNNY FOUNTAINS
Austria, Salzburg,
  Hellbrunn Pleasure Castle, 7
Belgium, Brussels,
  Jeanneke-Pis, 23
Belgium, Brussels,
  Mannekin-Pis Costume Collection, 23
West Germany, Augsburg,
  Statues in the Augustus Fountain, 107
West Germany, Duisburg,
  Urinating Statue, 108
West Germany, Nuremberg,
  Fountain of Virtues, 116–117
Italy, Collodi,
  Pinocchio Park—Shark Fountain, 192
Italy, Pescia,
  Urinating Statue, 194
Italy, Tivoli,
  Villa d'Este, 206
Portugal, Braga,
  The Stairway to Bom Jesus do Monte de Santa Marta Sanctuary, 234–235
Portugal, Lisbon,
  Illuminated Fountain Show, 240
Spain, Barcelona,
  Illuminated Fountain Show, 251–252
Spain, Madrid,
  Monument to the Fallen Angel, 257–258
Switzerland, Bern,
  Child-Eater Fountain, 282
Switzerland, Bern,
  Justice Fountain, 283

HOLY RELICS
Austria, Vienna,
  Holy Lance With Holy Nail, and Holy Grail, 12
Belgium, Brugge,
  Procession of the Holy Blood, 21
Belgium, Liège,
  Piece of the True Cross, 31
France, Paris,
  The Crown of Thorns, 59
France, Fécamp,
  Holy Blood, 69–70
West Germany, Rothenburg ob der Tauber,
  Holy Blood, 118
Ireland, Thurles,
  Piece of the True Cross, 188
Italy, Sarzana,
  Holy Blood, 195
Italy, Rome,
  Holy Relics, 202–203
Italy, Rome,
  Holy Stairs, 203

HOLY RELICS (cont.)
Spain, Alicante,
  Piece of St. Veronica's Veil, 254
Spain, Jaen,
  St. Veronica's Veil, 255
Spain, Valencia
  Holy Grail, 260
Spain, Potes,
  Pieces of the True Cross, 264–265

POSTCARD TOWNS
Belgium, Silly, 34
Finland, Rovaniemi,
  Santa Claus Land, 54
France, Condom, 86
West Germany, Wank, 121
Great Britain, Llanfair P.G., 147
Great Britain,
  Postcard Towns Box, 167
Norway, Hell, 227

STRANGE ART
Austria, Kaag,
  Franz Gsellmann's World Machine, 4–5
Denmark, Billund,
  Legoland, 39–40
Denmark, Hobro,
  World Map Garden, 42–43
France, Granville,
  Seashell Fairyland, Mineral Palace and Butterfly Garden, 70
France, Plouharnel,
  Le Galion Shellcraft Museum, 73
France, St-Malo,
  Sculptured Rocks, 74
France, Cheillé,
  Beardless Jesus, 78
France, Dénezé-sous-Doué,
  The Sculpted Cavern, 79
France, Plessis-Bourré,
  Strange Ceiling, 81
France, La Villedieu,
  The Little Museum of the Bizarre, 91
France, Chamonix,
  Ice Sculpture Cave, 96
Great Britain, Kendal,
  Levens Hall Topiary Garden, 162
Italy, Florence,
  Pratolino Sculpture Garden, 193
Italy, Bomarzo,
  Bomarzo Monster Park, 197–198
The Netherlands, The Hague,
  Panorama Mesdag, 217–218

The Netherlands, Valkenburg,
  Town Cave, 223
The Netherlands, Volendam,
  Cigar Band "Golden Room", 223–224
Norway, Lillehammer,
  Hunderfossen Lekeland, 227–228
Norway, Oslo,
  Emanuel Vigeland's Museum, 228
Norway, Oslo,
  The International Museum of Children's Art, 229
Norway, Oslo,
  Vigeland Sculpture Park, 230–231
Spain, Figueres,
  Salvador Dalí's Own Museum, 252
Spain, Valencia,
  Fallas Museum, 260
Sweden, Jönköping,
  Giant Sculptures, 270
Switzerland, Interlaken,
  Jungfraujoch Ice Palace, 286
Switzerland, Lausanne,
  Collection of "Art Brut", 289

UNUSUAL CHURCHES
Austria, Hallstatt,
  Chapel Bonehouse, 3
Austria, Stadl Paura,
  Church of the Holy Trinity, 9
Finland, Salo,
  Helisnummi Chapel, 54
France, Tréhorenteuc,
  Church with Bizarre Decorations, 75–76
France, St-Emilion,
  Church Carved From Solid Rock, 90
France, Vence,
  Matisse Chapel, 94
France, Villefranche-sur-Mer,
  Jean Cocteau Chapel, 94–95
France, Ronchamp,
  Le Corbusier Chapel, 102
Great Britain, Lamb Holm Island,
  Italian Nissen Hut Chapel, 169
The Netherlands, Amsterdam,
  Our Lord in the Attic, 213–214
Portugal, Evora,
  Chapel of Bones, 237
Portugal, Faro,
  Chapel of Bones, 238
Spain, Barcelona,
  Holy Family Cathedral, 250–251
Spain, Santiago de Compostela,
  Leaning Church, 265

Specialized Indexes / 313

Calendar of Festival Dates

	1988	1989	1990
Saturday preceding Mardi Gras	Feb. 13	Feb. 4	Feb. 24
Shrove Tuesday (Carnival)	Feb. 16	Feb. 7	Feb. 27
Ash Wednesday	Feb. 17	Feb. 8	Feb. 28
Tuesday after Ash Wednesday	Feb. 23	Feb. 14	Mar. 6
Good Friday	Apr. 1	Mar. 24	Apr. 13
Easter	Apr. 3	Mar. 26	Apr. 15
Easter Monday	Apr. 4	Mar. 27	Apr. 16
Ascension Day	May 12	May 4	May 24
Pentecost (Whitsunday)	May 22	May 14	June 3
Whitsuntide	May 22–29	May 14–21	June 3–10
Whit Tuesday	May 24	May 16	June 5
Trinity Sunday	May 29	May 21	June 10
Eighth day of Corpus Christi	June 9	June 1	June 21
Sunday following August 24	Aug. 27	Aug. 26	Aug. 25
First Monday after first Sunday after Sept. 4	Sept. 12	Sept. 11	Sept. 10
Saturday nearest October 18	Oct. 15	Oct. 21	Oct. 20

If, in your travels, you've discovered something off-the-wall that's not mentioned in this book, please tell us about it. We'll do our best to visit your suggestion for possible inclusion in future editions of *Europe Off The Wall*. If we've never heard of the place before and it turns out to be undeniably strange, we'll mention you in the edition in which your suggested item appears. Send all correspondence to: *Europe Off The Wall*, c/o Katherine Schowalter, John Wiley and Sons, 605 Third Avenue, New York, NY 10158.